11-26-01

TEXTS IN COMPUTER SCIENCE

Editors
David Gries
Fred B. Schneider

Springer
New York
Berlin
Heidelberg
Barcelona
Hong Kong
London
Milan
Paris
Singapore
Tokyo

TEXTS IN COMPUTER SCIENCE

(continued after index)

Doron A. Peled

SOFTWARE RELIABILITY METHODS

Foreword by Edmund M. Clarke

With 50 Illustrations

Springer

Doron A. Peled
Computing Sciences
Bell Labs/Lucent Technologies
Murray Hill, NJ 07974, USA
doron@research.bell-labs.com

Series Editors

David Gries
Department of Computer Science
415 Boyd Graduate Studies Research
    Center
The University of Georgia
Athens, GA 30602-7404, USA

Fred B. Schneider
Department of Computer Science
Upson Hall
Cornell University
Ithaca, NY 14853-7501, USA

Library of Congress Cataloging-in-Publication Data
Peled, Doron, 1962–
    Software reliability methods / Doron A. Peled.
        p. cm. — (Texts in computer science)
    Includes bibliographical references and index.
    ISBN 0-387-95106-7 (alk. paper)
        1. Computer software—Reliability.   I. Title.   II. Series.
QA76.76.R44 P317 2001
005—dc21   2001018395

Printed on acid-free paper.

Production managed by Allan Abrams; manufacturing supervised by Jerome Basma.
Photocomposed copy prepared from the author's LaTeX files.
Printed and bound by Maple-Vail Book Manufacturing Group, York, PA.
Printed in the United States of America.

9 8 7 6 5 4 3 2 1

ISBN 0-387-95106-7   SPIN 10774651

Springer-Verlag   New York Berlin Heidelberg
A member of BertelsmannSpringer Science+Business Media GmbH

To my parents, Priva and Zeev

Foreword by Edmund M. Clarke

It is a great pleasure for me to write the foreword for Doron Peled's new book on software reliability methods. When I first opened the book, I was immediately impressed by the breadth of its coverage. It covers

- specification and modeling,
- deductive verification,
- model checking,
- process algebra,
- program testing, and
- state and message sequence charts.

In addition to describing the individual methods in considerable depth, it also discusses when each method is appropriate and the tradeoffs that are necessary in selecting among them. The different techniques are illustrated by many challenging exercises that can be used in conjunction with state of the art tools. It even tells where to access the tools on the web! I do not know of any other book that covers the same topics with such depth.

The book also describes the process of applying formal methods, starting with modeling and specification, then selecting an appropriate verification technique, and, finally, testing the resulting program. This knowledge is essential in practice, but is rarely covered in software engineering texts. Most books focus on a particular technique like program testing and do not cover other validation techniques or how several techniques can be used in combination. Because Doron has made significant contributions to the development of many of the validation techniques described in the book, his insights are particularly important on this critical issue.

The book is appropriate for a wide spectrum of people involved in the development of software. It is particularly appropriate for an upper level undergraduate level course on software reliability or a master's degree course in software engineering. In fact, it is sufficiently well annotated with pointers to other more advanced papers that it can be used as a reference source for software engineers engaged in code validation or by researchers in formal methods.

Having just completed a book on model checking with Doron, I am immensely impressed with both his talent as a computer scientist and his skill as a writer. I am sure that the present book will be an enormous success. I recommend it with great enthusiasm for anyone who is interested in the problem of software reliability.

Preface

Many books focus on increasing the quality of software through the use of formal methods. However, most books embrace one particular method, and present it as *the* suggested solution for the software reliability problem. This book presents a wider picture of formal methods, through a collection of notations and techniques. It compares them, and discusses their advantages and disadvantages.

One of the main challenges of formal methods is in transferring the technology developed by researchers to the software development community. Recently, we seem to be starting to have a better understanding of the important ingredients of formal methods tools. This manifests itself in the growing acceptance of such tools in the software and hardware development industry. Ideally, formal methods need to be intuitive to use (preferably using graphical interfaces), do not impose on the user an extensive learning period, and incur only small overhead to the development process. Formal methods are much more acceptable today than ten or twenty years ago, in particular in the hardware industry. Yet there is still a lively contention between different approaches.

The focus of this book is on describing the main principles of formal methods, through a collection of techniques. At the time of writing this book, there are already many advanced techniques that are not covered here. Techniques that deal with real-time and hybrid systems, advanced specification formalisms, and special data structures such as binary decision diagrams, were not included. The exclusion of specific material does not mean that the methods presented here are superior to the ones omitted. Nevertheless, the algorithms and methods described here are being used in state-of-the-art software reliability tools. The selection is merely intended to present the subject of formal methods in a way that seems deductive. However, it is impossible to refrain from preferring to include subjects that are closer to one's own research The main themes used throughout this book are *logic* and *automata theory*. The interested reader can find details of advanced approaches in other books and research papers listed at the end of relevant chapters.

Studying formal methods is incomplete without hands-on experience with some tools. This book includes various exercises and projects, which may be performed using software reliability tools. There are several running examples that are used in different chapters. An effective way to learn formal methods and their strengths and weaknesses is to follow these examples throughout the different chapters in which they occur. In some cases, a later chapter further elaborates on a running example that was presented as an exercise in a previous chapter. This also serves the purpose of helping readers check their solutions to previous exercises (instead of providing an explicit solution). The readers are encouraged to check if some of the additional intuition gained about the running example may help in improving their solutions to previous exercises.

Most exercises and projects presented here can be performed using a choice of tools. While some of the software reliability tools are subject to nontrivial license fees, many of them can be used free of charge for nonprofit purposes. This usually involves downloading the tool from its worldwideweb page and installing it according to the instructions provided there. At the end of relevant chapters, some tools and their corresponding web pages are listed. Notice that even tools that can be used without acquiring a license often require an agreement letter to be sent to the developers of the tool, committing to their terms of use. In many cases, such terms restrict the use of the tool for academic purposes only, and maintain no responsibility for damage that may be incurred by using it. Since web pages and web addresses tend to change, and since new tools are constantly being constructed, replacing existing ones, one cannot guarantee that the provided web information will remain up to date for long. Moreover, it is not guaranteed that the tools will work under any particular environment.

Different communities have different interests in formal methods. It is of course impossible to present a book that will appeal equally to managers, software developers, quality assurance teams and researchers alike. Nevertheless, I tried to include material that would be interesting to members of each one of these groups. Consequently, the reader may want to skip sections that may seem too theoretical, or too technical. It should be pointed out that the focus of this book is mainly on *techniques* rather than on *methodology*.

Some of the formal methods presented in this book are described together with the corresponding algorithm. Understanding the algorithms is usually not crucial for using the methods, but may give a deeper perspective on how they work. Most of the mathematical proofs involving the methods described were omitted. In some cases, proof sketches are included, to add more intuition.

The author would like to thank the following people for enlightening discussions and comments related to this book: Nina Amla, Christel Baier, David Basin, Shai Ben-David, Roderick Bloem, Glenn Bruns, Ed Clarke, Dennis Dams, Xiaoqun Du, Kousha Etessami, Amy Felty, Elsa Gunter, Doug Howe, Orna Kupferman, Bart Knaack, Bob Kurshan, Bengt Jonsson, Leonid Libkin, Anca Muscholl, Kedar Namjoshi, Wojciech Penczek, Kavita Ravi, Natarajan Shankar, Natasha Sharygina, Marian Srenby, Richard Tefler, Wolfgang

Thomas, Moshe Vardi, Igor Walukiewicz, Thomas Wilke, Mihalis Yannakakis and Lenore Zuck. Indeed, one of the great benefits of writing such a book is the opportunity to further learn from the suggestions and comments of practitioners and experts of the particular subject.

Quoting from Lewis Carroll's adventure books is hardly original. However, it is little known that Charles Lutwidge Dodgson, who wrote under the pen name Lewis Carroll, was a mathematician interested in the visual representation of logic. His 'biliteral' and 'triliteral' diagrams are predecessors of Karnaugh maps, representing logic in a way that can be easily taught and understood, a recent trend in many formal methods.

Doron Peled, March 2001, Murray Hill, NJ

Contents

List of Figures

1. Introduction

> *'Where shall I begin, please your Majesty?' he asked. 'Begin at the beginning,' the King said, very gravely, 'and go on till you come to the end; then stop.'*
>
> Lewis Carroll, *Alice's Adventures in Wonderland*

During late 1999, the world waited, with growing concern, for the change of the calendar into the year 2000. The focus was on some potential damage from online computers that control vital systems. This damage could occur because of the mere change of the calendar year and the way years of the twentieth century were traditionally represented in computer memory, using only the least two significant digits from 00 to 99. This surprisingly small detail made some people expect extreme damage. It could have affected electronic systems driven by software, such as verifying traffic control, atomic missiles, nuclear reactors, banking systems, pension plans, electricity and water supply. The US alone spent over 100 billion dollars on combating this, so called, 'Y2K-bug.' Just prior to that date change, some people had escaped into self made shelters, while flashlights and bottled water were a popular demand. Joint teams of the US and Russian military spent the night of December 31 1999 at the North American Aerospace Defense Command (NORAD). Together they monitored the world's skies, as a precaution against a possible computer error that could cause an unruly launch of missiles. Midnight, December 31 1999 has passed into the new millenium with no significant events, except for a few minor glitches.

Computer systems control many aspects of our lives. Telephone systems, store checkout registers, ticket reservation systems, medical systems, financial systems, are all highly computerized. Data communication between computers replaces, in most cases, the use of actual paper money transfer. Computers are even responsible for many of the activities required for flying commercial airplanes. Failure of computerized systems have already caused grave consequences, including fatal accidents, shutting down of vital systems, and loss of money.

The software development industry has grown over the last few decades at an unprecedented pace. Hardware, and in particular memory costs, kept decreasing. The internet has practically transformed the world into a big computer network, where communication, information and business are constantly taking place on-line. With these technological changes, the software development industry has also transformed. It is no longer feasible for a talented individual to single-handedly develop a whole software system. Instead, tens or even thousands of programmers are taking part in joint development efforts. Different parts of programs are being developed by programmers who may be working in different locations, and perhaps have never seen each other, producing thousands or even millions of lines of code.

It is thus not surprising that controlling the quality of the software production process has become significantly difficult. Assuring that the products of different software development groups will successfully work together is a nontrivial task. One of the main techniques to combat this problem is the application of appropriate design methodologies. Software engineering suggests various techniques for increasing the quality of software products.

Even when coping with many rules of good design and programming, as dictated by various software engineering methods, programs may still contain errors. Different statistics show that a few errors are highly likely to occur per every thousand lines of code, even in code developed by very experienced and highly skilled programmers. It is thus very important to use methods that attempt to remove man-made mistakes from program code. This is the goal of *formal methods techniques*. While various software engineering methods try to guide the software development, formal methods attempt to accompany the development with techniques and tools for finding and point out potential problems.

1.1 Formal Methods

Formal methods are a collection of notations and techniques for describing and analyzing systems. These methods are *formal* in the sense that they are based on some mathematical theories, such as logic, automata or graph theory. They are aimed at enhancing the quality of systems. Formal specification techniques introduce a precise and unambiguous description of the properties of systems. This is useful in eliminating misunderstandings, and can be used further for debugging systems. Formal analysis techniques can be used to verify that a system satisfies its specification, or to systematically seek for cases where it fails to do so. Formal methods can reduce the time it takes to find design or coding errors. They also significantly reduce the risk of damage incurred by not finding an error in a system before deploying it. In this book we will focus on formal methods for software, which we will also refer to as *software reliability methods*.

These techniques are sometimes used by the programmers themselves, but often are the responsibility of special software quality assurance teams. In the latter case, the separation and cooperation between the developers and the people taking care of reliability (e.g., testing teams) creates a beneficial synergy towards the development of more reliable software. In many cases, the quality assurance team is, in fact, bigger than the development team.

In the early years of formal methods research, the focus was on assuring the *correctness* of systems. Correctness of a system as used here means that the system satisfies its provided specification. *Deductive software verification* was one of the main formal methods techniques studied. Pioneers in the field, such as Dijkstra, Floyd, Gries, Hoare, Lamport, Manna, Owicki, Pnueli and others, developed different proof systems that could be applied for verifying the correctness of programs. The goal of such techniques was to formally verify critical systems, e.g., missiles, air traffic control. It was also suggested that verification methods could be used to assist with the development of software and hardware systems [94]. According to this suggestion, the programs were supposed to be refined in a stepwise manner, starting from their formal specification, and ending with actual code, in a way that would preserve the correctness of each refinement step.

Some limitations of formal methods were soon realized. Software verification methods do not guarantee the correctness of *actual* code, but rather allow one to verify some abstract *model* of it. Hence, due to possible differences between the actual system and its abstract model, the correctness of the proof may not carry over. In addition, the correctness proof can itself be incorrect. The verification process often captures only a small part of the functionality of the system. The reason is that the verification is done with respect to a given specification, which is formed manually, and is sometimes incomplete, omiting some important properties of the system. In fact, it is often very hard or even impossible to assess when a given specification is complete. Although some parts of deductive verification can be automated, it is, in principle, a manual technique. As such, deductive verification was demonstrated mainly for rather small examples and requires a lot of time and expertise.

Despite its limitations, deductive software verification has had several important successes. It has affected the software development process, by defining the notion of an *invariant*. An invariant is a correctness assertion that needs to hold at certain control points during execution. It asserts some connections between the program variables. When programmers add invariants to the code of a program, they gain more intuition about the way it works. Moreover, they can insert simple run-time checks that the invariant assertions really hold at the appropriate control points of the program. If an invariant fails to hold, the normal execution of the program is interrupted with a warning message.

Recently, new and powerful tools are being developed for supporting deductive software verification. These tools attempt to mechanize parts of the proofs. The cleanroom method [98, 99] (which will be described later in this book) is an example of an informal use of software verification. It is used within a methodology, together with other software reliability methods, and aims at providing high quality software.

Early automatic verification techniques were suggested by West and Zafiropulo [146, 150]. These methods could be applied to various *finite state systems*, such as hardware circuits and communication protocols. *Model checking*, i.e., verifying a finite state system against a given temporal specification, was pioneered by Clarke and Emerson [28, 42] in the US, and Quielle and Sifakis [120] in France. Starting with modest examples such as traffic light controllers, these methods have matured into a multimillion dollar industry of tools.

New automatic and semi-automatic verification techniques, such as binary decision diagrams [24], partial order reduction [55, 113, 142], symmetry reduction [43], induction [81, 149], abstraction and others, demonstrated the scalability of automatic verification methods. These techniques gave evidence that verification can work well in practice, and not only in theory. However, several limitations still need to be taken into account when using automatic verification. These include severe inefficiency in handling nontrivial data structures, e.g., queues or trees. Furthermore, automatic verification methods are usually restricted to finite state systems. Thus, they are most appropriate for verifying communication protocols or some abstract representation of algorithms. They may fail to handle full fledged programs with *real* and *integer* variables and with pointer and array references. Like deductive verification, the automatic verification techniques also require modeling the system rather than verifying it directly. This may again create a discrepancy between the verified object and the actual system.

Software testing is perhaps the most frequently used quality assurance method. Instead of trying to provide a comprehensive check of a system, testing is focused on sampling the executions, according to some coverage criteria, and comparing the actual behavior with the behavior that is expected according to the specification. This is often done based on experimental evidence and experience, and is frequently performed in a rather informal way. Testing methods have the advantage of being able to check an actual system, rather than a model of it. Unlike model checking, testing is not limited to finite state systems. However, testing is not as comprehensive a technique as deductive verification or model checking. It does not cover all the possible executions. Thus, even code that has been thoroughly tested can still contain errors.

Some Formal Methods Terminology

The term *verification* is used in different ways by researchers and practitioners of diverse formal methods. In some cases, verification is used to refer only to the process of obtaining the formal correctness proof of a system, thus suggesting the narrow meaning of using deductive verification. In other contexts, verification is used to describe any action that is taken in an attempt to find errors in a program, including model checking and testing.

Since this book describes different formal methods techniques, we will sometimes have to choose interpretations of terms that may not be consistent across all the different communities. By means of *verification*, we will refer to the process of applying a manual or an automatic technique that is supposed to establish whether the code either satisfies a given property or behaves in accordance with some higher-level description of it. By this we will mostly refer to the activities of deductive verification and model checking, but not to testing, since the latter is more akin to *sampling* than to an exhaustive correctness checking.

We will distinguish between verifying that a software satisfies certain specification *properties* (this is sometimes called *validation* [70]), and verifying the *conformance* between two descriptions of the software. In the latter case, one description is often less detailed, i.e., more abstract.

1.2 Developing and Acquiring Formal Methods

Formal methods include specification, verification and testing techniques. These methods are used to enhance the quality of software development and hardware design. In the past two decades, the benefits, advantages, trade-offs and limitations of using different methods were realized. Understanding the limitations of formal methods is not less important than presenting their success stories. For example, experience shows that algorithmic methods are usually preferred over methods that require considerable human skills. On the other hand, automatic methods are limited in scope, e.g., are often restricted to finite state systems of moderate size. As a manifestation of the maturity of formal methods research, methods that attempt to *guarantee* correctness are treated with suspicion, while methods that are aimed at finding errors are preferred.

Tools and support for various formal methods were first pioneered by researchers in universities and in research laboratories. In recent years, we have witnessed companies, especially in the communication and in the hardware industries, where reliability is critical, developing their own formal methods and tools. In other cases, an interface is developed for translating the software into a form that is acceptable by some existing tool. The output of that tool may be translated back into some required format. We are also starting to see available tools that can enhance software reliability. However, the majority of these tools are related to various tasks of software testing or software modeling.

The research in formal methods is relatively new. Selecting the right technique and tool is difficult. Developing a new verification or testing tool requires considerable effort. In this book, we will try to point out the similarities and differences between the various formal methods, and how they can be combined and complement each other.

When a new software product is developed, a decision must be made on whether to use a particular software reliability tool or technique. In some cases, an attempt should be made to develop a new tool or tailor an existing one to some specific needs. Different considerations may be taken into account by people in different roles in software development organizations. Some of the relevant issues are listed below.

- **Project manager**
  - What are the benefits of using formal methods in my software project?
  - What is the investment in time, human resources, money?
  - Should I start an in-house formal methods group to develop new tools that will match my organization needs?
- **Head of quality assurance team**
  - In what stages of the development should we use formal methods?
  - How do I schedule the use of formal methods with the other development activities?
  - How much human resources do we need for this task? What are their qualifications?
  - How do we hire or train people to apply formal methods?
- **Engineer (User)**
  - What are the best tools or techniques for achieving better reliability?
  - How much would it cost?
  - What is the support that is provided with the tools?
  - What is the most appropriate formal representation of the system that is being developed?
  - What is the probability of finding errors by using the different formal methods?
  - Which specification formalism will best suit the developed system?
  - How much time would it take to develop new methods or improve and fit existing ones to my organization's purposes?
  - Do we need special equipment or software to support such tools?
  - How do we model the developed system or a part of it using the particular method or tool selected?
  - How can we interpret the results, i.e., is there really an error when the tool reports one, and how assured are we when no errors are found?
  - What do we do when the tool we use fails, e.g., when the verification does not terminate in a reasonable time or when it runs out of memory?
  - Are our specifications correct? Do they include internal contradictions? Do they include all the necessary requirements from the system?
- **Formal methods researcher**
  - How can I increase the *expressiveness* of formal methods techniques, allowing the specification and verification of more system requirements?

– How can I increase the *efficiency* of the techniques, making the methods and tools faster and capable of handling larger instances?
– Are there good *heuristics* that work better than standard methods in many practical cases?
– How do I transfer new technology to potential users?
– What is the common notation used by software developers? How do I integrate it into the techniques and tools I develop?

We cannot answer in this book all of these questions, as some of them are strongly dependent on the particular system being developed, the environment and the organization. However, we will attempt to address these issues by providing information about some of the modern formal methods, their uses and limitations. Our goal is to describe the main methods, and present their strengths and weaknesses. This will allow potential users to acquire more knowledge about their capabilities and limitations in order to select the right approach for their own purposes, and use it effectively and efficiently.

1.3 Using Formal Methods

The use of formal methods can achieve various goals:

• Obtaining a common and formal description of a system, at the various stages of its development. Formal *specification* allows a common and agreed upon description of the system or its properties that is used by the different groups involved in the development. This description has a clear and unambiguous meaning. It gives the designers, the programmers, the quality assurance teams, and later the users, a collection of documents that can be used to resolve misunderstandings and disputes regarding the intended behavior of the system.
• Formal methods were developed for the purpose of finding errors that are introduced during the development of systems. They are used to help the designer and the developer detect, pinpoint and analyze the errors. Thus, they increase the reliability of the system.
• Formal methods can be integrated with, and assist in, the development process. Some software reliability tools not only allow modeling and capturing the design of a system, but also provide some means of automatically or semiautomatically converting the design into an initial implementation. For example, tools that capture the dynamics of the behavior of a system may attempt to automatically generate code that will exhibit the desired behavior.

Formal methods can be used in almost every stage of a software development project. One can use formal specification to capture the desired features and the system specification. Testing and verification can already start at this early stage. The initial design, be it even a collection of possible scenarios within a feasibility study, can already be subjected to early fault-detection algorithms. These can alert the developer to some potential problems, such as unexpected interactions between features (feature interaction), or with the environment.

Testing and verification can be applied in different stages of the development. The earlier in the process an error is caught, the less damage it has done, and the cheaper it is to fix it. Yet, even if formal methods were extensively used in early development stages, new errors can still penetrate into the developed system. The repeated use of formal methods in later stages is thus a useful practice.

Software development *methodologies* can prescribe how to compose the system's requirements, plan the timetable, estimate the costs and human resources, divide the work between the different groups, etc. Formal methods are most effectively used within a project when properly used under such a methodology. Specific time and human resources should be reserved for enhancing the reliability of the developed software.

In reality it is still frequently the case that the advocates of formal methods need to compete with other development activities. There are several factors contributing to this situation:

- Formal methods are relatively new. Some of the methods were suggested only recently (twenty years ago, or even less).
- There is an ever-growing inclination to finish the development and ship the products as fast as possible, with tight deadlines on different development activities. On face of it, it seems that formal methods require additional investment in time, money and human resources. The fact that formal methods may save time and money by finding errors is often discounted, in particular in organizations that have not yet had experience with this technology.
- Research in formal methods is frequently focused on improving the expressiveness and efficiency of the techniques. This has often resulted in the neglect of human interface issues, which are crucial in attracting new users. Since formal methods are based on the mathematical analysis of systems, some techniques require the potential users to educate themselves in using a new mathematical framework and notation. It has only recently become widely accepted that the developers of formal methods need to adopt the framework and notation already used by the potential users.

Many software developers and software engineers still have some qualms about the use of formal methods. Perhaps one of the main reasons for this is the use of words such as 'verification,' which suggests some absolute guarantees about the inspected software. Such absolute guarantees cannot be achieved. In particular, a license for a software verification tool typically proclaims no responsibility whatsoever for the detection of some or all of the problems in the inspected software. This seems to be a marketing problem;

it may be solved by better explaining the benefits of using formal methods *and* their limitations.

There are various common misconceptions and prejudices about using formal methods:

Formal methods can be used only by mathematicians.

The fact that formal methods are based on mathematics means that the developers of the methods are likely to be mathematicians, computer scientists or electrical engineers. Indeed, some of the methods, such as deductive verification, require a high level of mathematical skill. However, many of the modern formal methods are designed so that a software engineer can use them with minimal training. This is due to the fact that developers of formal methods have realized that they are often successful when they base their methods on the formalisms and tools of their intended users, rather than requesting that the users learn new formalisms.

Using formal methods will slow down projects.

It is true that using formal methods takes a nonnegligible amount of time. Adding the use of formal methods to the development process requires scheduling a certain number of people to be engaged in this activity for some amount of time. However, experience shows that the use of formal methods, in particular in the early development stages, reduces considerably the time it takes to debug and deliver a system. Verifying or testing a system is time well spent, since customers are frequently willing to pay for reliability.

The verification process itself is prone to errors, so why bother at all?

Indeed, one cannot achieve absolute certainty with regard to the correctness of software. Mistakes can be made during the modeling of software and the translation done in order to fit verification and testing tools. Formal methods tools may also contain bugs, and human verification is obviously prone to errors. In fact, these problems are not merely theoretical and do occur in practice when using formal methods. The important point to realize is that formal methods are not intended to provide *absolute* reliability. The strengths of formal methods are thus in *increasing* the reliability. Statistical studies show that they indeed succeed in achieving this goal.

1.4 Applying Formal Methods

Formal methods can be used in various stages of the software development process, from early design to the acceptance tests of the completed product. Optimally, the use of such methods is integrated into the development process through a methodology. The development timetable should include specific time slots for performing testing and verification tasks. Certifying that the software has passed certain validity checks can be used as milestones for the development process.

Unfortunately, the effectiveness of formal methods tends to diminish with the size of the checked object. This problem, sometimes called the *state space explosion*, will be discussed at length in this book. Therefore, it is more effective to apply formal methods in the early design and development stages, where the checked objects are relatively small. Another reason for the early use of formal methods is that errors that are found in early stages have less chance of causing a lot of damage and are usually cheaper to fix.

The size of a software system consists nowadays of thousands to millions of lines of code. To cope with the deadlines for software development, software development is often shared among different groups of programmers, sometimes located in different places. Thus, it is often difficult, if not impossible, to apply formal methods to a complete system. Therefore, the tendency is to look for *compositional* methods, which attempt to verify or test different parts of the code separately, and then make conclusions about the system as a whole.

Consider, for example, an idealized case, where a system consists of two subsystems, A and B. We would like to check that the system satisfies some property p. During a compositional verification attempt, we may try to show that A satisfies some property p_1, and B satisfies some property p_2. Then, we want to show that given that p_1 and p_2 hold for A and B, respectively, implies that p holds for the complete system. Sometimes, when the development of subsystems A and B is done independently, there is one team that checks A against p_1, and another team that checks B against p_2. This allows various interesting possibilities, such as allowing the team that developed A to check B, while the team that developed B checks A (letting the developers check their own code is usually not a good idea, as will be explained in Chapter 9). On the other hand, compositional verification and testing allows increased flexibility in setting the system development schedule. Compositional formal methods are thus very desirable. Unfortunately, as we will see later, there are some difficult cases, where achieving compositionality is hard.

The use of formal methods is not restricted to the code of software systems. One may start by checking the requirements for possible contradictions. The early design, even when it consists merely of a few examples, can also be verified for consistency. Some development methodologies, such as *cleanroom* [98, 99] use formal methods throughout the process to refine the code in a way that attempts to preserve its correctness from one development stage to another. Ideally, one can start from the system specification, and by repeatedly refining it, while preserving the correctness at each stage, obtain code that satisfies the specification.

Some of the methods presented in this book are also used for specifying, verifying and testing hardware. In particular, some variants of these methods include optimizations that are most effective for hardware [24]. With the recent progress in software and hardware design, systems that include both hardware and software components are being developed. Critical software is sometimes implemented on a chip, and hardware design is nowadays done using programming languages. With the blurring of the distinction between software and hardware, and the growing trend of developing systems that include both hardware and software components, we need to provide efficient formal methods techniques that will be able to fit both [80].

Applying formal methods costs money. There is no way around this, although more efficient methods may help in reducing the costs. On the other hand, using formal methods may prevent some unfortunate situations caused by errors, and thus overall, may save money, or in some extreme cases, human life. It is thus not unreasonable to find out that in some cases the investment in applying formal methods may be equivalent or even greater than the investment in all other development activities. Achieving reliability is quite often a good investment, and sometimes is priceless.

1.5 Overview of the Book

Research in formal methods has produced many interesting and useful results. The basic methods demonstrated the capabilities of software analysis. Current improvements are aimed at achieving more efficiency and automatization, in order to apply these methods to a wider range of systems. As the area of formal methods matures, we witness many versions of the basic techniques, some of which are optimized towards more specific applications. It is not possible to cover in an introductory book all the recent results. However, the principles presented in this book are common to many of the basic and current methods.

The two main components of formal methods that are emphasized in this book are *logic* and *automata theory*. With the understanding of these concepts and their use in the formal analysis of systems, it is easy to grasp the basic ideas, as well as the new developments in this area.

We start with some preliminary background from mathematics (Chapter 2). Logic (Chapter 3) is a concisely defined syntax, equipped with a formal semantics and a deductive capability of inferring new facts from given facts. It can be used for formalizing systems and their properties. Certain instances, such as first order logic (Chapter 3) or linear temporal logic (Chapter 5), are frequently used for software specification. Related concepts, such as process algebra (Chapter 8), are used to analyze the subtle issues of interaction within a system or of the system with its environment. Using logical notation is not limited to providing a precise and unambiguous specification. Logics are often equipped with proof systems, which allow one to make inferences manually, or automatically. Such proof systems can be used for program verification (Chapter 7).

Another mathematical theory that plays an important role in formal methods is automata theory (Chapters 5, 6). An automaton is a mathematical structure that can be used to model different behaviors based on the states of the system and the transitions between them. Different versions of automata are often used to model software systems. Automata theory is one of the cornerstones of computer science, and thus many mathematical tools are available for the analysis of automata. Such tools are used in formal methods in order to perform the automatic analysis of systems.

The use of formal methods usually starts with modeling the checked system as a mathematical object (Chapter 4). Formal specification of the modeled system and its required properties (Chapter 5) are given using some selected formalism. Then, one can apply some techniques for obtaining a higher-level of confidence in the correctness of the system. The main methods are model checking (Chapter 6) deductive verification (Chapter 7), and testing (Chapter 9). One can also enhance reliability by stepwise refinement of a design, while maintaining the appropriate conformance between the versions (Chapter 8).

The last chapters of the book describe some more advanced techniques. We show how to combine the strength of different formal methods (Chapter 10). A recent successful trend in formal methods is to use visual formalisms (Chapter 11). We conclude with a discussion of the methods presented, and some new directions in formal methods research (Chapter 12).

2. Preliminaries

As she said this, she looked up, and there was the Cat again, sitting on a branch of a tree.

Lewis Carroll, *Alice's Adventures in Wonderland*

Software reliability methods are based on mathematical principles. It is usually not necessary for users of these methods to master the relevant mathematical theories. In this book we are going to present both the techniques and some of the principles comprising them. We will thus necessarily use some mathematical terminology. This chapter surveys some concepts and theories that are used later in the book. Having a prior knowledge of basic notions from set theory, graph theory, complexity theory and computability is sufficient to allow the reader to skip this chapter.

2.1 Set Notation

A *set* is a finite or infinite collection of elements. Repetitions of elements in a set are ignored. For finite sets, the elements can be listed between a matching pair of braces, as in $\{1, 3, 5, 9\}$. Another notation for sets is $\{x|R(x)\}$, where R is some description that restricts the possible values of x. For example, $\{x|even(x) \text{ and } x > 0 \text{ and } x < 200\}$ is the set of even numbers between 2 and 198. One special set is the *empty set*, denoted $\emptyset$, which does not contain any elements. The *size* of a set is the number of elements it contains. The size of a set A is denoted by $|A|$. Obviously, $|\emptyset| = 0$.

There are several operations that can be performed on sets:

Intersection. The elements that are both in A and in B are denoted by $A \cap B$.

Union. The elements that are in A or in B (or in both) are denoted by $A \cup B$.

Difference. The elements that are in A but not in B are denoted by $A \setminus B$.

Powerset. All the sets that can be formed from elements of A are denoted by 2^A. Note that 2^A is a set whose elements are also sets, the *subsets* of A. If A has finitely many elements, then the size of 2^A is $2^{|A|}$.

For example, if $A = \{1, 3, 5, 6, 8\}$ and $B = \{3, 6, 9\}$, then $A \cap B = \{3, 6\}$, $A \cup B = \{1, 3, 5, 6, 8, 9\}$, and $A \setminus B = \{1, 5, 8\}$. The powerset of B, 2^B is

$$\{\emptyset, \{3\}, \{6\}, \{9\}, \{3, 6\}, \{3, 9\}, \{6, 9\}, \{3, 6, 9\}\}.$$

When the elements under discussion are taken from a given domain $\mathcal{D}$ that is understood from the context, e.g., the *integers*,

$$Int = \{\ldots, -2, -1, 0, 1, 2, \ldots\},$$

or the *naturals*,

$$Nat = \{0, 1, 2, \ldots\},$$

one can take the *complement* of a set. The complement of A (with respect to $\mathcal{D}$), is the set containing all the elements of $\mathcal{D}$ that are not in A. This is denoted by $\overline{A}$. In other words, $\overline{A}$ is $\mathcal{D} \setminus A$.

To denote that an element x belongs to a set A, we write $x \in A$. If x does not belong to A, we write $x \notin A$. One can compare a pair of sets as follows:

- $A \subseteq B$ if for every element $x \in A$ it is also the case that $x \in B$. We say that A is *contained* in B or that A is a *subset* of B. In this case we can also write $B \supseteq A$.
- $A = B$ if both A is contained in B and B is contained in A. We say that A and B are *equal*.
- $A \subset B$ if A is contained in B but A is not equal to B (thus, B must include at least one element that is not in A). We say that A is *properly contained* in B or that A is a *proper subset* of B. We can also write $B \supset A$.

For example, let $B = \{1, 2, 3, 4, 5\}$ and $A = \{2, 4, 5\}$. Then we have that $A \subseteq B$. In fact, since $A \neq B$, we also have $A \subset B$.

The *Cartesian product* of two sets A and B, denoted by $A \times B$, is a set of *ordered pairs*. Each pair in $A \times B$ includes a first element from A and a second element from B. For example, if $A = \{q_0, q_1\}$ and $B = \{s_2, s_3\}$, then $A \times B = \{\langle q_0, s_2 \rangle, \langle q_0, s_3 \rangle, \langle q_1, s_2 \rangle, \langle q_1, s_3 \rangle\}$. For finite sets A and B, if $|A| = m$ and $|B| = n$, then $|A \times B| = m \times n$. We denote pairs by listing two elements in between angle ('$\langle$' and '$\rangle$') or round ('(' and ')') brackets. By a repeated application of the Cartesian product, we can obtain more complicated elements, e.g., triples, quadruples, quintuples, sextuples, or in general n-tuples.

A *relation* of arity n is a set of n-tuples over some domain. Each n-tuple is an object with exactly n ordered elements. An example of a relation is the 'greater than' order between *integers*, usually denoted by '$>$'. This is a *binary* relation, i.e., a relation of pairs. We have the following pairs belonging to the relation:

$$(3, 5), (7, 9), (3, 11)$$

while the following do not belong to it:

$$(3, 3), (7, 3), (0, -1)$$

A relation can also be defined over multiple domains, such that the value in each location of the n-tuple is taken from a particular domain.

For a binary relation $R \subseteq \mathcal{D}_1 \times \mathcal{D}_2$, we denote by R^{-1} the relation $\{\langle x, y \rangle | \langle y, x \rangle \in R\}$. Notice that $R^{-1} \subseteq \mathcal{D}_2 \times \mathcal{D}_1$. We sometimes say that R^{-1} is the *transpose* of R. We often denote the fact that $(x_1, \ldots, x_n) \in R$ by $R(x_1, \ldots, x_n)$. For binary relations, we also use *infix* notation and write $x_1 R x_2$.

The *transitive closure* of a binary relation $R \subseteq \mathcal{D} \times \mathcal{D}$ is denoted R^*. It is defined as follows: $(x, y) \in R^*$ when there is a sequence $z_0, z_1, \ldots, z_n$ such that $(z_i, z_{i+1}) \in R$ for $0 \leq i < n$, $z_0 = x$ and $z_n = y$.

A *function* (or a *mapping*) of arity n can be viewed as a constrained relation, containing $(n + 1)$-tuples, where the first n elements uniquely define the $(n+1)$st element. That is, we cannot have two $(n+1)$-tuples that agree on their first n elements but differ in their $(n + 1)$st element. A function f over the domains $\mathcal{D}_1, \mathcal{D}_2, \ldots, \mathcal{D}_n$ that results in a value from the domain $\mathcal{D}_{n+1}$ will be denoted by $f : \mathcal{D}_1 \times \mathcal{D}_2 \times \ldots \times \mathcal{D}_n \to \mathcal{D}_{n+1}$. *Integer* addition, denoted by '$+$' is a function of arity 2, i.e., $+ : int \times int \to int$. One can also view a relation of arity n as a function of the same arity, which returns either TRUE or FALSE. Thus, each n-tuple is extended to an $(n + 1)$ tuple, where the last Boolean element is uniquely defined by the previous n elements. Notice that relation and function symbols are often 'overloaded' with multiple interpretation. For example, the relation symbol '$>$' stands for 'greater than' over the *integers* and also over the *real* numbers.

An *equivalence relation* $\sim$ is a binary relation over some domain $\mathcal{D}$ satisfying the following:

reflexive For each element $x \in \mathcal{D}$, $x \sim x$.
symmetric For each two elements $x, y \in \mathcal{D}$, if $x \sim y$ then $y \sim x$.
transitive For each three elements $x, y, z \in \mathcal{D}$, if $x \sim y$ and $y \sim z$ then $x \sim z$.

A function $f : \mathcal{D}_1 \to \mathcal{D}_2$ is said to be

one-one (or *injective*) if for every two elements $d_1, d_2 \in \mathcal{D}_1$, $d_1 \neq d_2$ we have $f(d_1) \neq f(d_2)$.
onto if for each element $c \in \mathcal{D}_2$ there is an element $d \in \mathcal{D}_1$ such that $f(d) = c$.
injective if it is both one-one and onto.

2.2 Strings and Languages

A *string* is a (finite or infinite) sequence over some predefined set called an *alphabet*. It is a common practice to use the character Σ to denote an alphabet. The elements of Σ are called *letters*. A (finite or infinite) set L of strings over some alphabet is called a *language*. A string is typically denoted by listing the sequence of letters appearing in it. For example, if $\Sigma = \{a, b, c\}$, i.e., the first three English alphabet letters, then *aabacca* and *babacca* are strings over Σ. Since a language is a set (of strings), we can define it using the usual set notation. A special string, denoted ε (where ε is not in the alphabet Σ), is the *empty* string, containing no letters. There are several useful operations on strings that we will use in the sequel:

Concatenation Connecting two or more strings together in some order is usually denoted by writing them in the required order, and separating them with the '.' operator. For example, we can concatenate three strings *abba*, *acca* and *baa*, writing *abba.acca.baa*. This results in the string *abbaaccabaa*. Concatenation of strings is extended to sets of strings such that $U.V$ is defined as $\{u.v | u \in U \land v \in V\}$. In many cases the concatenation operator '.' is omitted.

Repetition If σ is a string, then σ^* is a set of strings (a language), each of which contains zero or more repetitions of σ. For example, the language $(abac)^*$ contains the strings ε, *abac*, *abacabac*, etc. Given a language L, we denote by L^* the language obtained from L by repeatedly concatenating zero or more words from L. For example, if $L = \{ab, bc\}$ then L^* includes ε, *ab*, *bc*, *abab*, *abbc*, *ababbc*, *bcbcab*, etc. Notice that the strings in L^* are not limited to taking a single string $\sigma \in L$ and repeating it. Once the operator '*' is defined, we can now denote a language L over an alphabet Σ as $L \subseteq \Sigma^*$. A variant of '*' is the operator '+'. It behaves in a similar way, except for excluding the empty string (i.e., zero repetitions). Another variant is the 'ω' operator, which is used to form infinite strings by imposing infinitely many repetitions.

Set operators Set operators, such as '$\cup$', '$\cap$' or '$\backslash$' may be used to form a language from other given languages. Since languages are sets of strings, we can also use the set comparison relations '$\subseteq$', '$=$' and '$\supseteq$' to compare between them.

If a string v can be decomposed into $u.w$ (where u or w can be the empty string), we call u a *prefix* of v, and w a *suffix* of v.

2.3 Graphs

Graphs are a common representation for a collection of objects S with some (binary) relation Δ connecting them. We denote such a graph as a pair $\langle S, \Delta \rangle$. The objects in S are usually called *nodes* or *vertices*. Nodes are usually represented visually as ovals or other shapes. Each related pair $(s, r) \in \Delta$ is called an *edge*. If the relation Δ is symmetric, meaning that if for each $(s, r) \in \Delta$ we also have $(r, s) \in \Delta$, then the graph is *undirected*, and the edges are represented by lines or arcs stretched between the ovals representing related nodes. If the relation Δ is not symmetric, the graph is *directed*, and each edge (s, r) is represented by an arrow from the oval representing s to the oval representing r. If $e = (s, r)$ is an edge in Δ, then s is the *source* of e and r is the *target* of e. We also say that e is an *out-edge* of s and an *in-edge* of r.

An example of a directed graph appears in Figure 2.1. The set of nodes is $\{r_1, r_2, \ldots, r_9\}$. The edges are

$$\{\, (r_1, r_2),\ (r_2, r_3),\ (r_3, r_1),\ (r_2, r_5),\ (r_3, r_4),\ (r_4, r_4),\ (r_5, r_6),$$
$$(r_6, r_7),\ (r_7, r_8),\ (r_8, r_5), (r_5, r_9),\ (r_9, r_7),\ (r_4, r_8)\, \}$$

An edge, such as (r_4, r_4), from one node (in this case r_4) back to itself, is called a *self edge* or a *self loop*.

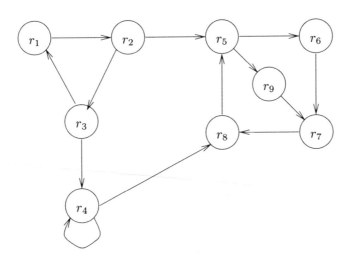

Fig. 2.1. A directed graph

We may include in a graph additional components to S and Δ. A graph may contain *labels* on the nodes, the edges, or both. Given a set of labels D, an *edge labeling function* $L : \Delta \to D$ assigns each edge in Δ an element of D. This is usually represented by putting next to each edge its corresponding label. The graph in this case is a quadruple (S, Δ, D, L). Labels can allow us to distinguish between edges when there is more than one edge between certain pairs of nodes. Then the edges can also be redefined as triples over $S \times D \times S$, so that each edge contains the source node, the label and the target node. In this case the edge labeling function L for an edge (s, a, r) returns the projection on the middle component a of the edge.

A *path* is a (finite or infinite) sequence of nodes of S, $s_0, s_1, s_2, \ldots, s_n, \ldots$ such that each adjacent pair of nodes s_i, s_{i+1} forms an edge $(s_i, s_{i+1}) \in \Delta$. A path is *simple* if no node on it appears more than once. Notice that in an infinite path over a finite graph, at least one of the nodes must repeat infinitely many times. A *cycle* is a finite path that begins and ends with the same node. The *length* of a path is the number of edges that appear on it, including repetitions (hence, the number of nodes on a path is one more than the length of the path). Consequently, for each node there is a trivial path from the node to itself of length 0. In the graph of Figure 2.1, there is a simple path $r_1, r_2, r_3, r_4, r_8, r_5, r_9, r_7$ of length 7. The path r_5, r_6, r_7, r_8, r_5 is a cycle, whose length is 4. The *distance* between two nodes in a graph is the length of the shortest path between them. The distance between r_2 and r_5 is then 1, and the distance between r_1 and r_7 is 4.

A subset of nodes $S' \subseteq S$ in a graph is *strongly-connected* if there is a path between any pair of nodes in S', passing only through nodes in S'. A *strongly-connected component* is a maximal set of such nodes, i.e., one cannot add any node to that set of nodes and still maintain strong connectivity. The graph in Figure 2.1 has three strongly-connected components: $\{r_1, r_2, r_3\}$, $\{r_4\}$ and $\{r_5, r_6, r_7, r_8, r_9\}$. A *trivial strongly-connected component* is a strongly connected component consisting of one node without a self loop.

There are many graph algorithms [33] that can be used to find important information related to finite graphs. Such algorithms can, for example, check whether there is a path between two nodes, and return the distance between them. One algorithm that will be of particular interest for automatic verification of programs is Tarjan's DFS algorithm for finding strongly-connected components [139]. Another important algorithm is the Floyd-Warshall algorithm [145] for calculating the *transitive closure* of a graph, i.e., the set of pairs of nodes (s, r) such that there is a path from s to r.

A *tree* is a cycle-free directed graph that has one node distinguished to be its *root* with no in-edges, while every other has exactly one in-edge. Thus, there is a path (in fact a unique one) from the root to any other node in the tree. The *outdegree* of each node is the number of its outgoing edges. One common way to draw a tree is to put the root at the top, then all the nodes accessible from the root via one edge appearing horizontally below, then all the nodes accessible from the latter nodes via one edge further below, and so forth, as in Figure 2.2. Each such horizontal collection of nodes is called a *level*. Then, the root is the only node in level 0, and nodes on the ith level have a path of length i from the root. If there is a path from a node r to a node r' in a tree, then r' is called a *successor* of r and r is a *predecessor* of r'. The node r is an *immediate predecessor* of r', and r' is an *immediate successor* of r if that path has length 1. A tree node that does not have any successors is called a *leaf*.

It is sometimes useful to look at an *unfolding* of a graph G, from a given node ι. An unfolding is a tree, whose nodes are labeled with the nodes of G, as described below. We will call each node of the unfolding that is labeled with s an *occurrence* of s. In the unfolding, there can be multiple occurrences of a single node of G. The root of the unfolding is an occurrence of the node ι of G. If there is an occurrence of a node s at the ith level of the unfolding, and there is an edge in G from s to s', then there will be an occurrence of s' in the

$(i+1)$th level and an edge from the occurrence of s to the occurrence of s' in the tree. Suppose that both s_1 and s_2 occur in the ith level of the unfolding, and both have an edge in G to some node s. Then there will be different occurrences of s in the $(i+1)$th level of the unfolding, one as an immediate successor of s_1, and one as an immediate successor of s_2. Figure 2.2 is a part of the infinite unfolding of the graph in Figure 2.1, from r_1.

Formally, we define $Tr = \langle \iota, \hat{S}, \hat{\Delta}, L \rangle$ to be an unfolding of a graph $G = \langle S, \Delta \rangle$ from some node ι of S, when the following hold:

- Tr is a tree, with root ι, a set of nodes $\hat{S}$, set of edges $\hat{\Delta}$, and a labeling function $L : \hat{S} \to S$.
- If $r \in \hat{S}$ such that $L(r) = s$, and s has m out-edges to nodes $s_1, \ldots, s_m$ in G, then r has according to $\hat{\Delta}$ exactly m immediate successors, $r_1, \ldots, r_m \in \hat{S}$, such that $L(r_i) = s_i$ for $1 \leq i \leq m$.

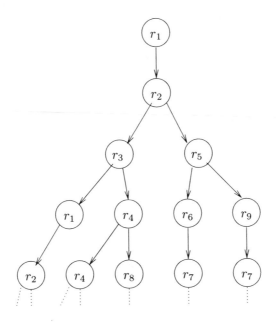

Fig. 2.2. An unfolding of the graph in Figure 2.1

An important fact about trees is König's Lemma (see, e.g., [33]):

Every infinite tree (i.e., a tree with infinitely many nodes) such that the outdegree of each node is finite, must have an infinite path.

2.4 Computational Complexity and Computability

The *complexity* of an algorithm is a measure that estimates how much time or memory (space) is required to execute it. One can also talk about the complexity of a computational problem, expressing the complexity of the best algorithm for solving it. In certain cases, complexity measures can be used to evaluate the hardware that is needed for that task. In other cases, they are used to show that a certain algorithm is impractical, or even that a certain problem has no chance of being solved efficiently.

Since there is a variety of computing devices, complexity is commonly measured with respect to the abstract model of *Turing machines* [69]. A Turing machine is a mathematical model of a computer program, which uses a linear *tape* as a storage device. The tape is divided into cells. Each cell is labeled by a tape symbol from a given alphabet Σ. The alphabet includes a special blank symbol $b̸$. The tape has a fixed left end, and is infinite on the right. The *read and write head* can read and change the tape symbol that is in the current tape location, namely the location pointed to by the head (see Figure 2.3). The head can also move one place to the left or to the right. Initially, the tape head is pointing at the leftmost cell.

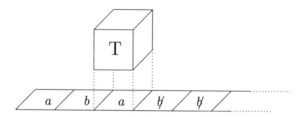

Fig. 2.3. A Turing Machine

The control of the Turing machine is a finite table, describing for each pair of a state and a current input symbol the following: (1) the next state, (2) a replacement symbol for the current tape location, and (3) a direction for the move of the head, left or right. At each step, depending on the current machine state and the symbol in the current tape location, the machine can change the symbol in the current location, move the head, and change the current state according to the control table.

The input to the machine is available at the beginning of the execution at the leftmost tape positions. It does not include any blank symbols $b̸$, and it is followed by an infinite contiguous sequence of blank symbols to the right. The *input size* is the number of cells the input occupies. In some cases, we use a slightly more complicated Turing machine with multiple tapes. Then, the input resides on one tape, which cannot be overwritten, while the other tapes are accounted as the memory used. Many other variants of Turing machines exist.

A Turing machine can act as an *acceptor* to input words. It accepts a word if the computation terminates in a state that is distinguished as *accepting*, and rejects a word if it the computation either does not terminate or terminates in a state marked *rejecting*. Alternatively, a Turing machine can also act as a *transducer*, transforming its input to a corresponding output that resides at the end of the computation on the tape.

The Turing machine model is a very abstract representation of an algorithm. Real computers are of course capable of performing much more complicated operations than moving the head, changing the current symbol and the state. However, the Turing machine model is still a good mathematical tool that is used as a yardstick to compare different algorithms and computation problems. Furthermore, although the operations of a real computer are more complicated than that of a Turing machine, the overall computation that is performed by them is the same.

The computational model of a Turing machine has several advantages. It is rather simple and abstract, eliminating the need to consider many details of actual computers. This also means that we do not have to analyze a computational problem or an algorithm again when moving from one actual computer to another. This model also allows viewing a computational problem as a language of accepted input words. In this way, it is related to other models of computation that are commonly used in computer science, such as finite automata (see Section 5.5). In fact, a Turing machine can be considered as a finite state automaton (referring to the finite control of the machine) with infinite memory (referring to the infinite tape).

Measuring the efficiency of an algorithm is done with respect to either *time* or *space* (i.e., memory) *complexity*. The time refers to the number of steps executed by a Turing machine, and the space refers to the number of tape symbols used. (When space is measured, we use multiple-tape machines, mentioned above. The reason for this is that, in this way, the space can be also a fraction of the size of the input.)

Complexity measures are given as a function of the size of the input n. We denote the worst-case complexity using the 'big-oh' notation, $\mathcal{O}(f(n))$, where f is a function. For example, $\mathcal{O}(n^2)$ (for quadratic complexity) or $\mathcal{O}(2^n)$ (for exponential complexity), where n refers to the input size. The '$\mathcal{O}(f(n))$' notation is interpreted as follows:

An algorithm or a computational problem is of complexity $\mathcal{O}(f(n))$ if there exist two constants, c_0 and c_1, such that for each instance of the input of size $n > c_0$, the time/space needed to run the algorithm (solving the problem) on a Turing machine is *no more* than $c_1 \times f(n)$.

The reasons for this interpretation are as follows:

- One *usually* does not care if there is a finite number of instances of the problem, smaller than some constant c_0, where the complexity does not behave according to $f(n)$.
- The complexity measure is given only up to some constant factor c_1. This is because we *usually* do not want to take into account in our calculations the speed of the execution of the machine, or the word size. If we buy later a faster computer, or a computer where each memory element is twice as large as the current one (e.g., 64 bits, instead of 32 bits), the complexity will still remain the same. (Actually, one can eliminate the constant c_0 by fixing a big enough constant c_1. However, this may result in some unnecessary large c_1.)
- There can be instances of size n (even $n > c_0$), where the calculation will be faster or require less memory than $c_n \times f(n)$. It is only the worst cases instances of size n which count. This is because we agree to commit only to the worst case in the complexity measure. Users of a computer system will not complain about instances of the input where the algorithm runs faster or consumes less memory than anticipated.

Note that if an algorithm is of complexity $\mathcal{O}(f(n))$ and for each $n \geq 0$, $f(n) \leq g(n)$ then it is also of complexity measure $\mathcal{O}(g(n))$. It is not necessarily the case that the algorithm that is most efficient with respect to the time complexity is also the algorithm that is most efficient with respect to space complexity.

We measure here the *worst case complexity* of algorithms, i.e., the measure for the worst instances. It is sometimes interesting also to provide the average complexity of algorithms. Average complexity is based on a probability distribution. In practice, one seldom has experimental results that substantiate the claim that instances of the problem distribute in a particular way. Thus, this is often less meaningful than the worst case complexity.

In this book, we will provide the complexity of the algorithms that are being presented. We will usually avoid the complicated complexity analysis of algorithms, and will refer the reader to the literature. We will survey here some essential facts from complexity theory, which can help in gaining some intuition about the efficiency of algorithms.

Let $P(n)$ denote some polynomial. That is, a function of n of the form $a_k n^k + a_{k-1} n^{k-1} + a_{k-2} n^{k-2} + \ldots + a_0$, for some *integers* constants $a_0, \ldots, a_k$. The *degree* of a polynomial is the highest power that appears in it. For example, $3n^7 + 9n^4 + 3$ is a polynomial of degree 7. A *complexity class* is a class of computational problems, whose complexity satisfies some given specification. Some of the main complexity classes are given below.

log – problems of complexity $\mathcal{O}(\log n)$.

polylog – problems of complexity $(P(\log n))$.

linear – problems of complexity $\mathcal{O}(n)$.

polynomial – problems of complexity $\mathcal{O}(P(n))$.

exponential – problems of complexity $\mathcal{O}(2^{P(n)})$.

doubly exponential – problems of complexity $\mathcal{O}(2^{2^{P(n)}})$.

NONELEMENTARY – problems for which there is no fixed k, such that the complexity is in $\mathcal{O}(2^{2^{\cdot^{\cdot^{2^n}}}})$, i.e., a tower of k exponents.

It can be shown using simple arithmetic arguments that for polynomial complexity, the only important factor for the complexity measure is the one with the highest (fixed) exponent. According to this, $\mathcal{O}(3n^7 + 9n^4 + 3)$ is the same as $\mathcal{O}(n^7)$.

To demonstrate the complexity measures, consider problem instances of sizes $n = 5$, 10, 50, 100 and 500. For simplicity, assume that the constants c_0 and c_1 are 0 and 1, respectively, in all of the following cases. The time it takes to calculate an $\mathcal{O}(n)$ algorithm is 5, 10, 50, 100 and 500, respectively of some time units, say milliseconds. For the complexity measure $\mathcal{O}(n^2)$, the execution time will be 25, 100, 2500, 10000 and 250000 milliseconds, respectively. For $\mathcal{O}(n^3)$, this is 125, 1000, 125000, 1000000 and 125000000, respectively. For exponential complexity, $\mathcal{O}(2^n)$ this is 32, 124, then a number that is greater than 1125 followed by 26 zeros, then a number that is greater than 3 followed by 150 zeros, etc. For doubly exponential complexity $\mathcal{O}(2^{2^n})$, even the first instance, where $n = 5$, will take 4294967296 milliseconds, which is more than 7 weeks.

Buying a faster computer, say a computer that is m times faster than the one we already have, would speed up the computation by m, which is a constant factor. If we buy such a machine, we can solve a problem of linear complexity $\mathcal{O}(n)$ in $1/m$th of the time it took us before, or we can solve a problem that is m times bigger in the same time. However, if our problem is of complexity $\mathcal{O}(n^2)$, and we buy the faster machine, we can solve in the same amount of time a problem that is only $sqrt(m)$ bigger. The faster machine will not help that much in solving problems of exponential complexity. For the same time it took to solve a problem with instance n, we will be able to solve instances that are $log(m)$ times bigger. Thus, for the 100-times increase of computing power, we may perhaps solve problems that are almost eight times as big (*log* means in this context log_2). A 1000-times increase in computing speed would solve within the same time problems whose size is only about 10 times bigger. Using an array of computers would not help much either. If we use 100 computers instead of one, we can speed up the execution by at most a factor of 100. This is provided that we have algorithms that can parallelize the problem and utilize the array of machines in an optimal way. Unfortunately, this is often not the case. Consider, for example in the case where we can parallelize an algorithm only for half of the duration of its execution, our 100 machines will reduce the execution time to $1/2 + 1/200 = 101/200$ of the original time. That is, in this case, the speedup is only about twice the original speed. In general, we can benefit from parallelization only if we can parallelize *almost all* of the algorithm.

Another classification is between *deterministic* and *nondeterministic* complexity measures. Deterministic complexity refers to the conventional computation model, where at each point the program has at most one choice of progress. Notice that an if-then-else statement or a while-loop offers only a single choice, depending on the current values of the variables.

Nondeterministics is merely a mathematical model. It refers to an execution model where we are allowed to make nondeterministic choices for the way to continue the execution. In particular, in a Turing machine, there can be more than a single transition that can be taken, given the current state and symbol in the current tape location. A nondeterministic Turing machine accepts an input if among all the possible executions for this input, *at least one* is accepting. For nondeterministic algorithms, one measures the time or space of a single terminating computation. This execution model usually incurs an exponential blowup in time when simulated by an equivalent deterministic algorithm. It is currently an open problem (perhaps the most important one in computer science) whether one can implement various nondeterministic algorithms in a deterministic way without incurring this exponential blowup. It is suspected that this is impossible, yet no one has been able to prove this formally.

This kind of nondeterminism asserts that *there is* a computation that gives the right result within the given amount of time. This is a different kind of nondeterminism than the one used in concurrency theory, and will be discussed later, in Chapter 4. In concurrency theory, the nondeterminism arises due to interprocess communication, or the use of shared variables. Then, in order that the program will satisfy its specification, we expect that no matter what choice is made, the program will *always* satisfy the specification.

Of course, in practice, we do not want to run a nondeterministic algorithm, where there is a computation that gives the right result and other computations which may not even guarantee to terminate. The use of nondeterminism in complexity theory only helps to classify the complexity of some problems. It largely reflects the lack of additional knowledge about the more informative deterministic complexity of certain important computational problems. We will follow the common dialect of computational complexity and use both deterministic and nondeterministic classes, wherever appropriate.

Complexity classes often include the following three indications: (a) space or time, (b) the measure (e.g., polynomial, exponential), and (c) a choice between the deterministic or the nondeterministic model of execution. The names of the complexity classes reflect these choices. Consider the following common classes:

NL nondeterministic logarithmic space. Notice that space complexity measures do not take into account the size of the input (thus the complexity can be less than linear). Algorithms of this class are usually quite efficient.

P Deterministic polynomial time. An algorithm in this class is considered to be efficient, in particular when the polynomial is of some low degree. In practice, most problems in this class do have complexity measures with fixed small degree, e.g., $\mathcal{O}(n^2)$ (quadratic), or $\mathcal{O}(n^3)$ (cubic), and hence are practical. Nevertheless, an algorithm of complexity $\mathcal{O}(n^{150})$ would still be considered polynomial, but is certainly not practical.

NP Nondeterministic polynomial time. Problems in this class are usually not efficient, due to the exponential explosion obtained when translating them into deterministic algorithms. However, experience shows that various heuristic solutions exist for solving some difficult NP problems efficiently in many practical cases.

PSPACE Polynomial space. (It is known that the deterministic and nondeterministic polynomial space classes are the same [125].) Problems with this complexity require quite a large and fast computer. We still do not know whether there are polynomial algorithms for solving all the PSPACE problems. It is suspected that this open problem will eventually be answered negatively.

EXPTIME Deterministic exponential time. Can be applied in practice only to small instances.

EXPSPACE Exponential space. These and problems of higher complexity can be solved only when the input is limited to being a very small instance, e.g., $n < 10$.

NONELEMENTARY Both space and time are the same here. Algorithms with such complexity are considered to be unreasonably difficult.

One can observe that the letter N at the beginning of the class name corresponds to a nondeterministic measure, while its absence corresponds to a deterministic one. The words TIME and SPACE are sometimes omitted, and common practice refers to one of them, as in NP, which stands for NPTIME.

It is known that

$$NL \subseteq P \subseteq NP \subseteq PSPACE \subseteq EXPTIME \subseteq EXSPACE$$

Some strict containment between classes are known, such as $P \subset EXPTIME$. But it is not known whether $P \subset PSPACE$.

A complexity measure of a computation problem can be given as an *upper bound* or as a *lower bound*. An upper bound is a complexity measure known to be achievable for the problem, via some specific algorithm. It is still possible that a better algorithm (although yet unknown) exists. A lower bound of a computational problem specifies that the problem is at least as hard to solve as the given complexity measure. However, it does not have to be the case that a specific algorithm that meets the lower bound complexity measure exists. To specify lower bounds, we need to define the Ω notation $\Omega(f(n))$ as follows:

> An algorithm or a computational problem is of complexity $\Omega(f(n))$ if there exist two constants, c_0 and c_1, such that for each instance of the input of size $n > c_0$, the time/space needed to run the algorithm (solve the problem) on a Turing machine is *at least* $c_1 \times f(n)$.

If the lower and upper bounds for a problem are the same, we say that it is a *tight* complexity bound. Otherwise, there is a complexity *gap*, which calls for further research. For many basic problems in computer science, tight bounds are still unknown.

There are interesting classes of problems with mutual complexity gaps. The problems in such a class are related to each other using *reductions*. Reductions are direct translations that are "efficient," e.g., translations that are polynomial in time (different complexity classes may have different notions of efficiency). A problem is *complete* for a complexity class if it belongs to that class and every other problem in that class can be efficiently reduced to that problem. In some intuitive sense, a complete problem is at least as difficult as any other problem in that class. Such complexity classes include for example, PSPACE-complete and NP-complete. Problems in PSPACE-complete can be solved with polynomial space, while problems in NP-complete can be solved with nondeterministic polynomial time. No one knows the tight lower bound complexity of any of the problems in these classes. Furthermore, if one will ever find a deterministic polynomial time algorithm for at least one problem in one of these classes, then this will automatically provide polynomial time algorithms for all the other problems in that class.

If NONELEMENTARY complexity seems bad enough, it is not the worst case. The theory of *computability* [69] shows that some problems cannot be solved by any algorithm. We say that these problems are *undecidable*. Such problems are often quite general, e.g., deciding whether a program terminates on every legal input. Although this may seem initially a rather theoretical issue, this problem strikes hard at software reliability methods. Guaranteeing that a given program terminates is certainly one property we may want to verify.

Some problems, such as checking whether a program terminates on a given input are *semi-decidable* (and are also called *recursive enumerable*). This means that an algorithm that terminates with the correct answer when the answer is positive exists, but this algorithm does not necessarily stop when the answer is negative. For the particular problem of checking whether an algorithm terminates on some input, we can simply simulate the program on the given input, and wait to see if the simulation terminates. Semi-decidable decision problems do not have complexity measures attached to them. If there were such a measure, we could have produced a decision procedure, in contradiction with the semi-decidability. To do that, we would have executed the semi-decision procedure until it either terminates, or until the time prescribed by the complexity measure expires. In the latter case, we would know that the answer is negative.

As will be shown in later chapters, complexity and undecidability issues have important consequences on the applicability of software reliability methods. Undecidability results have grave consequences on deductive verification. They imply that most of the properties we may want to prove for actual systems, such as termination, granting of service, and others, cannot be fully verified in an algorithmic way. As we will see, this does not prevent the trained engineer, mathematician or logician from coming up with a formal proof. However, there is no time bound that can be put on the verification process. Nevertheless, in practice, correctness proofs are usually attempted for systems that work due to principles that are well understood. In such cases, the experienced user of such methods, possibly exploiting the intuition of the developer, should be able to perform the verification.

High complexity, or even undecidability of some computational problems, should not deter researchers from trying to find heuristic solutions, i.e., solutions that work efficiently, for *some* important practical cases.

2.5 Further Reading

Textbooks on set theory include:

P. R. Halmos, *Naive Set Theory*, Springer-Verlag, 1987.

K. Devlin, *The Joy of Sets: Fundamentals of Contemporary Set Theory*, 2nd edition, Springer-Verlag, 1993.

Books on graph theory include:

R. Diestel, *Graph Theory*, Springer-Verlag, 2nd edition, 2000.

A. Gibbons, *Algorithmic Graph Theory*, Cambridge University Press, 1985.

Books on computability and complexity theory include:

J. E. Hopcroft, J. D. Ullman, *Introduction to Automata Theory, Languages and Computation*, Addison-Wesley, 1979.

H. R. Lewis, Ch. Papadimitiou, *Elements of the Theory of Computation*, Prentice-Hall, 2nd edition, 1997.

Ch. Papadimitiou, *Computational Complexity*, Addison-Wesley, 1994.

M. Sipser, *Introduction to the Theory of Computation*, PWS, 1996.

3. Logic and Theorem Proving

'Contrariwise,' continued Tweedledee, 'if it was so, it might be; and if it were so, it would be; but as it isn't, it ain't. That's logic.'

Lewis Carroll, *Through the Looking Glass*

Mathematical logic provides the basis of software verification methods. Like a programming language, a logic combines syntax, dictating *how* to write legal formulas, with semantics, which gives precise *meaning* to each formula. Mathematical logic formalizes the notion of a *proof*. In this chapter, we will survey first order and propositional logic. We will then study the essentials of mechanized theorem proving. Theorem proving tools usually do not provide full automation for obtaining proofs. Rather they are used to assist the user by imposing rigor and providing guidance during the proof process. In later chapters, we will show various logics and proof systems that can be used to prove properties of programs in a manual, computer-assisted or fully automatic way.

3.1 First Order Logic

First order logic is a formalism widely used in mathematics, e.g., in calculus and geometry, and in computer science, e.g., in databases and artificial intelligence. As we will see in Chapter 7, first order logic is extensively used in program verification. Predicates, which occur in *if-then-else* statements or in *while-loops*, are basically a restricted form of first order logic formulas. First order logic uses variables that range over specific domains such as the *integers* or the *reals*, relations such as '$\leq$', and functions like '$\times$' or '$+$'. It can be used to reason about *all* the objects in the domain, or to assert that *there exists* an object satisfying a property.

The reason that this logic is called *first order* is that all the variables used in its formulas range directly over the predefined domain (e.g., the *integers*). In *second order* logic, one can have both simple variables and *set variables*. The latter can range over sets of objects. Thus, if x is a simple variable and Y is a set variable, one can express in second order logic the formula $x \in Y$, meaning that the value that is represented by the variable x is included in the set that is represented by the variable Y. Third order logic includes even more complicated variables, representing sets of sets, and so forth.

First order logic forms the theoretical basis for database theory [2]. The programming language PROLOG [32] and its descendant DATALOG take their syntax and semantics from first order logic. Their execution mechanism is based on logical inference. Using programming languages based on logic automatically provides an increased level of reliability, as the program may then be viewed as its own specification. However, this does not guarantee the termination of such programs, which may require a separate proof.

3.2 Terms

First order *terms* are expressions denoted according to the precise syntax of first order logic. We will first define the syntax of terms, and later will provide their semantic interpretation. A *signature* $\mathcal{G} = (V, F, R)$ includes three disjoint sets: a set of variable symbols V, function symbols F, and relation symbols R. These are merely syntactic objects, and a priori have no special meaning. Since technically we can use a limited number of printed characters, it is difficult to denote each function or relation using a different character. Thus, we will often denote symbols with the usual syntax of programming languages: starting with a letter, followed by any combination of letters, digits and the underscore '_' character. We henceforth assume that it is clear from the context which symbols represent variables, functions and relations.

With each function or relation symbol that belongs to a signature, we associate its *arity*, i.e., the number of parameters or arguments it has. For example, the addition function *add* has arity of 2, the *sine* function symbol has arity 1, and the relation symbol *ge* (for 'greater than or equals') has arity of 2. A constant symbol, e.g., *zero* or *one*, is also considered to be a function symbol of arity 0.

Terms are expressions formed using function symbols and variables. For example, let $v1$ be a variable, *zero*, *one* be constants, and *add* be a function symbol with arity 2. Then, *add(one, one)*, *add(add(one, one), v1)* are terms. We use BNF notation, which is often used for defining programming language constructs, to define the syntax of terms:

$$term ::= var \mid const \mid func(term, term, \ldots, term)$$

where *var* is a variable symbol, *func* is a function symbol, and *const* is a constant symbol. In BNF notation, '::=' means *is defined as*. It uses the vertical bar to separate different options in the definition. Thus, a term can consist of either (1) a variable symbol, (2) a constant symbol, or (3) a function symbol followed by an open parenthesis, a list of terms, separated by commas, and finally a closed parenthesis. In case (3), each term is recursively defined using the same BNF definition. In conjunction with the BNF definition, we have the following constraint: following a function symbol with arity n, we must have n terms, separated by commas and enclosed within parentheses.

Accordingly, *v1* is a term since it is a variable, *one* is a term since it is a constant, *add(one, one)* applies a function symbol with arity 2 to two terms (which were shown already to be terms), and finally *add(add(one, one), v1)* is also a term, obtained by again applying the function symbol *add* to two previous terms. In the following discussion we will relax our notation, allowing the use of the common mathematical and programming languages function and constant symbols, such as '+' or 175. Moreover, in doing so, we will allow infix notation, i.e., putting the relation symbol in between the operands, as in $v1 + 1$.

So far, no particular meaning (semantics) was assigned to the defined objects. It may seem intuitive that the term *add(v1, add(one, one))* should represent the value of the variable *v1* plus 2. However, such a connection between the written symbols and the intended meaning requires formal definition. In order to interpret terms, we first assume a given domain, i.e., a set, $\mathcal{D}$, of values. For example, this domain can be

- the *integers*,
- the *natural* numbers, i.e., the positive *integers* and 0,
- the *rational* numbers, i.e., numbers that can be formed by dividing one *integer* by another (except for dividing by 0), or
- *strings* over some alphabet.

A first order *structure* is defined over a given signature. A structure $\mathcal{S} = (\mathcal{G}, \mathcal{D}, \mathcal{F}, \mathcal{R}, f)$ includes a signature $\mathcal{G} = (V, F, R)$, a domain (i.e., a set) $\mathcal{D}$, a set of functions $\mathcal{F}$ (including constants), a set of relations $\mathcal{R}$, and a mapping $f : F \cup R \to \mathcal{F} \cup \mathcal{R}$ from the function and relation symbols in the signature to actual functions and relations over the domain $\mathcal{D}$, respectively. For example, the function symbol *sub* can be mapped by f into the subtraction function over the *integers*. The relation symbol *ge* can be mapped by f into a relation that includes all the pairs of *integers* such that the first is greater than or equal to the second. The mapping f must preserve the arity of the function and relation symbols. That is, f maps a function symbol of arity n to a function with n parameters, and a relation symbol of arity n to a relation with n arguments.

The syntax of a logic dictates how to denote a function or a relation symbol, and some more complex objects such as terms and formulas on a piece of paper, or represent it in a computer memory. The semantics connects or maps the notation to mathematical objects. Accordingly, the signature of a first order logic dictates the syntactic objects (symbols) that can be used to refer to functions and relations; the components $\mathcal{D}$, $\mathcal{F}$ and $\mathcal{R}$ are used for providing the corresponding mathematical objects. The semantic interpretation function f is used to connect the syntactic objects in the signature with the corresponding mathematical objects.

For example, f can map the function symbol *add* to addition over the *integers*, that we often denote with '+'. Note that '+' itself is again only a syntactic object, a symbol that can be generated by a printer. We often attach to '+' the meaning of addition. This symbol is in fact overloaded and denotes, for example, the addition function over *integers*, *reals*, *rational* and *complex* numbers. We often assume that the appropriate domain is understood from the context.

Assignments and Interpretations

An *assignment* a maps a set V of variables to values in the domain $\mathcal{D}$. We denote this by $a : V \to \mathcal{D}$. For example, if $\mathcal{D}$ is the set of *integers*, and the set of variables V is $\{v1, v2, v3\}$, we can have $a = \{v1 \mapsto 3,\ v2 \mapsto 0,\ v3 \mapsto -5\}$. In this book we distinguish between *logical* (or *functional*) assignments, which maps each member of a set of variables to a variable of some given domain, and assignments in programming languages, whose effect is to change the value of a specified variable during the execution of a program.

Denote the terms of a signature $\mathcal{G}$ by $terms(\mathcal{G})$. We can now define the *semantic interpretation* $T_a : terms(\mathcal{G}) \to \mathcal{D}$, which maps each term to a value in the domain. Note that the interpretation depends also on the assignment a. The definition is recursive:

$$
\begin{aligned}
T_a(v) &= a(v), \text{ for } v \in V \\
T_a(func(e_1, e_2, \ldots, e_n)) &= f(func)(T_a(e_1), T_a(e_2), \ldots, T_a(e_n))
\end{aligned}
$$

The first line defines the interpretation of a variable to be its value under the assignment a. The second line is a recursive definition of a term. The interpretation of a term of the form $e = func(e_1, \ldots, e_n)$ is done as follows. We take the function $f(func)$, i.e., the actual function associated with *func* from the first order structure $\mathcal{S}$. Since the terms $e_1, \ldots, e_n$ are shorter than e, we assume that we already know how to interpret them by applying the definition of T_a recursively, obtaining the values $T_a(e_1), \ldots, T_a(e_n)$. We then apply $f(func)$ to these n values.

Consider for example the domain of *integers*, and the assignment $a = \{v1 \mapsto 2,\ v2 \mapsto 3,\ v3 \mapsto 4\}$. Let f map *add* to the addition function over the *integers*. Then we have:

$$
\begin{aligned}
T_a(v1) &= a(v1) = 2 \\
T_a(v2) &= a(v2) = 3 \\
T_a(v3) &= a(v3) = 4 \\
T_a(add(v1, v2)) &= f(add)(T_a(v1), T_a(v2)) = 2 + 3 = 5 \\
T_a(add(add(v1, v2), v3)) &= f(add)(T_a(add(v1, v2)), T_a(v3)) \\
&= 5 + 4 = 9
\end{aligned}
$$

The elaborate separation between syntax and semantics may seem at first complicated or unnecessary. However, it is a very practical distinction:

by identifying the relationship between the notation (the syntax) and its meaning (the semantics), first order logic allows us to *prove* properties of the domain under discussion. Such a proof is syntactic, as it manipulates the formulas, written on paper or represented in a computer memory. Yet the result of such string manipulation operations can be projected immediately back to the mathematical objects under discussion using the semantic interpretation.

Structures with Multiple Domains

Specific to our goal, i.e., reasoning about software systems, we may need to use more than a single domain. For example, we may need to reason both on the *integers* and the *strings*. In these cases, care must be taken to apply functions and relations to the appropriate types of arguments. Under this extension, each variable may be assigned a value from a particular domain.

The functions and relation symbols can range over multiple domains. Each parameter to a function, each argument of a relation, and the result of a function, need to be fixed over some domain. For example, we may have a function *length* over the domain of *strings*, resulting in the length of a string, which is a *natural* number. For more details of first order logics over multiple domains see, e.g., [38].

3.3 First Order Formulas

We again start by introducing new syntax. *Simple formulas* are constructed using relation symbols applied to terms. The syntax is

$$simp\_form ::= rel(term, term, \ldots, term) \mid term \equiv term$$

where *rel* is a relation symbol. For example, *ge(add(one, one), zero)* is a simple formula, since the relation *ge* with arity 2 was applied to the two terms *add(one, one)* and *zero*. We always include the special relation '$\equiv$', which stands for 'equals to'.

First order formulas include the simple formulas described above. In addition, they can be formed by applying recursively the Boolean operators '$\wedge$' (*and*), '$\vee$' (*or*), '$\neg$' (*not*) and '$\rightarrow$' (*implies*), or by prefixing a formula by one of the *quantifiers* '$\forall$' (*for all*) or '$\exists$' (*there exists*) and a variable name, as follows:

$$form ::= simp\_form \mid (form \wedge form) \mid (form \vee form) \mid (form \rightarrow form) \mid$$
$$(\neg form) \mid \forall var(form) \mid \exists var(form) \mid true \mid false$$

For example,

$$(ge(one, zero) \wedge ge(add(one, one), v1)) \tag{3.1}$$

is a formula, as well as $\forall v1\ (\exists v2\ (ge(v2,v1)))$. A subformula is any part of a formula that is itself a formula. Thus, $ge(one, zero)$, $ge(add(one, one), v1)$ and (3.1) itself are the subformulas of (3.1).

As in many programming languages, precedence between Boolean operators can be used to avoid including some of the parentheses. For example, the negation symbol '$\neg$' usually has higher precedence over the conjunction symbol '$\wedge$', which in turn has higher precedence over the disjunction symbol '$\vee$'. The Boolean operators '$\vee$' and '$\wedge$' are *left associative*, i.e., $\nu_1 \vee \nu_2 \vee \nu_3$ is the same as $((\nu_1 \vee \nu_2) \vee \nu_3)$. (A closer look at the semantics of the Boolean operators reveals that the result of a multiple conjunction or disjunction is independent of the placement of the parentheses.) It is always possible to ignore the outermost parentheses.

We also allow the use of the common mathematical and programming languages relation symbols, such as '$\geq$', and the use of infix notation. Accordingly (3.1) can also be expressed as

$$1 \geq 0 \wedge 1 + 1 \geq v1. \tag{3.2}$$

In a formula or a subformula of the form $\mu_1 \wedge \mu_2 \wedge \ldots \wedge \mu_n$, we say that each μ_i is a *conjunct*. Similarly, in a formula or a subformula of the form $\nu_1 \vee \nu_2 \vee \ldots \vee \nu_m$, each ν_i is a *disjunct*. In later chapters, we also use the forms $\bigwedge_{i=1,n} \mu_i$ and $\bigvee_{i=1,m} \nu_i$.

We will describe now the semantic interpretation of first order formulas. First, the relation symbol '$\equiv$' is interpreted as the standard 'equals to' relation. Thus, $v1 \equiv v2$ holds if and only if $v1$ is assigned the same value as $v2$, i.e., if $a(v1) = a(v2)$. Henceforth, we are careful to use the symbol '$\equiv$' to denote equality *within* the logic, while '=' denotes equality of objects *outside* of the logic. This distinction is typical of logic formalisms, where care should be taken not to confuse assertions *within* the intended logic with assertions *about* the logic. However, many logic books use the same symbol for '=' and '$\equiv$'. (In program texts, we will follow the usual programming languages syntax, and will denote equivalence by '='.) Assertions about the logic are expressed in a natural language (such as English), often referred to as the *meta language*.

Recall that f is an arity-preserving mapping from relation symbols to relations, e.g., from *leq* (less or equals) to the standard relation between pairs of *integers*, which is usually denoted by '$\leq$'. Let *forms*($\mathcal{G}$) be the set of first order formulas over a signature $\mathcal{G}$. The interpretation mapping $M_a : forms(\mathcal{G}) \rightarrow \{\text{TRUE, FALSE}\}$ assigns a Boolean (or *truth*) value, i.e., TRUE or FALSE, to each formula. Again, the interpretation will depend on the assignment a. We will first present the interpretation of formulas that do not contain the quantifiers '$\forall$' and '$\exists$'.

$$
\begin{aligned}
M_a(pred(e_1,\ldots,e_n)) &= f(pred)(T_a(e_1),\ldots,T_a(e_n)) \\
M_a(e_1 \equiv e_2) &= (T_a(e_1)\!=\!T_a(e_2)) \\
M_a(f1 \wedge f2) &= \text{TRUE iff } (M_a(f1)\!=\!\text{TRUE and } M_a(f2)\!=\!\text{TRUE}) \\
M_a(f1 \vee f2) &= \text{TRUE iff } (M_a(f1)\!=\!\text{TRUE or } M_a(f2)\!=\!\text{TRUE}) \\
M_a(f1 \rightarrow f2) &= \text{TRUE iff } (M_a(f1)\!=\!\text{FALSE or } M_a(f2)\!=\!\text{TRUE}) \\
M_a(\neg f1) &= \text{TRUE iff } (M_a(f1)\!=\!\text{FALSE}) \\
M_a(true) &= \text{TRUE} \\
M_a(false) &= \text{FALSE}
\end{aligned}
$$

The first line of the semantic interpretation of formulas should be understood as follows: first, we interpret the terms e_1, ..., e_n using the term interpretation function T_a. This results in the values $T_a(e_1)$, ..., $T_a(e_n)$. Now, $f(rel)$ is the relation that corresponds to the syntactic symbol *rel*. This relation is applied to the above values to obtain either TRUE or FALSE.

The constant relation symbols *true* and *false* are interpreted as TRUE and FALSE, respectively (according to the last two lines of the semantic definition above). We could have used the Boolean values TRUE and FALSE directly (as some books informally do). However, we carefully make the distinction between the syntactic constants and the semantic values. Notice that we could eliminate *true* by writing $\varphi \vee \neg\varphi$ for any formula φ, and similarly, could write $\varphi \wedge \neg\varphi$ to eliminate *false*. (Notice the notation *iff*, which reads as *if and only if* and has the same meaning as *exactly when*.)

Note that interpreting a simple formula uses the term-interpretation function T_a. Observe also that the second line of the above semantic interpretation of formulas, concerning $e_1 \equiv e_2$, includes three symbols for equivalence: the first is the '$\equiv$' symbol, denoting the first order symbol we use for equivalence in the logic. The second, denoted '=', means that the interpretation of the first order term on the left is defined using the equation on the right. The third, also denoted '=', requires an equivalence between the calculated values.

Interpreting the formula

$$\varphi = ge(add(add(v1,v2),v3),v2) \wedge ge(v3,zero)$$

under the assignment $a = \{v1 \mapsto 2,\, v2 \mapsto 3,\, v3 \mapsto 4\}$, can be done as follows:

$$
\begin{aligned}
T_a(add(add(v1,v2),v3)) &= 9 \text{ (as was shown in Section 3.2)} \\
T_a(v2) &= 3 \\
T_a(v3) &= 4 \\
T_a(zero) &= 0 \\
M_a(\,ge\,(add(add(v1,v2),v3),v2)\,) &= f(ge)(T_a(add(add(v1,v2),v3)), \\
&\qquad T_a(v2)) = 9 > 3 = \text{TRUE} \\
M_a(ge(v3,zero)) &= f(ge)(T_a(v3),T_a(zero)) = \\
&\qquad 4 \geq 0 = \text{TRUE} \\
M_a(\varphi) &= \text{TRUE}
\end{aligned}
$$

In preparation for the definition of the semantics of formulas with existential ('$\exists$') and universal ('$\forall$') quantifiers, we first define the notion of a *variant*.

Let a be an assignment, v a variable, and d a value of the chosen domain $\mathcal{D}$. A variant $a[d/v]$ is an assignment that is the same as the assignment a, except that it assigns the value d to the variable v. Formally,

$$a[d/v](u) = \begin{cases} a(u) & \text{if } u \neq v \\ d & \text{if } u = v \end{cases}$$

The semantics of quantified formulas is defined as follows:

$M_a(\forall v(\varphi)) = \text{TRUE}$ iff for each d in $\mathcal{D}$, $M_{a[d/v]}(\varphi) = \text{TRUE}$
$M_a(\exists v(\varphi)) = \text{TRUE}$ iff there exists d in $\mathcal{D}$ such that $M_{a[d/v]}(\varphi) = \text{TRUE}$

The first line asserts that $\forall v(\varphi)$ is TRUE under an assignment a if φ is TRUE under any variant of a that may differ from a with respect to the value of the variable v. We read this as *for every value of v, φ*. Similarly, we read $\exists v(\varphi)$ as *there exists a value of v for which φ*.

The fact that $M_a(\varphi) = \text{TRUE}$, where the structure $\mathcal{S}$ is known from the context, is often denoted as $a \models^{\mathcal{S}} \varphi$, and is read as *a satisfies φ under the structure $\mathcal{S}$*. If $a \models^{\mathcal{S}} \varphi$ for each assignment a, then $\mathcal{S}$ is a *model* of φ. This is denoted as $\models^{\mathcal{S}} \varphi$. If $\models^{\mathcal{S}} \varphi$ for every structure $\mathcal{S}$, then φ is a *tautology*. This is denoted as $\models \varphi$. If $a \models^{\mathcal{S}} \varphi$ does not hold (we denote this fact by $a \not\models^{\mathcal{S}} \varphi$) for any assignment a and any structure $\mathcal{S}$, then φ is a *contradiction*. Notice that φ is a tautology exactly when $\neg\varphi$ is a contradiction.

The subtle distinctions between the above three uses of the '$\models$' symbol are important. We demonstrate this with examples:

- Consider $a \models^{\mathcal{S}} x \equiv y \times 2$, where $\mathcal{S}$ is the structure that includes the domain of *integers*, and the binary function '$\times$' is interpreted as multiplication. This holds for example when a assigns 6 to x and 3 to y. However, $x \equiv y \times 2$ does not hold in general. For example, it does not hold when a assigns 2 to x and 3 to y.
- Consider $\models^{\mathcal{S}} x \times 2 \equiv x + x$, where the structure $\mathcal{S}$ includes the domain of *integers*, and the binary functions '$\times$', and '$+$' are interpreted as the usual *integer* multiplication and addition, respectively. The first order property $x \times 2 \equiv x + x$ holds in this structure, regardless of the actual assignment of value to the variable x. Consequently, $\mathcal{S}$ is a model of this formula. On the other hand, $\models x \times 2 \equiv x + x$ does not hold. For example, given the model $\mathcal{S}'$, over the *integers*, where '$\times$' represents applying the bitwise *and* operator to the binary representation of its arguments (i.e., the constant 2 corresponds to 0010), and '$+$' represents applying the bitwise *or* operator.
- Finally, consider $\models (x \equiv y \wedge y \equiv z) \to x \equiv z$. The latter formula expresses the *transitivity* property of the standard equivalence, and it does not depend on the structure or assignment. Thus, it is a tautology.

In a first order formula, any occurrence of a variable v in a subformula of the form $\forall v(\varphi)$ or $\exists v(\varphi)$ is called a *quantified* occurrence. Any other occurrence is called a *free occurrence*. From the above discussion, it follows that if $\models \varphi$ or $\models^S \varphi$, the truth value of φ does not depend on the values of the free variables that appear in it. Therefore, in these cases, this is the same as writing $\models \varphi'$ or $\models^S \varphi'$, respectively, where φ' is obtained from φ by applying a universal quantifier to each one of the free variables. For example, $\exists x \, (y < x \wedge x < z)$ becomes $\forall y \, \forall z \, \exists x \, (y < x \wedge x < z)$. In fact, if φ contains no free variables, then the truth value of φ under S does not depend on any assignment a. Thus, if $a \models^S \varphi$ for *some* assignment a, then $\models^S \varphi$. Conversely, by definition, if $\models^S \varphi$ then $a \models^S \varphi$ for *every* assignment a.

An interesting observation is that for a given structure S, for every first order formula φ, either $a \models^S \varphi$ or $a \models^S \neg\varphi$. When there are no free variables in φ, we further have that either $\models^S \varphi$ or $\models^S \neg\varphi$. On the other hand, if φ is not a tautology nor a contradiction, then it can happen that neither $\models \varphi$, nor $\models \neg\varphi$.

To demonstrate the difference between the syntax and the semantics of the logic, consider the following formula:

$$\varphi = \forall v1 \, \forall v2 \, (v1 < v2 \rightarrow \exists v3(v1 < v3 \wedge v3 < v2))$$

Without having further information about the structure under which this formula is interpreted, we cannot tell whether the formula holds or not. Although we may guess that '<' represents the relation '*less than*,' this is not necessarily the case for every structure. Moreover, even if indeed '<' is 'less than', we need to recall that this relation can be interpreted over different domains. Suppose that the intended domain is the *reals*. Then the formula expresses that for every two values assigned to $v1$ and $v2$, such that $v1$ is smaller than $v2$, there is a *real* value $v3$ in between. This formula happens to hold for the *real* numbers. Now, suppose that the domain is the *integers*. The same formula does not hold, as there are no *integer* numbers between any two successive *integers*, e.g., between 2 and 3.

For a formula φ, a term e and a variable v, define $\varphi[e/v]$ to be the formula obtained from φ by substituting the term e for each free occurrence of v. (Note that the quantified occurrences are not substituted.) Furthermore, we do not allow a free occurrence of v to be substituted by a term that contains, in the place of the substitution, a quantified variable. As an example that motivates this restriction, consider the formula $\forall x(x > y \rightarrow x > z)$. Interpreted over the *integers*, with the 'greater than' relation '>', it expresses that y is greater or equal to z. Now, if we were allowed to substitute y by $x-1$, we would have obtained $\forall x(x > x - 1 \rightarrow x > z)$. Since $x > x - 1$ holds for any *integer*, this formula asserts that any number is bigger than z. This is a false statement, as there is no minimum among the *integers*.

Notice that a substituted variable may also appear in the term replacing it. Thus, the substitution must not be repeatedly applied after it has already replaced the variable with the corresponding term. For example, if $\varphi = v1 \geq v2$, then $\varphi[v1 + 1/v1]$ is $v1 + 1 \geq v2$. Without the above consideration, this substitution will never terminate.

It is not coincidental that substitution to both an assignment and a formula are denoted using a similar notation. One can show by induction on the size of the formula (see e.g., [38]) that for each first order formula φ, term e and variable v, where the substitution $\varphi[e/v]$ is permitted,

$$a[T_a(e)/v] \models^{\mathcal{S}} \varphi \text{ if and only if } a \models^{\mathcal{S}} \varphi[e/v].$$

This connection shows the relationship between the syntactic and the semantic substitution. On the semantic side (left), we are obtaining a variant of the assignment a by setting v to the value $T_a(e)$ of the expression e (under the original assignment a). On the syntactic side (right), we are replacing each occurrence of the variable v by the expression e.

We sometimes write $\varphi(v_1, v_2, \ldots, v_n)$ to emphasize that the variables $v_1, v_2 \ldots, v_n$ are among the free variables in the formula φ. Accordingly, we can denote by $\varphi(e_1, e_2, \ldots, e_n)$ the formula obtained from φ by substituting each free occurrence of the variable v_i by the term e_i. Thus, we can write $\varphi(y, z) = \exists x\,(y < x \wedge x < z)$. Then $\varphi(3, t + 4)$ is $\exists x\,(3 < x \wedge x < t + 4)$.

When $\models \varphi \rightarrow \psi$, or $\models^{\mathcal{S}} \varphi \rightarrow \psi$, we often say that φ is *stronger* than ψ, or that ψ is *weaker*. In terms of structures, $\models \varphi \rightarrow \psi$ means that ψ is satisfied by all the structures and assignments that satisfy φ, and possibly some other structures. When both φ is stronger than ψ and ψ is stronger than φ, we say that φ is ψ are *logically equivalent*.

It is quite misleading to look at old books on logic, where the implication symbol '$\rightarrow$' is sometimes replaced by '$\supset$', which is usually used nowadays for set containment. Using this notation in $\varphi \supset \psi$ is exactly opposite to the fact that the structures that satisfy φ are *included* among the structures that satisfy ψ. That is, if $\models \varphi \rightarrow \psi$, then $\{\mathcal{S}| \models^{\mathcal{S}} \varphi\} \subseteq \{\mathcal{S}| \models^{\mathcal{S}} \psi\}$.

Expressiveness

An important property of a formalism is its *expressiveness*. Expressiveness refers to the descriptive power of the formalism. Consider a given signature $\mathcal{G}$. Let $\mathcal{H}$ be a class of structures over $\mathcal{G}$. which have a special property that we want to specify, while the other structures over $\mathcal{G}$ do not satisfy this property. A logic can *express* this property if it allows writing a formula φ over $\mathcal{G}$ such that φ holds exactly for the structures in $\mathcal{H}$.

For example, consider a signature that includes a binary relation R, representing a graph. We can express in first order logic the following properties:

- The graph is undirected (i.e., the relation R is symmetric).

$$\forall x\, \forall y\, (x\,R\,y \rightarrow y\,R\,x)$$

- There are no isolated nodes, i.e., nodes that are not connected to any other node.

$$\forall x\, \exists y\, (x\,R\,y \vee y\,R\,x)$$

On the other hand, there are interesting properties that we cannot express in first order logic.

- The graph is finite.
- The graph contains cycles.
- The graph is connected (i.e., contains a single strongly connected component).

3.4 Propositional Logic

Propositional logic is a simpler formalism than first order logic. It does not have quantification, nor does it allow function and relation symbols (including the equality symbol '$\equiv$'). It has a set of *propositional variables AP*. Each such variable ranges over the Boolean values {TRUE, FALSE}. The syntactic definition of the logic is as follows:

$$form ::= prop \mid (form \wedge form) \mid (form \vee form) \mid$$
$$(form \rightarrow form) \mid \neg form \mid true \mid false$$

where *prop* is a propositional variable a set of variables AP. An assignment a is redefined here to be $a : AP \rightarrow \{\text{TRUE, FALSE}\}$, i.e., every propositional variable in AP is mapped into a Boolean value. The semantics of the Boolean operators is as in first order logic. There are no signatures or structures involved. Thus, we can write $a \models \varphi$ when $M_a(\varphi) = \text{TRUE}$, and say that a satisfies φ. A propositional formula is a tautology if it is satisfied by any assignment, and is a contradiction if there is no assignment satisfying it. It can be easily shown that the truth value of a formula only depends on the assignment to the variables that appear in it.

For example, let P, Q be propositional variables. The formula $P \wedge \neg P$ is a simple contradiction. Any assignment would result in a FALSE interpretation. Similarly, $P \vee \neg P$ is a tautology. It is interpreted as TRUE under each assignment. The formula $\varphi = \neg P \wedge (Q \vee P)$ is not a tautology, nor a contradiction. Under the assignment $a = \{P \mapsto \text{FALSE}, Q \mapsto \text{TRUE}\}$, we have $a \models \varphi$. On the other hand, under $b = \{P \mapsto \text{TRUE}, Q \mapsto \text{TRUE}\}$, we have $b \not\models \varphi$. Notice that either $a \models \varphi$ or $a \models \neg \varphi$.

Propositional logic is useful in specifying hardware circuits, since digital systems are often based on two valued entities 0 and 1, which can be mapped into FALSE and TRUE respectively. The '$\wedge$', '$\vee$' and '$\neg$' operators are analogous to the electronic gates *and, or* and *not*, respectively.

3.5 Proving First Order Logic Formulas

Given a logic, we may want to prove that a formula φ holds for (every assignment and) a given structure S, i.e., that S is a model of φ. In some cases, we may want to prove that φ is a tautology, i.e., it holds for every structure and every assignment for that structure.

We may also want to prove that a formula holds under a certain given set of assumptions. Formally, let Γ be a set of first order formulas and φ be a first order formula. We say that φ *follows from* Γ *under a structure* $\mathcal{S}$, if when all the formulas in Γ hold, it follows that φ holds. That is, for every assignment a, if for each $\psi \in \Gamma$, $M_a(\psi) = \text{TRUE}$, then $M_a(\varphi) = \text{TRUE}$. We call Γ the set of *hypotheses* and φ the *conclusion*. We denote this fact by $\Gamma \models^{\mathcal{S}} \varphi$. This is a generalization of the formally defined notation $\models^{\mathcal{S}} \varphi$, which coincides with the new notation when $\Gamma = \emptyset$.

When $\Gamma \models^{\mathcal{S}} \varphi$ for every structure $\mathcal{S}$, we say that φ *follows from* Γ, and write $\Gamma \models \varphi$. For example, we may want to prove $\{v1 \equiv v2\} \models f(v1) \equiv f(v2)$. From the definitions, both the hypotheses and the conclusion are interpreted over the same assignment. Thus, the intended meaning is that $v1$ and $v2$ have the same values in the hypotheses and the conclusion.

We are interested in proving that $\Gamma \models \varphi$. The proof must consist of simple steps, whose correctness is clear. The fact that φ is *provable* from the hypotheses Γ is denoted by $\Gamma \vdash \varphi$. Recall that the fact that φ is a tautology is denoted by $\models \varphi$. Correspondingly, $\vdash \varphi$ means that φ can be *proved* to hold in every structure and for every assignment.

A *proof system* consists of a set of *axioms* and *proof rules*. Each axiom is a *template* for a formula; a template formula may contain *template variables*, instead of subformulas. An *instance* of the axiom can be obtained by replacing the template variables by actual subformulas (or terms, respectively). For example, consider the template formula $\varphi \rightarrow (\psi \rightarrow \varphi)$. It contains two template variables: φ and ψ. These variables can stand for subformulas. If we replace φ by $P(x)$ and ψ by $Q(y) \vee P(y)$ (where P and Q are unary relation symbols), we obtain $P(x) \rightarrow ((Q(y) \vee P(y)) \rightarrow P(x))$. (Note that the outermost parentheses that were omitted from $Q(y) \vee P(y)$ were restored during the substitution, in order to obtain a well structured formula.) Any instantiated axiom must be a tautology.

A proof rule includes a finite set of template formulas, called *premises*, and an additional template formula, called a *consequent*. We usually denote a proof rule by writing the premises above a horizontal line, and the consequent below it. Often the premises and the consequent share some template variables. We can substitute the template variables in a proof rule such that all the occurrences of each variable are substituted by the same subformulas (terms). After the substitution, we obtain from the premises a set of first order formulas Γ, and from the consequent a formula φ. For the proof rule to be valid, we must have that $\Gamma \models \varphi$. An axiom can also be considered as a special case of a proof rule, where there is a consequent by no premises.

For example, in the following proof rule

$$\frac{\varphi, \; \varphi \rightarrow \psi}{\psi}$$

we can substitute φ by $P(x)$ and ψ by $Q(y) \vee P(y)$. We obtain the following instance:

$$\frac{P(x),\ P(x) \rightarrow (Q(y) \vee P(y))}{Q(y) \vee P(y)}$$

Indeed, we have that $\{P(x),\ P(x) \rightarrow (Q(y) \vee P(y))\} \models Q(y) \vee P(y)$.

We will present an example of a proof system, which assumes that the only Boolean operators are '$\rightarrow$' and $\neg$. This is sufficient, because it is easy to check that the operators '$\wedge$' and '$\vee$' can be eliminated: instead of $\varphi \vee \psi$, we can write $(\neg\varphi) \rightarrow \psi$, and instead of $\varphi \wedge \psi$, we can write $\neg(\varphi \rightarrow \neg\psi)$.

The proof system includes the following axioms:

Ax1	$\varphi \rightarrow (\psi \rightarrow \varphi)$
Ax2	$(\varphi \rightarrow (\psi \rightarrow \eta)) \rightarrow ((\varphi \rightarrow \psi) \rightarrow (\varphi \rightarrow \eta))$
Ax3	$((\neg\varphi \rightarrow \psi) \rightarrow ((\neg\varphi \rightarrow \neg\psi) \rightarrow \varphi))$
Ax4	$(\forall v(\varphi \rightarrow \psi)) \rightarrow (\varphi \rightarrow \forall v\psi)$, v not free in φ
Ax5	$(\forall v\varphi(v)) \rightarrow \varphi(e)$

In the last axiom, e is a template variable that stands for a term that is to be substituted for every free occurrence of v in φ. The following three additional axioms deal with equality:

Ax6	$e \equiv e$
Ax7	$e_i \equiv e_i' \rightarrow f(e_1, \ldots, e_i, \ldots, e_n) \equiv f(e_1, \ldots, e_i', \ldots, e_n)$, $f \in F$
Ax8	$e_i \equiv e_i' \rightarrow (r(e_1, \ldots, e_i, \ldots, e_n) \rightarrow r(e_1, \ldots, e_i', \ldots, e_n))$
	$r \in R \cup \{\equiv\}$

In addition to axioms, we have the following proof rules:

MP (Modus Ponens) :

$$\frac{\varphi,\ \varphi \rightarrow \psi}{\psi}$$

GEN (Generalization):

$$\frac{\varphi}{\forall v\varphi}$$

provided that v does not appear free in any hypothesis of the proof.

Forward Reasoning

Proofs can be performed by *forward reasoning* or *backward reasoning*. In forward reasoning, a proof of $\Gamma \vdash \varphi$ consists of a sequence of numbered formulas, ending with the formula φ. Each line in a forward proof is justified in one of the following ways:

1. It consists of a *hypothesis*, taken from the set of hypotheses Γ.
2. It is an instantiation of an *axiom* of the proof system, obtained by replacing the template variables by appropriate subformulas or terms.

3. It follows from some previous lines using a *proof rule* of the proof system in the following way: after instantiating the template variables appearing in a proof rule, all the premises appear as previous lines in the proof. The instantiated consequent becomes the new line.

We demonstrate the proof system by proving the trivial property $P(x) \rightarrow P(x)$.

1	$P(x) \rightarrow ((P(x) \rightarrow P(x)) \rightarrow P(x))$	Ax1
2	$(P(x) \rightarrow ((P(x) \rightarrow P(x)) \rightarrow P(x))) \rightarrow$	
	$\quad ((P(x) \rightarrow (P(x) \rightarrow P(x))) \rightarrow (P(x) \rightarrow P(x)))$	Ax2
3	$(P(x) \rightarrow (P(x) \rightarrow P(x))) \rightarrow (P(x) \rightarrow P(x))$	MP 1, 2
4	$P(x) \rightarrow (P(x) \rightarrow P(x))$	Ax1
5	$P(x) \rightarrow P(x)$	MP 3, 4

Line 1 was obtained from the axiom Ax1 by instantiating φ with $P(x)$ and ψ with $P(x) \rightarrow P(x)$. Line 2 was obtained from the axiom Ax2 by instantiating both φ and η with $P(x)$ and ψ with $P(x) \rightarrow P(x)$. Line 3 was obtained by using the proof rule MP and the instantiating φ with $P(x) \rightarrow ((P(x) \rightarrow P(x)) \rightarrow P(x))$ and ψ with $(P(x) \rightarrow (P(x) \rightarrow P(x))) \rightarrow (P(x) \rightarrow P(x))$. After this instantiation, the first premise φ of MP corresponds to Line 1 of the proof, while the second premise, $\varphi \rightarrow \psi$ corresponds to line 2. Line 3 corresponds to the consequent of MP under the same assignment. Thus, the justification for line 3 is the use of MP, and the previous lines 1 and 2. Line 4 was obtained again from axiom Ax1 by instantiating both φ and ψ with $P(x)$. Finally, line 5 was obtained by instantiating φ of MP with $P(x) \rightarrow (P(x) \rightarrow P(x))$ and ψ with $P(x) \rightarrow P(x)$. Thus, the premises φ and $\varphi \rightarrow \psi$ of MP correspond to lines 4 and 3, respectively and Line 5 corresponds to the consequent.

Backward Reasoning

In backward reasoning, we 'read' each proof rule backwards: it prescribes how to reduce the task of proving the consequent to the tasks of proving the premises. Intuitively, we want to start with a proof goal that needs to be proved, and justify it using simpler subgoals. To demonstrate this, consider the simple proof rule CONJ:

$$\frac{\varphi, \ \psi}{\varphi \wedge \psi}$$

This rule states that in order to prove $\varphi \wedge \psi$, we can prove φ and ψ separately. In forward proof reasoning, we use such a rule by proving first φ and ψ, and then apply CONJ to conclude $\varphi \wedge \psi$. In backward reasoning, we try to prove the goal $\varphi \wedge \psi$ by creating two *subgoals*, φ and ψ. Then we try to verify these two subgoals separately. When we prove a subgoal φ or ψ, it can be *discharged* from the list of subgoals that are still waiting to be verified. When both subgoals, φ and ψ, are discharged, the goal $\varphi \wedge \psi$ is proved and can be discharged as well.

In general, when using a proof rule in backward reasoning, there is one subgoal for each premise. These are the subgoals of the goal that corresponds to the consequent. When all the subgoals are discharged, the goal itself is discharged. A subgoal that is an instance of an axiom can be discharged immediately.

Backwards reasoning strategy is often more intuitive and easy to use for the person performing the verification than forward reasoning. This applies, in particular, to proof rules that break the goal into shorter subgoals, such as the rule CONJ. The rule MP, presented above, is much harder to use in backward reasoning than CONJ: for proving ψ, we need to suggest some formula φ and prove both φ and $\varphi \rightarrow \psi$. We will see examples of backward reasoning in Sections 3.8 and 3.9.

It is sometimes convenient to be able to change the list of assumptions used in the proof in a dynamic way. Consider for example the *deduction theorem*, which states that

$$\Gamma \models \varphi \rightarrow \psi \ \textit{iff} \ \ \Gamma \cup \{\varphi\} \models \psi.$$

We may want to take advantage of this theorem in the following way: in order to prove that $\Gamma \models \varphi \rightarrow \psi$, we add φ as another hypothesis to the set of already existing hypotheses and then prove $\Gamma \cup \{\varphi\} \models \psi$.

We can add this flexibility to our proof system by formulating axioms and proof rules where the premises and the consequent are of the form $\Gamma \vdash \varphi$, where $\Gamma \cup \{\varphi\}$ are template formulas. For example, a proof rule that represents the deduction theorem can be denoted as

$$\frac{\Gamma \cup \{\varphi\} \vdash \psi}{\Gamma \vdash \varphi \rightarrow \psi}$$

Using this format, we can rewrite the proof rule CONJ as

$$\frac{\Gamma \vdash \varphi, \ \Gamma \vdash \psi}{\Gamma \vdash \varphi \wedge \psi}$$

to indicate that there is no change in the set of hypotheses assumed for the goal (corresponding to the consequent) and the subgoal (corresponding to the premises).

Exercise 3.5.1. Prove $P(x) \rightarrow P(x)$ using backward reasoning.

3.6 Properties of Proof Systems

In this section we will address some fundamental issues concerning formal proofs in mathematics, and in particular the issues of provability in first order logic. To motivate this discussion, consider the well known Fermat's conjecture:

There are no naturals l, m, n such that $l^x + m^x = n^x$ for $x > 2$.

This conjecture was open for over 350 years, and was proved only recently [130]. Now, consider the following plan: we start by defining a first order signature and structure that includes the *naturals*, and the appropriate relations and functions participating in Fermat's conjecture. Then we write Fermat's conjecture as a formula:

$$\neg \exists x \, \exists l \, \exists m \, \exists n \, (x > 2 \wedge l^x + m^x \equiv n^x)$$

We would like to be able to define a proof system for which this conjecture can be proved. Furthermore, we would like to find an algorithm that will automatically find such a proof. The fact that Fermat's conjecture was open for so long, even during times where fast computers were already available, gives evidence that there are some problems with this plan.

We will formalize and discuss here some important properties of proof systems. These properties reflect natural questions about the ability to perform formal mathematical proofs, such as:

- Is a proof system 'correct'?
- Can we use a given proof system to prove all the facts about some structure?
- Is there an algorithm that can decide if a given formula φ is a tautology, or follows from Γ? S is a model of φ?

Soundness

Soundness of a proof system means that it can only be used to prove correct facts. That is, if $\Gamma \vdash \varphi$, then it must be the case that $\Gamma \models \varphi$. First order logic has many different proof systems that are sound. However, care should be taken, since mistakes in formalizing axioms or proof rules can and do occur.

Consider for example the proof system presented in Section 3.5. Assume that we have forgotten to provide the constraint on the proof rule **GEN** that the universal quantifier cannot be applied to a variable that appears free in any given hypothesis. Then, given the hypothesis $v1 \equiv v2$, we can deduce that $f(v1) \equiv f(v2)$ (using **Ax7** and **MP**). Without the restriction on **GEN**, we can use **GEN** twice to prove that $\forall v1 \forall v2 (f(v1) \equiv f(v2))$. That is, we have just incorrectly 'proved' that if $v1 \equiv v2$ (for *some* assignment a), then the function f gives a constant value for every argument. Notice that the quantified $v1$ and $v2$ in the conclusion have nothing to do with the free occurrences of $v1$ and $v2$ in the hypothesis. Obviously, the proof system without the above constraint is not sound.

Completeness

Completeness of a proof system means the following: if $\Gamma \models \varphi$, then $\Gamma \vdash \varphi$. Gödel showed that first order logic is complete. Many of the proof systems for first order logic are complete, allowing one to prove any correct claim of the form $\Gamma \models \varphi$. A complete proof system was presented in Section 3.5. Showing that a proof system is complete is not trivial, see, e.g., [38].

Notice that completeness means that any such claim that uniformly holds (i.e., is interpreted to TRUE) for all the possible first order structures can be proved. However, this does not mean that we can prove all the correct properties of a particular structure, e.g., the *integers* with addition and multiplication, as discussed below.

Decidability

First order logic is *semi-decidable*. That is, there is no algorithm for checking whether $\Gamma \models \varphi$ holds or not. However, there exists an algorithm that constructs a proof of $\Gamma \vdash \varphi$, when $\Gamma \models \varphi$ holds. This algorithm is not even guaranteed to terminate when $\Gamma \not\models \varphi$ holds. Such a proof $\Gamma \vdash \varphi$ can be constructed, provided that we can always increase our memory capacity as needed. (This is not a problem with the theoretical model of Turing machines, see Section 2.4. But on an actual machine, with limited memory, we may run out of memory). As explained in Section 2.4, an algorithm for a semidecidable problem does not have any complexity bound.

Structure Completeness

Given a structure $\mathcal{S}$, we would like to be able to algorithmically provide a set of formulas $\Gamma_{\mathcal{S}}$ such that $\Gamma_{\mathcal{S}} \vdash \varphi$ exactly when $\models^{\mathcal{S}} \varphi$. Adding $\Gamma_{\mathcal{S}}$ as additional axioms to our complete proof system can be used to prove any property that holds for the structure $\mathcal{S}$.

There are some first order structures for which one can provide structural completeness [38]. One example of such a structure includes the *integers* with the addition function and comparison relations, but *without* multiplication. This structure is called *Presburger Arithmetic*. For this structure, one can decide which properties hold and which do not. The complexity of the best known decision procedure for Presburger arithmetic is triple exponential, i.e., the execution time complexity will be $\mathcal{O}(2^{2^{2^{P(n)}}})$, where n is the length of the formula. The known lower bound of this problem is only doubly exponential, i.e., $\mathcal{O}(2^{2^{P(n)}})$, but there is no known algorithm with this complexity. Thus there is an open complexity gap, which calls for additional research [107].

For some other structures there is no complete axiomatization. This includes the *natural* numbers, i.e., the positive *integers* with zero, with both addition and multiplication, called *Peano arithmetic*. Another such structure consists of the *integers* with addition and multiplication. In fact, by a famous result of Gödel, this is not coincidental, or a result of not investing enough resources in finding such axiomatization: it is provable that no such axiomatization exists! Thus, one cannot hope to prove, or decide or even enumerate all the first order formulas that hold for these structure.

Even in light of Gödel's incompleteness theorem, (incomplete) first order logic proof systems for the *naturals* or the *integers* are still very useful. There are useful collections of axioms that hold for the domain of *naturals*, which can be used to prove many important properties. In fact, practice shows that most of the important properties for the *naturals* (and the *integers* alike) can be proved using first order proof systems.

There is often a tradeoff between the expressiveness of a logic and properties such as the availability of a complete proof system, or decidability. For example, second order logic is more expressive than first order logic. It can be used to express the property that there is a path in a graph between two nodes. On the other hand, there is no complete proof system for second order logic. Moreover, second order logic is not even semi-decidable.

3.7 Proving Propositional Logic Properties

Propositional logic is decidable. The problem of checking whether there *exists* an assignment that satisfies a given propositional logic formula, known as the *satisfiability problem*, is in the complexity class NP-complete [51] (see Chapter 2). This means that the best known algorithm performs, in the worst case, in time exponential in the size of the formula. A naive algorithm can check a propositional formula against all possible truth values of the propositional variables that appear in it. Since only finitely many variables appear in a formula, it is guaranteed to terminate. In fact, if there are n variables, checking all the 2^n Boolean assignment combinations requires exponential time.

Notice that a propositional formula φ is a tautology exactly when $\neg\varphi$ is unsatisfiable (i.e., there is no assignment that results in that $\neg\varphi$ calculates to TRUE). Thus, it is sufficient to find one satisfying assignment for $\neg\varphi$ to refute the assumption that φ is a tautology. Some effective heuristic methods for checking satisfiability were developed, e.g., SATO [151], GRASP [129], and Stalmark's method [136].

It is possible to provide a relatively complete proof system for proving propositional logic tautologies. One example is Hilbert's system, which includes the axioms **Ax1**–**Ax3** and the proof rule **MP**, from Section 3.5. The variables that appear in these axioms and proof rule can be substituted by any propositional formula. It is assumed that all the propositional formulas are first translated to include only the negation ('¬') and implication ('→') operators. However, in light of the existence of appropriate algorithms, the use of proof rules in propositional logic with manual or computer-assisted proof is rare.

3.8 A Practical Proof System

We present a simple proof system, similar to the PVS system [109], for first order logic. A *sequent* is a formula of the form

$$(\varphi_1 \wedge \varphi_2 \wedge \ldots \wedge \varphi_n) \rightarrow (\psi_1 \vee \psi_2 \vee \ldots \vee \psi_m)$$

Each subformula φ_i in a sequent is an *antecedent*, and each subformula ψ is a *succedent*. The formulas $\varphi_1, \ldots, \varphi_n$ and $\psi_1, \ldots, \psi_m$ are not limited to any particular form. Thus, each first order formula is essentially of this form, as we can always select $n = 0$ and $m = 1$. We will now present a proof system, which takes advantage of this form.

We will write the formula vertically, where the antecedents will be written first, one per line, above the horizontal line, and will be numbered by negative values -1, -2, etc. The succedents will be written below the line, numbered by positive values 1, 2, etc.

$$
\begin{array}{rl}
-1 & \varphi_1 \\
-2 & \varphi_2 \\
\vdots & \vdots \\
-n & \varphi_n \\
\hline
1 & \psi_1 \\
2 & \psi_2 \\
\vdots & \vdots \\
m & \psi_m
\end{array}
$$

In a proof, we will mark, for convenience, the most recent lines that were changed during the proof with an asterisk '*'.

The proof $\Gamma \vdash \psi$ starts with a sequent with no hypotheses and a single succedent ψ. This is the *initial goal*. This goal is now waiting to be verified. Thus, initially, the list of pending goals includes exactly ψ. We use an axiom to discharge a goal from the list of pending goals, or a proof rule to reduce it to some simpler subgoals, which are added to the list of pending goals by using a proof rule. If we can discharge all of the pending subgoals that were generated from some previous goal, then the goal itself is discharged. Our aim is thus to continue this process until we can discharge the original initial goal.

Trees, described in Section 2.3, can be used to represent the current stage of the proof. A *proof tree* has the initial goal ψ as its root. The immediate successors of any tree node are the subgoals that were obtained from it using a proof rule. One of the leafs of the tree is the *current goal*. During the proof, we may find a proof rule that will reduce this goal to some subgoals. This causes the tree to grow, adding the new subgoals as the immediate successors of the current goal. We may also discharge the current goal using an appropriate axiom. Discharging all the successors (subgoals) of a node allows discharging the node itself. The proof process can be seen as a series of tree transformations (see e.g., Figure 3.1). The goal is to shrink the tree completely, into an empty tree (i.e., a tree without nodes). We will see examples of proofs that involve tree transformations in Section 3.9.

The proof rules that will be presented here are taken from the PVS system. The PVS system is based on a logic that is more general than first order logic. This *higher order logic* is based on *type theory* [27] and will not be discussed here further. We will restrict ourselves to a subset of the proof system that can handle first order logic. Instead of presenting the proof rules themselves, we present PVS *commands* that can control the mechanized theorem prover. Each command is based on a single proof rule or an axiom. (It is an interesting and not a difficult exercise to try to write the corresponding proof rule for each command.)

eliminate Removes the current goal, i.e., a sequent of the form $(\varphi_1 \wedge \ldots \wedge \varphi_n) \to (\psi_1 \vee \ldots \vee \psi_m)$, provided that at least one of the following conditions hold:

- One of the antecedents $\varphi_1, \ldots, \varphi_n$ is *false*.
- One of the succedents $\psi_1, \ldots, \psi_n$ is *true*.
- One of the antecedents is the same as one of the succedents, i.e., for some $1 \le i \le n$ and $1 \le j \le m$, we have $\varphi_i = \psi_j$.
- One of the succedents is of the form $e \equiv e$, where e is a term.

The *eliminate* command corresponds to applying an axiom (since it removes a goal). In the PVS system, it is in fact applied automatically, whenever a new goal is created.

flatten Creates one immediate subgoal, by simplifying the current goal, based on the special form of the sequent. It attempts to produce a sequent with shorter subformulas by performing one or more of the following simplifications:

- Removing negation. One way to remove negation is to replace an antecedent of the form $\neg\psi$ with a succedent of the form ψ. This is based on the fact that $(\varphi \wedge \neg\psi) \to \eta$ is logically equivalent to $\varphi \to (\psi \vee \eta)$. Another way is to replace a succedent of the form $\neg\psi$ with an antecedent of the form ψ. This is based on the fact that $\varphi \to (\neg\psi \vee \eta)$ is logically equivalent to $(\varphi \wedge \psi) \to \eta$.
- Breaking a conjunction by replacing an antecedent of the form $\varphi_1 \wedge \varphi_2$ with two antecedents, φ_1 and φ_2.
- Breaking a disjunction by replacing a succedent of the form $\varphi_1 \vee \varphi_2$ by two succedents, φ_1 and φ_2.
- Replacing a succedent of the form $\varphi_1 \to \varphi_2$ with an antecedent φ_1 and a succedent φ_2. This is based on the fact that $\varphi_1 \to \varphi_2$ is the same as $(\neg\varphi_1) \vee \varphi_2$. This involves the combination of two of the above steps: breaking the disjunction, and removing negation.

The *flatten* command specifies the line number in the current goal where the flattening needs to occur. Similar to other commands, if flattening fails, i.e., the line provided fails to be one of the above cases, the current goal is kept unchanged.

split Splits a subgoal according to one of the following cases:

- If the current goal s has an antecedent of the form $\varphi_1 \vee \varphi_2 \vee \ldots \vee \varphi_l$, the rule can create l subgoals, where in the ith new subgoal, the above antecedent is replaced with φ_i.
- If the current goal s has a succedent of the form $\varphi_1 \wedge \varphi_2 \wedge \ldots \wedge \varphi_l$, the rule can create l subgoals, where in the the ith new subgoal, the above succedent is replaced with φ_i.

The *split* command specifies the line number of the current goal, where the splitting needs to occur.

assumption Takes a subgoal and creates a single immediate subgoal, where one of the formulas from Γ is added as an additional antecedent. The *assumption* command specifies the name of the formula in Γ that is added.

Skolemize Eliminate the external universal quantification in a succedent, or the external existential quantification in an antecedent. There are two possibilities:

- There is some succedent of the form $\forall v \psi$. The Skolemization creates a single subgoal by replacing that succedent with $\psi[c/v]$ for some new constant c that did not appear before in the proof. The justification for using this rule is as follows: if the proof of the new subgoal succeeds, since c was chosen without loss of generality (i.e., without any restriction on it, since it was new when selected and did not have any special constraint on it), we can deduce that the original subgoal, which had the universal quantification, holds.
- There is some antecedent of the form $\exists v \varphi$. The Skolemization creates a single subgoal by replacing that antecedent with $\varphi[c/v]$ for some new constant c that did not appear before. If the proof of the new subgoal succeeds, then we can argue again that we did not use any specific constraint on c, except that it has to satisfy the subformula φ. Thus (without loss of generality) the existence of a value satisfying φ proves the implication, obtaining the original subgoal, with the existential quantification.

The *Skolemize* command specifies the line that needs to be Skolemized and the constant name c.

instantiate This is in some sense the complement of Skolemization, as it allows the removal of an outermost universal quantification in an antecedent, or an outermost existential quantification in a succedent. Again, there are two cases:

- There is some antecedent of the form $\forall v \varphi$. Then we can pick any term e, and create a single subgoal with that antecedent replaced by $\varphi[e/v]$. If we can later prove that the implication holds when we require φ to hold with specific term e, then it obviously holds when we require φ to hold for any value of the domain.

- There is some succedent of the form $\exists v \psi$. Then we can pick up any term e, and create a single subgoal with that antecedent replaced by $\psi[e/v]$. The justification for the use of the proof rule is as follows: if the implication holds with ψ satisfied for a specific value of the term e, then we know that there exists a value for which ψ holds. That is, the term e was used to give an evidence that ψ holds (once the antecedents hold).

Notice that in both cases, the definition of substitution (from Section 3.3) does not allow us to substitute a free variable by an expression that includes a variable that is quantified at the place of the substitution. The *instantiate* command includes the line that needs to be instantiated, and the term e. Note that Skolemization is less liberal than instantiation; it only allows substituting with a new variables.

substitution Given an antecedent of the form $e_1 \equiv e_2$, we can create a subgoal, where e_1 is replaced by e_2, or e_2 is replaced by e_1 in either an antecedent or a succedent. This captures the fact that the equality symbol '$\equiv$' has the usual semantics for equality.

The substitution command specifies the line from which the equality $e_1 \equiv e_2$ is retrieved, the line where the substitution should be applied, and an indication of whether to replace e_1 by e_2 or vice versa.

The proof system selects one of the leafs of the proof tree to be the current goal. We can alter this choice using the command *postpone*, which cyclically traverses between the current leafs. Its effect is to select a new leaf as the current goal (if there are multiple leafs in the current tree), postponing the process of proving the current leaf for a later stage of the proof.

3.9 Example Proofs

In the first example, we will prove the following propositional tautology:

$$((A \to C) \land (B \to C)) \to ((A \lor B) \to C)$$

Thus, our initial goal, numbered 1, is

$$\overline{1 \quad ((A \to C) \land (B \to C)) \to ((A \lor B) \to C)}$$

The initial proof tree, Tree 1 on the top left in Figure 3.1, contains this single node. Notice that the succedent of the initial goal is of the form $\varphi \to \psi$, where $\varphi = (A \to C) \land (B \to C)$ and $\psi = ((A \lor B) \to C)$. Thus, applying *flatten* to line 1, we can obtain the following subgoal for the initial goal

$$
\begin{array}{rrl}
* & -1 & (A \to C) \land (B \to C) \\
\hline
* & 1 & (A \lor B) \to C
\end{array}
$$

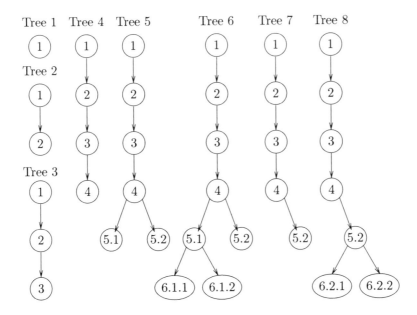

Fig. 3.1. Proof trees

The current proof tree, Tree 2 in Figure 3.1, contains the subgoal as node 2, which is the only leaf of the tree, and is an immediate successor of the initial goal, numbered 1.

Applying *flatten* to line -1, we obtain the following subgoal, numbered 3.

$$
\begin{array}{rl}
* & -1 \quad A \to C \\
* & -2 \quad B \to C \\
\hline
& 1 \quad ((A \lor B) \to C)
\end{array}
$$

The proof tree, Tree 3, includes a path containing three nodes, with the new leaf as the current subgoal. Applying *flatten* to line 1, we obtain the following subgoal, numbered 4.

$$
\begin{array}{rl}
& -1 \quad A \to C \\
& -2 \quad B \to C \\
* & -3 \quad A \lor B \\
\hline
* & 1 \quad C
\end{array}
$$

This adds a new leaf to the proof tree, obtaining Tree 4. We cannot use *flatten* any more to simplify the new current goal in node 4. But we can apply *split* to line -3, obtaining two subgoals:

$$
\begin{array}{rl}
& -1 \quad A \to C \\
& -2 \quad B \to C \\
* & -3 \quad A \\
\hline
& 1 \quad C
\end{array}
\qquad\qquad
\begin{array}{rl}
& -1 \quad A \to C \\
& -2 \quad B \to C \\
* & -3 \quad B \\
\hline
& 1 \quad C
\end{array}
$$

These subgoals appear as the two immediate successors of node 4, and are labeled 5.1 and 5.2 in the new proof tree, Tree 5. We need to treat each of these subgoals separately. We will start with the left subgoal, in node 5.1, as the new current goal. We will split according to line -1. Recall that $A \to C$ is logically equivalent to $(\neg A) \vee C$, so splitting will either negate A and put it as an additional succedent, or will put C as an additional antecedent. The two subgoals that are obtained are:

$$
\begin{array}{cl}
-1 & B \to C \\
-2 & A \\
\hline
1 & C \\
* \quad 2 & A
\end{array}
\qquad\qquad
\begin{array}{cl}
* \quad -1 & C \\
-2 & B \to C \\
-3 & A \\
\hline
1 & C
\end{array}
$$

These subgoals of node 5.1 are numbered 6.1.1 and 6.1.2 in the new proof tree, Tree 6. Notice that we leave the leaf 5.2 alone for the time being. We will have to return to this node in order to complete the proof. In both nodes, 6.1.1. and 6.1.2, there is a subformula that appears both as an antecedent and as a succedent. Thus, these nodes can be discharged in some (arbitrary) order, using *eliminate*. Their discharge causes their parent subgoal in node 5.1 to be discharged. This result in the proof tree, Tree 7. The transformation from Tree 6 to Tree 7 thus involves three steps: (1) discharging node 6.1, (2) discharging node 6.2, and (3) discharging node 5.1.

The only leaf of this new tree, Tree 7, is node 5.2. Thus, it becomes the current goal. Recall that this node contains the sequent

$$
\begin{array}{cl}
-1 & A \to C \\
-2 & B \to C \\
* \quad -3 & B \\
\hline
1 & C
\end{array}
$$

We can now handle the new current goal by splitting according to line -2. We obtain two subgoals

$$
\begin{array}{cl}
-1 & A \to C \\
* \quad -2 & C \\
-3 & A \\
\hline
1 & C
\end{array}
\qquad\qquad
\begin{array}{cl}
-1 & A \to C \\
-2 & B \\
\hline
1 & C \\
* \quad 2 & B
\end{array}
$$

These two subgoals, 6.2.1 and 6.2.2, are the new leafs in Tree 8. Again, the nodes are discharged using *eliminate*, because of the mutual antecedent and succedent. The discharging now spreads all the way to the root of the proof tree: node 5.1 is discharged once its predecessors 6.2.1 and 6.2.2 are discharged. For the same reason, node 4 is discharged, and then in reverse order to their creation, the nodes 3, 2 and 1. Once the root node is discharged, the proof is completed.

Exercise 3.9.1. Prove the following:

- $(A \wedge (\neg A)) \rightarrow B$
- Given the hypotheses $A \rightarrow B$ and $B \rightarrow C$, we can conclude that $A \rightarrow C$.

As another, more complicated example, we will prove a simple property of group theory. This time, the proof uses first order logic. The proof will demonstrate the use of instantiation and Skolemization. The signature of group theory includes the group multiplication symbol '$\times$' (which is another overloading of the same mathematical symbol that is used for multiplication of *real* or *integer* numbers), and the unit element *unit*. A group satisfies the following three axioms:

unity There is a special element *unit* such that $x \times unit \equiv x$ for each x.
$\forall x \; x \times unit \equiv x$
associativity The operator $\times$ is associative, meaning that in a repeated application of this operation, the ordering of the parentheses does not matter.
$\forall x \, \forall y \, \forall z \, (x \times y) \times z \equiv x \times (y \times z)$
right-complement Each element x has a *complement* y such that $x \times y$ gives the unit element *unit*. $\forall x \, \exists y \, (x \times y \equiv unit)$ Notice that y is a *right* complement of x.

We want to prove that for each element x there is a *left* complement y such that $y \times x$ gives the unit element *unit*. Formally, $\forall x \, \exists y \, (y \times x \equiv unit)$. We will give first the informal proof, as is done in mathematics classes or books on algebra.

Start by choosing x arbitrarily. Since we do not restrict x, our proof is done for every possible value of x (or 'without loss of generality'). By the 'right-complement' axiom, there exists some value y such that

$$x \times y \equiv unit. \tag{3.3}$$

Using the 'right-complement' axiom again, there exists some value z such that

$$y \times z \equiv unit. \tag{3.4}$$

We argue using the following equations:

$$
\begin{array}{lll}
& y \times x & \\
\equiv & (y \times x) \times unit & \text{by 'unity'} \\
\equiv & (y \times x) \times (y \times z) & \text{by Equation (3.4)} \\
\equiv & y \times (x \times (y \times z)) & \text{by 'associativity'} \\
\equiv & y \times ((x \times y) \times z) & \text{by 'associativity'} \\
\equiv & y \times (unit \times z) & \text{by Equation (3.3)} \\
\equiv & (y \times unit) \times z & \text{by 'associativity'} \\
\equiv & y \times z & \text{by 'unity'} \\
\equiv & unit & \text{by Equation (3.4)}
\end{array}
$$

The formal proof, obtained by using the PVS proof system, and lightly edited for presentation here, follows the same arguments as the informal one. However, it is done in a much more detailed and rigorous way. The proof in this case is 'linear', in the sense that the current tree always grows by exactly one single node, which becomes the new current subgoal. At the very last step in the proof, the last subgoal is discharged, which causes all the nodes in the tree to be discharged in the reverse order of their creation.

We start with the following initial goal:

$$\overline{\quad 1 \quad \forall x \exists y \, y \times x \equiv unit \quad}$$

Thus, we obtain a tree consisting of one node, which is also the current subgoal. Skolemizing the variable y in succedent 1 with a new constant x', we obtain a single subgoal

$$\overline{\quad * \quad 1 \quad \exists y \, y \times x' \equiv unit \quad}$$

Applying assumption 'right complement'

$$\frac{* \quad -1 \quad \forall x \, \exists y x \times y \equiv unit}{1 \quad \exists y \, y \times x' \equiv unit}$$

Instantiating variable x in antecedent -1 with the constant x'.

$$\frac{* \quad -1 \quad \exists y \, x' \times y \equiv unit}{1 \quad \exists y \, y \times x' \equiv unit}$$

Skolemizing the variable y in antecedent -1 with the new constant y'.

$$\frac{* \quad -1 \quad x' \times y' \equiv unit}{1 \quad \exists y \, y \times x' \equiv unit}$$

Applying assumption 'right-complement'

$$\frac{\begin{array}{rl} * & -1 \quad \forall x \, \exists y \, x \times y \equiv unit \\ & -2 \quad x' \times y' \equiv unit \end{array}}{1 \quad \exists y \, y \times x' \equiv unit}$$

Instantiating variable x in antecedent -1 with the constant y'.

$$\frac{\begin{array}{rl} * & -1 \quad \exists y \, y' \times y \equiv unit \\ & -2 \quad x' \times y' \equiv unit \end{array}}{1 \quad \exists y \, y \times x' \equiv unit}$$

Skolemizing the variable y in antecedent -1 with the new constant z'.

$$\frac{\begin{array}{rl} * & -1 \quad y' \times z' \equiv unit \\ & -2 \quad x' \times y' \equiv unit \end{array}}{1 \quad \exists y \, y \times x' \equiv unit}$$

Applying assumption 'unity'

$$
\begin{array}{lll}
* & -1 & \forall x\; x \times unit \equiv x \\
& -2 & y' \times z' \equiv unit \\
& -3 & x' \times y' \equiv unit \\
\hline
& 1 & \exists y\; y \times x' \equiv unit
\end{array}
$$

Instantiating variable x in antecedent -1 with the term $(y' \times x')$.

$$
\begin{array}{lll}
* & -1 & (y' \times x') \times unit \equiv (y' \times x') \\
& -2 & y' \times z' \equiv unit \\
& -3 & x' \times y' \equiv unit \\
\hline
& 1 & \exists y\; y \times x' \equiv unit
\end{array}
$$

Replacing $unit$ in antecedent -1 by $(y' \times z')$, according to antecedent -2.

$$
\begin{array}{lll}
* & -1 & (y' \times x') \times (y' \times z') \equiv (y' \times x') \\
& -2 & y' \times z' \equiv unit \\
& -3 & x' \times y' \equiv unit \\
\hline
& 1 & \exists y\; y \times x' \equiv unit
\end{array}
$$

Applying assumption 'associativity'

$$
\begin{array}{lll}
* & -1 & \forall x \,\forall y \,\forall z\; (x \times y) \times z \equiv x \times (y \times z) \\
& -2 & (y' \times x') \times (y' \times z') \equiv (y' \times x') \\
& -3 & y' \times z' \equiv unit \\
& -4 & x' \times y' \equiv unit \\
\hline
& 1 & \exists y\; y \times x' \equiv unit
\end{array}
$$

Instantiating x to y' in antecedent -1.

$$
\begin{array}{lll}
* & -1 & \forall y \,\forall z\; (y' \times y) \times z \equiv y' \times (y \times z) \\
& -2 & (y' \times x') \times (y' \times z') \equiv (y' \times x') \\
& -3 & y' \times z' \equiv unit \\
& -4 & x' \times y' \equiv unit \\
\hline
& 1 & \exists y\; y \times x' \equiv unit
\end{array}
$$

Instantiating y to x' in antecedent -1.

$$
\begin{array}{lll}
* & -1 & \forall z\; (y' \times x') \times z \equiv y' \times (x' \times z) \\
& -2 & (y' \times x') \times (y' \times z') \equiv (y' \times x') \\
& -3 & y' \times z' \equiv unit \\
& -4 & x' \times y' \equiv unit \\
\hline
& 1 & \exists y\; y \times x' \equiv unit
\end{array}
$$

Instantiating z to $(y' \times z')$ in antecedent -1.

$$\begin{array}{ll} * & -1 \quad (y' \times x') \times (y' \times z') \equiv y' \times (x' \times (y' \times z')) \\ & -2 \quad (y' \times x') \times (y' \times z') \equiv (y' \times x') \\ & -3 \quad y' \times z' \equiv unit \\ & \underline{-4 \quad x' \times y' \equiv unit} \\ & 1 \quad \exists y \, y \times x' \equiv unit \end{array}$$

Replacing $(y' \times x') \times (y' \times z')$ by $(y' \times x')$ in antecedent -1, according to antecedent -2.

$$\begin{array}{ll} * & -1 \quad (y' \times x') \equiv y' \times (x' \times (y' \times z')) \\ & -2 \quad (y' \times x') \times (y' \times z') \equiv (y' \times x') \\ & -3 \quad y' \times z' \equiv unit \\ & \underline{-4 \quad x' \times y' \equiv unit} \\ & 1 \quad \exists y \, y \times x' \equiv unit \end{array}$$

Applying assumption 'associativity'

$$\begin{array}{ll} * & -1 \quad \forall x \, \forall y \, \forall z \, (x \times y) \times z \equiv x \times (y \times z) \\ & -2 \quad (y' \times x') \equiv y' \times (x' \times (y' \times z')) \\ & -3 \quad (y' \times x') \times (y' \times z') \equiv (y' \times x') \\ & -4 \quad y' \times z' \equiv unit \\ & \underline{-5 \quad x' \times y' \equiv unit} \\ & 1 \quad \exists y \, y \times x' \equiv unit \end{array}$$

Instantiating x with x', y with y' and z with z' in antecedent -1 (we combine these three trivial steps into one).

$$\begin{array}{ll} * & -1 \quad (x' \times y') \times z' \equiv x' \times (y' \times z') \\ & -2 \quad (y' \times x') \equiv y' \times (x' \times (y' \times z')) \\ & -3 \quad (y' \times x') \times (y' \times z') \equiv (y' \times x') \\ & -4 \quad y' \times z' \equiv unit \\ & \underline{-5 \quad x' \times y' \equiv unit} \\ & 1 \quad \exists y \, y \times x' \equiv unit \end{array}$$

Replacing $(x' \times (y' \times z'))$ by $((x' \times y') \times z')$ in antecedent -2, using antecedent -1.

$$\begin{array}{ll} & -1 \quad (x' \times y') \times z' \equiv x' \times (y' \times z') \\ * & -2 \quad (y' \times x') \equiv y' \times ((x' \times y') \times z') \\ & -3 \quad (y' \times x') \times (y' \times z') \equiv (y' \times x') \\ & -4 \quad y' \times z' \equiv unit \\ & \underline{-5 \quad x' \times y' \equiv unit} \\ & 1 \quad \exists y \, y \times x' \equiv unit \end{array}$$

Replacing $(x' \times y')$ by $unit$ in antecedent -2, using antecedent -5.

$$-1 \quad (x' \times y') \times z' \equiv x' \times (y' \times z')$$
$$* \quad -2 \quad (y' \times x') \equiv (y' \times (unit \times z'))$$
$$-3 \quad (y' \times x') \times (y' \times z') \equiv (y' \times x')$$
$$-4 \quad y' \times z' \equiv unit$$
$$-5 \quad x' \times y' \equiv unit$$
$$\overline{\quad 1 \quad \exists y\, y \times x' \equiv unit \quad}$$

Applying assumption 'associativity'.

$$* \quad -1 \quad \forall x\, \forall y\, \forall z\, (x \times y) \times z \equiv x \times (y \times z)$$
$$-2 \quad (x' \times y') \times z' \equiv x' \times (y' \times z')$$
$$-3 \quad (y' \times x') \equiv (y' \times (unit \times z'))$$
$$-4 \quad (y' \times x') \times (y' \times z') \equiv (y' \times x')$$
$$-5 \quad y' \times z' \equiv unit$$
$$-6 \quad x' \times y' \equiv unit$$
$$\overline{\quad 1 \quad \exists y\, y \times x' \equiv unit \quad}$$

Instantiating x with y', y with $unit$ and z with z' in antecedent -1.

$$* \quad -1 \quad (y' \times unit) \times z' \equiv y' \times (unit \times z')$$
$$-2 \quad (x' \times y') \times z' \equiv x' \times (y' \times z')$$
$$-3 \quad (y' \times x') \equiv (y' \times (unit \times z'))$$
$$-4 \quad (y' \times x') \times (y' \times z') \equiv (y' \times x')$$
$$-5 \quad y' \times z' \equiv unit$$
$$-6 \quad x' \times y' \equiv unit$$
$$\overline{\quad 1 \quad \exists y\, y \times x' \equiv unit \quad}$$

Replacing $y' \times (unit \times z')$ by $(y' \times unit) \times z'$ in antecedent -3 using antecedent -1.

$$-1 \quad (y' \times unit) \times z' \equiv y' \times (unit \times z')$$
$$-2 \quad (x' \times y') \times z' \equiv x' \times (y' \times z')$$
$$* \quad -3 \quad (y' \times x') \equiv ((y' \times unit) \times z')$$
$$-4 \quad (y' \times x') \times (y' \times z') \equiv (y' \times x')$$
$$-5 \quad y' \times z' \equiv unit$$
$$-6 \quad x' \times y' \equiv unit$$
$$\overline{\quad 1 \quad \exists y\, y \times x' \equiv unit \quad}$$

Applying assumption 'unity'.

$$* \quad -1 \quad \forall x\, x \times unit \equiv x$$
$$-2 \quad (y' \times unit) \times z' \equiv y' \times (unit \times z')$$
$$-3 \quad (x' \times y') \times z' \equiv x' \times (y' \times z')$$
$$-4 \quad (y' \times x') \equiv ((y' \times unit) \times z')$$
$$-5 \quad (y' \times x') \times (y' \times z') \equiv (y' \times x')$$
$$-6 \quad y' \times z' \equiv unit$$
$$-7 \quad x' \times y' \equiv unit$$
$$\overline{\quad 1 \quad \exists y\, y \times x' \equiv unit \quad}$$

Instantiating x with y' in antecedent -1.

$$
\begin{array}{rl}
* \quad -1 & y' \times unit \equiv y' \\
-2 & (y' \times unit) \times z' \equiv y' \times (unit \times z') \\
-3 & (x' \times y') \times z' \equiv x' \times (y' \times z') \\
-4 & (y' \times x') \equiv ((y' \times unit) \times z') \\
-5 & (y' \times x') \times (y' \times z') \equiv (y' \times x') \\
-6 & y' \times z' \equiv unit \\
-7 & x' \times y' \equiv unit \\
\hline
1 & \exists y \; y \times x' \equiv unit
\end{array}
$$

Replacing $y' \times unit$ by y' in antecedent -4, using antecedent -1.

$$
\begin{array}{rl}
-1 & y' \times unit \equiv y' \\
-2 & (y' \times unit) \times z' \equiv y' \times (unit \times z') \\
-3 & (x' \times y') \times z' \equiv x' \times (y' \times z') \\
* \quad -4 & (y' \times x') \equiv (y' \times z') \\
-5 & (y' \times x') \times (y' \times z') \equiv (y' \times x') \\
-6 & y' \times z' \equiv unit \\
-7 & x' \times y' \equiv unit \\
\hline
1 & \exists y \; y \times x' \equiv unit
\end{array}
$$

Replacing $y' \times z'$ by $unit$ in antecedent -4, using antecedent -6.

$$
\begin{array}{rl}
-1 & y' \times unit \equiv y' \\
-2 & (y' \times unit) \times z' \equiv y' \times (unit \times z') \\
-3 & (x' \times y') \times z' \equiv x' \times (y' \times z') \\
* \quad -4 & y' \times x' \equiv unit \\
-5 & (y' \times x') \times (y' \times z') \equiv (y' \times x') \\
-6 & y' \times z' \equiv unit \\
-7 & x' \times y' \equiv unit \\
\hline
1 & \exists y \; y \times x' \equiv unit
\end{array}
$$

Instantiating y to y' in succedent 1.

$$
\begin{array}{rl}
-1 & y' \times unit \equiv y' \\
-2 & (y' \times unit) \times z' \equiv y' \times (unit \times z') \\
-3 & (x' \times y') \times z' \equiv x' \times (y' \times z') \\
-4 & y' \times x' \equiv unit \\
-5 & (y' \times x') \times (y' \times z') \equiv (y' \times x') \\
-6 & y' \times z' \equiv unit \\
-7 & x' \times y' \equiv unit \\
\hline
* \quad 1 & y' \times x' \equiv unit
\end{array}
$$

We can now discharge the last goal using *eliminate*, since antecedent -4 and succedent 1 are the same. Since the structure of the proof is linear (each goal has exactly one subgoal), the entire proof tree (which has a single path in this case), will be discharged, and the proof is completed.

3.10 Machine Assisted Proofs

Due to undecidability and structure incompleteness issues, discussed in Section 3.6, mathematical proofs are subjected to the ingenuity and the skills of an educated human. However, computer systems called *mechanized theorem provers* can be of great assistance in obtaining and checking proofs. Obtaining a proof is often the result of an interactive collaboration between a human *prover*, who may be a mathematician, a logician, or a trained engineer, and a mechanized theorem prover.

One of the ways in which a theorem prover program can help the human prover is by enforcing rigor. A proof consists of many formulas, including axioms, interconnected in a precise way using proof rules. The human prover is often prone to making mistakes. It is only natural that, after spending some time on a proof, the prover will start making 'shortcuts' in places that seem obvious and too trivial to prove. Using a mechanized theorem prover does not allow that, and makes sure that every intermediate step is obtained exactly according to the proof system used.

Although all theorem proving tools enforce rigor, the theorem proving community is split over the question of how much rigor must be enforced. On one extreme, there are supporters of the 'purist' approach. They believe that all of the mathematics that is used within a theorem prover must be verified, up to some very small number of elementary axioms and proof rules. According to this approach, if, for example, someone wants to prove properties of character strings, and the theorem prover was not used before for this domain, the human prover must first map the domain of character strings to some domain that exists within the theorem prover. He cannot add new axioms for character strings, but needs to prove theorems about them, using the theorem prover, based on theorems that were already proved. Only after doing that can he use these theorems within other proofs.

The aim of the purist approach is obviously to increase the reliability of the correctness of the proofs. Indeed, the goal of a theorem prover is to provide a reasonable amount of certainty. Under the purist approach, the entire proof is then based on a very small number of axioms and proof rules that are well understood, and where contradiction is unlikely (at least not more likely than having contradictions in known mathematics, based on *set theory* or *type theory* [27]). To avoid the undesirable possibility that using such systems will be painfully time consuming, the theorem prover collects the different mathematical theories that were already proved and organizes them in libraries, for reuse in future proofs. An example of such a system is HOL [97], which stands for *higher order logic*.

On the opposite end, the 'practical' approach focuses on helping the user to obtain a proof quickly. The user is allowed to provide axiomatization for new domains, and immediately use them to construct proofs. It is the user's responsibility to ensure that the axioms indeed reflect the properties of the intended domain. The user is free to start using the mechanized theorem prover after a minimal investment of time. This can involve looking for appropriate axioms of the given domain in books, and converting them into the syntax allowed by the theorem prover.

This approach is often very effective for engineering purposes. However, the user must be aware of the risks involved. It is an observed phenomenon that human provers tend to add, during the verification process, more axioms, whenever they think that the proof will become easier. A human prover may mistakenly believe that a given property is correct for the given domain. Such 'wishful thinking' tends to produce proofs that are much weaker than what is intended: the added axioms may in fact be additional assumptions, which may or may not hold. Therefore, in reality, instead of proving that some property φ holds in some domain, the prover has only showed that φ holds under the assumptions added during the proof. At worst, if the added assumptions contain some internal contradictions, the proof that φ holds has no value whatsoever. An example of a theorem prover that is built using the 'practical' approach is PVS [109]. The example proofs in this chapter follow this tool quite closely.

Another way in which theorem provers can assist the human prover is by suggesting how to continue the proof from a given point. Although the mechanized theorem prover may not be able to complete the proof itself, it may suggest various useful ways to continue it. Even though theorem proving cannot be performed automatically for many of the important mathematical structures, there are still many heuristics that can be used to help the user decide how to progress.

A *tactic* is a small procedure that combines the (possibly conditional and repeated) application of several axioms and proof rules. Tactics allow the prover to make substantial progress towards proving a theorem, rather than applying one axiom or one proof rule at a time. Here too, the purist and the practical approaches differ. The purist approach allows constructing tactics by combining existing axioms and proof rules that are already represented in the system. The practical approach often allows the tactics to be implemented as external programs that are applied to some subgoal in the proof and returns another subgoal.

Mechanized theorem provers can be of great assistance in navigating the proof. They can keep track of various incomplete alternative proofs, alternate between subgoals that are still unproven, and keep record of the completed proof for further update, or for use in another proof. Many provers include the important feature of 'pretty printing' a proof. Once the proof is completed, this feature can be used to produce a text of the proof that is easy to read, or can even be included in a paper or a book.

Exercise 3.10.1. *Equivalence relations* are often used in conjunction with formal methods. Their uses will be further discussed in later chapters. Recall from Section 2.1 that an equivalence relation '$\cong$' over some domain satisfies the following three axioms:

Reflexivity $\forall x\, x \cong x.$
Symmetry $\forall x\, \forall y\, (x \cong y \to y \cong x).$
Transitivity $\forall x\, \forall y\, \forall z\, ((x \cong y \land y \cong z) \to x \cong z).$

Use the axioms to prove informally that the following property holds:

If x is not equivalent to y, then any value z that is equivalent to z is not equivalent to y.

Use a mechanized theorem prover (e.g., obtain one by using the list of URLs below) to formally prove the above property. Formally, prove

$$\forall x\, \forall y\, ((\neg x \cong y) \to \forall z\, (x \cong z \to \neg y \cong z)).$$

3.11 Mechanized Theorem Provers

The ACL2 system is available from University of Texas at Austin using the URL
http://www.cs.utexas.edu/users/moore/acl2
The Coq system is available from Inria using the URL
http://pauillac.inria.fr/coq
The HOL system is available from Cambridge using the URL
http://www.cl.cam.ac.uk/Research/HVG/HOL
The Isabelle system [106] is available from Cambridge using the URL
http://www.cl.cam.ac.uk/Research/HVG/Isabelle
The Larch system is available from MIT using the URL
http://larch.lcs.mit.edu
The Nuprl system is available from Cornell using the URL
http://www.cs.cornell.edu/Info/Projects/NuPrl
The PVS system is available from Stanford Research Institute (SRI) using the URL
http://pvs.csl.sri.com
The TPS system is available from Carnegie Mellon University using the URL
http://www.cs.cmu.edu/ andrews/tps.html
   Notice: the use of formal methods systems often requires filling out and sending an appropriate release form, committing to some terms of use.

3.12 Further Reading

The following books can be used for an excellent introduction to mathematical logic:

G. S. Boolos, D. J. Richard, *Computability and Logic*, Cambridge University Press, (3rd edition), 1989.
D. van Dalen, *Logic and Structure*, Springer-Verlag, 3rd edition, 1994.

H. D. Ebbinghaus, J. Flum, W. Thomas, *Mathematical Logic*, Springer-Verlag, 1994.

Several books describe a particular deductive theorem prover:

R. S. Boyer, J. S. Moore, *The Computational Logic Handbook*, Academic Press, 1998.

T. F. Melham, M. J. C. Gordon, *Introduction to HOL: A Theorem Proving Environment for Higher Order Logic*, Cambridge University Press, 1993.

L. C. Paulson, *Logic and Computation: Interactive Proof with Cambridge LCF*, Cambridge, 1990.

N. Shankar, *Mathematics, Machines and Godel's Proof*, Cambridge, 1997.

L. Wos, *The Automatic Reasoning: An Experimenter's Notebook with Otter, Tutorial*, Academic Press, 1996.

L. Wos, *Automated Reasoning: Introduction and Application*, 2nd edition, McGraw-Hill, 1992.

4. Modeling Software Systems

'Be what you would seem to be' – or if you'd like it put more simply – 'Never imagine yourself not to be otherwise than what it might appear to others that what you were or might have been was not otherwise than what you had been would have appeared to them to be otherwise.'

Lewis Carroll, *Alice's Adventures in Wonderland*

Applying tools and techniques for increasing the reliability of a software system usually requires first *modeling* it. That is, representing the system in terms of mathematical objects that reflect its observed properties. In physics, it is helpful to use a model of a system (e.g., an atom, a planet) in order to analyze *some* of its aspects. Modeling usually involves the process of *abstraction*, i.e., simplifying the description of the system, while preserving only a limited number of the original details. This allows one to focus only on the main properties and better manage the complexity of the system. In software, as in physics, it is often much more convenient and manageable to deal with an abstract model, which is simplified and idealized, than to reason about the whole system. Issues such as high complexity can often prohibit analyzing software code directly, while a model can often be made small and simple enough for applying formal methods. From a different perspective, modeling is required since mathematical methods cannot handle physical entities (e.g., computer memory), but rather mathematical abstractions of them.

Modeling of software can also be a consequence of software diversity. Since there are many different programming languages, software packages, operating systems and computer hardware, software reliability tools cannot support all the possible combinations. It is thus typical that tools are being developed with a particular syntax, often different from any syntax used for actual programming. Applying formal methods thus often starts with translating the actual software to the particular syntax allowed by the tool that is used.

Automatic translation from a software system into a model, represented within some formalism, can sometimes be obtained via the usual compilation techniques. However, a direct translation is usually impossible or impractical since formal methods specification languages are often more restrictive in the number of constructs they offer than are programming languages. An automatic translation can result in a largely inefficient representation, preventing some optimizations, which the target technique or tool could take advantage of. Consequently, translating the code in order to make it fit the limitations of formal methods tools usually requires the manual assistance of an experienced engineer.

A model is not necessarily a scaled down version of an actual system. In many cases, a model of a system may be constructed *before* or *in parallel* with the development of the system. This allows the performance of preliminary checks, such as testing the design before the actual code is written. One can use such a preliminary model to conduct a feasibility study, or to check the consistency of the informal specification. This model can be *concretized* into actual code. When a substantial part of the system is constructed, it is useful to check the conformance of the actual system with the preliminary model.

It is important that a model will truthfully reflect properties of the actual system. One of the goals of modeling is simplifying and scaling down the checked object. To achieve this, a model may require the preservation of only *some* of the properties of the modeled system. In fact, it is sometimes useful to construct different models for the same system, each preserving a different aspect of it.

Modeling systems is a subtle task. Issues such as handling concurrency or using the right level of abstraction are easily prone to errors. If the modeling is done incorrectly, the fact that the model was verified or tested to satisfy a property may not carry over to the actual system. We may use some additional techniques to increase the probability that the translation between a system and a model preserves the verified properties. However, it is important to note that it is impossible to obtain an absolute guarantee for the correctness of the translation.

We carefully distinguish two uses of the word *model* in formal methods literature in general, and this book in particular. A *mathematical model* is a concept, a *class* of objects, satisfying some set of constraints and observations. In this sense, we talk about the *automata model* or the *interleaving model*. On the other hand, a particular *model of a system* is a single mathematical object, representing an abstraction of the physical system. In this sense, we can talk, for example, about a *model of the X11 windowing system*. Unfortunately, the two uses of the word model are strongly rooted in the jargon of formal methods and we will need to use them both.

4.1 Sequential, Concurrent and Reactive Systems

A model of a system should reflect the properties of that system that are of interest. In order to effectively model software systems, we need to observe their typical features that may be of relevance for our analysis. We start by describing different types of software systems that may be subjected to modeling and subsequently to formal analysis.

A sequential system can usually be described using its input-output relation, i.e., the condition that connects the possible initial states to the possible result of the computation. This relation can be denoted, for example, using first order logic. Thus, verifying the correctness of a sequential program or algorithm usually means proving an assertion of the following form: if the program starts at a state that satisfies a certain condition, then it eventually terminates, and the program variables at the final state satisfy some given relation with the corresponding values at the beginning of the execution. (We will formalize this kind of specification and show relevant proof techniques in Chapter 7.)

Many concurrent systems use parallelism in order to make calculations more efficient. Parallelism can be used to distribute the burden of the computation between different computers, possibly achieving a faster overall computation time. Concurrent systems are often much more involved than just input-output transducers. They include sequential components called *processes* that interact with each other. The input-output relation is often not enough for specifying the behavior of such software systems

One mode of concurrent computation is that of *multiprogramming*. In early days of computing, concurrency was simulated on a single processor using a scheduler. The goal was to allow better utilization of the expensive (in those days) resource of computer time. This would allow the machine to perform more calculations while another task or process waited for the typical slower operations of input or output to complete. This also allowed multiple people to work on the same machine simultaneously, each having the impression of having his own machine. A multiprogramming system has a scheduler that controls how to slice the execution time between the processes, preempting one process by swapping it with another.

Nowadays, although multiprogramming is still very common, there are many applications where there are distributed components that collaborate to perform a joint task composed of multiple processes. Such *multiprocessing* allows both speeding up the computation, and distributing the system in order to serve people in different places at the same time in a consistent way. In such systems too, the input-output relation may be of secondary importance. In fact, some software systems, such as operating systems or airline reservation systems, are designed to terminate only during exceptional conditions such as power shortage. In multiprocessing systems, the interaction between the different processes is influenced by the relative speeds between the different processors used to run the processes. There are many combinations where a system with n processors is used to run some $m > n$ processes, requiring both multiprogramming and multiprocessing.

Systems in which the *interaction* between the different components or between the system and its environment is important are often called *reactive systems* [90]. Reactive systems can be either sequential or concurrent. Specifying and verifying concurrent or reactive systems may include, for example, the response to requests, or the availability of services.

Consider for example, a specification for an airline reservation system. It may assert that if a flight is not completely booked, and a customer wants a ticket, then he will eventually obtain it. However, if there is only one remaining seat and two customers want the ticket, the system should prevent the case where both customers get the same seat. Alternatively, the system should just prevent overbooking beyond a certain threshold. Commonly, the customers are located in different parts of the world when the reservation is made. Such an airline reservation system may thus contain many software components that are partly autonomous, but coordinate with each other over some communication medium to maintain some overall consistency. Such systems are said to be *distributed*.

Concurrent systems are usually more difficult to model and analyze than simple sequential systems. They contain different components that can interact with each other. At any given moment there can be different activities happening, and alternative ways of continuing the computation. Because of the different speed and load of the computing components, the actions of different concurrent components may 'compete' with each other. Such a competition may be resolved differently in separate executions. This means that, at some points in the execution, there are more than a single way to proceed. This can happen, for example, when each one of two processes can change the value of a shared variable, or when a communication from two or more different processes is expected. This phenomenon is called *nondeterminism*. It complicates the modeling of concurrent systems, and consequently their specification and verification.

It is important to describe systems using an appropriate abstraction, keeping the essential details and omitting unimportant aspects. Many mathematical formalisms that are used for modeling software ignore the actual timing information, i.e., the amount of time it takes to transfer from one state to another. Accordingly, they maintain only the order between states. The reason for this is that the actual time may be of less importance (as long as it is reasonable, which is an assumption that may be tested independently). Furthermore, timing is difficult to analyze and subject to change when parts of the system are being replaced. Consequently, verification that abstracts away the timing constants is easier to obtain, and more robust for hardware change. Nevertheless, sometimes systems do depend on specific timing constraints. Recently, a variety of formal methods were designed to deal with the actual timing information, and are aimed at being used in time critical systems (see for example, [6]).

The following are some of the topics one may consider when modeling a software system:

Representing concurrency How do we model systems where transitions can be executed by different, concurrent processes?

- Allow one transition at a time (this is called the *interleaving model*)?
- Allow multiple transitions to change the state (this is allowed by *maximal concurrency* models used mainly in hardware)?
- Use a partial order between the events, reflecting the causal order on their occurrence?

Granularity What is the appropriate level of description of the transitions? Is it a single assignment or a decision predicate in the code of the verified program, a single machine code instruction executed in any of the participating processes, or a physical change such as the change of the voltage level in a processor that executes the code?

The execution model Should the model include a set of all possible complete executions? Or, should we observe all the different ways to continue from every point in the execution, due to the nondeterministic choices or the possible interactions with the environment?

Global or local states In concurrent and distributed systems, should we use global states that represent an instantaneous description of the entire system, or should we use local states, each representing only the assignment of values to variables of a single concurrent processor?

4.2 States

The notion of a *state* is central to the description of a system. It captures some information about the program at a certain moment in the execution. A state can be simply an abstract entity describing the system at a given point, e.g., using the proposition *waiting_for_input_from_user*, which can be either TRUE or FALSE at any point during the execution. Frequently, a state is represented as an assignment (in the sense of first order logic, see Section 3.2) to each one of the program variables. Sometimes, one needs to represent additional variables that may not be mentioned directly by the program, such as the program counters that hold the current position of the control of the program, or the message queues that represent messages that are in transition between the processes.

An example of a specification formalism that can express properties of the program states is first order logic, studied in Chapter 3. A first order formula that uses program variables as free variables can represent the set of program states where this formula is satisfied. Each state corresponds to an assignment to the program variables. An appropriate first order signature and structure, which allows asserting properties over the domain of the program, should be used.

A propositional formula can also be used to describe states. This requires that propositions be defined according to some state propositions. For example, we may not be interested in the individual values of the variables x and

y, but we may be interested in distinguishing the states where the value of x is bigger than the value of y. We then may define a proposition p that is TRUE in states where $x > y$ and FALSE otherwise.

Two important sets of program states are the *initial states* and the *final states*. As mentioned above, the correctness criterion for sequential programs usually refers only to these sets of states. Other intermediate states correspond to points in the execution where the program is in the process of its evaluation. Correctness proofs that establish the relation between the program variables at the beginning and the end of the execution, or proofs about the program termination, use these intermediate states in assertions made about the progress of the program.

Expressing properties about concurrent, distributed or reactive systems usually requires the ability to describe the dynamic change between the program states. Formalisms that can be used to express such dynamic properties will be studied in Chapter 5.

4.3 State Spaces

It is often convenient to model systems, both sequential and concurrent, as *transition systems*. This allows one to describe the behavior of systems as if one atomic transition is executed at each time. A similar model is often used to describe hardware systems.

In a transition system, which will be formalized in Section 4.4, the system can be in one of a finite or infinite number of *states*. From each state, the system can execute one of a number of atomic *transitions*. These are the transitions that are *enabled* in that state. The other transitions are *disabled*. From each state, an enabled transition is selected, and is used to transform the system into a new state. This process continues as long as there is at least one enabled transition. This is called the *interleaving model* of computation.

The *state space* of a system is a graph $\langle S, \Delta, I \rangle$, where S is the set of states, $\Delta \subseteq S \times S$ is the transition relation between the states, and $I \subseteq S$ are the initial states. We also call such a graph an *automaton*. The name emphasizes the operational view of the model. It can be viewed as a simple machine that 'recognizes' the executions of the program. A *run* of the automaton is a sequence $s_0 s_1 s_2 \ldots$ that starts with a state $s_0 \in I$ and proceeds according to the relation Δ, i.e., for $i \geq 0$, $(s_i, s_{i+1}) \in \Delta$. Such a run must be maximal, i.e., either it is infinite, or it reaches a state with no successor. Notice that we do not actually use such an automaton to recognize executions, as these may be infinite. This is merely a mathematical model that can be used to allow us to analyze the system. We will add more structure to the automata model and discuss it at length in Chapter 5.

Additional components can be added, according to the need and relevance (as will be done in later chapters). For example, one may also label each edge in Δ by the identification of the transition that was executed. In finite state systems, one may want to label each state with a set of propositional variables, each one representing some state property. For example, such variables may represent that some process is within some section of the program, that some process has terminated, or that a particular variable has a value above a certain threshold.

The interleaving model, which will be formalized later, views an execution of a system as a sequence of states called an *interleaved sequence*, where one transition is executed at a time. The name reflects the fact that if the modeled system consists of multiple processes, the transitions of the various processes are interleaved to form a single thread of execution. Thus, each interleaved sequence forms a path in the state space graph. Because of its simplicity, the interleaving model is usually preferred over other models of executions such as the partial order model, which will be presented in Section 4.13. Many mathematical tools, such as automata and linear temporal logic, exist to support the interleaving model, simplifying the development of appropriate formal methods.

The following question is often raised when trying to explain why we can use the interleaving model for describing computations, in particular concurrent ones:

In reality, transitions of different processes may overlap in time. How is this reflected in the interleaving model?

To answer this question, consider two transitions α and β whose executions overlap. Suppose that executing α and β starts from some given state. Often, the effect of executing transitions concurrently is also *commutative*, meaning that whatever order we may choose to interleave them, α before β or β before α, the outcome of executing both of them will result in the same state. In this case, the interleaving model allows two executions, one in which α precedes β, and one in which β precedes α. Indeed, due to the relative speed of the machines that execute α and β, or due to the scheduling of these transitions under one multiprogrammed machine, they can be executed in either order. They can also be executed simultaneously, but this possibility is not explicitly described in the interleaving model.

In Figure 4.1, the transition α increments x by 1 and the transition β increments y by 1. Both are executed concurrently, from a state where $x = 1$ and $y = 1$. When interleaved in either order, the result is a state where $x = 2$ and $y = 2$.

There are instances where two transitions α and β belong to different processes, but those are not commutative. This can happen, for example, when both transitions change some mutual variable that belongs to both processes. Consider the case in Figure 4.2, where α increments x by 1 and β doubles x, and both can be executed from a state where $x = 1$. In the cases where α is executed before β, we obtain a state where $x = 4$. In the other case, where β is executed before α, we obtain $x = 3$.

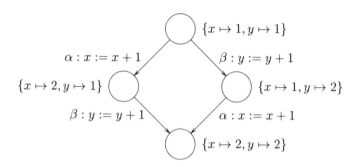

Fig. 4.1. Executing commutative transitions

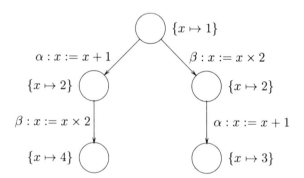

Fig. 4.2. Executing noncommutative transitions

In this case, the execution of α and β can not overlap, but would indeed be forced (by hardware arbitration) to be performed in one order or the other. In the interleaving model, it is not allowed that transitions that can execute concurrently interact with each other in a way that cannot be described by executing them one after the other. This is usually not a problem, as this interaction is not required for modeling software. There are some systems, including synchronous hardware, that do allow other outcomes than the ones obtained by executing the transitions in either order. In such cases, one has the choice of using a different model that allows such interaction. For example, in hardware, one often uses the maximal concurrency model that allows multiple transitions to execute at the same time. It is sometimes possible to model each collection of such intertransition interactions as one big transition, taking into account all the possible interactions.

4.4 Transition Systems

We will define here *transition systems*. A transition represents an atomic (i.e., elementary) action of a (sequential or concurrent) system. A transition system can be used to *generate* a state space describing the system. A state space contains information about the way the different states of the system are related to each other, while a transition system contains an information about the generators of the different states (the transitions). Thus, a transition system is somewhat more implicit than the corresponding state space.

Formally, a transition system $\langle S, T, \Theta \rangle$ is defined as follows:

- A first order *structure* S, which includes a first order signature $\mathcal{G}$, a domain (or multiple domains, as is usually the case for structures used for defining transition systems), relations and functions, and an interpretation function. The conditions and expressions used by a transition system, as defined below, are expressed over the signature $\mathcal{G}$, and are interpreted by the structure S. The signature $\mathcal{G}$ includes in particular a finite set of variables V. The set of variables includes those represented explicitly by the code of the program, and also the *program counters* (also called *location counters*). The latter variables, one for each concurrent process, are often implicit in the code of the program, and represent some internal values that point to the location of the next instruction, or set of instructions, which can be selected for execution by that process. In the process of modeling systems, one may need to 'invent' new names for each such program counter, and a set of values (program labels, the target of *goto* statements, if they do exist already in the original code) that each such program counter can undertake. This allows distinguishing between states where the values of the program variables are the same, but the control of at least one process is in different locations.

- A finite set T of *transitions*. Each transition $t \in T$ is of the form

$$p \longrightarrow (v_1, v_2, \ldots, v_n) := (e_1, e_2, \ldots, e_n)$$

The condition p is an unquantified first order formula whose variables are included in V. Furthermore, $v_1, \ldots, v_n \in V$, and $e_1, \ldots, e_n$ are first order expressions (terms) over the structure $\mathcal{G}$. Notice that there is only one set of transitions per program, thus all the transitions from all different processes are grouped together.

- An *initial condition* Θ, which is an unquantified first order formula over variables from V.

We may include in the structure $\mathcal{S}$ function and relations that do not occur in the modeled program and add appropriate symbols to the signature $\mathcal{G}$. The reason for this is that such functions and relations may be needed for the program specification. This is because the iterative nature of programs allows calculating mathematical structures that are not represented directly in the code. For example, a program may calculate the multiplication of two *integers* by a repeated iteration of addition.

Intuitively, a transition t of the form $p \longrightarrow (v_1, \ldots, v_n) := (e_1, \ldots, e_n)$ can execute from any state that satisfies the condition p. Thus, the condition p is called the *enabledness condition* of the transition t, and is also denoted by en_t. We say that t is *enabled* at a state s, if its condition p is satisfied by s, i.e., when $s \models^S p$. The effect of executing t from some state s is that the terms $e_1, e_2, \ldots, e_n$ are calculated based on the values of the variables according to the state s. Then these values are assigned to the variables $v_1, \ldots, v_n$, respectively, obtaining a new state s'. We sometimes denote the change of state incurred by executing a transition t to a state s, obtaining a new state s', by $s' = t(s)$. The order of the computation is important. First, *all* the terms are calculated according to the current state, and then all the values are assigned. Thus, the effect of $(x, y) := (y, x)$ is to replace x by y. If we did not calculate the expressions first and then make all the assignments of the calculated values, the result of the assignment would have been different. In particular, assigning y to x and then x to y, would result in assigning the old value of y, to both x and y.

At first it may seem that allowing multiple assignments to occur in atomic transitions goes contrary to the idea of atomicity, since intuitively, it is difficult to enforce several changes being made without some interference. However, observe that the program variables include the program counters; a typical assignment to a variable also involves setting the program counter to a new value, pointing to the next executable instruction(s) of the executed process.

An *execution* of a system is a sequence of states. It starts with one of the initial states, i.e., some state satisfying the initial condition Θ, and progresses from one state to another by selecting and executing transitions of the system. An execution can reach a state where the program *terminates* or *deadlocks*.

The distinction between termination and deadlock is made only according to whether the inability to make any progress in the execution from this state is according to plan (e.g., after the program's task has been completed and there are no further tasks to achieve), or unplanned (e.g., terminating before some of the tasks were achieved).

An execution may fail to terminate. This can be intentional, or due to failure to achieve the program's task in finite time. Of course, actual systems never execute indefinitely, as they may be interrupted, or eventually replaced by newer ones. Nevertheless, it is often a useful abstraction to view systems with no bound on their execution as ones that continue executing forever. We do not allow an execution to end at a state where at least one transition is enabled. Thus, executions correspond to *maximal* paths in the state space.

In defining executions, we need to note the important distinction between the actual execution of the real code, and a mathematical representation of it. It is important to observe that by 'executions', we refer in this book to a *mathematical construction* that is related to a *model* of the program, rather than to running the actual code.

Formally, an *execution* of a program is an infinite sequence of states $s_0, s_1, s_2, \ldots$ such that $s_0 \models^S \Theta$, i.e., the first state of the execution satisfies the initial condition. For each $i \geq 0$, one of the following two cases holds:

1. There exists some transition $p \longrightarrow (v_1, \ldots, v_n) := (e_1, \ldots, e_n)$ that is enabled at s_i, i.e., $s_i \models^S p$. Furthermore, let $l_1, \ldots, l_n$ be the values of the terms $e_1, \ldots, e_n$ at the state s_i. Then, $s_{i+1} = s_i[l_1/v_1, \ldots, l_n/v_n]$.
2. There is no enabled transition, i.e., a transition whose condition p is satisfied at s_i. Then for each $j > i$, we have that $s_j = s_i$.

In this way, when there is no transition that is enabled, the sequence is extended to an infinite one by repeating the last state indefinitely. This is of course just a technical convention, to avoid having both finite and infinite sequences. We could also force all the sequences to be infinite if we added to the set of transitions T a new transition t that is enabled exactly when all other transitions are disabled, and does not change the state. Thus, if the conditions of the transitions $t_1, t_2, \ldots, t_n$ in T are $p_1, p_2, \ldots, p_n$, respectively, then t can be defined as $\neg(p_1 \vee p_2 \vee \ldots \vee p_n) \longrightarrow (v_1 := v_1)$ for some arbitrary variable $v_1 \in V$.

States that appear in some execution of the program are called *reachable*. Not every state in the set of states S is necessarily reachable. For example, consider the case where the program is defined over variables that can hold (bounded) *natural* numbers, and the states in S correspond to all the possible assignments of *natural* numbers to the program variables. It can happen, for example, that the value of the variable $y1$ is always greater than the value of the variable $y2$. It is usually simpler to ignore the reachability issue when defining the state space, and define the set of states S according to the domains of the program variables, regardless of the special connection between them imposed by the code. This allows states that do not occur on any possible execution.

Variants of the above definition of executions may be used. For example, a more informative version defines an execution as an alternating sequence of states and transitions (or their labels). We will later see several examples where the additional information in such a model is useful. Another variant ignores the states altogether, concentrating on the transitions, and defines an execution as a sequence of transitions. We will usually take the point of view that the aspect of an execution we are interested in is the progress between states. In process algebra, described in Chapter 8, the focus is on the executed transitions.

The above definition of an execution can be described using a *scheduler* that can generate interleaved sequences for a program:

A Scheduler
Start from some initial state ι such that $\iota \models^S \Theta$. Set $s := \iota$
loop: if there is no enabled transition from s, goto *extend*.
Pick up a transition t that is currently enabled at s.
Apply the transition t to the current state s,
   obtaining a new current state $s := t(s)$.
goto *loop*.
extend: Repeat state s forever.

This scheduler is nondeterministic, as it has to choose first an initial state out of possibly multiple initial states. Furthermore, at each state it needs to select a transition enabled at that state. Again, there may be more than a single choice. The scheduler reaches its last instruction, which repeats the last state indefinitely, only if there are no more enabled transitions.

There is a subtle problem with the above schedule, as the scheduling can be unfair to one or more of the concurrent processes, repeatedly ignoring its enabled transitions in favor of other processes. This will be solved by imposing some constraints called fairness conditions on the execution of the scheduler. This issue will be discussed in Section 4.12.

Concurrent systems are composed of multiple processes, which usually interact with each other, using some mechanisms such as shared variables, synchronous or asynchronous message passing. One can model each process separately, and then combine them using appropriate operators. For example, one can construct a *local* state space for each process, and then define the *global* product of them. Each state in this product corresponds to a collection of local states, one per each process (and in case of a communication system, also the values of the message buffers, containing the messages that are in transit). Each transition of the product corresponds to a transition of a single process, or to a transition that is executed synchronously by several processes (for example, a handshake communication).

Notice that we did not limit a transition by forcing it to belong to a single concurrent process. Indeed, transitions that change some local or global variables often do belong to a particular process. However, some transitions require that multiple processes will be synchronized together. For example, a synchronous communication (as in Ada rendezvous) needs two processes to synchronize.

The interleaving model closely follows the multiprogramming model, where no two transitions ever execute simultaneously. In this model, there is a single time line, corresponding to the scheduling done within the process that executes all the processes. In distributed systems, there is actual simultaneity. Furthermore, it is not always the case that there are particular moments in time where global states actually exist across the entire system. We will later present the partial order execution model. This is a more realistic and intuitive model of execution for distributed systems. Thus it is often termed 'real concurrency'. It allows transitions to occur either ordered, when one causally follow the other, or unordered, when they can appear concurrently. It also introduces local states for the different concurrent agents (processes). Atomic transitions are executed from local states, or from combinations of local states.

A transition system is an *implicit* representation of a program, just like its code. In order to analyze the program, one may want to generate its state space. In general, one does not always have to explicitly construct a representation of the entire state space of a program. In fact, generating the state space is possible only when dealing with finite state systems. Automatic program verification, applied to finite state systems, may involve constructing the state space of a program, and analyzing it using graph algorithms, as will be shown in Section 6.1. However, even there, since state spaces tend to be large, one seeks various ways to avoid having to construct the entire state space.

4.5 Granularity of Transitions

One of the most common modeling errors is related to choosing the appropriate granularity of atomic transitions. This choice is subtle. When the granularity of the transitions is too small, e.g., the transitions are being described at the level of the electronic gates, their description contains more information than we may want to handle. When we allow for more information representing every state, we may distinguish more states from each other than is necessary for the purpose of analyzing the system. This contributes to the problem known as state space explosion, which will be described later. On the other hand, when the selected granularity is too large, we may lose some of the interaction that can appear between the processes, or with the environment, and as a result will not cover all the possible behaviors.

To demonstrate the difficulty in selecting the appropriate level of granularity, consider two processes P_1 and P_2 that have to execute the following instructions from some state where $x = 2$ and $y = 3$:

$$P_1: x:=x + y; \qquad\qquad P_2 : y:=y + x;$$

Now, consider a multiprocessing implementation, where those two processes share time on a single sequential computer. The variables x and y are held in registers $r1$ and $r2$, respectively, and the machine used can increment any pair of registers and put the result in the first one. In the assembly language, we may have the following code:

$$P_1: \text{add } r1, r2; \qquad\qquad P_2: \text{add } r2, r1 \ ;$$

If each transition describes one of the assembly code instructions, there are two possible executions, according to the order of execution of the two additions. One of them would add first the value 3 of $r2$ to $r1$, resulting in 5, and then add this new value to $r2$, resulting in $x = r1 = 5$ and $y = r2 = 8$. The other execution would add first the value 2 of $r1$ to $r2$, resulting in 5, and then add this new value to $r1$, resulting in $x = r1 = 7$ and $y = r2 = 5$. In this case, hardware is responsible for not allowing these two transitions to be executed simultaneously.

Suppose now that the variables A and B are stored in main memory instead of in registers, e.g., in locations $m100$ and $m111$, respectively. The assembly code would be in this case:

P_1 :   load r1, m100 P_2 :   load r2 , m111
          add r1, m111   add r2, m100
          store r1, m100   store r2, m111

If each transition corresponds to a single assembly language instruction, there are 20 ways to interleave them. In some of the interleavings, we have the same final result as in the previous case. However, there is an additional possibility. The following sequence alternates between states and transitions. We assume that the initial value of the registers $r1$ and $r2$ is 0.

$$\{r1 \mapsto 0,\ r2 \mapsto 0,\ m100 \mapsto 2,\ m111 \mapsto 3\}$$
$$\text{load } r1, m100$$
$$\{r1 \mapsto 2,\ r2 \mapsto 0,\ m100 \mapsto 2,\ m111 \mapsto 3\}$$
$$\text{load } r2, m111$$
$$\{r1 \mapsto 2,\ r2 \mapsto 3,\ m100 \mapsto 2,\ m111 \mapsto 3\}$$
$$\text{add } r1, m111$$
$$\{r1 \mapsto 5,\ r2 \mapsto 3,\ m100 \mapsto 2,\ m111 \mapsto 3\}$$
$$\text{add } r2, m100$$
$$\{r1 \mapsto 5,\ r2 \mapsto 5,\ m100 \mapsto 2,\ m111 \mapsto 3\}$$
$$\text{store } r1, m100$$
$$\{r1 \mapsto 5,\ r2 \mapsto 5,\ m100 \mapsto 5,\ m111 \mapsto 3\}$$
$$\text{store } r2, m111$$
$$\{r1 \mapsto 5,\ r2 \mapsto 5,\ m100 \mapsto 5,\ m111 \mapsto 5\}$$

Thus, at the end, $x = m100 = 5$ and $y = m111 = 5$. That is, first, the old values of the two variables are read internally, then these values are being added, and the result is stored back. If we choose to model the system with the same granularity as in the first case, consistent with the high level code of the addition, we will miss a possible interaction between the actual assembly code instructions. Verifying the code after modeling it using the bigger granularity may result in errors appearing within the additional behaviors that are not represented in this level of granularity, and thus are not found. Consequently, the verification may report that no errors were found, even when errors do occur.

Consider a system in which the implementation follows the bigger granularity case, but the model corresponds to the finer granularity description above. Then, the model includes behaviors that were not allowed by the actual code. The additional behavior may be erroneous (in this example, the specification does not allow that both values of x and y are 5 after the execution), and therefore reported as counterexamples by formal methods tools. These false alarms are called *false negatives*.

4.6 Examples of Modeling Programs

Modeling systems is an important part of using formal methods. In most cases, it is done manually. There is no 'generic recipe' for modeling systems, as different programs, especially concurrent ones, use various kinds of domains and programming constructs. We will demonstrate here modeling of several types of programs.

Integer Division

The first example is sequential a program for the *integer* division of the value in $x1$ by the value in $x2$. The result will reside in the end of the execution in the variable $y1$, while the remainder will be in $y2$. We will give a fully labeled version of this program.

```
m1: y1:=0;
m2: y2:=x1;
m3: while y2 >= x2 do
m4:    y1:=y1+1;
m5:    y2:=y2 - x2
m6: end
```

We first need to select the appropriate signature. We have the variables $\{y1, y2, x1, x2, pc\}$, the function symbols '$+$' and '$-$', and the relation symbol '$\geq$'. There are two domains: the *naturals*, and a finite domain of labels, $\{m1, m2, m3, m4, m5, m6\}$. In a similar way, we could have used the domain of *integers* instead of *integers*. We could have encoded the labels as small *naturals*, 1...6. The variables $y1$, $y2$, $x1$ and $x2$ can be assigned a *natural* value, while *pc* can be assigned a label. The function and relation symbols are interpreted over the domain of *naturals* in the standard way. One way of modeling the set of states S of this program is to allow any assignment of *natural* numbers to the variables $x1$, $x2$, $y1$ and $y2$. In addition, we also allow an assignment of one of the values from $\{m1, m2, m3, m4, m5, m6\}$ to the variable *pc*, representing the program counter. The initial states are those that satisfy the initial states $\Theta : x2 > 0 \land pc \equiv m1$.

Observe that not all of the states in S are reachable. A careful look into the program reveals some connections between the variables. For example, if $pc \equiv m4$, then $y1 \times x2 + y2 \equiv x1$. Such a connection will be very useful later in verifying the program. However, for modeling, one can use a state space that is properly bigger than the set of actual reachable states. The transition system includes the notation $if(b, e_1, e_2)$, where b is a first order formula and e_1 and e_2 are terms. It returns e_1 if b is TRUE and e_2 if it is FALSE.

$$pc \equiv m1 \longrightarrow (pc, y1) := (m2, 0)$$
$$pc \equiv m2 \longrightarrow (pc, y2) := (m3, x1)$$
$$pc \equiv m3 \longrightarrow pc := if(y2 \geq x2, m4, m6)$$
$$pc \equiv m4 \longrightarrow (pc, y1) := (m5, y1 + 1)$$
$$pc \equiv m5 \longrightarrow (pc, y2) := (m3, y2 - x2)$$

There are other choices of modeling the transitions of the program. For example, one can replace the third transition by a pair of transitions, each sending the program control to a different label, as follows:

$$pc = m3 \land y2 \geq x2 \longrightarrow pc := m4$$
$$pc = m3 \land y2 < x2 \longrightarrow pc := m6$$

According to the actual machine on which this code may run, it may also be possible to give a bound on the values that can be stored. In fact, the abstraction used in modeling this program, where the program variables contain arbitrary *naturals*, has the potential to fail to represent some actual executions of a program with a fixed word size: if a variable happens to fall out of the range of values that can be stored in the word size allocated to each variable, we may experience a behavior that differs from the ones prescribed with the above set of transitions. In this case, the program may abort with an error message, or some unexpected results may occur. A closer look at the code of the program reveals that this potential problem may never occur *for this particular code*: once the initial values fit into the variables $x1$ and $x2$, the values of the other variables, $y1$ and $y2$ will also fit (assuming that they have the same word size).

This suggests several possible approaches:

1. Ignore the problem of word size. Assume that the user will never use too large numbers. If he does, it is his own responsibility, as the verification that uses this model will not cover this case.

2. Model the possibility of value overflow. This may involve changing the set of transitions to allow the faulty behavior of the actual computer on this code. For example, allow a transition that is executed when an overflow occurs, and simulates the exceptional behavior of the computer in that case. Then, given this less abstract model, verify that an overflow cannot occur.

Calculating Combinations

The next program (which is a slight modification of a program in [92]) computes the number of possible combinations when choosing k out of n distinct elements without repetitions. It uses the formula

$$\binom{n}{k} = \frac{n \times (n-1) \times \cdots \times (n-k+1)}{1 \times 2 \times \cdots \times k}$$

The program consists of two parallel processes. The left process repeatedly multiplies the numerator, while the values of $y1$ range between n and $n-k+1$. The right process repeatedly divides the denominator, while the values of $y2$ range between 1 and k. At the end of the execution, the result resides in $y3$.

l_1:*if* $y1 = (n - k)$ *then halt*	r_1:*if* $y2 = k$ *then halt*
l_2:$y3 := y3 \times y1$	r_2:$y2 := y2 + 1$
l_3:$y1 := y1 - 1$	r_3:*await* $y2 <= n - y1$
l_4:*goto* l_1	r_4:$y3 := y3/y2$
	r_5:*goto* r_1

The initial condition is

$$\Theta : y1 \equiv n \wedge y2 \equiv 0 \wedge y3 \equiv 1 \wedge pc_l \equiv l_1 \wedge pc_r \equiv r_1 \wedge n > 0 \wedge k > 0$$

The *await* statement, labeled r_3 in the right process, allows the division in the statement labeled r_4 to be executed only when the number of values multiplied so far is greater than the number of values divided. This guarantees that the division will always produce an *integer* result with no reminder.

The first order structure that we use includes the function symbols '$\times$', '$+$', '$-$', '$/$' and the relation symbol '$\leq$' (which corresponds to $>=$ in the text of the program). The relation symbol for equivalence '$\equiv$' is included already in first order logic. We interpret these function and relation symbols in a standard way over the *naturals*.

The variables appearing in the program will be interpreted over the *naturals*, except for the variables pc_l and pc_r, which represent the program counters. The variable pc_l will range over the labels $\{l_1, \ldots, l_4, halt_l\}$, and the variable pc_r will range over $\{r_1, \ldots, r_5, halt_r\}$. Executing the command *halt* terminates the execution of a process. The special labels $halt_l$ and $halt_r$ represent the value of the program counters when the left or right process, respectively, terminates. The program can be translated to the following set of transitions:

$$t_1 : pc_l \equiv l_1 \longrightarrow pc_l := if(y1 \equiv (n-k), halt_l, l_2)$$
$$t_2 : pc_l \equiv l_2 \longrightarrow (pc_l, y3) := (l_3, y3 \times y1)$$
$$t_3 : pc_l \equiv l_3 \longrightarrow (pc_l, y1) := (l_4, y1 - 1)$$
$$t_4 : pc_l \equiv l_4 \longrightarrow pc_l := l_1$$
$$t_5 : pc_r \equiv r_1 \longrightarrow pc_r := if(y2 \equiv k, halt_r, r_2)$$
$$t_6 : pc_r \equiv r_2 \longrightarrow (pc_r, y2) := (r_3, y2 + 1)$$
$$t_7 : pc_r \equiv r_3 \wedge y2 \leq n - y1 \longrightarrow pc_r := r_4$$
$$t_8 : pc_r \equiv r_4 \longrightarrow (pc_r, y3) := (r_5, y3/y2)$$
$$t_9 : pc_r \equiv r_5 \longrightarrow pc_r := r_1$$

Of course, this does not have to be the only way to model this concurrent program. In modeling it as a set of transitions, we assumed a particular granularity. It is certainly possible that the code is translated into a different set of transitions, e.g., using finer granularity. In particular, consider the transitions t_2 and t_8. They both operate on the variable $y3$. In a way similar to the example in Section 4.5, it is possible that the program be translated into some machine code that first loads the value of $y3$ into some internal register, then makes the calculation (multiplication or division, respectively) on that register, and then puts the new value of that register into $y3$. Then, the actual program contains an error, while the verification assumes a model that behaves in a different way. Consequently, the error may remain undetected.

The Sieve of Eratosthenes

The *Sieve of Eratosthenes* is an algorithm for calculating prime numbers. In its parallel version, there is a leftmost process that is responsible for generating *integer* numbers, starting from 2, and up to some limit P. There are N middle processes, each responsible for keeping one prime number. The ith process is responsible for keeping the ith prime number. Each middle process receives numbers from its left. The first number it receives is a prime number, and it is kept by the receiving process. Subsequent numbers are checked against that first number: if dividing a new number arriving from left by the first number gives a remainder of 0, this cannot be a prime number, and hence it is discarded; otherwise the new value is sent to the process on the right. Thus, numbers that are not prime are being sifted-out. The rightmost process simply accepts values from the left. The first number it receives is kept (this is a prime number), while the other numbers are just being ignored. This allows overflow of numbers, when more prime numbers are generated by the leftmost process than there are processes. The algorithm is presented below in a parametric form, with parameters $P > 1$ and $N > 0$.

The command *ch!exp* means that the expression *exp* is calculated and is being sent via the queue *ch*. This is an asynchronous send, whose effect is to add the value of *exp* to the end of the queue, as the new last element (if the queue is not full). The notation *ch?var* can be executed when the queue *ch* is nonempty. Its effect is to remove the first (i.e., oldest) element of the queue *ch*, and to assign it to the variable *var*.

initially counter=2;
leftproc:: loop
    ch[1]!counter;
    counter:=counter+1
until counter>P
$||_{i=1,..,N}$
middleproc[i]:: ch[i]?myval;
while true do
    ch[i]?nextval
    if nextval mode myval≠0
        then ch[i+1]!nextval
end
||
rightproc:: ch[N+1]?biggest;
while true do
    ch[N+1]?next
end

We will not repeat here (and in further examples) the choice of some standard arithmetic functions and relations and their notations for modeling the program. However, in this program, we also need to model queues. We represent them as *lists* of *naturals*. In order to model this program as a transition system, we define functions that will help in describing operations on message queues.

    head Returns the head of a given list, i.e., its first element. (This is arbitrarily defined if the message queue is empty.)
    tail Returns the tail of a given list, i.e., its contents without the first element. (This is arbitrarily defined if the message queue is empty.)
    append This function takes a list and an element, and appends the element to the list to become its last element.

The list elements are enclosed between angle brackets, e.g., $\langle 5, 4, 7 \rangle$. The empty list is denoted as $\langle \rangle$.

    Like sets, lists require, in general, second order logic representation. However, our use of lists is restricted here. For example, we cannot express the fact that some values belong to a list (but we can express that some value is at the head of the list, and more generally, at the nth location, for every fixed n).

    There are a few issues of modeling that need to be addressed here. This example includes a parametrized number of concurrent processes. There are N middle processes, and $N + 1$ message queues used. While the communication queues are parametrized explicitly, i.e., $ch[i]$, each process has its own local variables, *myval* and *nextval*. Hence there are in effect N versions of these variables, referred to, in the transition system, by $myval_i$ and $nextval_i$, respectively. In order to convert the code into a transition system, we also need to invent new names of variables for program counters and new names of constants for program locations. These names are also parametrized, when related to the collection of middle processes. Notice that the location *haltleft* corresponds to the termination point of the left process.

$$pc_l \equiv l1 \quad \longrightarrow \quad (pc_l, ch1) := (l2, append(ch[1], counter))$$
$$pc_l \equiv l2 \quad \longrightarrow \quad (pc_l, counter) := (l3, counter + 1)$$
$$pc_l \equiv l3 \quad \longrightarrow \quad pc_l := if(counter > P, haltleft, l1)$$
$$pc_{m_i} \equiv m1_i \quad \longrightarrow \quad (pc_{m_i}, myval_i, ch[i]) := (m2_i, head(ch[i]), tail(ch[i]))$$
$$pc_{m_i} \equiv m2_i \quad \longrightarrow \quad (pc_{m_i}, nextval_i, ch[i]) := (m3_i, head(ch[i]), tail(ch[i]))$$
$$pc_{m_i} \equiv m3_i \quad \longrightarrow \quad pc_{m_i} := if(nextval \bmod myval \neq 0, m4_i, m2_i)$$
$$pc_{m_i} \equiv m4_i \quad \longrightarrow \quad (pc_{m_i}, ch_{i+1}) := (m2_i, append(ch_{i+1}, nextval_i))$$
$$pc_r \equiv r1 \quad \longrightarrow \quad (pc_r, ch[N+1], biggest) :=$$
$$(r2, tail(ch[N+1]), head(ch[N+1]))$$
$$pc_r \equiv r2 \quad \longrightarrow \quad (ch[N+1], next) := (tail(ch[N+1]), head(ch[N+1]))$$

The initial condition Θ is:

$$ch[1] \equiv \langle \rangle \wedge ch[2] \equiv \langle \rangle \wedge counter \equiv 2 \wedge pc_l \equiv l1 \wedge \bigwedge_{i \equiv 1, \ldots, N} pc_{m_i} \equiv m1_i \wedge pc_r \equiv r1$$

Consider an instance of the Sieve of Eratosthenes, with $N = 1$ and $P = 3$. The state space of this example grows up very quickly, when these parameters, especially the number of processes, grows. This problem, called the state space explosion, is the major challenge in automatic verification.

The assignments of part of the states for that example, $s1$–$s10$, are listed in a table in Figure 4.3. We denote variables that are not initialized by the special notation $\perp$. This is a common practice in modeling systems. The variables *biggest* and *next* have the value $\perp$ in each one of these states, and thus were not explicitly mentioned in the table. Since there is only one process of type $middle_i$, we omit the subscript i from the state variables pc_{m_1}, $myval_1$ and $nextval_1$ from the table.

state	pc_l	pc_m	pc_r	$ch[1]$	$ch[2]$	counter	myval	nextval
$s1$	$l1$	$m1$	$r1$	$\langle \rangle$	$\langle \rangle$	2	$\perp$	$\perp$
$s2$	$l2$	$m1$	$r1$	$\langle 2 \rangle$	$\langle \rangle$	2	$\perp$	$\perp$
$s3$	$l2$	$m2$	$r1$	$\langle \rangle$	$\langle \rangle$	2	2	$\perp$
$s4$	$l3$	$m1$	$r1$	$\langle 2 \rangle$	$\langle \rangle$	3	$\perp$	$\perp$
$s5$	$l3$	$m2$	$r1$	$\langle \rangle$	$\langle \rangle$	3	2	$\perp$
$s6$	$l1$	$m1$	$r1$	$\langle 2 \rangle$	$\langle \rangle$	3	$\perp$	$\perp$
$s7$	$l1$	$m2$	$r1$	$\langle \rangle$	$\langle \rangle$	3	2	$\perp$
$s8$	$l2$	$m2$	$r1$	$\langle 3 \rangle$	$\langle \rangle$	3	2	$\perp$
$s9$	$l2$	$m3$	$r1$	$\langle \rangle$	$\langle \rangle$	3	2	3
$s10$	$l3$	$m2$	$r1$	$\langle 3 \rangle$	$\langle \rangle$	4	2	$\perp$

Fig. 4.3. Some states of the Sieve of Eratosthenes for $N = 1$ and $P = 3$

Mutual Exclusion

Dijkstra is one of the first computer scientists who were concerned with correctness issues for multiprocess systems. In his seminal paper [37], he presented the problem of achieving *mutual exclusion* between processes in a didactic way, through a sequence of provisional attempts for a mutual exclusion protocol. In this problem, two (or more) processes are competing to enter a *critical section*, i.e., a segment of the code where they have access to some mutual resource. This access has to be exclusive. For example, the critical section may involve printing. Obviously, we do not want two processes to access the same printer simultaneously.

When not interested in entering its critical section, a process is performing some arbitrary local calculations, in its *noncritical section*. Then, when it wishes enter into its critical section, it participates in some mutual exclusion protocol. This concurrent protocol is responsible for keeping the processes outside their critical section until it is safe to allow exactly one of them to enter. After gaining access to the critical section, the process may need to participate again in (another part of) the critical section protocol, this time in order to allow another process to enter its critical section. There are several properties of the mutual exclusion problem that will be formally addressed in later chapters. Informally, one might want to achieve the following goals:

- *Exclusiveness.* No two processes can enter their critical section at the same time.
- *Liveness.* If a process wishes to enter its critical section, it will be allowed to do so within some finite time.

One of the provisional attempts to provide such a protocol is the following:

$$boolean\ c1,\ c2\ initially\ 1;$$

```
P1:: m1:while true do          P2:: n1:while true do
     m2:(* noncritical section 1*)    n2:(* noncritical section 2*)
     m3:c1:=0;                        n3:c2:=0;
     m4:wait until c2=1;              n4:wait until c1=1;
     m5:(* critical section 1 *)      n5:(* critical section 2 *)
     m6:c1:=1                         n6:c2:=1
end                            end
```

We assume that the critical and noncritical sections do not change any of the variables $c1$ and $c2$. We can represent this algorithm as a transition system as follows:

$$
\begin{aligned}
\tau_1 &: pc_1 \equiv m1 &\longrightarrow& \quad pc_1 := m2 \\
\tau_2 &: pc_1 \equiv m2 &\longrightarrow& \quad pc_1 := m3 \\
\tau_3 &: pc_1 \equiv m3 &\longrightarrow& \quad (pc_1, c1) := (m4, 0) \\
\tau_4 &: pc_1 \equiv m4 \wedge c2 \equiv 1 &\longrightarrow& \quad pc_1 := m5 \\
\tau_5 &: pc_1 \equiv m5 &\longrightarrow& \quad pc_1 := m6 \\
\tau_6 &: pc_1 \equiv m6 &\longrightarrow& \quad (pc_1, c1) := (m1, 1) \\
\tau_7 &: pc_2 \equiv n1 &\longrightarrow& \quad pc_2 := n2 \\
\tau_8 &: pc_2 \equiv n2 &\longrightarrow& \quad pc_2 := n3 \\
\tau_9 &: pc_2 \equiv n3 &\longrightarrow& \quad (pc_2, c2) := (n4, 0) \\
\tau_{10} &: pc_2 \equiv n4 \wedge c1 \equiv 1 &\longrightarrow& \quad pc_2 := n5 \\
\tau_{11} &: pc_2 \equiv n5 &\longrightarrow& \quad pc_2 := n6 \\
\tau_{12} &: pc_2 \equiv n6 &\longrightarrow& \quad (pc_2, c2) := (n1, 1)
\end{aligned}
$$

The initial condition is $\Theta : pc_1 \equiv m1 \wedge pc_2 \equiv n1 \wedge c1 \equiv 1 \wedge c2 \equiv 1$. Notice that the critical and noncritical sections are modeled by a simple transition each, according to τ_2, τ_5, τ_8 and τ_{11}. This is a subtle modeling issue, which requires careful consideration. As modeled, these critical and noncritical sections always terminate. We may want to allow the possibility that these sections would never terminate (theoretically, at least until the next power interruption). This calls for modeling these sections as loops with the possibility of a nondeterministic choice for exiting. For example, we may add the following transitions:

$$
\begin{aligned}
\tau_2' &= pc_1 \equiv m2 &\longrightarrow& \quad pc_1 := m2 \\
\tau_8' &= pc_2 \equiv n2 &\longrightarrow& \quad pc_2 := n2
\end{aligned}
$$

These transitions loop back to the same program counter location. In fact, a usual requirement is that the algorithm works under the assumption that noncritical sections, represented by τ_2 and τ_8 can loop forever, while the critical sections, represented by τ_5 and τ_{11} have to terminate eventually.

This raises another problem: if a noncritical section can be executed forever, can it postpone forever the execution of any transition of the other process? The mathematical possibility for such a scheduling should be countered by removing from further consideration and formal analysis such 'unfair' interleaving sequences. This is the motivation for the definition of *fairness* in Section 4.12.

Exercise 4.6.1. Construct the finite state space for the mutual exclusion algorithm.

Exercise 4.6.2. The solution for the mutual exclusion problem, given by the Dutch mathematician Dekker, appears in Figure 4.4. Translate Dekker's algorithm into a transition system.

boolean c1 initially 1;
boolean c2 initially 1;
integer (1..2) turn initially 1;

P1::while true do	*P2::while true do*
begin	*begin*
noncritical section 1	*noncritical section 2*
c1:=0;	*c2:=0;*
while c2=0 do	*while c1=0 do*
begin	*begin*
if turn=2 then	*if turn=1 then*
begin	*begin*
c1:=1;	*c2:=1;*
wait until turn=1;	*wait until turn=2;*
c1:=0	*c2:=0*
end	*end*
end;	*end;*
critical section 1	*critical section 2*
c1:=1;	*c2:=1;*
turn:=2	*turn:=1*
end	*end*

Fig. 4.4. Dekker's mutual exclusion solution

4.7 Nondeterministic Transitions

When modeling software using transition systems, as defined above, each transition that is enabled at a state can result in exactly one immediate successor state. Thus, transitions according to this model are *deterministic*. This does not mean that the modeled system is deterministic: there can be a nondeterministic choice between the execution of different transitions from the same state.

However, in some cases it is convenient to consider also nondeterministic transitions, i.e., transitions that, when applied to some state, have more than one possible successor state. For example, consider the case of getting input from the user. We may choose to represent this by a separate transition for each possible input value, or for convenience, may choose to represent it as a single, nondeterministic transition, grouping together all possible inputs.

Representing nondeterministic transitions requires a slight change of the definition of the model. Previously, a transition included an enabledness condition and a multiple assignment. Now, we add a new set of variables V', which includes exactly one primed version of each program variable from V. Thus, if $V = \{x_1, x_2, \ldots, x_n\}$, then $V' = \{x_1', x_2', \ldots, x_n'\}$. The variables V represent values of the program variables of the same name *before* the execution of a transition, while V' represent the values of the corresponding program variables *after* the execution. Each transition t is now represented by a first order formula r_t, which specifies the relation between the values of the program variables before and after the execution. A transition t is thus enabled at a state s exactly when it is possible to assign values to the variables in V according to s, and some values to V' that will satisfy the transition condition r_t. Expressing the enabledness condition of a transition t in terms of the values *before* the transition executes is thus given by the formula

$$\exists x_1' \exists x_2' \ldots \exists x_n' r_t.$$

Notice that after the existential quantification over all free variables of V', the enabledness condition contains only free variables from V.

Consider a nondeterministic transition over the variables $V = \{x, y\}$ represented by the formula

$$x > y \wedge x' = x + 1.$$

Then, $V' = \{x', y'\}$. The domain of the program variables is the *integers*. The enabledness condition $\exists x' \exists y' (x > y \wedge x' = x + 1)$ can be simplified to $x > y$. The effect of the transition is to increment the variable x. Since the transition does not provide any constraint over y', its value can be arbitrary. This can correspond, e.g., to getting some arbitrary *integer* input from the user. If this was not the intention, but actually that y does not change, we should have specified the transition formula

$$x > y \wedge x' = x + 1 \wedge y' = y.$$

This is a deterministic transition, which can be specified according to the previous notation as

$$x > y \longrightarrow x := x + 1.$$

Allowing the nondeterministic transitions format, it is sufficient to provide a single first order formula, representing all possible transitions. Specifically, let $r_1, r_2, \ldots, r_n$ be the (nondeterministic) transition formulas. Then, we can express them using a single formula $\varphi = \bigvee_{i=1,n} r_i$.

4.8 Assigning Propositional Variables to States

Propositional formalisms are commonly used for asserting properties of finite state systems. In order to use them for modeling systems, we need to connect the propositions used in the specification with the states S of the modeled system. Let AP be a finite set of propositional variables (sometimes called 'atomic propositions'). Each such variable represents some fixed property of the modeled system, which may hold or not hold in any of its states. Each state can be mapped to a subset of the propositions that hold in it.

Formally, let 2^{AP} be the collection of all the subsets of AP (including AP itself, and the empty subset $\emptyset$). We can define a labeling function $L_P : S \rightarrow$

2^{AP}, which maps each state in S to the subset of propositions that hold in it. We can denote the labeled transition system as $(S, \Delta, I, L_P, 2^{AP})$.

Equivalently, each state can also be considered as a Boolean assignment, assigning truth values to the propositions of AP. If a proposition p is in $L_P(s)$, then s assigns a truth value TRUE to p, otherwise, it assigns FALSE. Thus, in the former case, $s \models p$, while in the latter, $s \models \neg p$. This gives an alternative, but equivalent, definition of L_P, as a function from states and propositions to the truth values TRUE and FALSE. We can thus redefine $L_P : (S \times AP) \to \{\text{TRUE, FALSE}\}$.

For yet another, equivalent definition of L_P, we can map each proposition in AP to the subset of states in which it holds, redefining $L_P : AP \to 2^S$. All of the three definitions are equivalent and are used in the literature.

The labeling of states should reflect some conceptual meaning of the propositions. Thus, if a proposition ye corresponds to the fact that the *yellow* light in a traffic light is on, the proposition ye should be mapped to exactly the states that represent this case. The consequence of an incorrect mapping of propositions to states is the possibility that the verification result will be meaningless.

As an example, consider the state the Sieve program, in Section 4.6. Suppose that the property we want to assert about the program is that whenever the left process program counter is $l2$, the message queue $ch[1]$ is nonempty. We can use propositions such as at_l2 and $nonempty\_ch1$. We have to label each state in a way that corresponds to its intended meaning. In Figure 4.5, we provide such a mapping for the states $s1$–$s10$. The reader can compare this to the corresponding table in Figure 4.3.

state	at_l2	$nonempty\_ch1$
$s1$	FALSE	FALSE
$s2$	TRUE	TRUE
$s3$	TRUE	FALSE
$s4$	FALSE	TRUE
$s5$	FALSE	FALSE
$s6$	FALSE	TRUE
$s7$	FALSE	FALSE
$s8$	TRUE	TRUE
$s9$	TRUE	FALSE
$s10$	FALSE	TRUE

Fig. 4.5. Propositional values for the states in Figure 4.3

It is important to note that multiple states can have exactly the same propositional labelings. This reflects the fact that the propositional labeling may not contain all the relevant information about the states. However, it may contain enough information to perform the verification. It is therefore a mistake to try and combine states that are mapped to the same propositional values.

4.9 Combining State Spaces

A state space can be obtained from a transition system. It can represent the global states of the modeled system, and the transitions between them. A transition system, as defined in Section 4.4, encapsulates the transitions of all the components comprising the system. It is sometimes beneficial to construct first the local state spaces of different system components. A component can be, for example, a concurrent process, or even a single variable. Then, the global state space can be obtained by combining the different components.

Consider an extension of the definition of a transition system, where the set of transitions T is constructed from several *local* components $T_1, \ldots, T_n$. Each one of these sets of transitions, T_i, corresponds to a component of the computation, and represents, e.g., a concurrent process, a shared variable, or an interprocess communication queue.

In addition, we keep for each set of transitions T_i a set of *transition names* Σ_i, and a labeling function $L_i : T_i \to \Sigma_i$ that is a bijection. Such an extended transition system is not a simple partition of the set of transitions T of a transition system. In particular, it is typically the case that there are transitions that belong *different* sets, e.g., T_i and T_j, and are labeled by the same name.

The collection of the transitions that are labeled with the same name are always executed *together*, at the same time. Formally, from each global state s, we can execute all the transitions with a mutual name d (i.e., all the transitions t such that $L_i(t) = d$) provided that *all* their enabled conditions hold in s. The effect of executing these transitions is to apply all the assignments associated with them simultaneously. Thus, if we have two transitions $\alpha : p_\alpha \longrightarrow (v_1^\alpha, \ldots, v_n^\alpha) := (e_1^\alpha, \ldots, e_n^\alpha)$ and $\beta : p_\beta \longrightarrow (v_m^\beta, \ldots, v_m^\beta) := (e_m^\beta, \ldots, e_m^\beta)$ (and no other transition shares that name), then we can execute α and β from s provided that $s \models p_\alpha \land p_\beta$. The result would be a new state obtained from s by using the multiple assignment $(v_1^\alpha, \ldots, v_n^\alpha, v_m^\beta, \ldots, v_m^\beta) := (e_1^\alpha, \ldots, e_n^\alpha, e_1^\beta, \ldots, e_m^\beta)$

Suppose that each component of a system can be represented using a local state space $G_i = \langle S_i, \Sigma_i, \Delta_i, I_i \rangle$, corresponding to some local component T_i. We will provide now a way of obtaining the global state space by combining the local state spaces of the different components. We assume that the local states S_i of different components are disjoint, but the sets Σ_i of transition names may have a nonempty intersection. If the same transition name α appears in both Σ_i and Σ_j, then the components G_i and G_j need to synchronize in order to perform α. Performing such a *mutual transition*, can change the local states of both components. Such a collaboration can correspond to an exchange of a message between two processes, or to the use or change of a variable value, when one component represents a process, and the other represents the variable. Of course, a mutual transition can be shared by more than two components, but this is a rare situation in modeling software systems. A transition whose name belongs only to a single local component is a *local transition*.

We need an operator 'o' that combines local state spaces. Combining pairs of local state spaces $G_i \circ G_j$, we may want to require that certain conditions hold, e.g.,

Commutativity $G_i \circ G_j = G_j \circ G_i$.
Associativity $(G_i \circ G_j) \circ G_k = G_i \circ (G_j \circ G_k)$.

These conditions imply, for example, that the following different pieces of code behave in the same way:

parbegin	*parbegin*	*parbegin*
parbegin	*parbegin*	*P2::... end P2*
P1::... end P1	*P2::... end P2*	*parbegin*
P2::... end P2	*P1::... end P1*	*P1::... end P1*
parend	*parend*	*P3::... end P3*
P3::... end P3	*P3::... end P3*	*parend*
parend	*parend*	*parend*

We define an *asynchronous composition* operator '||' as one possible instance of an operator 'o' for combining local state spaces. The asynchronous composition is consistent with the interleaving semantics in the sense that local transitions of different components are interleaved, i.e., are taken one after the other in some arbitrary order.

Let $G_i = \langle S_i, \Sigma_i, \Delta_i, I_i \rangle$, for $i = 1, 2$. We define $G_1 || G_2 = \langle S, \Sigma, \Delta, I \rangle$ as follows:

- $S = S_1 \times S_2$. Each state of the composition is a pair of a local state of G_1 and a local state of G_2.
- $\Sigma = \Sigma_1 \cup \Sigma_2$. The transition names include those that belong to G_1 and those that belong to G_2. (Those that belong to both, i.e., are in $\Sigma_1 \cap \Sigma_2$ are also included in the union.)
- The set of transitions Δ is the union of three sets:
  1. $\{((s,r), \alpha, (s',r)) | (s, \alpha, s') \in \Delta_1 \wedge \alpha \in \Sigma_1 \setminus \Sigma_2 \wedge r \in S_2\}$. In this case there is a change in the G_1 component, while the state of the G_2 component remains unchanged.
  2. $\{((s,r), \beta, (s,r')) | (r, \beta, r') \in \Delta_2 \wedge \beta \in \Sigma_2 \setminus \Sigma_1 \wedge s \in S_1\}$. In this case there is a change in the G_2 component, while the state of the G_1 component remains unchanged.
  3. $\{((s,r), \gamma, (s',r')) | (s, \gamma, s') \in \Delta_1 \wedge (r, \gamma, r') \in \Delta_2\}$. In this case both components synchronize and make the transition together.
- $I = I_1 \times I_2$. Each local state of the composition consists of a pair of local initial states, one from each component.

An example of a asynchronous composition of two local state spaces appears in Figure 4.6.

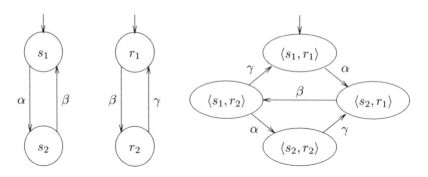

Fig. 4.6. Two local state spaces, and their asynchronous composition

It should be noted that in hardware, composing state spaces is usually done in a rather different way: in every single step, *each* of the components with enabled transitions is making a transition, all in one step (regardless of the transition names). Thus, the asynchronous composition operator '||' is not the only possible choice for a composition operator 'o'.

Composing a global state space from local state spaces has many advantages. First, it allows a more modular way of modeling the system, focusing on each component separately. It maintains the original structure of the system, proving a more intuitive representation of it. This can also be used to provide compositional specification of the system, which may be easier to understand than a monolithic global specification. Finally, some software reliability methods can take advantage of such modularity. For example, in some cases, it may be easier to specify, test or verify the local components of a system.

4.10 The Linear View

One way to observe the behaviors of a system is to study all the execution sequences that start from each initial state. With this view of the system, we typically want every interleaving to satisfy its intended specification. A specification can represent a set of allowed interleaved sequences SP. This set of sequences can be given using a specification formalism. (We will see such formalisms in Chapter 5.) Thus, if the set of executions of a program P is EP, we require that $EP \subseteq SP$. If there is an execution of the program that is not in SP, then the specification is violated. This can be demonstrated by the Venn diagrams in Figure 4.7.

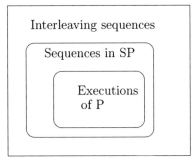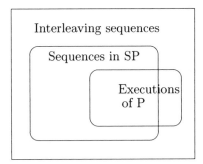

Program satisfies specification   Program does not satisfy specification

Fig. 4.7. The relation between executions and specification

According to the linear view, we do not take into account any relation between the different executions. In particular, we do not care if two interleavings have a common prefix, but then differ from a certain point in the execution due to some nondeterministic choice. The reason for adopting the interleaving view is that each time the program is executed, we want to be sure that the specification holds. If there is a nondeterministic choice involved, we want to guarantee that whatever choice is taken, the execution will still be allowed by the specification.

4.11 The Branching View

We can study the behavior of a system from a different point of view. Take an initial state $\iota \in I$ and consider the unfolding of the state space, starting at that state. This gives us a (possibly infinite) tree, with nodes labeled according to the corresponding states of the state space G. Each maximal path of this tree, starting from ι, corresponds to an execution of the program. If there are multiple successors from a node s in the tree, then the program can make a nondeterministic choice from s. Of course, if there is more than a single initial state, there are multiple branching trees.

This *branching semantics* allows one to observe where the program has a choice. A typical specification formalism is Computational Tree Logic CTL [42]. It allows one to specify that from a given state in the tree either *all* the executions behave in some way, or that there *exists* some execution behaving in a given way. The branching view has more information than the interleaving view, as one can obtain the interleaving view from it by ignoring the points of nondeterministic choice.

The importance of the branching view, is that we can specify that a system can make a choice. If the system interacts with another system or a user, the possibility of a choice may be of great importance. Consider a vending machine, where each item costs 60 cents. It is not only important that the machine dispenses a snack each time the correct amount of money is entered. The customers would be interested that it will allow them to *choose* among all types of snacks that are in stock after inserting sufficient amount of money.

There are many subtleties about what kind of branching information is required here. Although, intuitively, we need to make sure that the vending machine allows a choice, one may argue that there is no need to use all of the information enclosed in a branching unfolding of a system. This is because from each point, only the immediate choices, or in terms of transitions systems, the enabled transitions, are of interest. Thus, interleaving sequences that also maintain in each state the information about the enabled transitions may be sufficient in this case. A more complicated interface between the system and its environment may involve a multistep alternating interaction. In some cases, it may call for explicit distinction between the actions of the system and the actions of the interface [7].

There are many arguments in favor of either of the two paradigm, the linear and the branching views. Following arguments similar to the previous example of a vending machine, some researchers make the distinction that for *closed systems*, which make no interaction with the environment, one may prefer to use the interleaving view, while for *open systems*, which offer various alternative interactions, the branching view should be used.

The distinction between the linear and the branching view can be further sharpened. Researchers in the area of concurrency theory (and in particular, in process algebra) distinguish between different branching models. These subtle distinctions are discussed in Chapter 8. There, it is demonstrated that choosing the right model together with the appropriate criteria for comparing different models of systems can be quite subtle. It depends on the observations that we may want to make about the behaviors of the modeled system.

4.12 Fairness

Fairness is used generically to refer to semantic constraints imposed on interleaved executions of concurrent systems. To motivate fairness, consider a program with two concurrent processes, P_1 and P_2, which execute forever, and never interact with each other (through shared variables or an exchange of messages). An interleaving sequence representing an execution of this program is an infinite sequence of states of the two processes, where each state is obtained from its predecessor by executing either a transition of P_1 or a transition of P_2. Since there is no interaction between the processes, and both processes execute forever, there is always both a transition of P_1 and a transition of P_2 that is enabled. In each interleaved sequence, at any state, there is a choice of executing either a transition from P_1 or a transition from P_2.

One can observe a subtle flaw in the scheduler presented in Section 4.4: among all the execution sequences it allows, there are those where executing an enabled transition of a process can be deferred forever. For the above-mentioned program, the scheduler may decide to select from some point on only transitions of P_1, or only transitions of P_2, although both are available.

In the case of multiprogramming, this corresponds to a faulty scheduler. Actual schedulers would limit the time slice given for each process to execute before it is preempted. In multiprocessing, the lack of interaction between the processes usually allows each one of them to run in its own speed. Thus, in order to represent the behavior of the program faithfully, each execution should contain an infinite number of occurrences of transitions executed for each process. (Of course, there can be programs where one of the processes terminates while the other continues). With the scheduler presented in Section 4.4, this is not guaranteed; it also generates executions that ignore enabled transitions of one process forever.

An exact analysis of the execution must take into account the actual scheduler used, or the relative speed between the processors. This is obviously impractical. We would not like to use this level of detail for modeling, inasmuch as we do not want to reason about the program transitions on the level of electronic gates or transistors. Moreover, such analysis would result in a model that is too specific. Basing our testing or verification approaches on such a specific model may require that we repeat our analysis once a different operating system or a different hardware component is used. We usually want to analyze the software so that it can run on a large range of machines, rather than analyzing it for a particular machine.

Fairness assumptions are used to rule out infinite executions that are unreasonable for the architecture of systems that we model. For example, one may wish to use fairness to prohibit the above mentioned executions where P_1 (or P_2) is allowed to execute only finitely many times. There are many different fairness assumptions that are used within formal methods. Some of them are listed below. For the following definitions, it is important to distinguish both the states and the transitions that are executed. Thus, we assume a description of an execution that includes an indication (i.e., the name) of the executed transition between every pair of states.

Weak process fairness. Rules out an execution if from some state s on it and forever there is at least one transition of some process P_i that is enabled, but no transition of P_i is ever executed after s. (The enabled transitions of P_i can change from state to state.)

Strong process fairness. Rules out an execution if transitions of process P_i are enabled on it infinitely many times, but are executed only finitely many times.

Weak transition fairness. Rules an execution if from some state s on it and forever there is a transition that is enabled, but is never executed after s.

Strong transition fairness. Rules out an execution where there is a transition that is enabled on it infinitely many times but is executed only a finite number of times.

The diversity of fairness definitions raises the question of how to select the one we need. This in fact, depends on the characteristics of the system we want to model. One scheduler may correspond to one fairness assumption, while another will need a different assumption. Note that correspondence between a scheduler and a fairness assumption means that all the executions allowed by the scheduler are fair, but not the reverse. In fact, for many fairness assumptions (including the ones listed above) one can prove mathematically that without special provisions such as a way to generate true random numbers, it is impossible to construct a scheduler that will allow exactly the fair executions [11, 47].

To demonstrate this, and some of the above fairness conditions, consider a program with two processes P_1 and P_2:

$$P_1 :: x := 1; \quad || \quad P_2 :: while \ y = 0 \ do$$
$$[\ no\_op$$
$$[]$$
$$if \ x = 1 \ then \ y := 1 \ ]$$
$$end$$

These processes are assumed to have one shared variable x, initialized to 0. Process P_2 has also a local variable y, which is also initialized to 0. We will invent the new names pc_l and pc_r as program counters. The operator '$[]$', appearing within square brackets, represents a nondeterministic choice. Thus, the process P_2 can select between a *no_op* and an *if* statement. We allow the values l_0 and l_1 to the variable pc_l, and the values r_0 and r_1 to the variable pc_r. We model this program using the following transitions:

$$t_0 : pc_l \equiv l_0 \quad \longrightarrow \quad (pc_l, x) := (l_1, 1)$$
$$t_1 : pc_r \equiv r_0 \wedge y \equiv 0 \quad \longrightarrow \quad pc_r := r_1$$
$$t_2 : pc_r \equiv r_1 \quad \longrightarrow \quad pc_r := r_0$$
$$t_3 : pc_r \equiv r_1 \wedge x \equiv 1 \quad \longrightarrow \quad (pc_r, y) := (r_0, 1)$$

The initial condition is $\Theta : x \equiv 0 \wedge y \equiv 0 \wedge pc_l \equiv l_0 \wedge pc_r \equiv r_0$. The left process P_1 is modeled with one transition, t_0, setting the variable x to 1. The program counter of this process is then set to the value l_1, from which no transition is enabled. Thus P_1 terminates upon a single execution of t_0. Process P_2 is modeled with three transitions. Transition t_1 represents the head of the main loop. It checks whether y equals 0. If this is the case, it progress to the point where a nondeterministic choice between t_2 and t_3 is made. Transition t_2 is a *no_op*. It just loops back to the head of the main loop. Transition t_3 checks whether x is 1, whereupon it changes y to 1, and returns to the main loop. Process P_2 keeps executing the transitions t_1 and t_2, unless the value of x is changed to 1 by the transition t_0 in P_1.

Weak transition fairness (and weak process fairness alike) rules out an execution where process P_2 is repeatedly executing the transitions t_1 and t_2 forever without allowing process P_1, whose only transition t_0 is meanwhile enabled, to proceed. Notice that before transition t_0 of process P_1 is executed, transition t_3 cannot become enabled. Now, consider the case where P_1 executes its only transition. Then, x is set to 1. In this case, the transition t_1 and the pair of transitions t_2 and t_3 alternate in becoming enabled. In order for the loop of process P_2 to terminate, transition t_3 must be executed, setting y to 1.

Weak transition fairness does not guarantee termination, since in any execution, t_3 is not continuously enabled from some state and forever. In fact, it becomes disabled each time that t_1 is enabled. Strong (or weak) process fairness does not guarantee that t_3 will be executed either. It allows that the transition t_2 is always preferred over t_3 when both are enabled.

Under strong transition fairness, both processes will terminate. Transition t_0 is still guaranteed to execute, terminating process P_1, as before. Moreover, after executing t_0, if t_3 is not executed, the loop in process P_2 never terminates, and t_3 becomes enabled infinitely often. But strong transition fairness dictates that under this condition, transition t_3 must execute. Thus, in any case, transition t_3 executes. It sets y to 1 and the program counter pc_r to r_0. Thereafter, no transition can become enabled, i.e., the process P_2 terminates.

Notice that we used the fairness assumption to reason *by way of contradiction*. We assumed that there is an infinite execution of $P_1 \| P_2$. In this case, we used the fairness assumption to rule out that t_0 or t_3 may never execute. But when t_0 and t_3 execute, both processes terminate, ruling out the possibility that the execution is infinite.

We will now show that there cannot be a scheduler that will generate exactly the executions that satisfy strong transition fairness for the above program. If there was such a scheduler, we could have arranged the fair executions in a tree corresponding to the branching view of the behavior of the program. The tree has finitely many choices from each node (at most, the number of transitions). This tree is infinite, since as we saw before, there are infinitely many executions. Yet, as shown above, by the strong transition fairness assumption, each maximal path in this tree, corresponds to a finite execution. This is not allowed due to a famous result called König's lemma (see Chapter 2.3), which asserts that in an infinite tree with finitely many choices from each node there must be an infinite sequence. A similar analysis can show that no scheduler can exist for the other fairness assumptions presented above.

It is important to make the following distinction: the proof in the previous paragraph only means that one cannot construct a scheduler that can generate *any one* of the executions of a given program that satisfy the (strong transition) fairness assumption. However, we can certainly construct schedulers that will generate *only* (strongly) fair executions. Such a scheduler can thus generate a subset of the fair executions.

Exercise 4.12.1. Describe a scheduling algorithm that will guarantee that the scheduled executions will satisfy weak process fairness. Explain why your algorithm will not generate all the executions satisfying the weak process fairness assumption.

The choice of fairness assumption, like the choice of granularity of atomic transitions, is subtle for the correct modeling of concurrent systems. In multiprogramming systems, one might try to verify that a scheduler conforms with some fairness assumptions. This might be a difficult task (actual schedulers may contain a lot of timing details, and their code may not be available to the user).

There is no uniform way of deciding which fairness assumption to use. Researchers and practitioners of formal methods have different favorite fairness assumptions. Although some treat fairness only as a result of a mathematical abstraction, many people adopt a particular fairness assumption and in fact stipulate that concurrent systems actually behave according to it.

Since fairness assumptions are used to restrict the set of executions under discussion, using the right fairness constraint may be critical for obtaining reliable verification results. Suppose on the one hand that we use a fairness assumption that restricts the set of executions too much. Then verifying that this set satisfies a given property may not catch some errors that occurs in executions that were not supposed to be removed. On the other hand, suppose that we use a fairness assumption that does not restrict the set of executions enough. Then it might be the case that we fail to prove a property that holds for the modeled system, just because some executions that would have been removed by a more appropriate fairness assumption are still included.

Unfortunately, as in other modeling issues, we cannot *prove* that a given fairness assumption is indeed the right one that reflects reality. In the partial order model, which will be described in Section 4.13, we will give a more intuitive meaning, and hence a justification, for one particular fairness assumption.

One can define a hierarchy among fairness assumptions, where an assumption is *weaker* when it allows more executions. Proving the correctness of a system is best done using the *weakest* possible assumption. A stronger fairness assumption allows a subset of the executions of a weaker assumption. Thus, if some property is proved to hold for all the executions that satisfy a weaker fairness assumption, then that property must also hold for the subset of these executions that are allowed under a stronger assumption. Of course, proving that a system satisfies its specification under *no* fairness assumption implies that it does so under *any* fairness assumption, since fairness can only restrict the number of allowed executions.

For the fairness assumptions listed above, weak process fairness is weaker than strong process fairness (thus, the names *weak* and *strong*), and weak transition fairness is weaker than strong transition fairness. To see this, consider weak and strong transition fairness (for process fairness, the arguments are similar). If a sequence satisfies strong transition fairness, then for each transition, from some point, either it is never enabled, or it is executed infinitely many times. Obviously, in both cases, weak transition fairness holds.

We can show also that, under the assumption that there are finitely many transitions, strong transition fairness is stronger than strong process fairness. Take an arbitrary sequence ξ that satisfies strong transition fairness. We need to show that it also satisfies strong process fairness. Let P_i be some process such that in infinitely many states in ξ, at least one transition of P_i is enabled. Since each process has finitely many transitions, at least one transition of P_i is enabled infinitely often. Since the sequence satisfies strong transition fairness, there will be infinitely many occurrences of executions of this transition on the sequence. This means that there are infinitely many occurrences of transitions from P_i in ξ. The same reasoning holds for any process P_i. Thus, ξ satisfies strong process fairness.

One can show that no other relation holds among the four fairness conditions presented. The hierarchy can then be described as in Figure 4.8, where an arrow from one fairness condition to the other means the former is stronger than (i.e., implies) the latter.

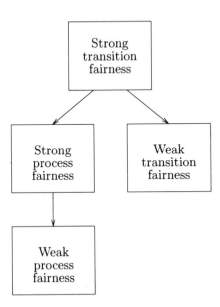

Fig. 4.8. A hierarchy of fairness criteria assumptions

4.13 The Partial Order View

Partial order executions of concurrent systems, give a more intuitive description of concurrent executions than interleaving executions, described previously. In fact, as we will see later, the interleaving executions of a program can be understood as a mathematical construction, obtained from its partial order executions. Despite the more intuitive flavor of the partial order execution model, the mathematical simplicity of interleaving sequences usually makes them a preferable model for representing concurrent programs. Although some formal methods techniques reason directly about partial order executions, interleaving sequences are much more often used in modeling. Using the interleaving model for representing concurrent executions is convenient because of the simplicity of manipulating sequences. Our goal in presenting this model here is restricted to obtaining a better understanding of modeling concurrent software.

One criticism of the interleaving model is that it does not distinguish between nondeterministic choice and concurrency; as we saw earlier, in Section 4.3, executing α and β concurrently is not distinguished from either executing α and then β or executing β and then α. The interleaving model imposes a total order on the *events*, resulting from executing atomic transitions.

Moreover, the interleaving model represents the *global* states of the *entire system*, before and after the execution of each transition. In reality, a system rarely passes through such global states. It does not execute one transition at a time (except for multiprogramming systems), as different concurrent actions happen concurrently. This is usually not a big problem: specifications of systems often omit constraints that force different parts to execute concurrently. However, as we will show later in this section, there are cases where a distinction between the actual states through which the system passes, and the artificial ones used in modeling the system using interleaving sequences, is important.

A Banking Example

To illustrate the problem with the interleaving model, consider two branches of a bank. Each of the branches starts the working day with a balance of one million dollars. At some point during the day, a customer enters one branch and deposits two million dollars. At about the same time, the other branch is robbed, and the one million dollars it had are being stolen. Both actions take place at roughly the same time. To model the bank, we let α be the transition representing the deposit, and β the transition representing the robbery. If $x1$ is the amount of money at the first bank, and $x2$ is the amount of money at the second, the state before α satisfies $x1 = 1,000,000$, and the state after α satisfies $x1 = 3,000,000$. Similarly, the state before β satisfies $x2 = 1,000,000$, and the one after β satisfies $x2 = 0$.

We can model the situation on that day using the global (state) space shown in Figure 4.9. This state space generates two interleaving sequences, with three states each.

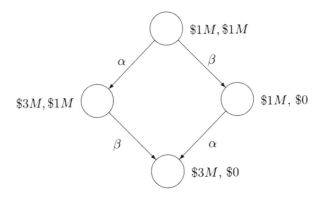

Fig. 4.9. A banking system

We can ask now what is the actual amount of money that the bank had during that day. The bank's stockholders may decide to buy or sell shares according to the current balance relative to the initial one. Suppose that they are using a web brokerage program that decides to buy shares when the balance goes over two million dollars, and sell if the balance is a million dollars or less. When the program recognizes the occurrence of the two transitions in the two different orders, it will behave in different ways. If it is informed that the deposit has happened before the robbery, it may suggest buying the bank's shares. If it is informed about the robbery happening before large deposit, it may suggest selling the shares, but later will suggest buying them back. The brokerage program behaves here as a possible specification for what is a good or a bad investment. Although both interleavings correspond to the same particular events that happened concurrently on the same day, the specification will have a totally different evaluation of the financial situation of the bank.

This hypothetical example illustrates that dealing with interleaved executions and with global states is sometimes misleading. To describe the banking system more faithfully, observe that each branch has its own balance, or in terms of modeling, its own local state. The transition representing the deposit acts on the local state of one of the branches, producing a new local state, while the transition representing the robbery acts on the other. This is described in Figure 4.10.

A *partial order execution* $(E, \prec)$ contains a finite or infinite set of events E. Each event represents an occurrence of an atomic transition. The events

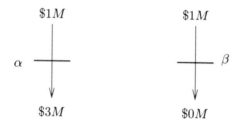

Fig. 4.10. A partial order description of the bank

are ordered by a partial order relation '$\prec$'. If $\alpha \prec \beta$ then α has to finish before β can start. The fact that '$\prec$' is a partial order means the following:

Transitivity if $\alpha \prec \beta$ and $\beta \prec \gamma$ then $\alpha \prec \gamma$. This captures the intuition behind the fact that if an event γ happens after β, and β happens after α, then γ happens after α.

Irreflexivity It is never the case that $\alpha \prec \alpha$. Obviously, an event cannot start after it has finished.

Asymmetry If $\alpha \prec \beta$ then we cannot have that $\beta \prec \alpha$. Thus, if β starts after α, it cannot also finish before α starts.

In the interleaving model, where each event corresponds to the execution of a transition, there is a *total order* between the events. That is, for each pair of events α and β, either α appears before β or β appears before α. In the partial order model, events for which $\alpha \prec \beta$ cannot overlap in time, as α must complete before β can start. It is possible that in the same partial order execution, neither $\alpha \prec \beta$, nor $\beta \prec \alpha$. This means that α and β *can* overlap in time. However, the lack of order does not force them to do so, although concurrent implementation may take advantage of the independency in their execution.

Modifying the bank example, suppose we have an execution with three events, α, β and γ, where α is the wealthy deposit event, β the robbery event, and γ is a new event where the first branch manager invites the depositor for a dinner that evening. The only ordered pair is $\alpha \prec \gamma$, so that α and γ are executed in that specific order. The order represents *causality*, in the sense that the fact that α occurred (to completion) caused γ to happen. The event β could have executed simultaneously with α, simultaneously with γ or concurrently with part of α and part of γ. Thus, the partial order model describes what *can* happen concurrently, but does not impose simultaneity. If we really wanted to say that α and β must coincide, we could have defined a single transition that represents both of them (or used a richer execution model).

To relate the partial order execution model to concurrent software, observe that concurrent programs usually have a number of components, each having its own *local* state space. For example, we may have a separate component for each

- process P_i (including the set of variables that can be used or changed only by P_i),
- global variable, or
- message queue.

Transition systems can be defined as in the interleaving model. Each such transition includes a condition that may depend on a subset of the components. Thus, in the partial order model of execution, a transition is enabled from a *collection of local states*, each taken from a different component, such that, when taken together, the enabling condition holds. Similarly, the execution of each transition can change a collection of local states, taken from different components. In the above banking example, the transitions α and β are each enabled depending only on the local state of one component, representing one branch of the bank. However, consider the enabledness of a transition μ, which reports at the end of the day whether one of the branches has a higher balance than the other. The execution of this transition depends on the local states of both components.

Consider the case where there are multiple transitions that are enabled, depending or changing at least one mutual local state. This represents a nondeterministic choice. For example, extend the banking example such that there is another person, making a fifty dollars deposit to the same branch where the two million dollars are deposited, on that day. Denote this event by δ. Since that branch has only one teller, the two deposits cannot execute concurrently, and the teller has to decide which one to process first. Both deposits depend and change the local state of one branch.

The partial order model distinguishes between nondeterminism that is due to concurrency and nondeterminism that is due to some choice in the code. In the latter case, there are two partial order executions. In the banking example, there is the choice of executing α before δ or δ before α. These choices will correspond to different partial order executions.

Linearizations and Global States

One can obtain interleaving sequences that correspond to each partial order execution. This is done by completing the partial order into total orders (in general there can be more than one way to do that), by adding order between pairs of unordered events. Each total (i.e., linear) order obtained in this way from a partial order is called a *linearization* of it. The additional order must satisfy two conditions:

- No cycles of ordered events are formed.
- Each event is preceded by only a finite number of other events.

Thus, a partial order execution can correspond to multiple interleaving sequences.

A global state can obtained in the partial order model of execution as a collection of local states, one for each different component. However, not every such collection can form a global state. Each global state s partitions the events of the partial order execution into two: those that occur before s (according to the partial order between the events), denoted $before(s)$, and those that occur after, denoted $after(s)$.

It only makes sense to take such a partition if the set $after(s)$ is finite and *left closed*. Given a partial order execution $(E, \prec)$, a left closed set $C \subseteq E$ must satisfy the following:

> If an event α is in C and for some event $\beta \in E$ we have that $\beta \prec \alpha$, then β is also in C.

We can also construct the assignment a attached to a global state s with $before(s) = C$. We assume that each event in the partial order execution $(E, \prec)$ corresponds to one or more local components (processes) of the system, and that each local component has an initial state. Moreover, for each event there is a local state that represents the value of the variables in the corresponding component after its occurrence. The global assignment a agrees with the local assignments after each maximal event in C. (An event $\alpha \in C$ is maximal if for no other event $\beta \in C$ we have that $\alpha \prec \beta$.) If C does not include any event for some some component (process), then for the variables of this component, the global assignment a is consistent with the initial values.

Consider the original version of the banking example and Figure 4.10. There are two unordered events, α and β. Thus, $E = (\{\alpha, \beta\}, \emptyset)$. The local initial state for the first branch is $x1 = 1,000,000$. The local initial state for the other branch is $x2 = 1,000,000$. The local state after executing α is $x1 = 3,000,000$. The local state after executing β is $x2 = 0$. There are 4 left closed subsets:

- $\emptyset$ (the empty set of events). Since there are no events, the two components (bank branches) are at their initial state. The global assignment is consistent with the local initial states, where $x1 = 1,000,000$ and $y1 = 1,000,000$.
- $\{\alpha\}$. Only one branch participates. The global assignment for this state satisfies has $x1 \mapsto 3,000,000$, which corresponds to the local state after executing α. Since the other branch stayed at its initial state, the global assignment also has $x2 \mapsto 1,000,000$, consistent with the local initial state of that branch.
- $\{\beta\}$. Only one branch participates. The global assignment for this state has $x2 \mapsto 0$, which corresponds to the local state after executing β. Since the other branch stayed at its initial state, it also has $x1 \mapsto 1,000,000$, consistent with the initial state of that branch.

• $\{\alpha, \beta\}$. Both branches participate. Since α and β are unordered they are both maximal. The global assignment is consistent with both the local state after α, thus $x1 \mapsto 3,000,000$, and the local state after β, hence $x2 \mapsto 0$.

This definition of a global state for the partial order model allows relating the notion of a global state back to the one defined in the interleaving semantics. However, notice that the global states of a partial order execution are not in general linearly ordered. In fact, the order between the global states, obtained from the partial order execution, corresponds to the set inclusion between their sets of events. That is, a global s_2 occurs after another global state s_1, if $before(s_1) \subset before(s_2)$. In the above example, the global state that corresponds to $\{\alpha\}$ happens after the one corresponding to $\emptyset$, and before the one corresponding to $\{\alpha, \beta\}$. However, the global states corresponding to $\{\alpha\}$ and $\{\beta\}$ are unordered, and thus their corresponding assignments cannot appear on the same linearization.

A Simple Example

An example of a simple program appears in Figure 4.11. It has two processes, $P1$ and $P2$. The process $P1$ starts with $x = 0$, and repeatedly increments x and sends the new value to $P2$ via a synchronous communication queue. The process $P2$ starts with $y = 0$. It receives each time a value into its variable z and adds it to y. To keep the example simple, we ignore practical issues such as the size of the data word. Hence, we assume that the two processes can run forever. Since the communication is synchronized, there is a single transition that represents the communication, effectively assigning the value of x to z. This transition is shared between the two processes. Hence, there are three transitions for this program:

$$\alpha : pc1 \equiv m0 \longrightarrow (pc1, x) := (m1, x + 1)$$
$$\beta : pc1 \equiv m1 \wedge pc2 \equiv n0 \longrightarrow (pc1, pc2, z) := (m0, n1, x)$$
$$\gamma : pc2 \equiv n1 \longrightarrow (pc2, y) := (n0, y + z)$$

Figure 4.12 describes a partial order execution of the program. It shows the order between the occurrence of transitions and the local states before and after each transition. Thus, the arrows in the graph do not represent directly the partial order between the events. Rather, the partial order is represented by the *paths* between the events. For example, the topmost occurrence of event α precedes an occurrence of β, which precedes another occurrence of α. Therefore, the former occurrence of α also precedes the latter occurrence of α. Some of the occurrences of α and γ are unordered, corresponding to the possibility that they can be executed concurrently. However, some occurrences of α are ordered before some later occurrences of γ, and vice versa.

Since there is no nondeterministic choice, there is actually only one partial order execution for this program. Two out of the infinite number of completions of the partial order execution into total orders appear in Figure 4.13.

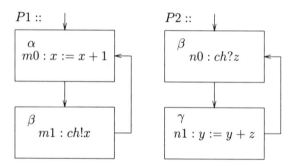

Fig. 4.11. Processes interacting by message passing

The dotted line in figure 4.12 corresponds to a global state. This state contains all the local states that appear above the line. It corresponds to the part of the execution that includes two occurrences of the event α, and a single occurrence of the event β. The corresponding global assignment can be formed by taking the assignments of the maximal local states below the line, namely,

$$\{pc1 \mapsto m1,\ x \mapsto 2,\ pc2 \mapsto n1,\ y \mapsto 0,\ z \mapsto 1\}.$$

A later global state that also includes in addition to the above events the first occurrence of the event γ corresponds to the global assignment

$$\{pc1 \mapsto m1,\ x \mapsto 2,\ pc2 \mapsto n0,\ y \mapsto 1,\ z \mapsto 1\}.$$

Applications of the Partial Order Model

Using the correspondence between partial order executions and interleaved sequences, we can regard each interleaving sequence as a mathematical construction. This allows us to use some of the many mathematical tools that deal with sequences. It is interesting to observe that many formalisms that are used to reason about interleaving sequences, including temporal logics, *can* distinguish between two interleaved executions that are constructed from the same partial order execution, in the same way that the brokerage program described in the above bank example could.

An interesting application of the relation between partial orders and interleavings is that of *partial order based verification* [76]. It exploits the fact that the specification often does not distinguish between the linearizations (interleavings) that correspond to the same partial order execution (since such a distinction would be artificial). Such verification methods reason about programs by selecting a convenient representative for each partial order execution. Consequently, we need to reason about fewer possibilities and the verification often becomes simpler. Similarly, *partial order reduction* [55, 113, 142]

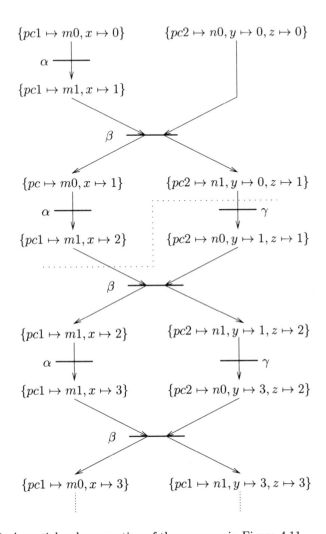

Fig. 4.12. A partial order execution of the program in Figure 4.11

attempts to use this phenomenon algorithmically to reduce the state space explosion problem (see Chapter 6), occurring in model checking algorithms.

$$\{m0, x \mapsto 0, n0, y \mapsto 0, z \mapsto 0\} \qquad \{m0, x \mapsto 0, n0, y \mapsto 0, z \mapsto 0\}$$
$$\alpha \downarrow \qquad\qquad\qquad \downarrow \alpha$$
$$\{m1, x \mapsto 1, n0, y \mapsto 0, z \mapsto 0\} \qquad \{m1, x \mapsto 1, n0, y \mapsto 0, z \mapsto 0\}$$
$$\beta \downarrow \qquad\qquad\qquad \downarrow \beta$$
$$\{m0, x \mapsto 1, n1, y \mapsto 0, z \mapsto 1\} \qquad \{m0, x \mapsto 1, n1, y \mapsto 0, z \mapsto 1\}$$
$$\gamma \downarrow \qquad\qquad\qquad \downarrow \alpha$$
$$\{m0, x \mapsto 1, n0, y \mapsto 1, z \mapsto 1\} \qquad \{m1, x \mapsto 2, n1, y \mapsto 0, z \mapsto 1\}$$
$$\alpha \downarrow \qquad\qquad\qquad \downarrow \gamma$$
$$\{m1, x \mapsto 2, n0, y \mapsto 1, z \mapsto 1\} \qquad \{m1, x \mapsto 2, n0, y \mapsto 1, z \mapsto 1\}$$
$$\beta \downarrow \qquad\qquad\qquad \downarrow \beta$$
$$\{m0, x \mapsto 2, n1, y \mapsto 1, z \mapsto 2\} \qquad \{m0, x \mapsto 2, n1, y \mapsto 1, z \mapsto 2\}$$
$$\gamma \downarrow \qquad\qquad\qquad \downarrow \gamma$$
$$\{m0, x \mapsto 2, n0, y \mapsto 3, z \mapsto 2\} \qquad \{m0, x \mapsto 2, n0, y \mapsto 3, z \mapsto 2\}$$

Fig. 4.13. Two interleavings

The same way that interleaving sequences are constrained by fairness assumptions, one may impose constraints on partial order executions. The most frequently used constraint is called *maximality*. It requires that a partial order execution cannot have a collection of local states that together enable a transition, while none of them has any immediately following event.

It is interesting to note that the seemingly natural constraint of maximality can be translated into a fairness assumption over the corresponding interleaving sequences that are generated from the partial order execution. Define a (symmetric and reflexive) *dependency* relation D between transitions such that $\alpha D \beta$ when any occurrences of α and β cannot be executed concurrently. That is, we cannot have unordered (with respect to '$\prec$') occurrences of these transitions. Then it is possible to prove (see [82, 115]) that maximality is equivalent to the following assumption:

There cannot be an infinite execution where, from some state s and forever, there is a transition α that is enabled, and remains enabled forever, but neither α, nor any transition dependent (according to D) on α, is executed after s.

This assumption is quite similar to weak process fairness. Here again, the correspondence between partial order and interleaving executions helps to explain modeling issues.

4.14 Modeling Formalisms

Many formalisms for representing software systems within software reliability tools are simple programming languages. The user has to *program* the abstract description of his system, before being able to use the tool. Other modeling formalisms are based on some extended forms of finite automata. In some cases, an automatic transition from the original representation of the system into the modeling formalism is directly available. However, due to complexity and computability related limitations of formal methods, this feature is usually quite restricted and not widely available. The common practice is, therefore, that a user of a software reliability tool *manually* abstracts the checked system, obtaining a description that is given using the specific modeling formalism of the tool used.

Modeling formalisms are designed to achieve certain goals:

- There is a simple and efficient translation between the modeling formalism and some internal representation. The software reliability tool is optimized to work efficiently using its internal representation.
- The formalism restricts the user to a domain in which the formal method can be applied. For example, it can limit the model to have finitely many states, or use a particular signature.
- The formalism is rich and easy to use. The process of modeling systems is often done manually. Hence it often comprises the bottleneck in using formal methods, and is highly prone to modeling mistakes. A rich formalism can simplify the modeling process and minimize the number of modeling errors.
- A modeling formalism needs to have a clearly and formally defined semantics. Software reliability tools are concerned with the correctness of software. Therefore, their developers must make effort that they do not introduce obscure or misleading constructs that would contribute to systematic modeling mistakes.

Several standard modeling formalisms were developed in order to relieve the developers of tools from having to design new programming languages, and in order to obtain uniformity and widely agreed upon semantics. This is done in particular in the case of formalisms for describing communication protocols. Such formalisms are often called 'formal description techniques' (FDTs). Some notable examples for such standard formalisms were defined by the ISO (International Standards Organization). These are ESTELLE [23],

LOTOS [17] and SDL [62]. It should be noted however, that standard formalisms are often developed independently from particular software reliability tools.

Process algebras are also used for modeling systems. One such formalism, called CCS [100], which is the origin of LOTOS. Both CCS and LOTOS will be described in Chapter 8. Another popular formalism is PROMELA [65]. This programming language is used within the model checker SPIN. It allows a large number of programming constructs, and different kinds of ways for concurrent interaction, including synchronous and asynchronous message passing and shared variables. The careful attention and the effort made to make PROMELA a rich modeling language has paid off by making SPIN a popular verification tool.

Translations are sometimes available from one formal modeling language used in one tool to another formal modeling language, used in another tool. Such translations allow using different formal methods and software reliability tools without having to repeat the modeling process. This is possible since many tools use the same assumptions about the computational model, in particular, having finitely many states. However, it should be noted that since formal methods are usually based on computationally hard problems, many tools use various heuristics that optimize them to work efficiently with the particular formalism they use. For example, a tool can include a particular heuristic that reduces the number of the states it needs to explore for a particular communication pattern. Such a pattern is then recognized during compilation of the model. Translating from one formalism to another often ignores such heuristics, and therefore produces a description of the system for which the target tool would perform poorly.

Another approach for modeling systems is to use *graphical interfaces* to capture the description of the system. The modeling involves putting together a visual description of the system, usually as a finite graph. This description is translated into some internal representation, which is transparent to the user. Such a description particularly suit for finite state systems. Infinite state systems can also be described in a similar way, using *extended finite state systems*: instead of representing the states of the system directly, one can represent a finite number of *parametrized states*, which include only a partial description of the state. The additional parameters, which can be, for example, program variables or message queues, are not described visually. The issue of visualization has become very important recently, and is partly responsible for an increase in the popularity of using software reliability tools.

Visualizing the specification using graphs and other diagrams helps provide a better intuitive understanding of the designed system. For example, the UML methodology [46], and similarly, the ROOM methodology [127], contain a collection of different diagrams, that are capable of presenting different aspects of the designed system. One type of diagrams is used to present the architecture of the system, including the different processes and the way they interact. Another type of diagrams is used to describe the behavior of each process in the system. This is often done using some kind of state space representation. Different behaviors of the system are often represented using other formalisms, e.g., message sequence charts, which describe the exchange of messages in different scenarios. Visual description techniques are further described in Chapter 11.

4.15 A Modeling Project

The following communication protocol is aimed at transmitting a message over lossy communication queue. This is part of the *data link layer*, according to the OSI (Open Systems Interconnection) communication model. The *sender* process sends a message, via an unreliable communication line, by sending a message (using the command *SendEnv*). The environment can either eventually forward the message to the *Receiver* process, or the message may get lost. The receiver process receives the message, if it is available, using the *EnvReceive* command. Because of the message loss problem, the sender process sends an indication of the message number using the bit *NextMessage*. This variable keeps a modulo 2 count of the messages being sent. The message sent from the *sender* to the *receiver* contains the contents of the message and the value of the *NextMessage* counter.

Since there is no indication that a message was lost, the *sender* uses a timer, which is set each time a message was sent, and is reset each time a message is received. The receiver waits for either the arrival of an acknowledgement, using an *AckReceive* command, or the expiration of the timer, using a *TimerUp* event. The latter triggers the *Sender* to try and resend. Of course, the timer can expire prematurely, if the *Receiver* or the environment is too slow. This calls for a formal verification (or conversely, *falsification*) of the algorithm.

Waiting for an event is indicated below using the construct *wait-event* [. . .]. If several events can occur, they are separated inside this construct by '[]'. A triggering event, e.g., a receiving event, or a timeout event, is followed by '−>' and the instructions that must be executed after the event has occurred.

Sender :: bool *NextSend*, *AckVal* =0;
    while true do
      prepare NextMessage;
      SendEnv NextSend,NextMessage;
      StartTimer;
      wait-event [
        AckReceive AckVal −>
          CancelTimer;
          if AckVal=NextSend then
            NextSend:=1−NextSend

```
    []
    TimerUp −> no_op ]
  end
||
Receiver :: bool MsgNum, FrameExpected=0;
  while true do
    wait-event {
      EnvReceive MsgNum,MsgContent −>
        if MsgNum=FrameExpected then
          FrameExpected:=1−FrameExpected;
        ReceiverAck!1−FrameExpected }
  end
```

More details of this protocol, and similar ones can be found in Tanenbaum's Computer Networks book [138].

Before modeling this protocol, the following points should be considered:

- The timer can be considered as a separate process, with transitions that set, reset and expire it. These transitions are also mutual to the *Sender* process.
- There is no need to impose an actual time constraint causing the timer to expire. This can be simply modeled using a nondeterministic choice between expiring or being cancelled by the *Sender*.
- The two communication lines: from the *Sender* to the *Receiver* for sending a message, and from the *Receiver* to the *Sender* for receiving a message, can be modeled by two additional processes, with transitions mutual with the corresponding processes.
- The actual message is irrelevant here. One possibility is to use a nondeterministic transition which puts no constraint on the value assigned to *NextMessage* in the transition corresponding to *prepare NextMessage*. Another possibility is to disregard the part related to the message contents. This process of *abstraction* is further discussed in Section 10.1, and in general may need some formal justification (although in practice, this is often done informally).

4.16 Further Reading

The following book by Manna and Pnueli gives a very comprehensive treatment of modeling systems:

  Z. Manna, A. Pnueli, *The Temporal Logic of Reactive and Concurrent Systems: Specification*, Springer-Verlag, 1991.

A comprehensive book devoted to the issue of modeling (and verifying) fairness is

N. Francez, *Fairness*, Springer-Verlag, 1986.

A survey of concurrent programming languages, examples of classical concurrent algorithms and further verification examples can be found in

M. Ben-Ari, *Principles of Concurrent and Distributed Programming*, Prentice-Hall, 1990.

5. Formal Specification

'If you knew Time as well as I do,' said the Hatter, 'you wouldn't talk about wasting it. It's him.'

Lewis Carroll, *Alice's Adventures in Wonderland*

Most software projects are developed over a period of several months or even years. Over its lifetime, a software product is often updated, new features are added, and adjustments are made at the request of the users. A complete system may include millions of lines of code. It is sometimes developed and maintained by hundreds of people, located in different places. A software system may consist of numerous parts, each responsible for performing some predefined tasks. Interfaces through which the different parts can interact with each other need to be defined. The right use of the interfaces between the different components is important for integrating them into a system that operates correctly.

Formally specifying the design, and promptly updating the specification, helps keep track of the consistency between the different parts of a project during its development and maintenance. It allows the distribution of a programming effort by clearly defining, for each group, the functionality of the code, which it is responsible for. An unambiguous specification of the interfaces allows partitioning of the programming effort. Each group of developers can focus on its own part, and use the other parts according to the given specification. The specification can be used to compare the design with the implementation or with archaic code, and as a reference, while implementing changes in the code.

The phrase 'a program is correct' is only meaningful with respect to a given specification. Thus, formal verification is necessarily connected to a given specification. Tools for performing various verification tasks use formal specification formalism. Tools can also check for internal consistency of the preliminary specification of a system.

Formal specification can be used as a contract between the developer and the customer. The customer may present some formal requirements, or review the specification suggested by the developer. Then the specification can be used in the same way as a legal binding contract. After the development is done, the customer can complain and argue if the product does not satisfy the specification. The developer may use the specification to argue back, and show that the delivered product meets the specification. Such arguments can be refuted or supported by verification tools.

In this chapter, we study formalisms that are used to specify *properties of systems*. Specifying the system itself and specifying its properties are distinct activities that should not be confused. Both kinds of specification may sometimes be given with similar or even the same formalisms. However, in many cases they are expressed by different formalisms. For example, the system specification can be given as a program, or as a state machine, which prescribes in detail how the system should behave. On the other hand, the system properties may be given in a simple and succinct logic-based notation.

5.1 Properties of Specification Formalisms

A specification needs to be precise and have a unique and agreed upon interpretation. Therefore, a specification formalism is required to have a well-defined syntax and precise semantics. In this way, a specification is unambiguous, and the question

Does the system satisfy its specification?

has a unique answer.

Natural languages, which are frequently used in requirements documents, are often ambiguous, and thus can be unsuitable for formally specifying software. Notice that ambiguity of a specification refers to the possibility of interpreting it in more than a single way. The fact that a specification formalism is unambiguous does not rule out the possibility that specifying a certain property can be given in more than one way. Although there can be certain advantages to a formalism that prescribes one canonical way of describing each property, this is a minor concern. A specification formalism does not have to be textual. A recent trend is to use formalisms that can be presented in a visual way. Such formalisms tend to give a more intuitive understanding of the specified system. Visual formalisms are presented in Chapter 11.

Specification formalisms need to be intuitive and easy to use. A specification can be written by a programmer, a system designer, a requirements engineer, etc. It needs to be understood by other people, including developers and testers. In formal methods applications the specification is often used by an algorithm and thus needs to be machine readable. However, its main purpose is to convey information between humans. Even if a specification formalism is subsequently used for testing or verification, there is no value in it if it does not reflect the property intended by the person performing the specification. Using a specification formalism requires learning it first. For practical purposes, the overhead involved in learning a new formalism should be compensated favorably by the time saved in reducing the debugging time while using it.

It is usually preferable to use a formalism that allows a *succinct* representation of the requirements. However, when conciseness is obtained by using intricate mathematical tricks, resulting in an incomprehensible specification, succinctness may be of no advantage.

A good specification formalism is *effective* in the sense that there is a way to check or verify that a system is consistent with its specification. In order to facilitate testing and simulation, the specification should only refer to objects that can be observed in actual experiments. An even better formalism allows an *efficient* automatic way of performing testing or verification. Choosing the right specification formalism is affected by the various checks that one might want to perform:

Check that the collection of specifications does not include a contradiction. For example, part of the specification might prescribe that task A must be performed before task B, while another part prescribes that task B must be performed before task A. Note that no execution satisfies a specification with a contradiction.

Check that the specification is implementable. For example, one may want to exclude a specification that requires a system response that cannot be supported because of some additional timing constraints.

Check the correctness of the implementation against the required specifications, or at least test it using an extensive set of test cases.

The *expressiveness* of a specification formalism is another important factor. One would obviously prefer a formalism that can express a wide range of properties. Here too, there is a tradeoff. A more expressive formalism deals with more instances of specifications. Hence, it may require more complicated automatic verification algorithms for checking the consistency of a specification, or for checking a system against such a specification. In some cases, selecting a more expressive formalism results in the complete loss of the ability to use an algorithmic method for performing various checks. Further expressiveness may even lead to the loss of the ability to apply manual verification. Thus, research is being conducted not only for finding more expressive specification formalisms, but also for finding less expressive, but more efficient ones.

A specification can sometimes be used to generate some initial version of the desired code. Some algorithms and tools can automatically translate a formal specification into some template code that can later be further refined by programmers into working code. This template can include, for example, the communication patterns of a protocol. Such a template still needs to be completed and massaged, before an actual program is obtained. A similar approach allows stepwise refinement of the specification into an actual program. At each stage of the refinement, a more concrete specification is obtained, and the conformance between successive stages in the refinement is being tested or verified.

Such approaches for converting specification into code allow obvious gain in development time, making the specification process part of the implementation task. Furthermore, code that is automatically generated from the specification naturally tends to be more reliable.

Unfortunately, there is no 'silver bullet' formalism that is preferable in all cases. In some cases, it is quite difficult to select exactly the right formalism to fit the specification needs. The right selection is often a combination of different formalisms. Since it is quite difficult to design a specification formalism that would meet all the requirements, there are many different formalisms, just as there are many different programming languages. Formalisms that are of frequent use or have been standardized offer an obvious advantage. In the rest of this chapter we focus on two formalisms that have a relatively large number of users: *linear temporal logic* and *automata*. In this book we concentrate more on specifying the *dynamic* behavior of a system, i.e., the way the system progresses during its execution. We put less emphasis on expressing the static properties of the system. Some formalisms, such as first order logic (described in Chapter 3) and the Z-notation place more emphasis on static properties (see e.g., [35]).

5.2 Linear Temporal Logic

First order and propositional logics, discussed in Chapter 3, are capable of expressing properties of states. Each formula represents a set of states that satisfy it. Thus, a formula in such a logic can express, for example, an initial condition, an assertion about the final states, or an *invariant*. By keeping two copies of the program variables we can also represent the relation between the initial and final states. However, such logics are *static* in the sense that they represent a collection of states, but not the dynamic evolution between them during the execution of a program.

Modal logics (see, e.g., [71]) extend static logics by allowing the description of the relation between different states during the execution. This is in particular appropriate for asserting about interactive, concurrent or distributed systems, where we are not only interested in the relation between the values at the beginning and the end of the execution, but also in other properties related to the sequence of states during an execution.

Linear Temporal Logic (abbreviated LTL) [91] is an instance of modal logic. LTL is often used to specify properties of interleaving sequences [119], modeling the execution of a program, e.g., as presented in Section 4.10. LTL is defined on top of a static logic $\mathcal{U}$. The logic $\mathcal{U}$ can describe properties of states, but not the changes between the different states. In this book, we will use propositional and first order logic as specific instances of $\mathcal{U}$. (For simplicity, we omit mentioning explicitly the first order structure $\mathcal{S}$ used within the logic $\mathcal{U}$. Accordingly, we write '$\models$' instead of '$\models^{\mathcal{S}}$'.) The syntax of LTL is as follows:

- Every formula of $\mathcal{U}$ is a formula of LTL,
- If φ and ψ are formulas, then so are $(\neg\varphi)$, $(\varphi \wedge \psi)$, $(\varphi \vee \psi)$, $(\bigcirc\varphi)$, $(\Diamond\varphi)$, $(\square\varphi)$, $(\varphi\mathsf{U}\psi)$, and $(\varphi\mathsf{V}\psi)$.

An LTL formula is interpreted over an infinite sequence of states $x_0 x_1 x_2 \dots$. We write ξ^k for the suffix of $\xi = x_0 x_1 x_2 \dots$ starting at x_k, i.e., the sequence $x_k x_{k+1} x_{k+2} \dots$. It is convenient to define the semantics of LTL for an arbitrary suffix ξ^k of a sequence ξ as follows:

- $\xi^k \models \eta$, where η is a formula in the static logic $\mathcal{U}$, exactly when $x_k \models \eta$
- $\xi^k \models (\neg\varphi)$ exactly when not $\xi^k \models \varphi$,
- $\xi^k \models (\varphi \wedge \psi)$ exactly when $\xi^k \models \varphi$ and $\xi^k \models \psi$,
- $\xi^k \models (\varphi \vee \psi)$ exactly when $\xi^k \models \varphi$ or $\xi^k \models \psi$,
- $\xi^k \models (\bigcirc\varphi)$ exactly when $\xi^{k+1} \models \varphi$,
- $\xi^k \models (\Diamond\psi)$ exactly when there is an $i \geq k$ such that $\xi^i \models \psi$,
- $\xi^k \models (\square\varphi)$ exactly when for every $i \geq k$, $\xi^i \models \eta$.
- $\xi^k \models (\varphi\mathsf{U}\psi)$ exactly when there is an $i \geq k$ such that $\xi^i \models \psi$ and for all j, where $k \leq j < i$, $\xi^j \models \varphi$
- $\xi^k \models (\varphi\mathsf{V}\psi)$ exactly when either for every $i \geq k$, $\xi^i \models \psi$, or for some $j \geq k$, $\xi^j \models \varphi$, and for every i, where $k \leq i \leq j$, $\xi^i \models \psi$.

The first line in the semantic definition states that a formula from the underlying logic $\mathcal{U}$, i.e., an LTL formula that contains no modal operators, is interpreted in the first state (x_k) of the sequence ($x_k x_{k+1} x_{k+2} \dots$). The next three lines give the interpretation of the familiar Boolean operators negation ('$\neg$'), conjunction ('$\wedge$') and disjunction ('$\vee$'). The rest of the definition deals with the modal operators.

The modal operator '$\bigcirc$' is called *nexttime*. The formula $\bigcirc\varphi$ holds in a sequence $x_k x_{k+1} x_{k+2} \dots$ when φ holds starting with the next state x_{k+1}, namely in the suffix sequence $x_{k+1} x_{k+2} \dots$. Similarly, $\bigcirc \bigcirc \varphi$ holds provided that φ holds in the sequence $x_{k+2} x_{k+3} \dots$. The modal operator '$\Diamond$' is called *eventually*. The formula $\Diamond\varphi$ holds in a sequence ξ provided that there is a suffix of ξ where φ holds. The modal operator '$\square$' is called *always*. The formula $\square\varphi$ holds in a sequence ξ provided that φ holds in every suffix of ξ.

We can already construct formulas that combine different modal operators. For example, the formula $\square \Diamond \varphi$ holds in a sequence ξ provided that for every suffix ξ' of ξ, $\Diamond\varphi$ holds. That is, there is a suffix ξ'' of ξ' where φ holds. Stated differently, no matter how far we progress in ξ (to produce a suffix ξ'), there is still a later suffix (ξ''), where φ holds. This means that there are infinitely many suffixes of ξ in which φ holds, or in other words, φ holds in ξ 'infinitely often'. Consider now the formula $\Diamond \square \varphi$. This formula holds in a sequence ξ provided that there is some suffix ξ' of ξ for which $\square\varphi$ holds. That is, φ holds for every suffix of ξ'. In other words, φ holds from some suffix of ξ and forever.

Two additional modal operators are defined, 'U' and 'V'. The operator 'U' is called *until*. Intuitively, $\varphi U \psi$ asserts that φ holds until some point (i.e., some suffix) where ψ holds. We can view '$\Diamond$' as a special case of 'U', that is, $\Diamond \varphi = true U \varphi$. The operator 'V' is called *release*. Intuitively, $\varphi V \psi$ holds in a sequence ξ if either ψ holds forever (i.e., for every suffix of ξ), or holds until some point (suffix) where both φ and ψ hold. Thus, φ 'releases' the requirement that ψ will need to hold later (although, it is not required that ψ must not hold at a later suffix). Here too, '$\Box$' is a special case of 'V', as $\Box \varphi = false V \varphi$.

We omit the suffix superscript, and denote $\xi \models \varphi$ when $\xi^0 \models \varphi$, i.e., when the complete sequence ξ satisfies φ. The notation $\xi \models \varphi$ means that a sequence ξ satisfies the LTL formula φ. Accordingly, $\xi \not\models \varphi$ means that ξ does not satisfy φ. It follows from the semantic definitions that $\xi \not\models \varphi$ exactly when $\xi \models \neg \varphi$. Thus, for each sequence ξ we have $\xi \models true$ and $\xi \not\models false$.

We will often omit parentheses in LTL specification. To do that, we will assume the following priority: '$\bigcirc$' has highest priority, then '$\Diamond$', '$\Box$', 'U' and 'V', in descending order. The binary 'U' operator binds stronger to the right, i.e., $\varphi U \psi U \eta = (\varphi U (\psi U \eta))$, while the operator 'V' binds stronger to the left. We have the following connections: $\varphi V \psi = \neg((\neg \varphi) \wedge (\neg \psi))$, $\varphi \rightarrow \psi = (\neg \varphi) \vee \psi$, $\varphi \leftrightarrow \psi = (\varphi \rightarrow \psi) \wedge (\psi \rightarrow \varphi)$ $\Diamond \varphi = true U \varphi$, $\Box \varphi = \neg \Diamond \neg \varphi$ and $\varphi V \psi = \neg((\neg \varphi) U (\neg \psi))$. It follows that we could have defined a smaller temporal logic, with only the modal operators '$\bigcirc$', 'U' and the Boolean operators '$\wedge$' and '$\neg$'. However, using the additional operators increases the readability of formulas.

Let P be a system that admits multiple executions. Such a system can be described, for example, as a transition system or an automaton. Each execution of P is represented by a sequence of states (see Section 4.10). We abuse notation and denote by P also the set of sequences generated for the system P. We write $P \models \varphi$ if *all* the executions of P, when represented as sequences of states, satisfy φ. We denote $P \not\models \varphi$ when not all the sequences of P satisfy φ. Notice that it is not always the case that $P \models \neg \varphi$ when $P \not\models \varphi$; it can happen that not *all* the sequences satisfy φ, but at the same time, *some* of them do satisfy φ.

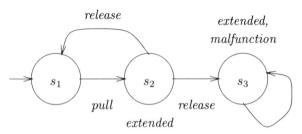

Fig. 5.1. A model of a spring

As an example, consider a simple model of a spring, described in Figure 5.1. One can pull the spring, and later release it. After being pulled, the spring may lose its elasticity and stay extended or return to its original form. The system has three states, s_1, s_2 and s_3, where s_1 is the initial state (marked with an incoming arrow that is not connected to any other node). This system is simple enough that the underlying logic $\mathcal{U}$ can be propositional logic. Accordingly, each one of the states is labeled by propositions from the set $AP = \{extended, malfunction\}$. The state s_1 is not labeled with any of the above propositions. That is, $s_1 \models \neg extended \wedge \neg malfunction$. The state s_2 is labeled with $extended$ only. Thus, $s_2 \models extended \wedge \neg malfunction$. Finally, s_3 is labeled by both $extended$ and $malfunction$, i.e., $s_3 \models extended \wedge malfunction$.

The system has an infinite number of sequences. This includes the following:

$$\xi_0 = s_1 s_2 s_1 s_2 s_1 s_2 s_1 \ldots$$

$$\xi_1 = s_1 s_2 s_3 s_3 s_3 s_3 s_3 s_3 \ldots$$

$$\xi_2 = s_1 s_2 s_1 s_2 s_3 s_3 s_3 s_3 \ldots$$

As an example, consider whether the sequence ξ_2 satisfies several LTL formulas.

$\xi_2 \not\models extended$. The formula $extended$ does not use any temporal operators. Hence it is interpreted over the first state in the sequence ξ_2, which is s_1. That state is not labeled by $extended$, thus the formula $extended$ does not hold in s_1 and consequently in ξ_2.

$\xi_2 \models \bigcirc extended$. The $nexttime$ operator $\bigcirc$ is used in this formula to assert that the second state in the sequence, which is s_2, satisfies (i.e., is labeled with) the proposition $extended$.

$\xi_2 \not\models \bigcirc \bigcirc extended$. The use of of $nexttime$ twice in $\bigcirc \bigcirc extended$ (which reads 'nexttime nexttime extended') asserts that the third state, i.e., the successor of the successor of the first state, is labeled with $extended$. However, this state, s_1, is not labeled with $extended$.

$\xi_2 \models \Diamond extended$. The formula $\Diamond extended$, which reads as 'eventually extended', asserts that there is some state in the sequence, where $extended$ holds. Indeed, the second state in the sequence is labeled with $extended$.

$\xi_2 \not\models \Box extended$ The formula $\Box extended$, which reads 'always extended', asserts that it is the case that for each state in the sequence, $extended$ holds. (Formally, it asserts that $extended$ holds for the first state in each suffix.) This does not hold for ξ_2 because the first and also the third state are not labeled with $extended$.

$\xi_2 \models \Diamond \Box extended$. The formula $\Diamond \Box extended$, which reads 'eventually always extended', asserts that there is some state in the sequence from which all the following states are labeled with $extended$. This happens to hold from the fourth state on the sequence ξ_2 (which is s_2) and onwards.

$\xi_2 \not\models (\neg extended) \mathsf{U} malfunction$. The formula $(\neg extended) \mathsf{U} malfunction$, which reads 'not extended until malfunction'. For it to hold in ξ_2, the spring must not be extended until there is a malfunction. According to the semantic definition, in order for this formula to hold, there must be a state in ξ_2 where *malfunction* holds. Furthermore, all the preceding states on ξ_2 must satisfy $\neg extended$. The first state of ξ_2 that satisfies *malfunction* is the fifth state, which is s_3. Examining the four previous states, we see that not all of them satisfy $\neg extended$. In particular, the second state of ξ_2, which is s_2, does not satisfy $\neg extended$.

We saw some examples of temporal formulas interpreted over a single sequence. We will see now examples of temporal formulas interpreted over a system P. Recall that $P \models \varphi$ holds provided that $\xi \models \varphi$ *for every* execution ξ of P. Consider now the following properties we are asserting about the execution sequences of the spring model P:

$P \models \Diamond extended$ Each execution of the system reaches a state in which the spring is *extended*. This holds because one cannot stay at the initial state s_1 forever. Notice that this situation can be changed by adding a self loop on s_1.

$P \models \Box(\neg extended \rightarrow \bigcirc extended)$ In each state, in each execution of P, if the spring is not *extended*, then it is *extended* in the next state. This holds because the only state where we have $\neg extended$ is s_1. According to the spring model, each occurrence of s_1 in any execution sequence of P is followed immediately by an occurrence of s_2.

$P \not\models \Diamond \Box extended$ The formula $\Diamond \Box extended$ asserts that eventually we reach a state where the spring remains extended forever. This does not hold for one particular sequence, namely the one we denoted above by ξ_0, which alternates between *extended* and $\neg extended$ forever.

$P \not\models \neg \Diamond \Box extended$ The formula $\neg \Diamond \Box extended$ is the negation of the previous one. To see why this formula does not hold for P, we will first write the formula in an equivalent form. We can use the following dualities between '$\Box$' and '$\Diamond$': $\neg \Diamond \varphi = \Box \neg \varphi$ and $\neg \Box \varphi = \Diamond \neg \varphi$. Thus, we obtain that $\neg \Diamond \Box extended = \Box \Diamond \neg extended$. This formula asserts that from every state in a sequence (due to the '$\Box$' modality) there is some future state (due to the '$\Diamond$' modality), including possibly the current one, where $\neg extended$ holds. That is, there are infinitely many states in which $\neg extended$ holds. Although this holds for the sequence ξ_0, it does not hold for all other sequences of P, where eventually the spring remains extended forever. Note that both the formula $\Diamond \Box extended$ and its negation do not hold for P.

$P \not\models \Box(extended \rightarrow \bigcirc \neg extended)$ The formula $\Box(extended \rightarrow \bigcirc \neg extended)$ asserts that after each state where the spring is extended, there is an immediate successor state where it is not extended. Although there is (exactly) one sequence, namely, ξ_1, where this property holds, this does not hold in general, since in all but this sequence, we eventually get stuck in state s_3.

Exercise 5.2.1. The above model is, of course, a very abstract description of a spring. It ignores the continuum of states, in which the spring passes through while being pulled or released. In fact, it assumes that each time the spring is extended, it gets to the same state, s_2. It also assumes that after being pulled, the spring cannot be pulled further, but has to be released. This is of course not the only model for the behavior of a spring. Consider another model, in which the spring may lose its elasticity while being extended. In this alternative model, there are two successor states for s_1: one in which the spring is extended but some physical damage has occurred to its elasticity, and another in which it is extended without the damage. Describe the alternative model as an automaton, and check which of the above properties hold for it.

As mentioned in Section 4.12, one may sometimes use fairness constraints to disallow some unreasonable executions of a system [3]. Consider, for example, a constraint that asserts that every execution must not remain forever in the strongly connected component $\{s_1, s_2\}$. This constraint rules out the execution ξ_0. In this case, the system P admits fewer executions, and thus may satisfy more properties. The property $\Diamond \Box \, extended$, which was not satisfied by P before, is satisfied under the additional constraint.

In some cases, the focus of the system's model is on the transitions rather than the states, or both the transitions and the states. Accordingly, we may interpret LTL formulas over sequences of transitions, or sequences that alternate between states and transitions. To do the latter, assume that we add to the structure of a model a set of *transition names* TN (disjoint from the propositions in AP). The syntax of LTL is extended to allow using a proposition from NT whenever a formula from the underlying logic $\mathcal{U}$ is allowed. Let $first(\xi)$ be the first transition in the sequence ξ. We add the following item to the semantic interpretation of LTL:

- $\xi^k \models t$ where $t \in TN$, exactly when $first(\xi^k) = t$.

5.3 Axiomatizing LTL

The axioms and proof rules below provide a complete axiomatization for propositional linear temporal logic [88]. They can be used to prove that a given formula φ is *valid*, i.e., is satisfied by every sequence (under the given set of propositions).

In this proof system we assume that all the occurrences of the *release* operator 'V' are removed, e.g., using the equivalence $\mu V \eta = \neg((\neg\mu)U(\neg\eta))$.

The axiomatization includes three parts. The first part consists of eight axioms, as follows:

$$A1 \quad \neg \Diamond \mu \leftrightarrow \Box \neg \mu$$

$$A2 \quad \Box(\mu \rightarrow \psi) \rightarrow (\Box \mu \rightarrow \Box \psi)$$

$$A3 \quad \Box \mu \rightarrow (\mu \wedge \bigcirc \Box \mu)$$

$$A4 \quad \bigcirc \neg \mu \leftrightarrow \neg \bigcirc \mu$$

$$A5 \quad \bigcirc(\mu \rightarrow \psi) \rightarrow (\bigcirc \mu \rightarrow \bigcirc \psi)$$

$$A6 \quad \Box(\mu \rightarrow \bigcirc \mu) \rightarrow (\mu \rightarrow \Box \mu)$$

$$A7 \quad (\mu \mathsf{U} \psi) \leftrightarrow (\psi \vee (\mu \wedge \bigcirc(\mu \mathsf{U} \psi)))$$

$$A8 \quad (\mu \mathsf{U} \psi) \rightarrow \Diamond \psi$$

The second part consists of a sound and complete axiomatization for propositional logic. However, instead of only allowing the template variables in the axioms and proof rules to be instantiated with propositional formulas, we can replace them consistently with any propositional LTL formula. This part of the axiomatization allows us to prove tautologies such as $\Box A \vee \neg \Box A$.

Finally, the proof system also includes the proof rule:

Gen (Temporal Generalization):

$$\frac{\mu}{\Box \mu}$$

(Note that this proof rule is different from the first order logic proof rule **GEN**, presented in Section 3.5.)

We will see in Section 6.6 that there is an attractive alternative to proving the validity of propositional LTL formulas. Namely, there is an algorithm that can check this automatically. In addition, experience shows that LTL specifications that are used for expressing properties of software are typically reasonably short. Because of this, propositional LTL is particularly appropriate for the automatic verification of properties of finite state systems.

First order linear temporal logic, where the state properties are expressed in first order logic, can express more properties. On the other hand, we lose decidability and completeness [1, 137]. First order linear temporal logic is often used within deductive verification (see Chapter 7).

5.4 Examples of LTL Specification

A Traffic Light

Consider a traffic light. It can change between the colors *green*, *yellow* and *red*. The underlying logic $\mathcal{U}$ will be in this case propositional logic. The propositions *re*, *ye* and *gr* correspond to the color of the traffic light being *red*, *yellow* and *green*, respectively. The lights in this traffic light keep changing according to the following order:

$$green \longrightarrow yellow \longrightarrow red \longrightarrow green$$

We assume that the traffic light continues to operate forever.

Specifying that the traffic light can only have exactly one of these lights at any given moment is an invariant and can be expressed in LTL as follows:

$$\Box(\neg(gr \wedge ye) \wedge \neg(ye \wedge re) \wedge \neg(re \wedge gr) \wedge (gr \vee ye \vee re))$$

Specifying that from a state where the light is *green* the green color continues until it changes to *yellow* can be expressed in LTL as

$$\Box\,(gr \rightarrow gr\mathsf{U}ye).$$

Thus, the correct change of colors is specified as

$$\Box((gr\mathsf{U}ye) \vee (ye\mathsf{U}re) \vee (re\mathsf{U}gr)) \tag{5.1}$$

Suppose that new regulations are made for traffic lights, and there is now a *yellow* light also in between the *red* and the *green* lights (signaling that the driver should 'get ready'). The above specification needs to be modified, as it does not allow for this possibility.

As a first attempt, we could try the specification

$$\Box(((gr \vee re)\mathsf{U}ye) \vee (ye\mathsf{U}(gr \vee re))).$$

This specification is incorrect; $(gr \vee re)\mathsf{U}ye$ allows the light to be switch several times between *green* and *red* before it becomes *yellow*. Moreover, this specification allows changing from *green* to *yellow* and then to *green* again. A correct specification is

$$\begin{aligned}\Box(\quad & (gr \rightarrow (gr\mathsf{U}(ye \wedge (ye\mathsf{U}re)))) \\ \wedge\quad & (re \rightarrow (re\mathsf{U}(ye \wedge (ye\mathsf{U}gr)))) \\ \wedge\quad & (ye \rightarrow (ye\mathsf{U}(gr \vee re)))).\end{aligned} \tag{5.2}$$

The first line allows the *green* $\longrightarrow$ *yellow* $\longrightarrow$ *red* sequencing. The second line allows the sequencing *red* $\longrightarrow$ *yellow* $\longrightarrow$ *green*. Although the first two lines of (5.2) refer to states where the *yellow* light is on, they deal only with the cases where the *yellow* light follows a *green* or a *red* light. They do not provide information about the behavior of the traffic light in the case that it *starts* with a *yellow* light. For this reason, the third line is added.

The specification given so far for the traffic light allows starting it from any color. If we want to specify that the initial color is *red* we can add a conjunct *re*. Note that if the traffic light must start with the *red* light on, there is no need in the third line of (5.2).

Properties of Sequential Programs

Assume that a program is modeled as a transition system, as in Section 4.4, and that the underlying logic $\mathcal{U}$ is the one used in defining the transition system. Consider the following additional notation:

en_α The enabling condition of transition α.

en_{P_i} At least one transition of P_i is enabled. If P_i also denotes the set of transitions of the process by the same name, then this can be denoted as $\bigvee_{\alpha \in P_i} en_\alpha$.

init   The current state is an initial state. In this book, we usually denote the initial condition of a transition system by Θ.

finish   The current state is a termination state. If T is the set of all transitions, then this can be expressed as $\bigwedge_{\alpha \in T} \neg en_\alpha$. (Recall that we assume that all the execution sequences are infinite, and thus extend finite sequences by an infinite repetition of the last state.)

In the following properties, we will use ψ as an assertion about states, expressed in the underlying logic $\mathcal{U}$.

Partial correctness, with respect to the initial condition and a final assertion ψ.

$$init \wedge \Box(finish \rightarrow \psi)$$

It asserts that the program starts with a state satisfying *init*, and if a termination state is reached, that state satisfies ψ.

Termination, with respect to the initial condition.

$$init \wedge \Diamond finish$$

It asserts that the program starts with a state satisfying *init* and that it reaches a termination state.

Total correctness with respect to the initial condition and a final assertion ψ.

$$init \wedge \Diamond(finish \wedge \psi)$$

It asserts that the program starts with a state satisfying *init* and that eventually it terminates with a state satisfying ψ.

The program starts with the initial condition init and ψ is an invariant, i.e., holds always throughout its execution.

$$init \wedge \Box\psi$$

Mutual Exclusion

The problem of mutual exclusion was discussed in Section 4.6. Consider a pair of processes P_1 and P_2 that are connected to a shared device, say a printer. They must not use the device simultaneously, as printing at the same time from both processes would result in a garbled printout. Thus, they voluntarily enter a regime, where each process must enter a special place in the code, called its *critical section*. A process can print only from within its critical section. To prevent simultaneous printing, the processes use a protocol for achieving mutual exclusion, i.e., to guarantee that it is not possible for both of them to enter their critical section. As part of this protocol, before entering its critical section, each process enters a *trying section*, where it notifies its intention to enter the critical section. The mutual exclusion protocol then takes into account various conditions, and permits a process to enter the critical section, or makes it stay and wait in its trying section before entering the critical section. There are several requirements one may impose on such a protocol. First, let us define some propositions that will be used in specifying these requirements.

$tryCS_i$ The process P_i is in its trying section, i.e., it attempts to enter its critical section.

$inCS_i$ The process P_i is in its critical section CS_i.

The first property is that of mutual exclusion: *only one process can be at its critical section at any time.*

$$\Box \neg (in\, CS_1 \wedge in\, CS_2)$$

Another property is that of *responsiveness.* We require that *each process that tries to enter its critical section will eventually be allowed to enter it.*

$$\Box (tryCS_i \rightarrow \Diamond inCS_i)$$

In order for the mutual exclusion protocol to operate correctly, we may further require that *when a process enters its trying section, it will remain there, unless it progresses to its critical section.*

$$\Box (tryCS_i \rightarrow ((tryCS_i \,\mathsf{U}\, inCS_i) \vee \Box tryCS_i))$$

Fairness Conditions

We will now formulate some of the fairness conditions presented in Section 4.12 using LTL. We will use the following *transition* propositions:

$exec_\alpha$ The transition α is executed. This is an example of the use of executions that include alternations of states and transitions, where α is a transition name. Expressing this proposition requires using propositions labeling the transitions, as explained at the end of Section 5.2 (or equivalently, augmenting the state with information about the transition that is executed next).

$execp_i$ A transition from P_i is executed. This is shorthand for $\bigvee_{\alpha \in P_i} exec_\alpha$.

Weak transition fairness.

$$WTF = \bigwedge_{\alpha \in T} \neg \Diamond \Box (en_\alpha \wedge \neg exec_\alpha)$$

This can also be expressed in the following equivalent way:

$$\bigwedge_{\alpha \in T} (\Diamond \Box en_\alpha \rightarrow \Box \Diamond exec_\alpha)$$

Strong transition fairness.

$$STF = \bigwedge_{\alpha \in T} (\Box \Diamond en_\alpha \rightarrow \Box \Diamond exec_\alpha)$$

Weak process fairness.

$$WPF = \bigwedge_{P_i} \neg \Diamond \Box (en_{P_i} \wedge \neg exec_{P_i})$$

This can also be expressed in the following equivalent way:

$$\bigwedge_{P_i} ((\Diamond \Box en_{P_i}) \rightarrow (\Box \Diamond exec_{P_i}))$$

Strong process fairness.

$$SPF = \bigwedge_{P_i} (\Box \Diamond en_{P_i} \rightarrow \Box \Diamond exec_{P_i})$$

The relation between the fairness conditions, illustrated in Figure 4.8 can now be stated in terms of logical implication. Recall that $\varphi \rightarrow \psi$ means that φ is stronger than ψ. We have $STF \rightarrow SPF$, $SPF \rightarrow WPF$ and $STF \rightarrow WTF$.

Exercise 5.4.1. Consider the following alternative specification for the traffic light specification (5.2).

$$\begin{aligned} \Box(\quad &(gr \rightarrow (gr \mathsf{U}(ye \mathsf{U} re))) \\ \wedge \quad &(re \rightarrow (re \mathsf{U}(ye \mathsf{U} gr))) \\ \wedge \quad &(ye \rightarrow (ye \mathsf{U}(gr \vee re)))) \end{aligned} \qquad (5.3)$$

Explain why this specification is not sufficient to capture the description of the order among the lights. (Hint: check the precise definition of the *until* 'U' operator.)

5.5 Automata on Infinite Words

Automata theory plays an important role in computer science. Various kinds of automata are used, for example, for compilation, natural language analysis, complexity theory and hardware design. Automata theory also fits well into the domain of modeling and verification of systems.

Finite automata are basically state machines over finite transition systems. Modeling programs using transition systems, and using automata to specify properties of programs is highly beneficial: it means using the same kind of representation to describe both programs and their specifications. One can then exploit graph algorithms to perform automatic verification, as will be shown in Chapter 6.

Finite automata over infinite words, called ω-automata, can be used to describe the executions of a program. The properties of the system can also be specified using ω-automata, or translated, e.g., from LTL to such automata, as we will see in Section 6.8.

Modeled systems can exhibit finite as well as infinite behaviors. As we have already discussed, in order to avoid dealing with two kinds of behaviors, we can translate finite behaviors into infinite ones. This can be done by using a special *no_op* transition that does not change the system state and is enabled exactly when all the other transitions are disabled. Thus, we can focus on finite automata over infinite words, i.e., words from Σ^ω, where Σ is some finite alphabet. The superscript 'ω' denotes an infinite number of iterations. The languages accepted by ω-automata are called ω-regular languages. Each such language can be described using expressions containing letters from the alphabet Σ, and the operators + (union), . (concatenation), $*$ (denoting zero or more repetitions) and ω (infinitely many repetitions).

We discussed in Chapter 4 different possibilities for modeling executions as sequences of states, sequences of transitions, or alternating sequences containing both. Consistent with a previous choice, we usually model executions as sequences of states. Accordingly, we will define automata that recognize sequences of states. Since automata commonly have labels on their transitions rather than on their states, our presentation is somewhat nontraditional. In this way, the translation from LTL to such automata, described in Section 6.8, is more direct. We can also extend our model, by labeling both the states and the transitions, allowing our automata to recognize alternating sequences of states and transitions. Since this extension is straightforward, we will omit the details of such an extended construction.

One should bear in mind that ω-automata are not really meant to actually recognize executions, since executions are infinite, and recognizing even one of them will never terminate. However, ω-automata provide a finite way of representing infinite executions, and have a finite structure. This finiteness allows providing algorithms for automatic verification.

The simplest class of ω automata over infinite words is that of Büchi automata [22]. We will describe a variant of it, where the labels are defined on the states rather than on the transitions. A Büchi automaton $\mathcal{A}$ is a sextuple $\langle \Sigma, S, \Delta, I, L, F \rangle$ such that

- Σ is the finite *alphabet*.
- S is the finite set of *states*.
- $\Delta \subseteq S \times S$ is the *transition relation*.
- $I \subseteq S$ are the *starting states*.
- $L : S \rightarrow \Sigma$ is a *labeling* of the *states*.
- $F \subseteq S$ is the set of *accepting states*.

In a graph representing a Büchi automaton, we mark initial states with an incoming arrow that is not connected to any other node. We mark accepting states with a double circle. An example of an automaton is shown in Figure 5.2. There, $\Sigma = \{a, b\}$, $S = \{s_1, s_2\}$, $I = \{s_1, s_2\}$. The labeling in this example is $L(s_1) = \alpha$ and $L(s_2) = \beta$, and $F = \{s_1\}$.

A *run* ρ of $\mathcal{A}$ on v corresponds to an infinite path in the automaton graph from an initial state, where the nodes on this path are labeled according to the letters in v. We say that v is an *input* to the automaton $\mathcal{A}$, or that $\mathcal{A}$ *reads* v. Formally, let v be a word (string, sequence) over Σ^ω. We can also represent v as a function $v : Nat \rightarrow \Sigma$, i.e., $v = v(0)\, v(1)\, v(2)\ldots$. A run of $\mathcal{A}$ over v is a mapping $\rho : Nat \rightarrow S$ such that

- $\rho(0) \in I$. The first state is an initial state.
- For $i \geq 0$, $(\rho(i), \rho(i+1)) \in \Delta$. Moving from the ith state $\rho(i)$ in the run to the $i+1$st state $\rho(i+1)$ is consistent with the transition relation Δ.
- The ith element on v, i.e., $v(i)$ and the labeling $L(\rho(i))$ of the state $\rho(i)$ are the same. That is, $v(i) = L(\rho(i))$.

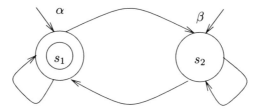

Fig. 5.2. A Büchi automaton

Let $inf(\rho)$ be the set of states that appear infinitely often in the run ρ (when treating the run as an infinite path). Notice that $inf(\rho)$ is finite. A run ρ of a Büchi automaton $\mathcal{A}$ over an infinite word is *accepting* when $inf(\rho) \cap F \neq \emptyset$. That is, when some accepting state appears in ρ infinitely often.

The *language* $\mathcal{L}(\mathcal{A}) \subseteq \Sigma^\omega$ of a Büchi automaton $\mathcal{A}$ consists of all the words accepted by $\mathcal{A}$. For the automaton in Figure 5.2 over $\Sigma = \{\alpha, \beta\}$, consider the infinite word α^ω which has only αs. A run of the automaton $\mathcal{A}$ over this word must start with the state s_1, since this is the only state labeled with an α. Then the run continues, passing through s_1 forever. The word α^ω is accepted by the automaton $\mathcal{A}$, and thus $\alpha^\omega \in \mathcal{L}(\mathcal{A})$. This is because the state s_1 is an accepting state, and it appears infinitely often.

Consider the word β^ω. This word consists of infinitely many βs. The (unique) run of the automaton over this word starts and stays in the state s_2. This is not an accepting run, because there is no accepting state that occurs infinitely many times. (In fact the only accepting state, which is s_1, does not occur at all.) Thus, $\beta^\omega \notin \mathcal{L}(\mathcal{A})$. Finally, consider the word that includes an alternation between αs and βs, denoted $(\alpha\beta)^\omega$. A corresponding run starts with s_1 and alternates between s_2 and s_1 forever. Since s_1 is an accepting state and it appears infinitely many times, that word is in $\mathcal{L}(\mathcal{A})$.

The language of the automaton in Figure 5.2 can be denoted using the ω-regular expression $(\beta^*a)^\omega$. This notation prescribes an infinite repetition of the following: a finite (possibly empty) sequence of βs, followed by a single α. Thus, an infinite word over $\Sigma = \{\alpha, \beta\}$ is accepted by this automaton if it contains infinitely many αs. As shown above, this includes the word $(\alpha\beta)^\omega$, i.e., an infinite alternation between αs and βs, starting with an α. The automaton $\mathcal{A}$ also accepts the words α^ω and $\beta\alpha\beta^2\alpha\beta^3\alpha\ldots$.

5.6 Specification using Büchi-automata

As mentioned above, one of the advantages of using automata is that both the modeled system and its properties can be represented in the same way. We can represent a system as a Büchi automaton $\mathcal{A} = \langle 2^{AP}, S, \Delta, I, L, S \rangle$. It contains a set of states S. The *immediate successor relation* between the states is $\Delta \subseteq S \times S$, i.e., $(s, r) \in \Delta$ where r is obtained from s by executing a single atomic transition. The set of initial states is $I \subseteq S$.

The labeling function $L : S \rightarrow 2^{AP}$ annotates each state with a set of propositions from the finite set AP. These are the propositions that hold in that states, while the rest of the propositions in AP do not hold in that state (see Section 4.8).

For automata that represent systems, we often set *all* the states S to be accepting. In fact, we distinguish between accepting and nonaccepting states only when modeling systems that impose some fairness conditions [3]. The set of accepting states are thus sometimes called the *fairness condition* of the system[1].

---

[1] For various fairness conditions, it is not sufficient to annotate the automaton with the Büchi acceptance conditions (although, due to the equivalence between various kinds of ω-automata, it is possible to transfer the automaton into one that expresses the fair sequences of the original system). One can use acceptance conditions that have more structure (e.g., Generalized Büchi conditions, described in Section 6.4.)

A Büchi automaton is nondeterministic if, given the next input letter from Σ it has a choice between the next states. That is, there are two states $r_1, r_2 \in S$ such that $L(r_1) = L(r_2)$, and either (1) $r_1, r_2 \in I$, or (2) there are at least two transitions $(s, r_1), (s, r_2) \in \Delta$ from the same state $s \in S$. Nondeterministic Büchi automata may have more than a single run for a given input. Note that according to the definition of acceptance, if *there is* an accepting run for v, then v is included in the language $\mathcal{L}(\mathcal{A})$ of $\mathcal{A}$.

A specification of a property of a system $\mathcal{A}$ can be given as an automaton $\mathcal{B}$ over the same alphabet as $\mathcal{A}$. The system $\mathcal{A}$ satisfies the specification $\mathcal{B}$ when there is an inclusion between the language of the system $\mathcal{A}$, and the language of the specification $\mathcal{B}$. That is, $\mathcal{L}(\mathcal{A}) \subseteq \mathcal{L}(\mathcal{B})$. Thus, each behavior of the modeled system must be included among the behaviors that are allowed by the specification. This simple formalism can be used as a basis for automatic verification, as explained in the next chapter.

In practice, it is sometimes inefficient to use specification automata where each state corresponds to a single assignment of the propositional variables AP. Consider the automaton on the left in Figure 5.3. It has three states, r_1, r_2 and r_3. These states have a common successor and predecessor, the state q. This situation, where several states have the same successors and predecessors is quite common. To obtain a smaller and a simpler representation of the automaton, we combine such states into one state. We do that by replacing the states that share the same successors and predecessor (in this case, r_1, r_2 and r_3, with assignments $\{A\}$, $\{A, B\}$ and $\emptyset$), by one state r, labeled with a propositional formula that is satisfied by exactly these assignments. The label $\{B\}$ of the state q is replaced by the corresponding propositional formula $(\neg A) \wedge B$. The simplified automaton is shown on the right in Figure 5.3.

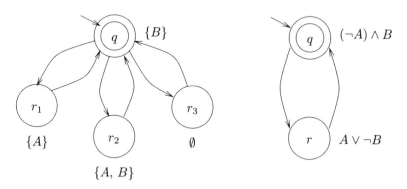

Fig. 5.3. Two representations for a Büchi automaton

Accordingly, we change the definition of an automaton. The only change is that each state now corresponds to several assignments over AP. Thus, our labeling function will be $L : S \rightarrow 2^{2^{AP}}$, where $2^{2^{AP}}$ denotes a set of subsets of AP. Such a set of subsets can be represented using a propositional formula. Each state $s \in S$ is then mapped into a formula φ_s. The labelings that are allowed by s are those that satisfy φ_s. In the example in Figure 5.3, the formula $A \vee (\neg B)$ corresponds to the states $\{\{A\}, \{A, B\}, \emptyset\}$. Each one of these states satisfies this formula, while the state $\{A\}$ does not. Note that with the redefined class of automata, we did not extend the languages we can recognize. Rather, we provided a way to achieve a more compact representation.

We need to redefine a run of such an automaton. The appropriate change is in the last condition of the definition of a run, i.e., the requirement that the input letters agree with the labeling on the states. The alphabet for the input word is still $\Sigma = 2^{AP}$. In the case where $L(\rho(i))$ is denoted as a propositional formula, we can write the corresponding condition as

$$v(i) \models L(\rho(i)).$$

Nondeterminism needs to be defined carefully in this extended context. Again, an automaton is nondeterministic if given the next input letter from Σ, it has a choice between between the next states. This happens when there are two states r_1, $r_2 \in S$ such that $L(r_1) \wedge L(r_2) \neq false$ ('$\neq$' means here 'not logically equivalent to', i.e., the conjunction is not a contradiction) and either (1) $r_1, r_2 \in I$, or (2) there are two transitions (s, r_1), $(s, r_2) \in \Delta$ from the same state $s \in S$. According to this definition, the automaton in Figure 5.5 is deterministic, while the one in Figure 5.6 is nondeterministic.

Of course, any state labeled by a condition that is logically equivalent to *false* can be removed, together with its in-edges and out-edges. This is because the state condition cannot be satisfied by any assignment, and therefore, cannot participate in any run. Additional simplifications of automata include the removing of nodes that cannot be reached from any initial state, again with all of their in-edges and out-edges.

Examples for Büchi Automata Specifications

Figure 5.4 shows an automaton that specifies the *mutual exclusion* property that the two processes cannot enter their critical sections (CR_0 and CR_1) at the same time. The proposition $inCR_0$ ($inCR_1$) labels the states where process P_0 (P_1, respectively) is in its critical section. The mutual exclusion requirement is expressed in LTL as $\Box \neg (inCR_0 \wedge inCR_1)$. Note that there is no state in this Büchi automaton that is labeled by $inCR_0 \wedge inCR_1$ Thus, according to the definition of a run of a Büchi automaton, there can be no run over a word that contains such a label. Thus, there cannot be an accepting run of this automaton over a word that reaches a state where $inCR_0 \wedge inCR_1$.

Figure 5.5 shows an automaton that specifies a liveness property. Informally, a liveness property requires something to eventually happen [83]. The property in Figure 5.5 asserts that a process will eventually enter its critical section, expressed in LTL as $\Diamond inCR_0$.

$$\neg(inCR_0 \wedge inCR_1)$$

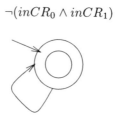

Fig. 5.4. Mutual exclusion

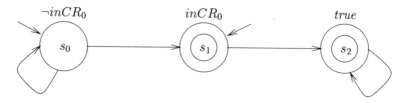

Fig. 5.5. A liveness property

5.7 Deterministic Büchi Automata

Deterministic Büchi automata seem conceptually simpler than nondeterministic ones. However, there exist nondeterministic Büchi automata for which there is no equivalent deterministic automaton.

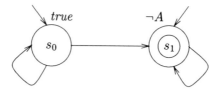

Fig. 5.6. An automaton accepting words where A holds finitely many times

Consider the language of infinite words over $AP = \{A\}$ that includes the words where A holds finitely many times. Note that this means that every word accepted by this automaton has some suffix where no state satisfies A. This language can be accepted by a nondeterministic Büchi automaton, as shown in Figure 5.6. The state s_0 is labeled by *true*, or equivalently by $A \vee \neg A$. Thus, given that the automaton is in state s_0 and the next input letter is A, it has the choice of either staying in s_0 or moving to s_1. On an input v, the automaton stays in the self loop s_0 until some point where it 'guesses' that there will be no more states satisfying A. Then it moves to s_1. Since the automaton is nondeterministic, it is sufficient that there will be one such correct guess in order to accept v.

We will show that there is no deterministic automaton that can recognize this language [141]. Suppose there were a deterministic Büchi automaton that recognized this language. Then it would have to reach some accepting state after a finite string $(\neg A)^{n_1}$ for some $n_1 \geq 0$ Otherwise, the word $(\neg A)^\omega$ could not be accepted. (Recall that in a deterministic automaton, for each input word there can be at most one run.) Continuing from this state, this deterministic automaton must reach an accepting state after $(\neg A)^{n_1} A(\neg A)^{n_2}$, for some $n_2 \geq 0$, and so forth. Thus, this automaton would accept a word of the form $(\neg A)^{n_1} A(\neg A)^{n_2} A(\neg A)^{n_3} \ldots$, which contains infinitely many states satisfying A, a contradiction.

It is interesting to notice that the complement of this language, i.e., the language of infinite words with infinitely many As can be recognized by a deterministic automaton. To see this, consider the automaton shown in Figure 5.2, and let $\alpha = A$ and $\beta = \neg A$. Thus, we can conclude that the set of languages accepted by deterministic Büchi automata is not closed under complementation.

A language $\mathcal{L}(\mathcal{A})$ over some alphabet Σ, recognized by a deterministic Büchi automaton $\mathcal{A}$, satisfies the following:

> For each infinite word σ over Σ, σ is in $\mathcal{L}(\mathcal{A})$ exactly when there are infinitely many finite prefixes of σ for which the corresponding finite run of $\mathcal{A}$ reaches an accepting state.

This stems from the fact that in a deterministic Büchi automaton, for each word, and thus for every prefix of a word, there at most one run.

5.8 Alternative Specification Formalisms

In Chapter 6 we will show that every propositional LTL specification can be translated into a corresponding Büchi automaton. Thus, the expressiveness of Büchi automata (the set of specifications or languages that can be described) is at least as big as for LTL. In fact, the former is strictly more expressive. For example, LTL cannot express the language of infinite words where A holds in *at least* the even states [147] (counting from 0). A Büchi automaton for recognizing this language appears in Figure 5.7. Note that we did not impose any restriction on the odd states, and thus A may hold also in some of the odd states. If, in addition, we required that A *does not* hold in any odd state, then we could have easily express this language within LTL.

The following formalisms are as expressive as Büchi automata:

Monadic second order logic [22]. This logic is interpreted over mathematical structures that include the following components:

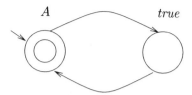

Fig. 5.7. Automaton for identifying words where A holds in even places

Nat The set of *natural* numbers.

$Q_A, Q_B, \ldots$ Unary ('monadic') relations. Each such relation defines a subset of the *naturals* where it holds. Such a relation Q_A is related to an LTL proposition A in the following sense: $Q_A(i)$ holds when A holds on the ith state of the sequence.

$<$ is the usual order relation on the *natural* numbers.

succ is the successor relation on the *natural* numbers.

0 is the constant denoting the smallest natural number.

Note that the use of both *succ* and 0 can be eliminated by using the relation $<$. As a second order logic, it allows quantification on both simple variables set variables. For example, we can write a monadic second order logic formula of the form $\exists X \, \varphi$, where X is a set of *naturals* variable (whereas $Q_A, Q_B, \ldots$ are unary relation 'constants'). Then, inside φ, we can use $y \in X$, where y is a simple variable (over the *naturals*). The property that A appears in (at least) all the even places can be expressed as follows:

$$\exists X (0 \in X \land \forall y \forall z (succ(y,z) \to (y \in X \leftrightarrow \neg z \in X))$$
$$\land \forall y (y \in X \to Q_A(y)))$$

This formula asserts that there is a set of *naturals* X which contains 0 (denoted $0 \in X$), and for each pair of *naturals* such that one of them is the successor of the other, it contains exactly one element. The set X is contained in the relation Q_A (corresponding to the proposition A). It is satisfied by the set of sequences that are accepted by the automaton in Figure 5.7.

LTL with quantification. One can extend LTL by allowing second order quantification. The quantified variables can be used as any other proposition within the scope of their quantifier. The above property can then be expressed in quantified LTL as

$$\exists X \left((X \land \Box(X \to \bigcirc \neg X) \land \Box(\neg X \to \bigcirc X)) \land \Box(X \to A)\right)$$

ω-**regular expressions.** These are regular expressions extended with the infinite-iteration operator 'ω'. The above property can be expressed using the ω-regular expression $(A\Sigma)^\omega$, where Σ denotes any state over 2^{AP}, and A denotes any state where A holds.

Monadic *first order logic* is obtained from monadic second order logic, shown above, by disallowing set variables (and hence quantification over such variables). It is equivalent in its expressive power to LTL.

Intuitively, Büchi automata use their finite state structure as a finite memory. A property that requires unbounded memory cannot be specified using this formalism, and hence also cannot be specified using the less expressive LTL. Although programs are in practice limited to finitely many states, the formal description of algorithms often uses unbounded structures for specification. This often gives a more intuitive and concise specification.

Consider fifo (first-in, first-out) message passing, where the messages are over some finite domain M. The abstract description of fifo queues does not put a constraint on the size of the buffer. We may add such a constraint if we want to do so; we can, in theory, use the knowledge that a particular fifo queue is limited to some given finite size to provide a finite state specification. Such a specification can provide an exact account of all the possible queue contents allowed under fifo regime, limited to some specific number of messages. However, this will lack the intuitive appeal of the abstract fifo representation that does not impose a particular constraint.

Many standard structures, such as fifo queues, cannot be expressed directly using Büchi automata or LTL formulas [133]. Suppose that the operation of inserting an element x into the queue is represented by the proposition add_x, and the operation of removing an element x from the top of the queue is represented by the proposition $remove_x$. In this case, the finite memory capability of Büchi automata is insufficient to describe the set of sequences of add_x and $remove_x$ that correspond to the fifo behavior.

The expressive power of a specification formalism is not the only important criterion one needs to consider. One should also consider the complexity of checking whether a given system (expressed in some formalism, e.g., as an automaton) satisfies its given specification. For example, although monadic first or second order logics have the same expressive power as LTL or Büchi automata, respectively, they are not often used for model checking. This is because they admit a too succinct representation of properties such that translating the representation into automata, or to an equivalent LTL formula, may result in a NONELEMENTARY explosion [134].

The complexity of checking monadic first or second order logic specification against a given finite state system is in general NONELEMENTARY in the size of the formula. This may prohibit the use of such succinct specification formalisms for model checking. On the other hand, checking LTL specification against a finite state system is in PSPACE-complete (see Section 6.9). However, one can show that some specifications that are expressed in monadic second (first, respectively) order formulas have equivalent Büchi automata (LTL formulas, respectively) of minimal size that are NONELEMENTARY bigger [134]. Thus, one can argue that the inherently hard complexity depends on the property to be verified rather than on the formalism used. Moreover, the

NONELEMENTARY explosion is not necessary the case for arbitrary monadic first or second order logic properties. Hence, systems such as MONA [41], can successfully verify properties expressed using monadic second order logic.

In practice, for most purposes, it is sufficient to use a limited number of small LTL properties to specify most of the requirements for both hardware and software.

5.9 Complicated Specifications

Experience shows that there is a small number of simple properties common to many system specifications [93]. On the other hand, there are cases where systems require some unique and nonstandard properties to hold.

One such case is in specifying *feature interaction*. A software system often has to provide a number of features. A typical example is a telephone switch, which handles many different services, such as simple calls, toll free calls, conference calls, etc. When adding a new feature, it is required that its behavior will not interfere in an unexpected way with that of existing features. Providing an exact specification for feature interaction is a difficult challenge.

Another example involves consistency with *legacy code*. We would like to keep the behavior of a newly developed code consistent with some old code. The specification of the old code may not exist in documentation, and may only be known implicitly by a few veteran developers.

In both of these examples, using a specification formalism to describe the required properties of the system provides only part of the solution. One may need to compare different versions or parts of systems, and show a correspondence in behavior. Comparing behavior of different systems can be done in the context of process algebra, described in Chapter 8. There, different systems can be compared using a variety of comparison criteria. Nevertheless, dealing with problems such as feature interaction and consistency with legacy code has not been completely resolved, and poses practical challenges to software engineers.

5.10 Completeness of Specification

It is clear that a system must satisfy its specification. However, it is difficult to determine when enough specification is given. It is not always the case that all the important requirements are imposed when a new system is designed. Sometimes, even after deploying the system, some important constraints are not considered. In many cases, it is possible to check algorithmically that a given set of requirements do not contradict each other (see Section 6.11). However, checking whether a set of constraints is *complete*, i.e., includes every reasonable requirement, is in general not feasible. This is because there can be additional requirements that we may impose on the system.

Consider, as an example of an incomplete specification, a system whose input is a sequence of array variables $A[1], \ldots, A[n]$ and whose output is a variable *sum*, containing their summation. We can specify the following: Initially, $A[1], \ldots, A[n]$ and n are *naturals*. At termination, we have $sum = \Sigma_{i=1}^{n} A[i]$.

This is not a complete specification. The implementation in which 0 is assigned to all the array variables and to *sum* satisfies the specification. What we 'forgot' to mention is that the array variables do not change during the execution. Are we complete now? Not yet, since we also need to specify that n is not changed during the execution as well.

The completeness of the specification depends basically on the ingenuity of the designer. Nevertheless, there are a number of 'standard' properties of software systems, several of them mentioned in this chapter, against which we can compare our set of requirements.

Specification Exercises

Exercise 5.10.1. Give an LTL specification for Dijkstra's provisional mutual exclusion algorithm in Section 4.6 and to Dekker's mutual exclusion algorithm in Section 4.6.

Exercise 5.10.2. Specify the properties of an elevator system. Use the following propositions:

at_i The elevator is at the ith floor.
go_up The elevator is going up.
go_down The elevator is going down.
$between_i$ The elevator is between the floor i and $i + 1$.
stop The elevator is not moving.
open The elevator door is open.
$press\_up_i$ Someone is pressing the *up* button on the ith floor.
$memory\_up_i$ The elevator 'remembers' that the *up* button was pressed on the ith floor.
$press\_down_i$ Someone is pressing the *down* button on the ith floor.
$memory\_down_i$ The elevator remembers that the *down* button was pressed on the ith floor.
$press_i$ Someone is pressing the button for the ith floor inside the elevator.
$memory\_press_i$ The elevator remembers that someone was pressing the button for the ith floor inside the elevator.
alarm The elevator alarm is sounding.

The specification should include at least the following properties:

• If a button is pushed on the third floor, the elevator will reach that floor.

- The elevator is never on the first and second floor at the same time.
- If the elevator is not moving, the door is open.
- If no button is pushed and the elevator is on the fourth floor, the elevator will wait on that floor until a button is pushed.
- Whenever the elevator becomes stuck between the floors, the alarm sounds until the elevator resumes moving.

Exercise 5.10.3. Specify properties required from the communication protocol in Section 4.15. In particular, specify the following properties:

- The *Sender* process does not send the next message as long as the previous message was not accepted by the *Receiver*.
- If every message sent by the *Sender* is lost only finitely many times, then each message sent eventually arrives at the *Receiver*.

5.11 Further Reading

A book on software specification is

V. S. Alagar, K. Periyasamy, *Specification of Software Systems*, Springer-Verlag, 1998.

Two surveys on Büchi automata and monadic second order logic by Wolfgang Thomas are

W. Thomas, Automata on infinite objects, in *Handbook of Theoretical Computer Science*, vol. B, J. van Leeuwen (ed)., Elsevier, (1990) 133–191.

W. Thomas, Languages, Automata, and Logic, in *Handbook of Formal Language Theory*, G. Rozenberg, A. Salomaa, (eds.), Volume 3, Springer-Verlag, 389–455.

The temporal approach for specification is extensively described in the following books:

Z. Manna, A. Pnueli, *The Temporal Logic of Reactive and Concurrent Systems: Specification*, Springer-Verlag, 1991.

F. Kröger, *Temporal Logic of Programs*, EATCS Monographs on Theoretical Computer Science, Springer-Verlag, 1992.

A more general perspective on temporal logic can be found in the following survey paper:

E. A. Emerson, Temporal and Modal Logic, in *Handbook of Theoretical Computer Science*, vol. B, J. van Leeuwen (ed.), Elsevier, (1990), 995–1072.

6. Automatic Verification

She went on and on, a long way, but wherever the road divided there were sure to be two finger-posts pointing the same way, one marked 'TO TWEEDLEDUM's HOUSE' and the other 'TO THE HOUSE OF TWEEDLEDEE.'
'I do believe,' said Alice at last, 'that they live in the same house!'

Lewis Carroll, *Through the Looking Glass*

Fully automated verification of software is certainly a very desirable goal: one would like to have a tool that accepts the inspected software, together with its specification, as input; the tool would check, without any human intervention, whether the given software satisfies its specification. However, from computability theory (see Section 2), we know that we cannot expect to build such a tool for a broad enough class of programs. Nevertheless, the theoretical restriction must not stop us from seeking a practical solution for checking the correctness of software.

Some possible ideas that can help to achieve this goal are:

- Restricting the focus of the verification to a smaller class of programs, for which an automatic verification algorithm is possible. In model checking, which will be described later in this chapter, such a class includes programs with finitely many states.
- Instead of verifying a whole system, focusing on simple, yet crucial parts of it. For example, one can verify:
  - the underlying basic algorithms,
  - a restricted version of the system, e.g., by setting (small) bounds to values of variables, message queue sizes, etc., or
  - the underlying communication protocols of a concurrent system.
- Using abstraction methods to hide or remove some of the details of the programs, resulting in a simpler program (e.g., again, a finite state system). The abstraction may be performed manually, since the existence of an abstraction algorithm that could *always* reduce the verification problem into a decidable one would contradict the undecidability result. As a consequence, there is a potential gap between the actual system and the verified version. Thus, the verification process achieves an enhanced, but not absolute, confidence in the correctness of the checked system.

- Using human assisted verification methods. For example, use manual deductive theorem proving to verify parts of the system, e.g., verifying a proposed abstraction transformation, and reduce the verification problem to a simpler and decidable one. This will be further discussed in Section 10.1.

This chapter presents a collection of techniques for automatically verifying properties of systems with finitely many states. One of the first suggestions to exploit finite state machines (automata) in formal methods was by Bochmann [16], who used them to model communication protocols. Zafiropulo [150] developed an algorithm based on state space search for analyzing communication protocols, modeled using finite state machines. West and Zafiropulo [146] used this algorithm for verifying the CCITT X.21 communication protocol. *Model checking*, i.e., the algorithmic verification of programs against temporal logic specifications, was pioneered independently by Clarke and Emerson [28, 42] in the US and by Quielle and Sifakis [120] in France.

Even when the focus is restricted to finite state systems, one often has to deal with an inherent high complexity involved in verification. A finite state program can still have an enormous number of states. Concurrent systems are in particular difficult, since the number of possible states can run as high as the product of the states in each one of their components. For this reason, model checking tools use a wide range of heuristics, intended to combat this state space explosion problem.

6.1 State Space Search

Consider a finite state system with a set of initial states I. The following algorithm searches the state space, visiting every state that is reachable from the initial states. It uses two lists of states, *new* and *old*.

State space search algorithm

1   Let *new* contain the set of initial states I and *old* be empty;
2   While *new* is not empty do
3   Choose some state s from *new*;
4   Remove s from *new*;
5   Add s to *old*;
6   For each transition t that is enabled at s do
7   Apply transition t to s, obtaining s';
8   If s' is not already in *new* or in *old* then
9   Add s' to *new*;

This algorithm does not specify how to choose the state s from *new* at line 3 and how to store new elements in *new* at line 9. There are several ways to do so. One of them is to implement *new* as a queue, i.e., remove elements from it on a first-in first-out basis. Thus, new elements are appended to the end of *new*. This search strategy is called *breadth-first search* (BFS). It can be shown that states are added to *new* in the following way: first, the queue *new* contains the initial states, then states whose distance (i.e., the length of the minimal path) from a state in I is 1 are added to the end of *new*. Then states with distance 2 are added, and so forth.

Consider a search of the graph in Figure 2.1 using BFS, with $I = \{r_1\}$. The columns *new*, s and *old* in the following table represent the values of these variables in successive iterations at line 4, and the last line represents their values at the end of the execution.

new	s	old
$\langle r_1 \rangle$	r_1	$\langle \rangle$
$\langle r_2 \rangle$	r_2	$\langle r_1 \rangle$
$\langle r_3, r_5 \rangle$	r_3	$\langle r_1, r_2 \rangle$
$\langle r_5, r_4 \rangle$	r_5	$\langle r_1, r_2, r_3 \rangle$
$\langle r_4, r_9, r_6 \rangle$	r_4	$\langle r_1, r_2, r_3, r_5 \rangle$
$\langle r_9, r_6, r_8 \rangle$	r_9	$\langle r_1, r_2, r_3, r_5, r_4 \rangle$
$\langle r_6, r_8, r_7 \rangle$	r_6	$\langle r_1, r_2, r_3, r_5, r_4, r_9 \rangle$
$\langle r_8, r_7 \rangle$	r_8	$\langle r_1, r_2, r_3, r_5, r_4, r_9, r_6 \rangle$
$\langle r_7 \rangle$	r_7	$\langle r_1, r_2, r_3, r_5, r_4, r_9, r_6, r_8 \rangle$
$\langle \rangle$		$\langle r_1, r_2, r_3, r_5, r_4, r_9, r_6, r_8, r_7 \rangle$

We expand the states (when we select them from the list *new*, according to line 4 of the algorithm) in the order r_1, r_2, r_3, r_5, r_4, r_9, r_6, r_8, r_7. This is not the only order possible under BFS, since different successors of the same state (e.g., r_3 and r_5, which are successors of r_2) may be added to *new* in a different order.

A different strategy is to implement *new* as a stack, i.e., removing the states on a last-in first-out basis. This strategy of search is called *depth-first search* (DFS). Consider again the case where we search the graph in Figure 2.1 using DFS, starting with $I = \{r_1\}$. The following table summarize the values of *new*, s and *old* at line 4 in each successive iteration, and at the end of the execution.

new	s	old
$\langle r_1 \rangle$	r_1	$\langle \rangle$
$\langle r_2 \rangle$	r_2	$\langle r_1 \rangle$
$\langle r_3, r_5 \rangle$	r_3	$\langle r_1, r_2 \rangle$
$\langle r_4, r_5 \rangle$	r_4	$\langle r_1, r_2, r_3 \rangle$
$\langle r_8, r_5 \rangle$	r_8	$\langle r_1, r_2, r_3, r_4 \rangle$
$\langle r_5 \rangle$	r_5	$\langle r_1, r_2, r_3, r_4, r_8 \rangle$
$\langle r_9, r_6 \rangle$	r_9	$\langle r_1, r_2, r_3, r_4, r_8, r_5 \rangle$
$\langle r_7, r_6 \rangle$	r_7	$\langle r_1, r_2, r_3, r_4, r_8, r_5, r_9 \rangle$
$\langle r_6 \rangle$	r_6	$\langle r_1, r_2, r_3, r_4, r_8, r_5, r_9, r_7 \rangle$
$\langle \rangle$		$\langle r_1, r_2, r_3, r_4, r_8, r_5, r_9, r_7, r_6 \rangle$

We thus expand the states in the order $r_1, r_2, r_3, r_5, r_4, r_8, r_9, r_6, r_7$. Again, this is not the only possible order in which the states are expanded in DFS.

A simple search, as performed by the above algorithm, can be used for checking invariants of finite state systems. These are properties that can be expressed as LTL formulas of the form $\Box\varphi$, where φ is a first order or propositional formula. The above search algorithm needs then to check whether the initial states (in line 1) and each new state (in line 9) added to the set *new* satisfy φ.

Suppose that a state that is reachable from the initial state and does not satisfy φ is found by the search algorithm. In addition to the knowledge about the existence of such a state, it is also interesting to know how such a state is generated. In other words, it is valuable to obtain a path that starts from some initial state in I and ends with a state that violates φ. Such a path corresponds to a prefix of an execution. This can help finding, in addition to the existence of an error, also the cause for its occurrence. We can recover such a path by keeping for each state a single edge, pointing backwards to the unique predecessor state from which it was first discovered during the search[1]. That is, in line 9, we keep a back pointer from s' to s (notice that this pointer direction goes contrary to the direction of edges in the state space graph). In Figure 6.1, the sequence of nodes generated under DFS are presented, together with the backward edges. If φ is violated, for example, in state r_9, we can trace back the path r_1, r_2, r_5, r_9, starting with the (unique, in this case) initial state.

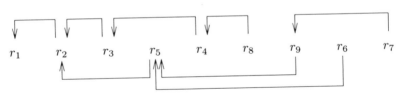

Fig. 6.1. A DFS traversal of nodes with backward edges

It is a property of the BFS algorithm that a counterexample generated in this way is of minimal length. For DFS, this does not necessarily hold. Checking properties other than invariants can be more complicated and will be described in the following sections.

---

[1] In a *recursive* implementation of DFS, common in model checking, the counter example resides on the recursion stack.

6.2 Representing States

For the purpose of the automatic verification algorithms presented in this chapter, it is important to represent each state with enough information that will allow us to calculate its successors with respect to the enabled transitions. It is also important to be able to distinguish each state from other, different states. Without being able to check when we reach the same state again, the search may not terminate.

A typical state representation includes an assignment of values to the program variables, the program counter, and for message passing systems, the message queues. Programs that use complicated data structures such as stacks and trees often result in a state space that is too large to be automatically analyzed.

A subtle point about representing states, which is often ignored, is that one should not use a representation that distinguishes between states that are essentially the same. To demonstrate this, consider the following example [67]: a system has two communication queues $qu0$ and $qu1$. Instead of using two different queue variables, the system is modeled with one list that includes the information of both. The messages are put into this list according to the order in which they arrive. Each message is tagged with either 0 or 1, so that it is possible to check and retrieve the head of each one of the original queues using a linear search of the single queue content.

This seemingly simple representation incurs a severe penalty. Consider the case where $qu0$ and $qu1$ receive n messages each. This could have been represented by a state that includes the corresponding queue contents using two separate queue variables. In the single list representation, there are many different ways of interleaving the messages of the two queues in the single list, according to the order in which the messages of the different queues arrived with respect to each other. This order is irrelevant here (it can be deduced from the sequence of states, if it is of any interest). Instead of a single state representing both queues, the single list representation can have $(2n)!/(n!^2)$ different states. For example, if $n = 5$, there can be 252 states with a single list representing the different ways to interleave the two separate queues.

The way states are stored in the computer memory has a profound effect on the efficiency of model checking. In order to be able to retrieve states quickly, while keeping the memory size manageable, the states are usually kept in a hash table. Compression techniques are also used to minimize the space used [65].

6.3 The Automata Framework

The model checking approach that we will present here is based on automata theory. It allows bringing both the checked system and the specification into the same representation, namely that of Büchi automata. The relationship between automata theory and other research areas, and the wealth of related results, helps in developing new model checking algorithms. Other useful connections relate automata theory with various logics [141], such as temporal logics, monadic first and second order logic and regular expressions. This helps in developing model checking algorithms for specifications expressed in these formalisms.

The automata theoretic framework for model checking was suggested independently by Kurshan [4] and Vardi and Wolper [144]. The presentation in this chapter is also influenced by the work of Alpern and Schneider [5]. We will present some basic facts from automata theory and demonstrate how model checking can be done in this framework. In particular, we will present model checking for linear temporal logic using automata.

Recall that we can represent both the state space and the specification as automata over the same alphabet. The system model $\mathcal{A}$ satisfies the specification $\mathcal{B}$ if there is an inclusion between the language of the system $\mathcal{A}$ and the language of the specification $\mathcal{B}$, i.e.,

$$\mathcal{L}(\mathcal{A}) \subseteq \mathcal{L}(\mathcal{B}) \tag{6.1}$$

(see also Figure 4.7).

Let $\overline{\mathcal{L}(\mathcal{B})}$ be the language $\Sigma^\omega \setminus \mathcal{L}(\mathcal{B})$ of words *not accepted* by $\mathcal{B}$, i.e., the *complement* of the language $\mathcal{L}(\mathcal{B})$. Then, the above inclusion (6.1) can be rewritten as

$$\mathcal{L}(\mathcal{A}) \cap \overline{\mathcal{L}(\mathcal{B})} = \emptyset \tag{6.2}$$

This means that there is no accepted word of $\mathcal{A}$ that is disallowed by $\mathcal{B}$. If the intersection is not empty, any element in it is a counterexample to (6.1).

Implementing the language intersection in (6.2) is simpler than implementing the language inclusion in (6.1); the algorithm for checking for the emptiness of the language obtained from the intersection of two automata is simpler than the algorithm for checking for language inclusion. Indeed, as we will see in Section 6.5, complementing a Büchi automaton is difficult. However, when the source of the specification is an LTL formula φ, we can avoid complementation. This is done by translating the negation of the checked formula φ, i.e., translating $\neg\varphi$ into an automaton $\overline{\mathcal{B}}$ directly rather than translating φ into an automaton $\mathcal{B}$ and then complementing.

Due to the possibility of introducing modeling errors while forming the model $\mathcal{A}$, representing the original checked system, one has to carefully evaluate the results of an automatic verification process. One possible problem may occur when $\mathcal{A}$ underspecifies the modeled system. Consequently, some of these executions are not included in $\mathcal{L}(\mathcal{A})$. This may allow the inclusion (6.1) to hold and the model checking process to report that the model satisfies the specification even when this is not the case for the actual system.

Conversely, $\mathcal{A}$ may overspecify the modeled system. Consequently, when a counterexample is reported, one has to check that modeling errors did not introduce an incorrect counterexample, called a *false negative*. This can happen when $\mathcal{L}(\mathcal{A})$ contains an execution that does not correspond to the behavior of the modeled system. Comparing a counterexample against the modeled system is rather simple. Thus, finding a counterexample during model checking is often considered much more valuable than a conclusion that the model of the program satisfies the specification.

As will be discussed in the next section, Büchi automata are closed under intersection, union and complementation. This means that there exists an automaton that accepts exactly the intersection or the union of the languages of the two given automata, and an automaton that recognizes exactly the complement of the language of a given automaton. We will sometimes informally say that we take the intersection or the union of two automata, meaning that we construct an automaton that recognizes the intersection or the union of the languages of these automata.

The formulation of the correctness criterion in (6.2) suggests the following general strategy for model checking:

> First, complement the automaton $\mathcal{B}$, i.e., construct an automaton $\overline{\mathcal{B}}$ that recognizes the language $\overline{\mathcal{L}(\mathcal{B})}$. (Alternatively, generate the complement specification $\overline{\mathcal{B}}$ directly.) Then, intersect the automata $\mathcal{A}$ and $\overline{\mathcal{B}}$. If the intersection is empty, the specification $\mathcal{B}$ holds for $\mathcal{A}$. Otherwise, use an accepted word of the nonempty intersection as a counterexample.

The following sections provide more specific details about implementing this strategy using Büchi automata.

6.4 Combining Büchi Automata

An important property for a specification formalism is its closure under the Boolean operators 'and', 'or' and 'not'. In terms of languages, these operators correspond to intersection, union and complementation, respectively. To see this, consider for example intersection. Let φ, ψ be some specification over sequences, such that $\mathcal{L}(\varphi)$ are the sequences that satisfy the property φ, i.e., $\{\sigma | \sigma \models \varphi\}$. Then

$$\mathcal{L}(\varphi \wedge \psi) = \{\sigma | \sigma \models \varphi \text{ and } \sigma \models \psi\} = \mathcal{L}(\varphi) \cap \mathcal{L}(\psi).$$

We will see that Büchi automata are indeed closed under these operators. This is particularly important, since we saw in (6.2) that model checking can be translated into intersection and complementation of automata.

Consider a pair of automata $\mathcal{A}_1 = \langle \Sigma, S_1, \Delta_1, I_1, L_1, F_1 \rangle$ and $\mathcal{A}_2 = \langle \Sigma, S_2, \Delta_2, I_2, L_2, F_2 \rangle$ over a joint alphabet Σ. One can build the union automaton $\mathcal{A}_1 \cup \mathcal{A}_2$, provided that $S_1 \cap S_2 = \emptyset$. (If $S_1 \cap S_2 \neq \emptyset$, one can rename states.) The language of $\mathcal{A}_1 \cup \mathcal{A}_2$ is the union of the languages of the individual automata, i.e., $\mathcal{L}(\mathcal{A}_1 \cup \mathcal{A}_2) = \mathcal{L}(\mathcal{A}_1) \cup \mathcal{L}(\mathcal{A}_2)$ (hence it is called the union automaton).

The union automaton $\mathcal{A}_1 \cup \mathcal{A}_2$ is

$$\langle \Sigma, \ S_1 \cup S_2, \ \Delta_1 \cup \Delta_2, \ I_1 \cup I_2, \ L_1 \cup L_2, \ F_1 \cup F_2 \rangle.$$

The labeling $L = L_1 \cup L_2$ agrees with L_1 and L_2, namely if $s \in S_1$, then $L(s) = L_1(s)$, and if $s \in S_2$, then $L(s) = L_2(s)$. The union automaton has a nondeterministic choice between behaving according to $\mathcal{A}_1$ or behaving according to $\mathcal{A}_2$. The choice is made by selecting an initial state from either I_1 or I_2, and thereafter behaving according to the appropriate automaton. When automata $\mathcal{A}_1$ and $\mathcal{A}_2$ represent specifications, their union corresponds to the disjunction of the specifications: either behaving according to the specification of $\mathcal{A}_1$, or behave according to the specification of $\mathcal{A}_2$. The union includes the languages of both automata, thus allows the specified system to behave in either way. Generalizing the union to n automata is clear.

An intersection automaton $\mathcal{A}_1 \cap \mathcal{A}_2$, which accepts the intersection $\mathcal{L}(\mathcal{A}_1) \cap \mathcal{L}(\mathcal{A}_2)$, corresponds to the conjunction of the specifications given by $\mathcal{A}_1$ and $\mathcal{A}_2$. The intersection contains only words accepted by both automata. Consequently, each run of the intersection automaton needs to simulate two simultaneous runs of the input, one on each automaton $\mathcal{A}_1$ and $\mathcal{A}_2$. We will ignore for the moment the acceptance conditions, and will deal with them later. Each state of the intersection automaton is related to both a state of $\mathcal{A}_1$ and a state of $\mathcal{A}_2$. In a simultaneous run of both automata, the input sequence must satisfy the state conditions (which are the labels on the states) in both, state by state. Thus, the condition on a state in the intersection is the conjunction of the conditions of the components.

Consider the two automata in Figure 6.2. The four combinations of the states are as follows:

$$
\begin{aligned}
L(\langle q_0, q_2 \rangle) &= L_1(q_0) \wedge L_2(q_2) = A \wedge (\neg B) \wedge (\neg A) \wedge B &&= \textit{false} \\
L(\langle q_0, q_3 \rangle) &= L_1(q_0) \wedge L_2(q_3) = A \wedge (\neg B) \wedge (A \vee (\neg B)) &&= A \wedge (\neg B) \\
L(\langle q_1, q_2 \rangle) &= L_1(q_1) \wedge L_2(q_2) = (\neg A) \wedge (\neg A) \wedge B &&= (\neg A) \wedge B \\
L(\langle q_1, q_3 \rangle) &= L_1(q_1) \wedge L_2(q_3) = (\neg A) \wedge (A \vee (\neg B)) &&= (\neg A) \wedge (\neg B)
\end{aligned}
$$

The left automaton in Figure 6.2 requires that in each state, either $A \wedge (\neg B)$ or $\neg A$ holds. In addition, for infinitely many states, $A \wedge (\neg B)$ holds. The right automaton requires that the initial state, and every even state (counting from 0), satisfy $(\neg A) \wedge B$. The rest of the states must satisfy $A \vee (\neg B)$.

Notice that for the pair $\langle q_0, q_2 \rangle$, the condition is $\textit{false}$. No run can pass through such a pair, since there is no assignment that can be satisfied by the formula $\textit{false}$. We can safely remove states labeled with $\textit{false}$, and their in-edges and out-edges. An edge between two states $\langle q, r \rangle$ and $\langle q', r' \rangle$ in the intersection exists when there is an edge between q and q' in $\mathcal{A}_1$, and an edge between r and r' in $\mathcal{A}_2$. The initial states are those pairs in which the components are initial states of $\mathcal{A}_1$ and $\mathcal{A}_2$, respectively. The resulting automaton, devoid of its accepting states, is shown in Figure 6.3.

It remains to be determined which states are accepting. This subtle issue will be demonstrated by first presenting two incorrect attempts. As a first

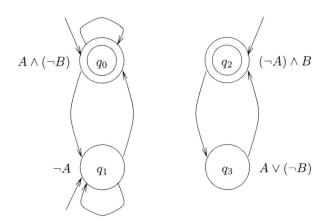

Fig. 6.2. Two automata to be intersected

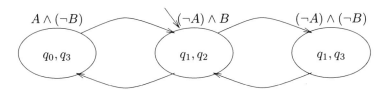

Fig. 6.3. Intermediate stage of intersection

attempt, suppose we set states of the intersection to be accepting when either the $\mathcal{A}_1$ component, *or* the $\mathcal{A}_2$ component is accepting. This will allow the automaton to accept a word if it visits the accepting states of one of the automata $\mathcal{A}_1$ or $\mathcal{A}_2$ infinitely often. In this case, the state $\langle q_0, q_3 \rangle$ will be accepting because of q_0, and $\langle q_1, q_2 \rangle$ will be accepting because of q_2. Under the Büchi acceptance condition, this will allow accepting an infinite sequence that passes through at least one of them, e.g., the sequence that cycles only through $\langle q_1, q_2 \rangle$ and $\langle q_1, q_3 \rangle$. Such a sequence will have no states satisfying $A \wedge \neg B$, as required to appear infinitely often by the left automaton in Figure 6.2.

In a second attempt, we set the accepting states of the intersection to be those where both components are accepting in $\mathcal{A}_1$ and $\mathcal{A}_2$, respectively. The problem in this case is that the two automata $\mathcal{A}_1$ and $\mathcal{A}_2$ may never reach their accepting states at the same time. In Figure 6.3, the pair $\langle q_0, q_3 \rangle$ includes the accepting state q_0 from $\mathcal{A}_1$, while q_3 is not accepting in $\mathcal{A}_2$. Similarly, the pair $\langle q_1, q_2 \rangle$ includes q_2, which is accepting in $\mathcal{A}_2$, and q_1, which is not accepting in $\mathcal{A}_1$. The third pair, $\langle q_1, q_3 \rangle$ includes states that are not accepting in either $\mathcal{A}_1$ and $\mathcal{A}_2$. Cosequently, in this example, no state will qualify to be accepting.

Thus, we need some way to make sure that we visit states from both accepting sets F_1 and F_2 infinitely often, although not necessarily simultaneously. The solution we provide is given in two stages: first we define a generalized version of Büchi automata, which will allow us dealing with multiple acceptance conditions. Next, we will show how to translate automata defined in the extended setting into simple Büchi automata. The definition of generalized Büchi automata will also be useful later, when a translation algorithm from LTL to automata will be presented.

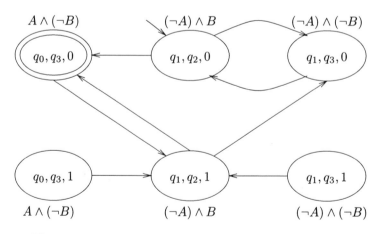

Fig. 6.4. The intersection of the automata in Figure 6.2

Generalized Büchi Automata

The structure of generalized Büchi automata differs from Büchi automata by allowing multiple accepting sets rather than only one. The structure is then a sextuple $\langle \Sigma, S, \Delta, I, L, F \rangle$, where $F = \{f_1, f_2, \ldots, f_m\}$, and each f_i, for $1 \leq i \leq m$, is a subset of S, namely $f_i \subseteq S$. The other components are the same as in simple Büchi automata. An accepting run needs to pass through each one of the sets in F infinitely often. Formally, a run ρ of a generalized Büchi automaton is accepting if *for each $f_i \in F$, $inf(\rho) \cap f_i \neq \emptyset$.*

The class of Büchi automata is clearly a special case of the class of generalized Büchi automata. However, we will show later that this definition of acceptance condition for generalized Büchi automata does not add expressive power over the usual Büchi automata. A translation from a generalized Büchi automaton to a simple Büchi automaton that accepts the same language will be given.

In the generalized Büchi automaton constructed for the intersection of two Büchi automata, we make one accepting set f_1 for states containing the first component from F_1, i.e., $F_1 \times S_2$, and another accepting set f_2 for states containing the second component from F_2, i.e., $S_1 \times F_2$. In the example of Figure 6.3, the first accepting set is the singleton $\{\langle q_0, q_3 \rangle\}$. (Notice that the state $\langle q_0, q_2 \rangle$ was removed due to its *false* condition). The second accepting set is the singleton $\{\langle q_1, q_2 \rangle\}$.

Translating from Generalized to Simple Büchi Automata

We present here a simple translation [34] from a generalized Büchi automaton $\langle \Sigma, S, \Delta, I, L, F \rangle$ to a (simple) Büchi automaton. If the number of accepting sets $|F|$ is m, we create m separate copies of the set of states S, namely, $\bigcup_{i=1,m} S_i$, where $S_i = S \times \{i\}$ for $1 \leq i \leq m$. Hence, a state of S_i will be of the form (s, i). Denote by $\oplus_m$ the addition operation changed such that $i \oplus_m 1 = i + 1$, when $1 \leq i < m$, and $m \oplus_m 1 = 1$. This operator allows us to count cyclically from 1 through m. In a run of the constructed Büchi automaton, when visiting the a states in S_i, if a copy of a state from f_i occurs, we move to the corresponding successor state in $S_{i \oplus_m 1}$. Otherwise, we move to the corresponding successor in S_i. Thus, visiting accepting states from all the sets in F in increasing order will make the automaton cycle through the m copies.

We need to select the accepting states such that each one of the copies S_1 through S_m is passed infinitely often. Since moving from one of the sets to the next one coincides with the occurrence of an accepting state from some f_i, this guarantees that all of the accepting sets occur infinitely often. We cannot choose one of the S_i sets to be the Büchi accepting set, since a run that would stay in S_i forever without any state from f_i ever occurring would then be accepted. But we can select the Cartesian product $f_i \times \{i\}$ for some arbitrary $1 \leq i \leq m$. This guarantees that we are passing through a state in $f_i \times \{i\}$ on our way to a state in $S_{i \oplus_m 1}$. In order to see a state in $f_i \times \{i\}$ again, we need to go cyclically through all the other copies once more. In the case where the set of accepting sets F of the generalized Büchi automaton is empty, we define the translation as $\langle \Sigma, S, \Delta, I, L, S \rangle$, i.e., all the states of the generated Büchi automaton are accepting.

It may seem strange at first that we imposed an order on the occurrence of the accepting states from the different sets. This does not mean that the accepting states from the different sets in F occur in the input sequence in that order. It only means that we take account of them in that order. For example, if a state $(s, 2) \in S_2$, where $s \in f_2$ occurs, we move to some state $(r, 3) \in S_3$. If then a state $(q, 3) \in S_3$ occurs, with $q \in f_2$, or in $q \in f_1$, we stay at S_3. The subtle point is that if there are infinitely many states with first component from each accepting set f_i, it does not matter that we do not exploit all of them to move between the different copies of states. If after some point, there are no more states from some f_i, we must not accept anyway.

Formally, the Büchi automaton obtained by the translation of a generalized Büchi automaton $\langle \Sigma, S, \Delta, I, L, \{f_1, \ldots, f_m\} \rangle$, with a nonempty set of acceptance conditions (the case where $m = 0$ was already given above), is therefore $\langle \Sigma, S \times \{1, \ldots, m\}, \Delta', I \times \{1\}, L', f_1 \times \{1\} \rangle$, where $L'(q, i) = L(q)$, and $(\langle q, i \rangle, \langle q', j \rangle) \in \Delta'$ exactly if $(q, q') \in \Delta$ and one of the following conditions holds:

1. $q \in f_i$ and $j = i \oplus_m 1$, or
2. $q \notin f_i$ and $j = i$.

We can now define the intersection of two Büchi automata as a generalized Büchi automaton. The intersection is constructed as follows:

$$\mathcal{A}_1 \cap \mathcal{A}_2 = \langle \Sigma, S_1 \times S_2, \Delta, I_1 \times I_2, L, \{F_1 \times S_2, S_1 \times F_2\} \rangle$$

The transition relation Δ of the intersection is defined by

$$(\langle l, q \rangle, \langle l', q' \rangle) \in \Delta \text{ iff } (l, l') \in \Delta_1, \text{ and } (q, q') \in \Delta_2.$$

The labeling of each state $\langle l, q \rangle$ in the intersection, denoted $L(l, q)$, is $L_1(l) \wedge L_2(q)$. States labeled with *false* are removed, together with their corresponding in-edges and out-edges. The result of the intersection of the automata in Figure 6.2, after converting the generalized Büchi automaton back into a simple Büchi automaton, appears in Figure 6.4.

Notice that the size of the union automaton is proportional to the sum of the sizes of the component automata. The size of the intersection automaton is proportional to the product of the sizes of the component automata.

The intersection in (6.2) usually corresponds to a more restricted case, where *all* the states of the automaton representing the modeled system are accepting. In this restricted case, where the automaton $\mathcal{A}_1$ has all its states accepting and the automaton $\mathcal{A}_2$ is unrestricted, we have

$$\mathcal{A}_1 \cap \mathcal{A}_2 = \langle \Sigma, \, S_1 \times S_2, \, \Delta, \, I_1 \times I_2, \, L, \, S_1 \times F_2 \rangle, \qquad (6.3)$$

where $(\langle l, q \rangle, \langle l', q' \rangle) \in \Delta$ iff $(l, l') \in \Delta_1$ and $(q, q') \in \Delta_2$, and for each state (l, q) in the intersection, $L(l, q) = L_1(l) \wedge L_2(q)$. This is a simple Büchi automaton. Thus, the accepting states are the pairs with accepting second component. Nevertheless, the more general case of intersection is useful for modeling systems where fairness constraints are imposed (see Section 6.10). In this case, not all the states of the system automaton are necessarily accepting.

The details of complementing a Büchi automaton are rather complicated. The main principles appear in the next section. More details can be found, e.g., in [134]. For a more efficient algorithm, see [124]. The complement automaton $\overline{\mathcal{B}}$ can be exponentially bigger than $\mathcal{B}$. In some implementations (e.g., [65]), the user is supposed to provide the automaton for $\overline{\mathcal{B}}$ directly, instead of providing the automaton for $\mathcal{B}$. In this case, the user is specifying the *bad behaviors* instead of the good ones. Another approach, taken in COSPAN [79], is to use a more involved version of ω-automata, which allows simple complementation.

Finally, the automaton $\mathcal{B}$ may be obtained by using a translation from some specification language, e.g., LTL or monadic second order logic. In this case, instead of translating a property φ into $\mathcal{B}$ and then complementing $\mathcal{B}$, one can simply translate $\neg\varphi$, which would immediately provide an automaton for the complement language, as required in (6.2). We will later provide an efficient translation from LTL.

6.5 Complementing a Büchi Automaton

For completeness, we will now explain the principles (but will not provide the full details) of complementing Büchi automata. As we saw in the previous section, some implementations avoid explicit complementation due to the possible exponential blowup. The reader can thus safely skip the following mathematical details and progress directly to the next section.

A *congruence* '$\sim$' over a set of strings is an equivalence relation satisfying $(x_1 \sim y_1 \wedge x_2 \sim y_2) \to x_1.x_2 \sim y_1.y_2$. Consider some Büchi automaton $\mathcal{A} = \langle \Sigma, S, \Delta, I, L, F \rangle$. Let $u \in \Sigma^*$, $q, q' \in S$. Denote by $q \overset{u}{\leadsto} q'$ a path whose edges are marked by the letters in u from the state q to the state q'. Denote by $q \overset{u,F}{\leadsto} q'$ such a path that passes through an accepting state from F. Let $u \cong v$ when for each $q, q' \in S$, $q \overset{u}{\leadsto} q'$ exactly when $q \overset{v}{\leadsto} q'$ and $q \overset{u,F}{\leadsto} q'$ exactly when $q \overset{v,F}{\leadsto} q'$. It is easy to check that '$\cong$' is an equivalence relation.

We show now that '$\cong$' is a congruence. We will give the proof for '$\overset{u}{\leadsto}$'. The case of '$\overset{u,F}{\leadsto}$' is similar. Let $u_1 \cong v_1$ and $u_2 \cong v_2$, and let q, q' be any pair of states. We need to show that there is a path labeled $u_1.u_2$ from q to q' exactly when there is a path labeled $v_1.v_2$ from q to q'. But this follows from the above equivalences, since we know that for any state r, $q \overset{u_1}{\leadsto} r$ if and only if $q \overset{v_1}{\leadsto} r$ and $r \overset{u_2}{\leadsto} q'$ if and only if $r \overset{v_2}{\leadsto} q'$.

From the definition of the relation '$\cong$', the number of its equivalence classes is finite (but can be large, namely exponential in the number of states of $\mathcal{A}$). Each equivalence class U of '$\cong$' is a set (or a language) of finite words.

For each pair U, V of equivalence classes of '$\cong$', either $U.V^\omega \subseteq \mathcal{L}(\mathcal{A})$ or $U.V^\omega \subseteq \overline{\mathcal{L}(\mathcal{A})}$. To see that, let $u.v_1.v_2 \ldots$ and $u'.v_1'.v_2' \ldots$ be two infinite strings in $U.V^\omega$. That is, u, $u' \in U$ and $v_i, v_i' \in V$ for $i \geq 1$. Then, since $u \cong u'$ and $v_i \cong v_i'$ for $i \geq 1$, we have that there is a run $q_0 \overset{u}{\leadsto} q_{j_1} \overset{v_1}{\leadsto} q_{j_2} \overset{v_2}{\leadsto} \ldots$ of $\mathcal{A}$ exactly when there is also a run $q_0 \overset{u'}{\leadsto} q_{j_1} \overset{v_1'}{\leadsto} q_{j_2} \overset{v_2'}{\leadsto} \ldots$. Furthermore, we can select these two runs such that for each $i \geq 1$, $q_{j_i} \overset{v_i,F}{\leadsto} q_{j_{i+1}}$ exactly when $q_{j_i} \overset{v_i',F}{\leadsto} q_{j_{i+1}}$. Therefore, the first run is accepting exactly when the second one is accepting. Consequently, $u.v_1.v_2 \ldots$ is in $\mathcal{L}(\mathcal{A})$ exactly when $u'.v_1'.v_2' \ldots$ is in $\mathcal{L}(\mathcal{A})$. Therefore, if one string in $U.V^\omega$ is in $\mathcal{L}(\mathcal{A})$ then all the strings in $U.V^\omega$ are in $\mathcal{L}(\mathcal{A})$.

Let w be an infinite word. Then there is a pair of equivalence classes U, V of '$\cong$' such that $w \in U.V^\omega$. To prove that, let $ix(x, y)$ be the equivalence class of '$\cong$' that contains the subword $w[x..y]$, from the xth to the yth letter. Thus, if $ix(x, y) = ix(x', y')$ then $w[x, y] \cong w[x', y']$. Since there are finitely many equivalence classes, ix maps infinitely many pairs into a finite set. Ramsey theory [57] shows that when an infinite set of pairs of *naturals* is partitioned into a finite number of sets, there exists an infinite sequence $m_1, m_2, m_3, \ldots$ of *naturals* such that each pair of numbers in this sequence, and in particular, each adjacent pair, is in the same set of the partition. Thus, there is an infinite sequence $m_1, m_2, m_3, \ldots$ such that $ix(m_i, m_{i+1} - 1) = ix(m_j, m_{j+1} - 1)$ for each $i, j \geq 1$. We can choose $U = ix(0, m_1 - 1)$ and $V = ix(m_1, m_2 - 1)$.

In order to complement $\mathcal{A}$, one can construct (following the above definition of '$\cong$') the union of the automata for the languages of the form $V U^\omega$, for U, V equivalence classes of '$\cong$' where $V U^\omega \cap \mathcal{L}(\mathcal{A}) = \emptyset$.

6.6 Checking Emptiness

Earlier in the book we saw how model checking can be translated into checking the emptiness of the intersection of two automata: one that represents the system, and another that represents the complement of the specification, as in (6.2). Thus, we need an algorithmic way to perform a check for emptiness. Moreover, if the intersection is nonempty, we would like to obtain a counterexample. Although an execution of a Büchi automaton can be infinite, we would like to obtain the counterexample in some finite representation.

Consider a Büchi automaton $\mathcal{A} = \langle \Sigma, S, \Delta, I, L, F \rangle$. As observed in Section 6.4, we can henceforth assume that no state of a Büchi automaton is labeled with a formula equivalent to *false*. In the most general form, each state can be labeled with an arbitrary Boolean formula over the propositional variables AP. This makes checking that the formula is equivalent to *false* a complex problem. The time complexity of this problem is in NP-complete, namely, no solution that is better than exponential time is yet known. Henceforth, the only state labelings that we will use will include a conjunction over propositional variables and negated propositional variables. In particular, the result of the automatic LTL translation algorithm in Section 6.8 adheres to this form. This also holds for the intersection of two automata of this form. Then, checking equivalence to *false* can be done in linear time in the length of each label.

Let ρ be an accepting run of $\mathcal{A}$. Then ρ contains infinitely many states from F. Since S is finite, there is some suffix ρ' of ρ such that every state on ρ' appears infinitely many times. This means that each state on ρ' is reachable from any other state on ρ'. Thus, the states on ρ' are contained in a strongly-connected component of the graph of $\mathcal{A}$. This component is reachable from an initial state and contains an accepting state. Conversely, any nontrivial strongly-connected component that is reachable from an initial state and contains an accepting state generates an accepting run of the automaton. Thus, checking nonemptiness of $\mathcal{L}(\mathcal{A})$ is equivalent to finding a strongly-connected component in the graph of $\mathcal{A}$ that is reachable from an initial state and contains an accepting state.

The significance of this observation is that if the language $\mathcal{L}(\mathcal{A})$ is nonempty, then there is a counterexample that can be represented in a finite way. The counterexample is a run, constructed from a finite prefix and a periodic sequence of states. That is, a counterexample is a sequence of the form $\sigma_1 \sigma_2{}^\omega$, where σ_1 and σ_2 are finite sequences. Such a sequence is called *ultimately periodic*. Tarjan's version of the *depth-first search* (DFS) algorithm [139] can be used for finding strongly-connected components. Model checking can thus be performed as follows:

1. Construct an automaton $\mathcal{A}$, representing the modeled system.
2. Construct the automaton $\overline{\mathcal{B}}$, representing the complement of the specification (e.g., translate $\neg\varphi$, where φ is the LTL specification).
3. Construct the intersection automaton $\mathcal{C} = \mathcal{A} \cap \overline{\mathcal{B}}$.
4. Apply Tarjan's algorithm to find strongly-connected components reachable from the initial states of $\mathcal{C}$.
5. If none of the strongly-connected components found contains an accepting state, announce that *the model $\mathcal{A}$ satisfies the specification $\mathcal{B}$*.
6. Otherwise, pick up some reachable strongly-connected component S of $\mathcal{C}$. Construct a path σ_1 from an initial state of $\mathcal{C}$ to some accepting state q of S. Construct a cycle from q and back to itself. Such a cycle exists, since S is a strongly-connected component. Let σ_2 be that cycle, excluding its first state q. Then, announce that $\sigma_1 \sigma_2{}^\omega$ is a counterexample that is accepted by $\mathcal{A}$, but is not allowed by the specification $\mathcal{B}$.

An important observation is that one does not necessarily need to complete the construction of the system or the intersection of the automata before starting to perform the intersection and to check for emptiness. This is sometimes called 'on-the-fly' model checking. New states of the system automaton are constructed *on demand*, when needed in calculating the intersection. In this way, it is sometimes possible to check some systems whose model, represented as an automaton, is too big to fit into memory. If an error is found before the intersection is completed, then there is no need to complete the state space construction. Moreover, since the construction of the product is guided by the property automaton, some parts of the system automaton might simply not be needed for the intersection. The details of such an algorithm can be found in [34].

6.7 A Model Checking Example

Consider the model for a traffic light system on the left side of Figure 6.5. This is a different kind of traffic light than the one in Section 5.4. Now, the *yellow* light starts to appear while the *green* light is still on. The propositional variables are re, ye and gr, for *red*, *yellow* and *green*, respectively. The system automaton has all of its states accepting. That is, any infinite sequence is an execution. In fact, there is only one execution in this example. Accordingly, we did not mark the accepting states of the model automaton in Figure 6.5.

The specification we want to check asserts that we always move from *yellow* to *red*. We form the LTL property, $\Box(ye \to \bigcirc re)$, which we check against the traffic light model. To model check this property, we check whether there is a sequence of the model that satisfies the negation of the property, namely $\neg \Box (ye \to \bigcirc re) = \Diamond(ye \wedge \bigcirc \neg re)$. An automaton that represents this property is shown in the right-hand side of Figure 6.5. Later, we will describe an algorithm for translating LTL properties into Büchi automata.

The intersection of the two automata is shown in Figure 6.6. Nodes whose label are equivalent to *false* are crossed over, and their edges are not shown. The initial state is $\langle s_1, q_1 \rangle$, as both state components are initial in the intersected automata. (The pair $\langle s_1, q_2 \rangle$ consists of two initial components, but is crossed off since $L(s_1) \wedge L(q_2) = false$.) There are also some non-initial states with no in-edges ($\langle s_2, q_3 \rangle$, $\langle s_3, q_3 \rangle$), and a state with no out-edges ($\langle s_4, q_2 \rangle$). These states are redundant, as they cannot participate in any accepting run. We are dealing with the simple (and common) case, where one of the intersected automata (the system) has all of its states accepting. Thus, the accepting states of the intersection are those where the second component, corresponding to the property automaton, is accepting. In this case, these are the states with second component q_4. There are two nontrivial strongly-connected components,

$$\{\langle s_1, q_1 \rangle, \langle s_2, q_1 \rangle, \langle s_3, q_1 \rangle, \langle s_4, q_1 \rangle\}$$

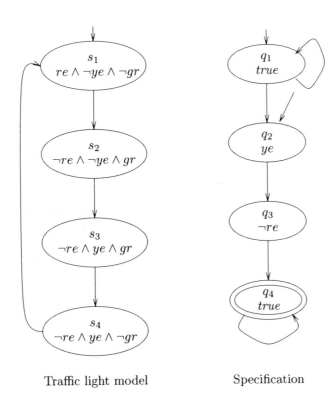

Traffic light model   Specification

Fig. 6.5. A traffic light model and the negation of a specification

and

$$\{\langle s_1, q_4 \rangle, \langle s_2, q_4 \rangle, \langle s_3, q_4 \rangle, \langle s_4, q_4 \rangle\}.$$

Both components are reachable from the initial state (in fact, the former component contains the initial state). The former strongly-connected component contains no accepting states, while all the states of the latter are accepting. The counterexample can be formed then by the finite prefix

$$\langle s_1, q_1 \rangle, \langle s_2, q_1 \rangle, \langle s_3, q_2 \rangle, \langle s_4, q_3 \rangle, \langle s_1, q_4 \rangle$$

and the periodic sequence

$$\langle s_2, q_4 \rangle, \langle s_3, q_4 \rangle, \langle s_4, q_4 \rangle, \langle s_1, q_4 \rangle.$$

Analyzing the counterexample reveals that the faulty step occurs in the prefix, when moving from the state $\langle s_3, q_2 \rangle$, in which both *yellow* and *green* are on, to the next state, $\langle s_4, q_3 \rangle$, in which *yellow* is still on, but not *red*.

Before running back to the engineers and complaining about an error, one needs to decide whether this is really an indication that something is wrong with the traffic light system. Looking closer at the counterexample shows that the *red* state did previously occur after an exclusively *yellow* state. In the first *yellow* state after the previous *red* state, the *green* light is still on. Now according to the above specification, in the next state we require that the *red* light be on. Instead, in the next state, the *green* light goes off, while the *yellow* light is still on. Only in the subsequent state, the *yellow* changed into *red*. It is quite plausible that the LTL property that was used does not represent the intended specification, and that the counterexample behavior does not pose any problem. In this case, the LTL property should be reformulated (perhaps as $\Box(ye \rightarrow ye\mathsf{U}re)$).

6.8 Translating LTL into Automata

We now present the algorithm for translating (propositional) LTL specifications into generalized Büchi automata [52]. Let φ be the LTL specification, which we want to translate into a generalized Büchi automaton. We start with an intuitive description of the algorithm.

With each node s in the generated automaton, we associate a formula $\eta(s)$. Given an accepting run over some sequence ξ, if the run reaches a state s with a suffix ξ^i remaining, we must have $\xi^i \models \eta(s)$. The formulas $\eta(s)$ are of the form

$$\left(\bigwedge_{i=1..m} \nu_i \right) \wedge \bigcirc \left(\bigwedge_{j=1..n} \kappa_j \right).$$

This helps in creating the successor nodes for s, which have to satisfy $\bigwedge_{j=1..n} \kappa_j$. Notice that each LTL formula can be brought into this form by selecting $m = 1$ and $n = 0$.

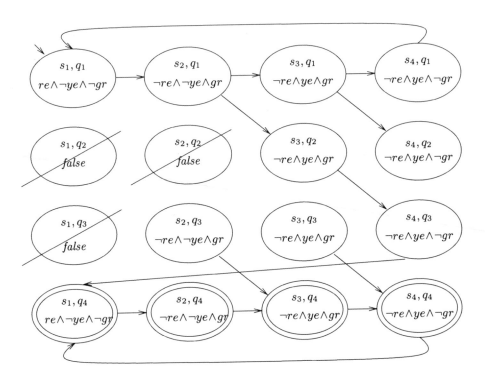

Fig. 6.6. The intersection of the automata in Figure 6.5

Our goal is to refine $\eta(s)$ into simpler (i.e., shorter) subformulas ν_i, until all the ν_i are either propositional variables or negated propositional variables.

Consider, for example a node s that contains a subformula $\nu_i = \mu \mathsf{U} \psi$. We will use the following characterization of the *until* operator 'U':

$$\mu \mathsf{U} \psi = \psi \vee (\mu \wedge \bigcirc \mu \mathsf{U} \psi)$$

(see axiom A7 in Section 5.3). This can be seen as a *fixpoint* or recursive definition of the U operator, as the expression on the right includes an occurrence of the defined formula itself. Consequently, there are two ways of satisfying $\mu \mathsf{U} \psi$. One way is by satisfying the right-hand part of the *until*, i.e., ψ. The other way is to postpone ψ, meaning that μ must hold for the current suffix, while $\mu \mathsf{U} \psi$ has to hold from the next state as well. Because of the two separate ways (or, equivalently, the existence of the disjunction operator '$\vee$'), we *split* the current node into two. In the first copy, we add a ν_i subformula ψ. In the second copy, we add a ν_i subformula μ and a κ_j subformula $\mu \mathsf{U} \psi$. Other types of formulas are treated similarly, as listed in Table 6.1 below.

When we split a node, we maintain the rest of the ν_i and κ_j formulas, and the list of its predecessor nodes. We separate between subformulas ν_i that were already refined, and ones that are yet to be processed. After completing the refinement or splitting of a node s, we generate a successor for it, s', where the ν_i formulas of s' are set to be the κ_j formula of the node s, and the set of κ_j formulas of s' is empty.

After the set of nodes is constructed, we need to assign acceptance conditions. These will enforce satisfying the right-hand side of each *until* subformula. That is, each time an *until* subformula of the form $\mu \mathsf{U} \psi$ has to be satisfied by a suffix ξ^i, there must be a suffix $\xi^j \models \psi$ with $j \geq i$. (Notice that $(\mu \mathsf{U} \psi) \rightarrow (\Diamond \psi)$.) This is important, as the split we presented before allows satisfying $\mu \mathsf{U} \psi$ by either satisfying ψ, or postponing $\mu \mathsf{U} \psi$ to the next state (while μ has to hold in the current suffix). We have to guarantee that the satisfaction of ψ will not be postponed forever. We achieve this by adding a set of Generalized Büchi conditions for each subformula of that type. Each such condition, corresponding to a subformula of the form $\mu \mathsf{U} \psi$, is a set that includes all the nodes which

- include some $\nu_i = \psi$, or
- do not include some $\nu_i = \mu \mathsf{U} \psi$.

We now present the algorithm formally. In order to apply the following translation algorithm, we first convert the formula φ into *negation normal form*, where negation can only be applied to the propositional variables. We first use Boolean equivalences so that only the Boolean operators *and* ('$\wedge$'), *or* ('$\vee$') and *not* ('$\neg$') remain. Negation are then pushed inwards, so that they can only precede propositional variables from AP. This is done using the LTL equivalences $\neg \bigcirc \mu = \bigcirc \neg \mu$, $\neg(\mu \vee \eta) = (\neg \mu) \wedge (\neg \eta)$, $\neg(\mu \wedge \eta) = (\neg \mu) \vee (\neg \eta)$, $\neg \neg \eta = \eta$, $\neg(\Box \psi) = \Diamond \neg \psi$, $\neg(\Diamond \psi) = \Box \neg \psi$, $\neg(\mu \mathsf{U} \eta) = (\neg \mu) \mathsf{V} (\neg \eta)$ and

$\neg(\mu V \eta) = (\neg\mu) U (\neg\eta)$. Finally, we replace each occurrence of the *eventually* ($\Diamond$) and *always* ($\Box$) operators by the *until* (U) and *release* (V) operators, using the equivalences $\Diamond\eta = true U \eta$ and $\Box\eta = false V \eta$, respectively.

In what follows, we will assume that φ is already in normal form. Notice that the conversion of an LTL formula to this normal form does not involve a significant (i.e., more than linear) increase in size.

For example, consider the formula $\neg\Box(\neg A \rightarrow (\Box B \wedge \Box C))$. We replace the implication by a disjunction, obtaining $\neg\Box(A \vee (\Box B \wedge \Box C))$. Pushing negation inwards we obtain $\Diamond(\neg A \wedge((\Diamond\neg B) \vee (\Diamond\neg C)))$. Then, we can eliminate the $\Diamond$ operators to obtain $true U(\neg A \wedge ((true U \neg B) \vee (true U \neg C)))$.

A *graph node* is the basic data structure of the algorithm (see Figure 6.8). Some of the nodes will be used as the states of the constructed automaton, while others will be discharged during the translation. A graph node contains the following fields:

Name. A unique identifier for the node.

Incoming. A list of the identifiers of nodes with edges that lead to the current node.

New, Old, Next. Each of these fields is a set of subformulas of φ. Each node represents the temporal properties of some suffixes of executions. The formulas in $New(s) \cup Old(s)$ are the ν_i formulas, in the above informal explanation of the algorithm. The set $New(s)$ contains subformulas that have not been processed yet, while $Old(s)$ contains subformulas that were processed. The subformulas in $Next(s)$ are the κ_j formulas in the explanation above.

We keep a set *Nodes_Set* of nodes whose construction was completed. These nodes constitute the states in the constructed automaton. The set *Nodes_Set* is initially empty.

The algorithm for translating an LTL formula into a generalized Büchi automaton appears in Figure 6.7.

The function **new_name()**, used in lines 9, 24 and 39 in the algorithm generates a new name for each successive call. The functions **New1(η)**, **New2(η)**, **Next1(η)** and **Next2(η)** are defined in Table 6.1.

η	**New1(η)**	**Next1(η)**	**New2(η)**	**Next2(η)**
$\mu U \psi$	$\{\mu\}$	$\{\mu U \psi\}$	$\{\psi\}$	$\emptyset$
$\mu V \psi$	$\{\psi\}$	$\{\mu V \psi\}$	$\{\mu, \psi\}$	$\emptyset$
$\mu \vee \psi$	$\{\mu\}$	$\emptyset$	$\{\psi\}$	$\emptyset$
$\mu \wedge \psi$	$\{\mu, \psi\}$	$\emptyset$	$-$	$-$
$\bigcirc\mu$	$\emptyset$	$\{\mu\}$	$-$	$-$

Table 6.1. The split table for the LTL translation algorithm

For translating the formula φ, the algorithm starts with a single node (lines 39–40) that has a single incoming edge, from a dummy special node init. In addition, $New=\{\varphi\}$ and $Old=Next=\emptyset$. For example, the node in Figure 6.8 is the one with which the algorithm for constructing the automaton for $AU(BUC)$ starts.

For the current node s, the algorithm checks if there are subformulas to be processed in the field New of s (line 4). If not, the processing of the current node is completed. The algorithm then checks whether the current node should be added to $Nodes\_Set$; if there is a node r in $Nodes\_Set$ with the same subformulas as s in both its Old and $Next$ fields (line 5–6), then the node s is no longer needed (and its space can be reused). In addition, the set of incoming edges of s are added to the incoming edges of r (line 7). Otherwise, i.e., if no such node exists in $Nodes\_Set$, the node s is added to $Nodes\_Set$, and a new current node s' is formed as follows (lines 9–11):

- There is an edge from s to s', i.e., s' is a successor of s.
- The field New of s' is initialized to $Next$ of s.
- The fields Old and $Next$ of s' are set to be empty.

An example of generating a new current node appears in Figure 6.11.

Each temporal formula, written with full parentheses, has a main modal or a main Boolean operator. This is the modal or operator that appears inside the outermost parentheses (when the formula is fully parenthesized). For example, in the formula $(\Box(A \vee (B \wedge C)))$, the main modal is '$\Box$'. In the formula $(A \vee ((\Box B \wedge C)))$, there is a main operator, which is '$\vee$'.

If the field New of s is not empty, a formula η in New is selected (line 13) and is removed from New. According to the main modal or Boolean operator of η, the node s can be split into two copies s_1 and s_2 (lines 20–28), or can just evolve (be refined) into a new version s' (lines 16–19 and 29–36). The new nodes are formed by first selecting new names for these nodes and copying from p the fields $Incoming$, Old, New and $Next$. Then, η is added to the set of formulas in Old. In addition, formulas can be added to the fields New and $Next$ of either s_1 and s_2, or s', according to the following cases:

η is a proposition, the negation of a proposition, or a Boolean constant. If η is false, or $\neg\eta$ is in Old (we identify $\neg\neg\eta$ with η), then the current node is discarded, since it contains a contradiction (lines 16–19) and thus cannot be satisfied. Otherwise, the node s evolves into s' according to the above description.

$\eta = \mu U\psi$ The node s is split into s_1 and s_2 (lines 20–28). For the first copy s_1, μ is added to New and $\mu U\psi$ to $Next$. In this and any other split, the first copy can reuse the space of the old node s. For the second copy s_2, ψ is added to New. This split corresponds to the fact that $\mu U\psi$ is equivalent to $\psi \vee (\mu \wedge \bigcirc(\mu U\psi))$. For example, a split occurs on the node in Figure 6.8, producing the two nodes in Figure 6.9. There, $\eta = AU(BUC)$, i.e., $\mu = A$

and $\psi = BUC$. A further split, of the node on the right in Figure 6.9, appears in Figure 6.10. In this case, $\eta = BUC$, thus, $\mu = B$ and $\psi = C$.

$\eta = \mu V \psi$ The node p is split into s_1, s_2 (lines 20–28). Then, ψ is added to New of both s_1 and s_2, μ is added to New of s_1, and $\mu V \psi$ is added to $Next$ of s_2. This split is explained by observing that $\mu V \psi$ is equivalent to $\psi \wedge (\mu \vee \bigcirc(\mu V \psi))$.

$\eta = \mu \vee \psi$ Then, p is split into s_1, s_2 (lines 20–28). μ is added to New of s_1, and ψ is added to New of s_2.

$\eta = \mu \wedge \psi$ Then, s evolves into s' (lines 29–32). Both μ and ψ are added to New of s', as both subformulas must hold in order for η to hold.

$\eta = \bigcirc \mu$ Then s evolves into s' (lines 33–36), and μ is added to $Next$ of s'.

The algorithm then recursively expands the new copies.

The set of nodes $Nodes\_Set$ constructed by the above algorithm can now be converted into a generalized Büchi automaton $\mathcal{B} = (\Sigma, S, \Delta, I, L, F)$ with the following components:

- The alphabet Σ includes propositional formulas that consist of conjunctions of negated and non-negated propositions from the set of propositions AP that appear in the translated formula φ.
- The set of states S consists of the nodes in $Nodes\_Set$.
- $(s, s') \in \Delta$ when $s \in Incoming(s')$.
- The set of initial states $I \subset S$ is the set of nodes that contain the special incoming edge init.
- $L(s)$ is the conjunction of the negated and non-negated propositions in $Old(s)$.
- The generalized Büchi acceptance condition contains a separate set of states $f \in F$ for each subformula of the form $\mu U \psi$; f contains all the states s such that either $\psi \in Old(s)$ or $\mu U \psi \notin Old(s)$.

The nodes constructed for the formula $AU(BUC)$ appears in Figure 6.12. The corresponding generalized Büchi automaton, in Figure 6.13, has two accepting sets, one for BUC and one for $AU(BUC)$.

The number of nodes constructed by the algorithm, and the time complexity are exponential in the size of the formula. However, experience shows that the constructed automaton is typically small. One can improve the above translation algorithm by observing that there is no need to store in Old the subformulas of the form $\mu \vee \nu$, $\mu \wedge \nu$ and $\bigcirc \mu$, unless they appear as the right-hand part of an *until* (U) subformula. The reason for the above constraint is that the right-hand part of an *until* subformula is used for defining the acceptance conditions.

Another improvement is based on a relation between states called *bisimulation*. Intuitively, it relates pairs of states that agree on the labeling and acceptance, and have successors that are related to each other. Furthermore, these successors must have successors that agree on the labeling and acceptance and are related to each other, and so on. The formal definition of bisim-

LTL translation algorithm

```
1    record graph_node = [Name:string, Incoming:set of string,
2        New:set of formula, Old:set of formula, Next:set of formula];
3    function expand (s, Nodes_Set)
4       if New(s)=∅ then
5          if exists node r in Nodes_Set with
6              Old(r)=Old(s) and Next(r) =Next(s)
7          then Incoming(r) = Incoming(r)∪ Incoming(s);
8              return(Nodes_Set);
9          else return(expand( [Name⇐new_name(),
10             Incoming⇐ {Name(s)}, New⇐Next(s),
11             Old⇐ ∅ , Next⇐ ∅], Nodes_Set∪ {s})))
12      else
13         let η ∈New(s);
14         New(s) := New(s)\{η}; Old(s) := Old(s)∪{η};
15         case η of
16         η = A, or ¬A, where A proposition, or η = true, or η =false=>
17             if η =false or ¬η ∈Old(s) then return(Nodes_Set)
18                 else return(expand([Name⇐Name(s), Incoming⇐Incoming(s),
19                     New⇐New(s), Old⇐Old(s), Next⇐Next(s)], Node_Set));
20         η = μUψ, or μVψ, or μ ∨ ψ =>
21             s₁:=[Name⇐ Name(s), Incoming⇐Incoming(s),
22                 New⇐New(s)∪({New1(η)}\Old(s)),
23                 Old⇐Old(s), Next=Next(s)∪{Next1(η)} ];
24             s₂:=new_node([Name⇐new_name(),
25                 Incoming⇐Incoming(s),
26                 New⇐New(s)∪({New2(η)}\Old(s)),
27                 Old⇐Old(s), Next⇐Next(s)]);
28             return(expand(s₂, expand(s₁, Nodes_Set)));
29         η = μ ∧ ψ =>
30             return(expand([Name⇐Name(s), Incoming⇐Incoming(s),
31                 New⇐New(s)∪({μ,ψ}\Old(s)),
32                 Old⇐Old(s), Next=Next(s)], Nodes_Set))
33         η = ○μ =>
34             return(expand([Name⇐Name(s), Incoming⇐Incoming(s),
35                 New⇐New(s), Old⇐Old(s),
36                 Next⇐Next(s)∪{μ}], Nodes_Set))
37   end expand;
38   function create_graph (φ)
39      return(expand([Name⇐new_name(), Incoming⇐ {init},
40          New⇐ {φ} , Old⇐ ∅, Next⇐ ∅], ∅))
41   end create_graph;
```

Fig. 6.7. The translation algorithm

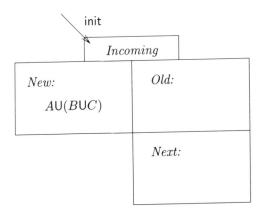

Fig. 6.8. The initial node

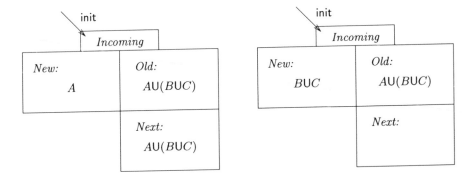

Fig. 6.9. Splitting the node in Figure 6.8

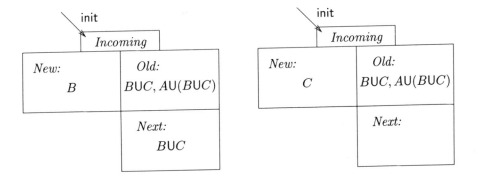

Fig. 6.10. Splitting the right node in Figure 6.9

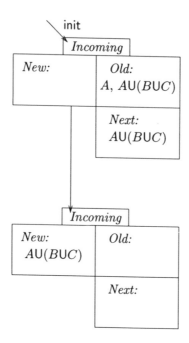

Fig. 6.11. Generating a successor node

ulation is given in Section 8.5.3, and a bisimulation minimization algorithm is given in Section 8.8.

Recall that according to Equation (6.2) in Section 6.3, we use in model checking the automaton representing the *bad behaviors*, i.e., the ones that are not allowed by the specification φ. First translating φ into an automaton and then complementing it may incur a doubly exponential size increase. A much better solution is to first negate φ by affixing a negation symbol in front of it. Then one can translate the negated specification $\neg\varphi$ to an automaton. This may, at worst, involve a single exponential explosion, although in practice the automata resulting from the above translation are often quite small.

6.9 The Complexity of Model Checking

In order to determine the complexity of model checking, we need first to decide how to measure the size of the input. The two inputs for a model checking algorithm are a model of the system, and a property specification. These can be given in various ways, which differ from each other considerably in size.

The property specification can be given, for example, using a Büchi automaton (accepting the disallowed sequences), in LTL, or in monadic first

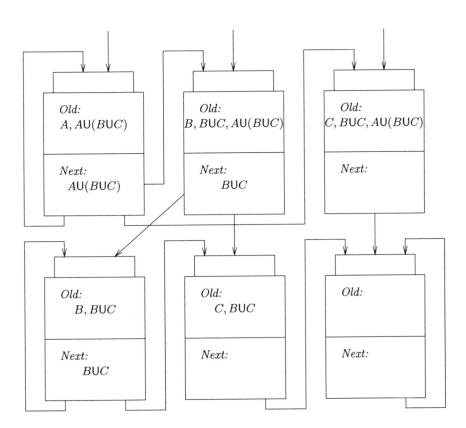

Fig. 6.12. The set *Nodes_Set* at termination

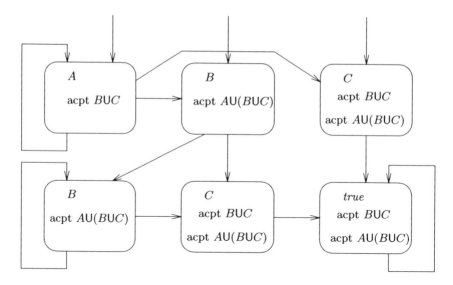

Fig. 6.13. The automaton with the accepting nodes

or second order logic (see Section 5.8). The complexity of model checking, as a function of the specification size, depends heavily on this choice: it is polynomial in time (in fact, it can be done in nondeterministic logarithmic space) for the Büchi automaton, it is in PSPACE for LTL representation, and NONELEMENTARY for monadic first and second order logic.

This may immediately raise the issue of choosing the specification formalism that gives the smallest model checking complexity. As discussed in Section 5.8, the smaller complexity may come at the expense of increasing the size of the specification. For example, model checking using Büchi automata can be exponentially faster than model checking LTL specifications of the same size.

On the other hand, LTL specifications may be exponentially smaller in size than their corresponding Büchi automata representation. Similarly, checking monadic first order logic specifications is NONELEMENTARY slower than checking LTL specifications of the same size. On the other hand, monadic first order logic specifications may be considerably smaller in size than their corresponding LTL representations [134].

In practice, a good specification formalism satisfies that many commonly used specifications are relatively short and are not hard to check. LTL specifications of common properties for software and hardware are usually relatively short (although there are cases where first order formulas can be considerably shorter than an LTL formula representing the same specification), well understood, and widely used. Accordingly, in analyzing the complexity of model checking, we will select LTL as the specification formalism.

The other parameter we need to consider for the complexity of model checking is the size of the system model. Assume a concurrent system, with n independent components (processes) $P_1, \ldots, P_n$, where P_i has m_i local states, combined using the concurrency '$\|$' operator, defined in Section 4.9. Thus, each state is a combination of n local states. The number of global states is therefore bounded by the product $\prod_{i=1}^{n} m_i$. If all the processes are of equal size m, we get a state space of up to m^n states, i.e., the state space is exponential in the number of processes. With the model checking algorithm described in this chapter, we can perform the verification in polynomial time (or in nondeterministic logarithmic space) in the size of the global state space.

However, measuring the input size using the global state space is a rather biased measure of the size of the input: the natural description of a system, e.g., using code written in some programming language, is proportional to the sizes of the components, i.e., to $\sum_{i=1}^{n} m_i$, rather than to the global state space. We will therefore measure the size of the checked model as the sum of the sizes of the local automata, rather than the product. Assume for simplicity that all the processes have an equal number of states m. Then an algorithm whose time complexity is polynomial in the size of the global state space, which is bounded by m^n, is actually exponential in the size of the input, which is $m \times n$.

The following is a rather theoretical treatment of the complexity of LTL model checking. The reader may want to skip to the end of this section. In order to present an upper bound on the complexity of LTL model checking, we briefly describe a different translation from an LTL formula to a Büchi automaton [144] than the one described in Section 6.8. With this translation, each state of the automaton for the property φ contains a *consistency* and a *liveness* component.

Instead of the negation normal form used for the translation given in Section 6.8, we use another normal form. We assume that the translated formula φ does not contain the *release* '$\vee$' operator. If it does, we can remove it, while increasing the size of the formula only by a constant factor, using the equivalence $\psi_1 \vee \psi_2 = \neg((\neg\psi_1) U (\neg\psi_2))$. Similarly, it does not include the *always* '$\square$' modal operator (since $\square\psi = \neg \Diamond \neg\psi = \neg(true U \neg\psi)$).

The *closure* of φ, denoted $cl(\varphi)$, includes the subformulas of φ and their negations. For *until* formulas, of the form $\psi U \eta$, the closure also includes $\bigcirc(\psi U \eta)$ and its negation. We will use temporal equivalences to represent $\neg \bigcirc \psi$ as $\bigcirc \neg\psi$, and $\neg\neg\varphi$ as φ. Each consistency component contains exactly one of ψ and $\neg\psi$ for each of the formulas in $cl(\varphi)$. Thus, for $\varphi = AU(BUC)$, $cl(\varphi)$ includes A, $\neg A$, B, $\neg B$, C, $\neg C$, BUC, $\neg BUC$, $\bigcirc(BUC)$, $\bigcirc\neg(BUC)$, $AU(BUC)$, $\neg(AU(BUC))$, $\bigcirc(AU(BUC))$ and $\bigcirc\neg(AU(BUC))$.

In addition, the consistency component must comply with the following constraints:

- If it contains an *until* formula $\mu U \psi$, then it must also contain either ψ, or both $\bigcirc(\mu U \psi)$ and μ.

- If it contains a formula of the form $\mu \vee \psi$, then it must contain either μ or ψ.
- If the component contains a formula of the form $\mu \wedge \psi$, then it must contain both μ and ψ.

When a state r is a successor of a state s, the following holds: if the consistency component of s contains a subformula of the form $\bigcirc \psi$, then the consistency component of r must contain ψ. The consistency component is thus responsible for guaranteeing consistency between adjacent states.

The liveness component of each state contains a subset of the *until* subformulas of φ of the form $\mu \mathsf{U} \psi$. Consider a state s and a successor r. If the liveness component of s is empty, then the liveness component of r contains all the *until* subformulas that appear in the consistency component of r. Otherwise (i.e., in the case that the liveness component of s is not empty), for each formula $\mu \mathsf{U} \psi$ appearing in the liveness component of s, $\mu \mathsf{U} \psi$ also appears in the liveness component of r, exactly when ψ does not appear in the consistency component of s. Intuitively, the liveness part maintains the set of *until* subformulas that still need to be satisfied. Whenever such a subformula $\mu \mathsf{U} \psi$ is satisfied from some state, due to ψ satisfied there, it is removed from the liveness component. Once all the *until* subformulas are satisfied, namely the liveness component is empty, a set of *until* subformulas that need to be satisfied is loaded from the consistency component. If there are no *until* formulas in $cl(\varphi)$, then all the states are accepting.

The initial states are those that contain the translated formula φ itself in their consistency component, and have an empty liveness component.

The translation given in Section 6.8 tends to generate in practice [49] substantially smaller automata than the algorithm described here. However, the advantage of using the alternative algorithm presented in this section for the complexity analysis is that it is possible to check in polynomial space (and time) (1) whether a given state belongs to the translation or not, and (2) whether a given state is a successor of another state according to the above constraints. This is done without having to first complete the construction of all the nodes and edges. Notice that each state in this translation is polynomial in the size of the translated LTL formula, although the number of states is exponential.

We can now conduct a search through the combined state space of the Cartesian product of the property automaton and the system automaton without actually fully constructing these automata. This is a search for some accepting state s that is reachable from an initial state, and then from s to itself. If such a state exists, then the system does not satisfy its specification. To be efficient in space, we conduct a *binary search*. Recursively, to find if there is a path of length no more than l (assume for simplicity that l is a power of 2) from a state s to a state r, we need to find a state q such that there is (1) a path of length no more than $l/2$ from s to q, and (2) a path of length no more than $l/2$ from q to r. When the length becomes 1, checking whether there is a path from s to r means checking whether r is a successor of s, and we already know how to do this in polynomial time.

The maximal number of states that need to be stored during the binary search is log l, where each state is polynomial in the size of φ and the number of processes n. The maximal length of the path is the product of the size of the state space automaton, which is m^n, and the size of the Büchi automaton for φ, which is $4^{|\varphi|}$, where $|\varphi|$ is the length of the formula φ. The size of each state is polynomial in $n \times$ log m and $|\varphi|$. A simple calculation shows that the overall space complexity for the binary search is polynomial in both $|\varphi|$ and n. This gives us the upper bound PSPACE complexity for model checking.

The PSPACE lower bound on the complexity, with respect to the size of the modeled system, is immediate, by a result of Kozen [77]. There, even the simple property of checking *reachability* of some state in the intersection of a finite set of automata is PSPACE-complete. Clarke and Sistla [132] showed that model checking is also PSPACE-complete with respect to the size of the checked LTL property. Thus, model checking for LTL properties is PSPACE-complete with respect to both the size of the system and the checked property.

6.10 Representing Fairness

If one wants to perform model checking under a fairness assumption, the model checking algorithm needs to be adapted accordingly.

One way of checking that a system S satisfies a property φ under a fairness assumption ψ, expressed in LTL, is to prove that S satisfies $\psi \rightarrow \varphi$. That is, each execution of S that is fair under ψ satisfies φ. This is not a very efficient way to check for fairness, since the fairness formula ψ may be large, and a translation may result in a rather large Büchi automaton.

A different way to verify a property under fairness is to modify the verification algorithm [88]. For example, consider the case of weak transition fairness. A fair execution is one in which each transition is disabled infinitely often or is executed infinitely often (or both). To check that, assume that different transitions have unique names. We label each edge with the name of the corresponding transition that is taken. We can now check each reachable strongly-connected component that is obtained by applying Tarjan's DFS algorithm. Such a component contains a counterexample exactly if for each transition t it contains either

- an edge that is labeled with t, or
- a state where t is disabled.

Again, we can show that if such a strongly-connected component exists, a fair counterexample exists. This counterexample will pass through *all* the states and edges of the component (with repetitions allowed) in a cyclic way. This, in fact, gives an ultimately periodic counterexample. Thus, it will include for each transition t infinitely many states where t is disabled, or infinitely many occurrences of t. Conversely, if there is a fair counterexample, it must be a part of a strongly-connected component satisfying the conditions above.

Similar algorithms exist for the other fairness assumptions, including the ones mentioned in 4.12. One can define acceptance conditions that are more involved than simple Büchi acceptance (but can be shown to describe the same set of languages) [141]. Such acceptance conditions can be used to denote various fairness conditions of the system automaton [3].

6.11 Checking the LTL Specifications

The LTL translation algorithm and the algorithm for checking emptiness in Büchi automata can be used to check the validity of LTL formulas. Recall that a propositional LTL formula is valid if and only if it holds for every possible sequence over the set of propositions appearing in the formula. This can be useful when we are interested in checking whether one specification φ is stronger than another ψ, i.e., whether $\varphi \to \psi$ is valid. In this case, if we verified that a system satisfies φ, then it also satisfies ψ.

We may also be interested in checking whether some specification φ is satisfiable by at least one sequence, i.e., if it contains no internal contradiction. If there is no execution satisfying the property, the specification is obviously not useful.

It is easy to see that there is a relation between validity and satisfiability: a formula φ is valid exactly when $\neg\varphi$ is not satisfiable. Thus, checking whether a formula φ is valid can be done by prefixing it with the negation symbol and checking whether $\neg\varphi$ is not satisfiable.

We therefore reduced (i.e., translated) the validity problem of a formula φ into a problem that we already know how to solve:

1. Translate $\neg\varphi$ into an automaton $\mathcal{A}$, as explained in Section 6.8.
2. Check for the emptiness of the language $\mathcal{L}(\mathcal{A})$ of $\mathcal{A}$, as explained in Section 6.6.

The language of $\mathcal{A}$ is exactly the set of executions satisfying the formula $\neg\varphi$. If it is empty, then $\neg\varphi$ is not satisfiable, i.e., φ is valid.

One may observe that the translation algorithm may produce an automaton that is exponentially larger than $\neg\varphi$. Checking for emptiness is linear in the size of the automaton. Hence the above algorithm is exponential in the size of the formula. One can check (un)satisfiability more efficiently in terms of the space complexity using a binary search technique, as discussed in section 6.9. There, a binary search through the state space of an automaton for $\neg\varphi$ is performed without completing the construction of the entire automaton [144]. Checking the (un)satisfiability of an LTL specification is also PSPACE-complete [132].

6.12 Safety Properties

An important class of temporal properties is called *safety properties*. Lamport [83] characterized safety properties informally by requiring that "nothing bad ever happen." There were many attempts to characterize these important properties formally, e.g., using topology or linear temporal logic with past modalities. We will adopt the definition of Alpern and Schneider [5], using automata. The simple structure of automata that describe safety can be immediately translated to a model checking algorithm [131].

To develop an intuition about safety properties, consider first the simpler case of an invariant. An invariant has to be satisfied throughout the execution. The "bad" thing that can happen is that we reach a state where the invariant does not hold. For example, this can be a state where two processes are in their critical section at the same time. An invariant is thus a safety property. However, safety can be more general than that. The bad thing, appearing in the informal definition of safety, does not have to be the result of having a single bad state in the execution of the program. It can correspond to a finite sequence of states, appearing in some order. For example, this can be the situation when one message arrives before the other to a message queue, but then the messages are being read in a reverse order.

We can develop a class of automata that will recognize the negation of safety properties. Such an automaton for a given safety property will identify prefixes of executions where the safety is violated. Such a prefix will include evidence that the bad thing has already occurred, hence the entire execution sequence is discarded as bad. The last state of a run on such a prefix will be a distinguished state marked as bad. Note that the states of the property automaton correspond to the information collected during the run of the automaton over the finite prefix of the input word. During a run of this automaton, when entering a bad state, the entire execution is considered as violating the safety condition. Thus, to recognize that safety has already been violated in an execution of the checked model, it is sufficient to follow a finite prefix of a run over that execution, which ends with a bad state. No matter how the (infinite) run over this (infinite) execution continues, safety was already violated.

A *safety automaton* is therefore a sextuple $\langle \Sigma, S, \Delta, I, L, B \rangle$. The components Σ, S, Δ, I and L are the same as in a Büchi automaton. The set $B \subseteq S$ is the set of *bad* states. We say that the states in $S \setminus B$ are the *good* states. We also have the following constraints:

1. A bad state does not have any successor. This is because when we reach a bad state, we know that safety is violated. For safety properties, it is enough to find that a prefix of the execution violates the property.
2. Let q be a good state, and $q_1, \ldots, q_n$ its immediate successors. Then $L(q_1) \vee \ldots \vee L(q_n) = true$. Thus, if safety is not yet violated, we cannot

yet make a conclusion about the execution, and thus there is always a successor automaton state.

Safety automata can be nondeterministic, although for each such safety property there is a corresponding deterministic automaton (which may be exponentially bigger). A run of the automaton is defined in a similar way to Büchi automaton. The only change is that an execution violates the safety property exactly if there is a run that enters a bad state in B after a finite prefix. Notice that in this case, since there are no successors for the states in B, the run is finite. A safety automaton $\overline{B}$ recognizes prefixes of executions that *violate* a safety property (hence we denoted the automaton by $\overline{B}$ instead of B). In the case of a nondeterministic safety automaton, it is enough to have a run that reaches a bad state in order to determine that the execution violates the safety property, even if there are other runs that never reach a bad state.

We can convert a safety automaton into a Büchi automaton in the following, simple way: add a single state l to the safety automaton, and label it with *true*. This state has a self loop. Add an edge from each bad state to l. The state l is the only accepting state of this automaton, and the bad states can now be ignored.

The safety automaton was constructed in such a way that it allows us to simplify the model checking algorithm. We would like to find finite prefixes of executions that violate the safety property. These are finite sequences that belong both to the automaton representing the system A and the safety automaton $\overline{B}$. The intersection of A and $\overline{B}$ is defined as follows: each state of the intersection is a pair consisting of a state from A and a state from $\overline{B}$. An initial state in the intersection is a pair of initial states from A and $\overline{B}$. The transition relation connects a pair of states with another pair such that the A component follows an A transition, and the $\overline{B}$ component follows a $\overline{B}$ transition. A state in the intersection is bad exactly if its $\overline{B}$ component is bad.

Replacing the Büchi conditions by a set of bad states gives a simpler model checking algorithm. In the general case, we search for a reachable Büchi accepting state inside a reachable strongly-connected component, and construct a counterexample that has a finite prefix followed by a cycle through the accepting state. Here, we seek a bad state that is reachable from an initial state in the intersection. As a counterexample, it is sufficient to give the prefix that leads from an initial state to a bad state, since the error already occurs in that prefix. Hence, a simple on-the-fly DFS, searching for such a state is sufficient. Notice that in this case there is no need to calculate the strongly-connected components of the intersection graph.

6.13 The State Space Explosion Problem

The main challenge in model checking is to alleviate the problem of state space explosion. This problem reflects the observation that a system comprised of concurrent components can have as many states as the multiplication of the numbers of states of the concurrent components. Recall that a system consisting of n identical components, each one of them with m states, and where the processes do not communicate or interact using shared variables, will have m^n states (n independent choices of m possibilities). Of course, in more realistic cases, the interaction between the processes may limit the number of possible states considerably. Still, the number of states may remain high.

There are several strategies that are used for attacking the state space explosion problem. None of them guarantees an efficient solution in combating the problem. Experience and experiments should be used in finding out which strategy or combination of strategies to use. Many model checking tools include at most one of these strategies.

We will list here some of the strategies. The interested reader may find more details in [30].

Binary Decision Diagrams [24]. One important technique to combat the state space explosion is to avoid having to calculate and store *separately* each state of the checked system. Instead of keeping each state in the state space as a separate entity, a collection of the states is kept in a cycle free diagram (DAG). Isomorphic subtrees, i.e., subtrees that can be mapped to each other such that the successor relation and the labeling are preserved, are combined together to save space. This data structure is often used within a search strategy other than depth-first search. The search progresses backwards rather than forwards. At each calculation step, the set of predecessors of the states represented by the current DAG are calculated, *all at once*, rather than state by state.

Partial Order Reduction [55, 113, 142]. This method allows checking only a subset of the executions, using a smaller state space. It exploits the commutativity between concurrent transitions. This is based on the observation that a typical specification does not distinguish between executions that are the same up to reordering of concurrently executed events (i.e., up to interleavings that are generated from the same partial order execution, see Section 4.13).

Symmetry [43]. This method is based on exploiting a permutation between the components of a state. It uses the observation that under some specifications (especially for hardware), one cannot distinguish between executions obtained from each other by permuting components that belong to different processes. Thus, in these cases one does not have to explore all the possible states, and can use one representative for each set of states that are equivalent up to permutation.

6.14 Advantages of Model Checking

Model checking is largely, but not completely, automatic. It may require modeling (although this can sometimes be automated as well) in order to represent the checked system in a form that can be manipulated by the tool used. Abstraction may be used to reduce the complexity of the verification problem. In addition, the user of model checking tools usually needs to set some verification parameters (for example, the estimated number of states). However, compared to other software reliability methods, the user's part in the verification process is rather small.

Model checking is based on ideas that are relatively easy to implement. A wealth of model checking tools exist (some are listed at the end of this chapter), which allow checking of a wide range of properties. Model checking tools provide important information when the checked property fails to hold. A counterexample can be generated that includes information about an execution where the property failed. This information can be used for debugging the code.

6.15 Weaknesses of Model Checking

Model checking is a collection of algorithms that should, in principle, be executed automatically by verification programs. In practice, because of the combinatorial complexity incurred in model checking, the user must often tune the verification by supplying various parameters such as the size of the search stack, the amount of memory allowed and the ordering between the model variables. This means that, in many cases, the user of a model checking tool is an expert in using the tool, and in some cases is the tool developer himself.

Model checking, like deductive verification, usually requires first modeling the checked system. Model checking tools often include an internal modeling language. Automatic translation is sometimes available between the original code and the syntax used by the verification tool. However, verification tools often include certain optimizations and heuristics for their internal syntax, which is typically lost in a mechanical translation. Moreover, the program that needs to be verified is often not originally a finite state system, and hence requires some abstraction to be applied before performing model checking. Such abstraction is often done manually. Consequently, if model checking is applied to the abstracted model of the program and an error is reported, one usually has to check, again manually, that the error is indeed a real one rather than a false negative, resulted from a discrepancy between the original program and the corresponding model.

The automatic verification of software is a computationally hard problem. Its complexity, as explored in Section 6.9, puts it together with problems that were not so long time ago considered to be prohibitively difficult. The quick advance of hardware, together with a wealth of special heuristics developed for model checking, contributed to the fact that automatic software verification can be applied in practice, at least to some abstract versions of the software products. Nevertheless, we must remember that the established complexity results still apply, and automatic software verification is still a very hard task, which can easily fail due to memory or time limitations.

Relying heavily on special heuristics, the existing automatic verification tools often fail to complete the verification task. It is even difficult to predict when a given tool will succeed or fail. One of the reasons is that the size of the state space required for verifying a program of a particular length varies considerably.

6.16 Selecting Automatic Verification Tools

Rules of thumb, based on practical observations and experiments, may suggest that some tools, based on a given set of techniques, can perform better than others. For example, many researchers believe that tools based on BDDs [24] are more suitable for the verification of hardware circuits, while tools based on on-the-fly [34] techniques, automata theory [144] and partial order reduction [113] are optimized for the interleaving model of software. However, these rough observations are not cast in stone.

Since the 'expertise' of verification tools is typically manifested by their special heuristics, it is not unusual that a tool is optimized for a particular form of software. For example, a verification tool can be optimized to work with programs that contain asynchronous message passing, while the existence of shared variables may neutralize most of its optimization. For this reason, automatic translations performed between formalisms used by different tools is usually much less efficient than using the specific syntax of a given tool directly. The translation often misses the particular form for which the particular target tool is optimized. The existence of a neutral and comprehensive 'benchmark' would help selecting among the different tools.

6.17 Model Checking Projects

Exercise 6.17.1. Consider again Dekker's algorithm for mutual exclusion from Section 4.6.
Task 1 Translate the algorithm into the modeling language of a model checking tool (e.g., use one of the tools that are listed in the next section).
Task 2 Formalize the following properties in the specification language of the tool, and perform the verification:

Exclusiveness The two processes cannot get into the critical section together.

Liveness Whenever a process tries to get into its critical section (by setting its own variable $c1$ or $c2$ to 0), it will eventually be able to do so.

Task 3 (advanced) Notice the following modeling variations:

Allow a self loop on the noncritical section of each process. Repeat the checking while disallowing this loop.

Allow two kinds of implementation for *wait until turn=1*:

1. Busy waiting: each process checks the value of *turn* until it is set by the other process to the value that allows it to progress.
2. Non-busy waiting: each process freezes itself until the value it needs to continue is being set by the other process.

Verify the above properties with all combinations. Check whether the algorithm satisfies its liveness property. Now, force it to satisfy the liveness property by imposing weak fairness conditions. Not every tool allows fairness, but some allow specifying a formula *fair*. In this case, instead of checking a property φ, check equivalently *fair* $\rightarrow \varphi$. (Compare the verification results to the discussion of this interesting phenomena, given in Section 8.4.)

Exercise 6.17.2. Consider the communication protocol in Section 4.15. Model it using the formalism used in one of the available model checking tools. Check the properties formalized in Exercise 5.10.3.

6.18 Model Checking Tools

The COSPAN and FORMALCHECK systems can be obtained from R. P. Kurshan at Bell Labs. His home URL is
http://cm.bell-labs.com/who/k/index.html
The MURPHY model checking tool can be obtained from Stanford University, using the URL
http://sprout.stanford.edu/dill/murphi.html
The SPIN model checking tool can be obtained from Bell Laboratories, using the URL
http://netlib.bell-labs.com/netlib/spin/whatispin.html
The SMV model checking tool can be obtained from CMU, using the URL
http://www.cs.cmu.edu/~modelcheck/code.html
The VIS model checking tool can be obtained from Berkeley, using the URL
http://www-cad.EECS.Berkeley.EDU/Respep/Research/vis
   Notice: the use of formal methods systems often requires filling out and sending an appropriate release form, committing to some terms of use.

6.19 Further Reading

A recent comprehensive book on model checking techniques is

E. M. Clarke, O. Grumberg, D. A. Peled, *Model Checking*, MIT Press 1999.

It deals with various techniques and heuristics and present several realistic case studies.

The automata approach to model checking is described in Kurshan's book

R. P. Kurshan, *Computer Aided Verification of Coordinating Processes: the Automata–Theoretic Approach*, Princeton University Press, 1995.

There are several books that cover model checking with the BDD approach, based on the CTL branching temporal logic. This approach is often used for verifying hardware, but can be applied to software as well.

K. L. McMillan, *Symbolic Model Checking*, Kluwer Academic Press, 1993.

Ch. Meinel, Th. Theobald, *Algorithms and Data Structures in VLSI Design*, Springer-Verlag, 1998.

7. Deductive Software Verification

'Please your Majesty,' said the Knave, 'I didn't write it, and they can't prove I did: there's no name signed at the end.'
'If you didn't sign it,' said the King, 'that only makes the matter worse. You MUST *have meant some mischief, or else you'd have signed your name like an honest man.'*
'That PROVES *his guilt,' said the Queen.*

Lewis Carroll, *Alice's Adventures in Wonderland*

In the late 1960's, several researchers, in particular Floyd [45] and Hoare [63], advocated the idea of formally verifying algorithms and computer programs. The techniques developed involved formalisms that combine program text and logic, used within specially developed proof systems. Later works considered the addition of various programming constructs such as array variables and procedure calls [85] and concurrency [86, 108]. It was also suggested that such proof systems will be used in the opposite way: applying methods and tools related to deductive verification to develop provably correct programs from a given specification. A collection of powerful mechanized theorem provers have been developed recently (see a list of some of these tools at the end of this chapter). These can assist in obtaining correctness proofs and enforcing the correct use of deductive verification.

In addition to enhancing program correctness, there are several beneficial ideas that originally came from deductive program verification. One of them is the use of *invariants*, i.e., assertions that need to hold throughout the execution of the code. Invariants can be used to check the consistency of the code during the different development stages. They can be inserted into the code as additional runtime checks so that the program will break with a warning message when an invariant is violated.

Another use of proof systems for software reliability is to define the semantics of various programming language constructs. One can understand a construct such as a *while-loop* through a corresponding proof rule.

Since deductive verification is often tedious, it is not performed frequently on actual code. However, it can be performed on the basic algorithms that are used, or on simplified abstractions of the code. The faithfulness of the translation from one program to a simpler, abstracted one can sometimes also be formally verified.

7.1 Verification of Flow Chart Programs

The first proof system to allow program verification, was developed by Floyd [45]. It deals with a simple class of programs, presented as *flowcharts*. These programs include simple assignments, of the form $v:=e$, for some program variable v and some expression e, and decision predicates. An expression e is a first order term over some given structure and signature. A decision predicate is an unquantified first order formula over that structure. A flowchart has four kinds of nodes (see Figure 7.1):

- An oval, with one outgoing edge and no incoming edges, represents a *begin* statement.
- An oval, with one incoming edge and no outgoing edges, represents an *end* statement.
- A parallelogram, with one or more incoming edges and one outgoing edge, represents an *assignment*.
- A rhombus, with one or more incoming edges and two outgoing edges marked with *true* and *false*, represents a *decision*.

An example of a flowchart program appears in Figure 7.2.

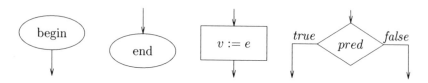

Fig. 7.1. Nodes in a flowchart

In early days of computing, programmers used to draw flowcharts of their algorithms before writing actual code. Although flowcharts are still in use, they are somewhat less common. Flowcharts can also be obtained automatically from programming languages by means of compilation. To present them in a reasonable visual form, while minimizing edge intersection, one can use special graph layout algorithms [50].

To simplify the notation, assume that the initial values of the program are stored in a set of input variables $x0$, $x1$, ..., and that these variables do not change their values during the execution of the program. Thus, the input variables may not appear on the lefthand side of an assignment.

With each program, we associate a first order assertion called the *initial condition*. The free variables of this assertion are among the input variables.

The initial condition restricts the set of values assigned to these variables at the beginning of each execution of the program.

A *state* of a program is simply an assignment to the program variables. Recall the fact that an assignment a (a state) that satisfies a formula φ is denoted by $M_a(\varphi) = \text{TRUE}$ (here, the structure S is not mentioned and is assumed to be understood from the context), or by $a \models^S \varphi$. An execution of a program is a finite or infinite sequence of states where the first state satisfies the initial condition, and each subsequent state b is obtained from its previous state a as follows:

- If a is a state on an in-edge of a decision node with a predicate p, b is a state on the out-edge labeled *true* from that node, and $a \models^S p$ holds, then b is the same as a.
- If a is a state on an in-edge of a decision node with predicate p, b is a state on the out-edge labeled *false* from that node, and $a \models^S \neg p$ holds, then b is the same of a.
- If a is a state before an assignment $v := e$ and b is a state just after that assignment, then b is $a[T_a[e]/v]$. Recall from Section 3.3 that $T_a[e]$ is the value of the expression e calculated according to the state a, and that $a[d/v]$ is an assignment similar to a, except for the value of v, which is set to d. Thus, the state b after the assignment is the same as a, except for the value of the variable v, which is changed to hold the value of the expression e, calculated in the previous state a.

A *polarized node* is a combination of a flowchart node and a specific choice of one of its out-edges. Thus, any assignment forms a polarized node, as it has only one out-edge. Each decision node forms two polarized nodes: a *positive* decision, with an outgoing edge marked *true* and a *negative* decision, with the outgoing edge marked *false*.

A *final assertion* of a program is a first order formula that needs to be satisfied by the final states of every execution, provided that the program was executed after being initialized with its initial condition. A *location* of a flowchart program is an edge connecting two flowchart nodes. The initial condition is attached to the location exiting from the *begin* node, and the final assertion is attached to the location entering the *end* node. Initial conditions and final assertions are just two out of many assertions that can be attached to the locations of a flowchart program. Assertions attached to flowchart locations are also called *invariants*, as they are supposed to hold for every state in which the control is exactly in the place where the invariant is attached. The usual meaning of an invariant is that it always holds throughout the execution of the program. An assertion φ attached to a flowchart location X is an invariant in the following sense: if we add a proposition $at(X)$, that holds exactly when the program control is at the location X, then $at(X) \to \varphi$ holds throughout the execution of the program. It holds in the control points other than x as well, since there $at(X)$ is FALSE and thus the entire implication becomes TRUE.

An invariant on an incoming edge of a node is said to be a *precondition* of that node, while an invariant on an outgoing edge of a node is a *postcondition* of the node. Notice that each decision node has two postconditions, while each polarized node has only one. The same invariant can be a precondition of one node and a postcondition of another. In the flowchart program in Figure 7.2, the initial condition, attached to the location A is $x1 \geq 0 \wedge x2 > 0$. The final assertion, attached to location F is $(x1 \equiv y1 \times x2 + y2) \wedge y2 \geq 0 \wedge y2 < x2$. We can attach additional assertions to the flowchart locations (i.e., edges), for example, at location C, we can attach the assertion $(x1 \equiv y1 \times x2 + y2) \wedge y2 \geq 0$. In fact, for correctness proofs, we will attach such an assertion to every flowchart location. Of course, attaching an assertion to a location does not mean immediately that this is an invariant. We still have to *prove*, in a manner that will be explained shortly, that the assertions attached are invariants.

We can view a sequential program P as a relation between input states and output states. Thus, $P(a, b)$ represents the fact that executing P from a state satisfying a, it terminates at the *end* node with a state satisfying b. For simplicity, we assume that P is deterministic. Consequently, for a given initial state a, either P never terminates, or terminates with a unique final state b.

Partial correctness of a program is an assertion that contains a triple: an initial condition φ, a program P and a final assertion ψ. This is usually denoted as $\{\varphi\}P\{\psi\}$. It expresses the fact that if a program starts with a state satisfying φ and then terminates at the *end* node, then the final state satisfies ψ. Formally, for every pair of program states a, b,

$$\text{if } P(a, b) \text{ and } a \models^S \varphi \text{ then } b \models^S \psi.$$

This formalization is subtly crafted. Careful observation reveals that it does not contain any claim about guaranteed termination of the program from the states satisfying the initial condition. This is not coincidental. It turns out that proving partial correctness separately is simpler than proving at the same time that the program also terminates. In fact, the name 'partial correctness' represents the fact that it does not give a complete account of the correctness of the program. *Total correctness*, which is the combination of partial correctness and termination, will be discussed later. A consequence of the formalization of partial correctness is that it allows the existence of states that satisfy the initial condition φ and from which the program does not terminate.

In order to prove partial correctness, we need to show that if the program starts with a state that satisfies the initial condition, and during an execution it reaches a particular location corresponding to some edge of the flowchart, then it satisfies the invariant at that location. To show that we need to prove consistency between the invariants annotating the flowchart program. Let c be a polarized node, with precondition $pre(c)$ and postcondition $post(c)$. We need to show the following:

If the control of the program is just before c, with a state satisfying $pre(c)$ and c is executed such that control moves to the edge annotated by $post(c)$, then the state after the move satisfies $post(c)$.

This can be denoted using the above notation as $\{pre(c)\}c\{post(c)\}$. For polarized flowchart nodes there are three cases for the *consistency conditions*:

1. c is a positive decision, i.e., $post(c)$ is the postcondition after taking the *true* out-edge of c, with predicate p. Then the state before and after the decision remains the same. Thus, we need to show that if $pre(c)$ holds at that state, and the decision predicate is interpreted as TRUE, then $post(c)$ holds. Hence, we have to prove the implication

$$(pre(c) \wedge p) \rightarrow post(c).$$

2. c is a negative decision, i.e., $post(c)$ is the postcondition after taking the *false* outgoing edge of c, with predicate p. As in the previous case, but now with $\neg p$ holding, we have to prove the implication

$$(pre(c) \wedge \neg p) \rightarrow post(c).$$

3. c is an assignment $v := e$. This case is more difficult, as the states before and after the assignment are different. In particular, the assertions $pre(c)$ and $post(c)$ do not reason about the same states. The first step is then to make these two formulas assert about the same state. We can do this by *relativizing* $post(c)$ to assert about the states before the assignment, obtaining an assertion $relpost(c)$. (We could also relativize $pre(c)$ to reason about the states after the assignment, but this happens to give a more complicated first order formula, which involves adding quantification, see e.g., [11].)

We define $relpost(c) = post(c)[e/v]$, for $c =$'$v := e$'. This construction may seem surprising at first. It prescribes taking the postcondition, and replaces each free occurrence of the variable v by the expression e. While the assignment works in the forward direction, this substitution works in the backward direction: from the postcondition to the precondition!

To see why this works, consider two sets of variables: the program variables, which will represent the values at the state just before the assignments, and another, primed copy of these variables, representing the program state just after executing the assignment. The relation between the two sets is that $u' \equiv u$ for each variable u other than v, and $v' \equiv e$. Notice that e is expressed using unprimed variables only, as the assigned expression uses the value according to the state *before* the assignment. Thus, $relpost(c)$ can be obtained as follows: first, rewrite $post(c)$ with the primed variables replacing free occurrences of the program variables by their primed counterparts. We need now to write the formula that represents the states prior to the assignment. This can be done by eliminating the primed variables, using the above relation between the primed and unprimed variables. That is, we replace each primed variable by its unprimed version, except for replacing v' by e. This gives $post(c)[e/v]$. Notice that in the actual substitution, one does not need to first translate the variables to their primed version, but only to replace v with e, since the primed variables were only introduced in order to explain the backward substitution.

In the partial correctness proof, we need to prove that each state satisfying $pre(c)$ also satisfies $relpost(c)$. If it satisfies $relpost(c)$, it is guaranteed that after executing the assignment, the resulting state satisfies $post(c)$. This implication $pre(c) \rightarrow relpost(c)$, can be denoted as

$$pre(c) \rightarrow post(c)[e/v].$$

We claim now that proving the consistency between each precondition and postcondition of a given polarized node of the flowchart program guarantees the partial correctness of the program. In fact, this guarantees a stronger property:

> In each execution that starts with a state satisfying the initial condition of the program, when the control of the program is at some location, the condition attached to that location holds.

In particular, when reaching the edge entering the *end* node of a program, the final assertion, which is attached to that location, must hold. The proof of the above property is based on a simple induction on the length of prefixes of the execution sequences that start from a state satisfying the initial condition. The base of the induction trivially holds. The induction step is explained as follows. Suppose such a prefix ends with a state a in some location with condition $pre(c)$ and then c is executed. In this case, by the induction hypothesis, $a \models^S pre(c)$. Then, the correspondence between the precondition and postcondition pairs, as prescribed by the above three cases, guarantees that if c is executed, we reach a state b satisfying $post(c)$. The state b can then extend the previous prefix into a prefix that is longer by one, where each state satisfies the corresponding location condition in the flowchart.

The flowchart program in Figure 7.2 calculates the *integer* division of $x1$ by $x2$ for *natural* numbers. The result is stored at the end of the computation in the variable $y1$, and the remainder is in $y2$. The initial condition is $x1 \geq 0 \wedge x2 > 0$. The final assertion is $(x1 \equiv y1 \times x2 + y2) \wedge y2 \geq 0 \wedge y2 < x2$.

Finding invariants for the proof may be a difficult task. There are several heuristics and tools that attempt to suggest invariants [75]. However, from the theory of computability, we know that there cannot be a fully automatic way of finding them, i.e., this problem is undecidable. The first step in seeking invariants is to look carefully at the program, and study its behavior, e.g., by simulating some executions. Then, we can try to figure out the relation between the different program variables at different locations.

This usually involves some trial and error. We may start with a preliminary set of location invariants, and try to verify the consistency conditions

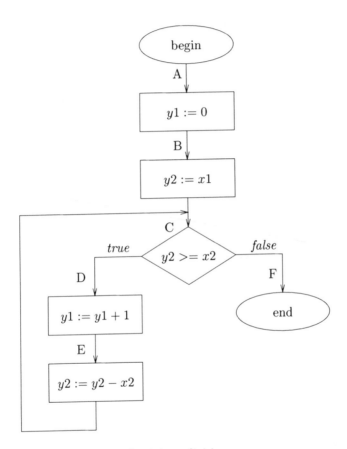

Fig. 7.2. A flowchart program for *integer* division

between the preconditions and the postconditions of the polarized nodes. Suppose that c is a positive decision polarized node, and we fail to prove that $pre(c) \land p \to post(c)$. This can happen since $pre(c)$ is too weak and does not contain enough connections between the program variables at the location entering c. Another possibility is that $post(c)$ is not a correct invariant at the location exiting c, and some of the connections it stipulates do not hold when the control of the program is at that location.

Example: Integer Division

The input for this program is a non-negative *integer* in $x1$ and a positive *integer* in $x2$. The result of this program is the *integer* division of $x2$ by $x1$ in $y1$ and the reminder of that division in $y2$. Thus, the initial condition is $x1 \geq 0 \land x2 > 0$. The final assertion is $(x1 \equiv y1 \times x2 + y2) \land y2 \geq 0 \land y2 < x2$.

The locations in Figure 7.2 are labeled with the letters A through F. We can first ascribe to the location A the initial condition, and to the location F the final assertion. We observe the following: at the beginning, $y2$ gets the value of $x1$. In the main loop, as long as $y2$ is not smaller than $x2$, we subtract $x2$ from $y2$ and add 1 to $y1$. At location C, the number of times we deducted $x2$ from $y2$ is $y1$. Overall, we so far subtracted $y1 \times x2$ from $y2$. If we add to this multiplication the number remained in $y2$, this should sum up to the initial (and also current) value in $x1$. That is, at location C, we have $x1 \equiv y1 \times x2 + y2$. Moreover, it is easy to see that $y2 \geq 0$ holds there. In a similar way, we assign the following invariants:

$$\varphi(A) = x1 \geq 0 \land x2 > 0$$
$$\varphi(B) = x1 \geq 0 \land x2 > 0 \land y1 \equiv 0$$
$$\varphi(C) = (x1 \equiv y1 \times x2 + y2) \land y2 \geq 0$$
$$\varphi(D) = (x1 \equiv y1 \times x2 + y2) \land y2 \geq x2$$
$$\varphi(E) = (x1 \equiv y1 \times x2 + y2 - x2) \land y2 - x2 \geq 0$$
$$\varphi(F) = (x1 \equiv y1 \times x2 + y2) \land y2 \geq 0 \land y2 < x2$$

To show consistency, we need to prove the following implications using some first order logic proof system:

$\varphi(A) \to \varphi(B)[0/y1] =$
$\quad (x1 \geq 0 \land x2 > 0) \to (x1 \geq 0 \land x2 > 0 \land 0 \equiv 0)$

$\varphi(B) \to \varphi(C)[x1/y2] =$
$\quad (x1 \geq 0 \land x2 > 0 \land y1 \equiv 0) \to ((x1 \equiv y1 \times x2 + x1) \land x1 \geq 0)$

$(\varphi(C) \land y2 \geq x2) \to \varphi(D) =$
$\quad ((x1 \equiv y1 \times x2 + y2) \land y2 \geq 0 \land y2 \geq x2) \to$
$\quad ((x1 \equiv y1 \times x2 + y2) \land y2 \geq x2)$

$(\varphi(C) \wedge \neg y2 \geq x2) \to \varphi(F) =$
  $((x1 \equiv y1 \times x2 + y2) \wedge y2 \geq 0 \wedge \neg y2 \geq x2) \to$
  $((x1 \equiv y1 \times x2 + y2) \wedge y2 \geq 0 \wedge y2 < x2)$

$\varphi(D) \to \varphi(E)[y1 + 1/y1] =$
  $((x1 \equiv y1 \times x2 + y2) \wedge y2 \geq x2) \to$
  $((x1 \equiv (y1 + 1) \times x2 + y2 - x2) \wedge y2 - x2 \geq 0)$

$\varphi(E) \to \varphi(C)[y2 - x2/y2] =$
  $((x1 \equiv y1 \times x2 + y2 - x2) \wedge y2 - x2 \geq 0) \to$
  $((x1 \equiv y1 \times x2 + y2 - x2) \wedge y2 - x2 \geq 0)$

Exercise 7.1.1. Use a mechanized theorem prover to prove the implication that shows the consistency between points D and E and between E and C.

7.2 Verification with Array Variables

The proof system presented in the previous section deals only with simple variables over some domain $\mathcal{D}$. When array variables are allowed, the proof system needs to be modified. This, more advanced section, can be safely skipped.

The Problem with Array Variable Assignment

To see the problem involved, consider the assignment $x[x[1]] := 2$. It assigns the value 2 to $x[x[1]]$, where the *index* $x[1]$ is calculated according to the state *before the assignment*. However, it may also have the side effect of assigning 2 to $x[1]$, in the case that $x[1] = 1$ before the assignment (since then $x[1]$ and $x[x[1]]$ are two references to the same memory location). Suppose that the precondition for c is $pre(c) = x[1] \equiv 1$ and the postcondition is $post(c) = x[x[1]] \equiv 2$. The assertion

$$\{x[1] \equiv 1 \wedge x[2] \equiv 3\}x[x[1]] := 2\{x[x[1]] \equiv 2\} \tag{7.1}$$

is not correct. It suggests that after the assignment, we have $x[x[1]] \equiv 2$. However, since $x[1] \equiv 1$ initially, we have now $x[1] \equiv 2$, and hence $x[x[1]]$ is now $x[2]$, which is 3 and not 2.

A naive application of the proof system presented in the previous section allows 'proving' the incorrect assertion (7.1) as follows. Let us relativize $post(c)$ to the state before the assignment according to the formalization in the previous section. We obtain

$$relpost(c) = x[x[1]] \equiv 2[2/x[x[1]]] = 2 \equiv 2 = true \tag{7.2}$$

Now, using (7.2) we obtain that $pre(c) \to relpost(c)$ is $x[1] \equiv 1 \to true$, which is logically equivalent to *true*. This establishes (7.1). Our proof system, as used here, allows us to prove incorrect facts, and is thus invalid. Thus, we need to change it. We do that by changing the relativization of array assignments.

Modifying the Proof System

To correctly handle array variables, we will extend the first order logic defined in Chapter 3. The syntactic entity *term* (defined in Section 3.2) will also include references to array elements. In addition, a new kind of terms, which behave in a similar way the to *if-then-else* construct in functional programming languages, is introduced. The extended BNF definition for terms is then

$$term ::= var \mid func(term, term, \dots, term) \mid const \mid$$
$$if(form, term, term) \mid arr\_var[term] \mid (arr\_var, term : term)$$

The construct *arr_var* refers to a name of an array variable. We assume that the set of array variables used in the program is disjoint from simple variables. We do not allow quantifying over them in our first order logic assertions.

Assignments are extended to return values for elements in arrays. Accordingly, if x is an array, i is an index (we ignore here the problem of out-of-bound indexing), and a is an assignment, then $a(\langle x, i \rangle)$ gives a value in the domain $\mathcal{D}$. The interpretation function T_a is extended as follows:

$$T_a[x[e]] \;=\; a(\langle x, T_a[e] \rangle)$$
$$T_a[if(\varphi, e1, e2)] \;=\; \begin{cases} T_a[e1] & if\ M_a[\varphi] = \text{TRUE} \\ T_a[e2] & otherwise \end{cases}$$

The *if* construct does not add any expressiveness to the logic, since it can be eliminated. However, dispensing with it may involve a considerable (exponential) increase in the size of the formula. Consider a formula ψ with an *if* construct $if(\varphi, e1, e2)$. This formula can be translated into an intermediate form η such that the subformula $if(\varphi, e1, e2)$ is replaced by a new variable v. Then, the original formula ψ is equivalent to

$$(\varphi \wedge \eta[e1/v]) \vee (\neg\varphi \wedge \eta[e2/v]). \tag{7.3}$$

This process can be repeated until all of the *if* constructs are eliminated (notice that multiple identical occurrences of an *if* subformula should be eliminated simultaneously).

For example, consider the formula

$$x1 > if(x2 > 3,\ x4,\ if(x3 > x5, 2, 4)). \tag{7.4}$$

According to the above translation, when replacing the innermost *if* in (7.4) with the new variable v we obtain that the following formula:

$$\eta = x1 > if(x2 > 3,\ x4,\ v),\ \varphi = x3 > x5,\ e1 = 2,\ e2 = 4.$$

According to (7.3) we obtain the following formula, which is equivalent to (7.4):

$$(x3 > x5) \land (x1 > if(x2 > 3, x4, 2)) \lor$$
$$\neg(x3 > x5) \land (x1 > if(x2 > 3, x4, 4)).$$

Notice that the formula obtained now includes two *if* constructs, which need to be eliminated.

Exercise 7.2.1. Eliminate all the *if* constructs from the above formula.

The extended definition for terms, given in this section, includes another construct: for an array variable x, let $(x; e1 : e2)$, where $e1$ and $e2$ are expressions, be a *variant* of x. Informally, the variant $(x; e1 : e2)$ is different from x only in the value of its $e1$ element, which is set to $e2$. We can use a variant in a first order formula in place of an array variable (notice that a variant is an array, not an array element). The formal semantics is as follows:

$$T_a[(x; e1 : e2)[e3]] = \begin{cases} T_a[e2] & if \ T_a[e1] = T_a[e3] \\ a(\langle x, T_a[e3] \rangle) & otherwise \end{cases}$$

The variant notation can also be eliminated from formulas, using the following translation:

$$(x; e1 : e2)[e3] = if(e1 \equiv e3, e2, x[e3]) \tag{7.5}$$

To obtain the correct substitution for array assignments, again write the variables after the assignment using their primed version, and then replace them by expressions representing these values using the unprimed variables. The subtle point is that we need to work with the primed and unprimed version of *array variables*, rather than with the primed and unprimed version of *elements of arrays*. The definition of an array variant will help us to make this connection.

If the assigned variable is a simple one, then the substitution works just as in the previous section. However, if the assigned variable is an array variable, it must be substituted by a variant. Thus, if the assignment c is $x[e1] := e2$, then x' after the assignment is the same as $(x; e1 : e2)$ before. As in the simple assignment case, described in the previous section, one does not need to substitute variables by their primed values first, as this is done only to explain the proof system. In the above assignment, one can directly substitute x by its variant $(x; e1 : e2)$. The relativization substitution is then

$$relpost(c) = post(c)[(x; e1 : e2)/x]$$

Then, all the instances of variants are eliminated by using the translation rule (7.5).

We will return now to the case where c is $x[x[1]] := 2$ and $post(c) = x[x[1]] \equiv 2$. The relativized postcondition $relpost(c)$ is

$$x[x[1]] \equiv 2[(x; x[1] : 2)/x]$$

Performing the substitution of the variant for x, we obtain

$$(x; x[1] : 2)[(x; x[1] : 2)[1]] \equiv 2$$

Now, we can eliminate the second occurrence of the variant notation and replace it with an *if* construct as explained above. We obtain

$$(x; x[1] : 2)[if(x[1] \equiv 1, 2, x[1])] \equiv 2 \tag{7.6}$$

Eliminating the remaining occurrence of the variant, we have

$$if(x[1] \equiv \underline{if(x[1] \equiv 1, 2, x[1])}, 2, x[\underline{if(x[1] \equiv 1, 2, x[1])}]) \equiv 2 \tag{7.7}$$

We underlined two occurrences of an *if* construct that are identical. Thus, we can eliminate both of them at the same time. Replacing the underlined occurrences with v, we obtain $\eta = if(x[1] \equiv v, 2, x[v]) \equiv 2$, $\varphi = x[1] \equiv 1$, $e1 = 2$, $e2 = x[1]$. Then, according to the transformation in (7.3), we obtain

$$(x[1] \equiv 1 \wedge if(x[1] \equiv 2, 2, x[2]) \equiv 2) \vee (x[1] \neq 1 \wedge if(x[1] \equiv x[1], 2, x[x[1]]) \equiv 2).$$

We can make some logical simplifications. First, $if(x[1] \equiv x[1], 2, x[x[1]]) \equiv 2$. Further, given that $x[1] \equiv 1$, we have that $if(x[1] \equiv 2, 2, x[2]) \equiv x[2]$. Thus, we obtain the simpler formula

$$(x[1] \equiv 1 \wedge x[2] \equiv 2) \vee (x[1] \neq 1) \tag{7.8}$$

By applying some logical equivalence on (7.8), we can finally obtain

$$relpost(c) = x[1] \equiv 1 \rightarrow x[2] \equiv 2$$

It is obvious that the above logical manipulations required for obtaining the relativized postcondition are quite difficult, and hard to follow. A mechanized theorem prover can help in performing or in checking the correctness of these manipulations.

7.3 Total Correctness

The *total correctness* of a program, denoted as $\langle\varphi\rangle P\langle\psi\rangle$ asserts that if the program P is executed starting from a state satisfying the initial condition φ, then it *terminates* with a state satisfying the formula ψ. Formally, for every pair of program states a, b,

if $a \models^S \varphi$ then there exists a state b such that $P(a, b)$ and $b \models^S \psi$.

(This definition is based on the fact that flowchart programs are *deterministic*.) One can establish total correctness by proving separately partial correctness *and* termination (although we will explain later how total correctness can be proved directly). In general, the justification behind the partial correctness of a program may differ from the justification for termination. Thus, this separation, although not necessary, may help simplify the proofs. Termination (again, for deterministic programs) is defined formally as,

If $a \models^S \varphi$ then there is a state b such that $P(a, b)$.

In Section 7.1, a method for proving partial correctness that uses a simple induction over finite prefixes of executions was presented. The induction stated that if consistency between adjacent preconditions and postconditions was proved, then each state in an execution, initialized with a state satisfying the initial condition, satisfies some invariant associated with some program location. In particular, if the program terminates, then the last state must satisfy the invariant associated with the location that enters the *end* node, which happens to be the final assertion of the program.

This kind of inductive reasoning is not sufficient to show termination, as it deals with *finite* prefixes of arbitrary length. What we need is an induction principle that takes into account the possibility of having an infinite execution, and then ruling it out. We thus employ in termination proofs another reasoning principle, which involves well founded domains.

A *partially ordered domain* is a pair $(W, \succ)$, where W is a set and '$\succ$' is a partial order relation over W. Recall that the following conditions must hold for a partial order relation '$\succ$':

Irreflexivity. for no $u \in W$ it holds that $u \succ u$.
Asymmetry. For each $u, v \in W$, if $u \succ v$ then $v \succ u$ does not hold (we write also $v \not\succ u$).
Transitivity. if $u \succ v$ and $v \succ w$ for some $u, v, w \in W$ then $u \succ w$.

We denote $u \succeq v$ when $u \succ v$ or $u \equiv v$. When $u \succ v$, we also write $v \prec u$. Similarly, $u \succeq v$ and $v \preceq u$ are the same.

Some examples of partially ordered domains are:

- The set of *integers* with the usual 'greater than' relation '$>$'.
- The set of finite sets of *integers*, with set inclusion relation '$\supset$'.
- The set of *strings* over some finite alphabet, where $u \succ w$ if w is a *substring* of u. That is, there are strings v_1 and v_2 such that $u = v_1.w.v_2$.
- Strings over some finite alphabets (e.g., the Latin alphabet), with the lexicographic order, i.e., the order in which words would have appeared in a dictionary.
- Tuples of *natural* numbers, e.g., pairs or triples, with the alphabetic ordered between tuples. Similar to alphabetic order in dictionaries, the alphabetic order between tuples gives precedence to the order between the two first component elements. If they are not the same, the tuples are ordered according to the order between these elements. If these elements are the same, priority is given to the second component, and so forth. For example, for pairs, $(u_1, u_2) \succ (v_1, v_2)$ if $u_1 > v_1$ or if $u_1 \equiv v_1$ and $u_2 > v_2$.

A *well founded domain* is a partially ordered domain that contains no infinite decreasing sequence, i.e., no sequence of the form $w_0 \succ w_1 \succ \ldots \succ w_n \succ \ldots$. The first partially ordered domain presented above is not well founded. This is because for the *integers* with the usual 'greater than' relation, there is an infinite decreasing chain, e.g., $0 > -1 > -2 > \ldots$. If we replace the set of *integers* by *naturals*, we obtain a well founded domain. The strings with lexicographic order are also not founded, for example, consider the infinite sequence $ab > aab > aaab > \ldots$. The other partially ordered domains presented above are well founded.

To prove termination we need to follow the following steps.

- Select a well founded domain $(W, \succ)$. It is required that $W \subseteq \mathcal{D}$, and the relation $\succ$ must be expressible using the signature of the program.
- Attach to each location in the flowchart a formula (an invariant) and an expression. The formula attached to the edge outgoing from the *begin* node is the initial condition. (It is possible to prove termination together with partial correctness, achieving total correctness, by attaching the final assertion to the edge that enters the *end* node.) During any execution of the program, whenever the control of the program is at a certain location with an attached expression e and a state a, the value $T_a(e)$ is associated with the current state.
- Show consistency between the precondition and postcondition of each polarized node, as in the partial correctness proof.
- Show that the value associated with each state in the execution satisfies the following conditions:
  - When an expression e, attached to a flowchart location, is calculated in some state in the execution (when the program counter is in that location), it is within the set W.
  - In each execution of the program, when progressing from one location to a successor location, the value of the associated expression does not increase.
  - In each execution of the program, during a traversal of a cycle (a loop) in the flowchart there is some point where a decrease occurs in the value of the associated expression from one location to its successor.

Let c be some polarized node, $pre(c)$ and $post(c)$ its precondition and postcondition, respectively, and e_1 and e_2 the expressions attached to the entering and exiting edges, respectively. We will now formalize the conditions that need to be proved.

First, the consistency conditions between the precondition and the postcondition are the same as in the partial correctness proof. There are three cases:

- A positive decision p. Then

$$(pre(c) \wedge p) \rightarrow post(c). \tag{7.9}$$

- A negative decision p. Then

$$(pre(c) \wedge \neg p) \rightarrow post(c). \tag{7.10}$$

- An assignment $v := e$. Then

$$pre(c) \rightarrow post(c)[e/v]. \tag{7.11}$$

This establishes that each time the execution reaches some particular location, the invariant associated with that location holds.

To show that the value attached to a location using an expression e is from the set W, one needs to show that

$$\varphi \rightarrow (e \in W). \tag{7.12}$$

Recall that $e \in W$ in not, in general, a first order logic formula. However, in this context, it can often be translated into a first order term, depending on the verified program. For example, when the program domain is the *integers*, it may be the case that the well founded domain consists of the *natural numbers* with the usual '>' relation. In this case, (7.12) becomes $\varphi \rightarrow (e \geq 0)$.

To prove that $T_a(e_1) \succeq T_b(e_1)$ for each state a such that $a \models^{\mathcal{S}} pre(c)$ and a successor state b such that $b \models^{\mathcal{S}} post(c)$, one needs to *relativize* one of the expressions e_1 or e_2 so that both are expressed with respect to the same state. We choose to relativize e_2, obtaining $rel_c(e_2)$. As in section 7.1, we can use a primed set of variables to represent the values of the program variables after executing c. Then according to the type of the (polarized) node c we replace the prime variables by expressions with unprimed variables.

- For a positive or negative decision c, we have $u \equiv u'$ for each program variable v. Thus, $rel_c(e_2) \equiv e_2$.
- For an assignment $v := e$, we have that $u \equiv u'$ for every $u \neq v$, and $v' \equiv e$. This results in $rel_{v:=e}(e_2) \equiv e_2[e/v]$.

To show a non-increase in the value attached to each location using the expression e, during the execution of a polarized node c, one proves the implication

$$pre(c) \rightarrow (e_1 \succeq rel_c(e_2)). \tag{7.13}$$

To show a decrease along each cycle in the flowchart , one proves that there is at least one polarized node c where

$$pre(c) \rightarrow (e_1 \succ rel_c(e_2)). \tag{7.14}$$

Now we can argue that the program must terminate. This will be based on a contradiction argument. Suppose that (7.9)–(7.14) are proved for a program P, yet P does not terminate. Consider the sequence of attached values for some nonterminated execution of P. Since the domain $(W, \succ)$ is well founded, this cannot form an infinite decreasing sequence. Since it was established by (7.13) that this is a nondecreasing sequence, it must reach at some point a constant value. Consider the execution from the point where the associated value remains constant. Since the program has only finitely many locations, it cannot pass in this suffix through infinitely many nodes, hence it must

pass some cycle. But then according to (7.14), there must be a decrease in
the attached values, a contradiction.

We will now prove the termination of the flowchart program in Figure 7.2.
We select the well founded domain $(Nat, >)$, i.e., the *naturals* with the usual
ordering relation. The annotation of invariants and expressions for the location A through F is as follows:

$$\varphi(A) = x1 \geq 0 \wedge x2 > 0 \qquad e(A) = x1$$
$$\varphi(B) = x1 \geq 0 \wedge x2 > 0 \qquad e(B) = x1$$
$$\varphi(C) = x2 > 0 \wedge y2 \geq 0 \qquad e(C) = y2$$
$$\varphi(D) = x2 > 0 \wedge y2 \geq x2 \qquad e(D) = y2$$
$$\varphi(E) = x2 > 0 \wedge y2 \geq x2 \qquad e(E) = y2$$
$$\varphi(F) = y2 \geq 0 \qquad\qquad\quad e(F) \equiv y2$$

To show that the expression returns a value from the well founded domain,
we have immediately that

$$\varphi(A) \rightarrow x1 \in Nat \quad \varphi(B) \rightarrow x1 \in Nat$$
$$\varphi(C) \rightarrow y2 \in Nat \quad \varphi(D) \rightarrow y2 \in Nat$$
$$\varphi(E) \rightarrow y2 \in Nat \quad \varphi(F) \rightarrow y2 \in Nat$$

To show consistency, we need to prove the following implications:

$$\varphi(A) \rightarrow \varphi(B)[0/y1] =$$
$$(x1 \geq 0 \wedge x2 > 0) \rightarrow (x1 \geq 0 \wedge x2 > 0)$$

$$\varphi(B) \rightarrow \varphi(C)[x1/y2] =$$
$$(x1 \geq 0 \wedge x2 > 0) \rightarrow (x2 > 0 \wedge x1 \geq 0)$$

$$(\varphi(C) \wedge y2 \geq x2) \rightarrow \varphi(D) =$$
$$(x2 > 0 \wedge y2 \geq 0 \wedge y2 \geq x2) \rightarrow (x2 > 0 \wedge y2 \geq x2)$$

$$(\varphi(C) \wedge \neg y2 \geq x2) \rightarrow \varphi(F) =$$
$$(x2 > 0 \wedge y2 \geq 0 \wedge \neg y2 \geq x2) \rightarrow y2 \geq 0$$

$$\varphi(D) \rightarrow \varphi(E)[y1 + 1/y1] =$$
$$(x2 > 0 \wedge y2 \geq x) \rightarrow (x2 > 0 \wedge y2 \geq x2)$$

$$\varphi(E) \rightarrow \varphi(C)[y2 - x2/y2] =$$
$$(x2 > 0 \wedge y2 \geq x2) \rightarrow (x2 > 0 \wedge y2 - x2 \geq 0)$$

To show nondecreasing of the values attached to the states between successive pairs of locations, and a proper decrease along the loop $C \rightarrow D \rightarrow$
$E \rightarrow C$, which occurs when moving from E to C, we have:

$$\varphi(A) \rightarrow e(A) \succeq e(B)[0/y1] =$$
$$(x1 \geq 0 \wedge x2 > 0) \rightarrow x1 \geq x1$$

$$\varphi(B) \rightarrow e(B) \succeq e(C)[x1/y2] =$$
$$(x1 \geq 0 \wedge x2 > 0) \rightarrow x1 \geq x1$$

$$(\varphi(C) \wedge y2 \geq x2) \rightarrow e(C) \succeq e(D) =$$
$$(x2 > 0 \wedge y2 \geq 0 \wedge y2 \geq x2) \rightarrow y2 \geq y2$$

$$(\varphi(C) \wedge \neg y2 \geq x2) \rightarrow e(C) \succeq e(F) =$$
$$(x2 > 0 \wedge y2 \geq 0 \wedge \neg y2 \geq x2) \rightarrow y2 \geq y2$$

$$\varphi(D) \rightarrow e(D) \succeq e(E)[(y1+1)/y1] =$$
$$(x2 > 0 \wedge y2 \geq x2) \rightarrow y2 \geq y2$$

$$\varphi(E) \rightarrow e(E) \succ e(C)[(y2-x2)/y2] =$$
$$(x2 > 0 \wedge y2 \geq x2 \wedge x2 > 0) \rightarrow y2 > y2 - x2$$

7.4 Axiomatic Program Verification

Verifying flowchart programs suffers from the disadvantage that one needs to first translate the program from textual code into a flowchart. Flowcharts are less frequently used nowadays, perhaps because it is difficult to use them for large programs. Hoare [63] developed a proof system that included both logic and pieces of code. This proof system allows us to verify the code of the program directly. Moreover, it motivates compositional verification, by allowing us to prove different sequential parts of the program separately and later combining the proofs.

The logic is constructed on top of some first order deduction system. In addition to first order assertions, the logic allows assertions of the form $\{\varphi\}S\{\psi\}$, where S is a part of a program and φ, ψ are first order formulas. These assertions are called *Hoare triples*. The syntax of the allowed programs (and program segments) is given in BNF:

$$S ::= v := e \mid skip \mid S; S \mid$$
$$if \ p \ then \ S \ else \ S \ fi \mid while \ p \ do \ S$$

where v is a variable, e is a first order expression, and p is an unquantified first order assertion. The meaning of the Hoare triple $\{\varphi\}S\{\psi\}$ is as follows: if execution of S starts with a state satisfying φ, and S terminates from that state, then a state satisfying ψ is reached. Obviously, if S is the entire program, then $\{\varphi\}S\{\psi\}$ is exactly the partial correctness claim, with initial condition φ and final assertion ψ.

Notice that the allowed programs do not contain any *goto* statement. Thus, any part of a program S formed using the above syntax can be entered upon execution only at the beginning of S, and if terminated, exit at the end of S. This assumption is essential to the formulation of the following proof rules. For a treatment of *goto* statements in Hoare's logic, see [12]. The axioms and proof rules of Hoare's logic are given below.

Assignment axiom

This axiom is reminiscent of the way the consistency between the precondition and the postcondition of assignments is proved under the Floyd proof system, as described in Section 7.1. It takes the postcondition φ, describing states after the execution of the assignment $v := e$, and translates it to a corresponding precondition, stated in terms of the variables before the assignment.

$$\{\varphi[e/v]\}v := e\{\varphi\}$$

If array variables are involved, the same considerations discussed in Section 7.2 need to be taken.

Skip axiom

$$\{\varphi\}skip\{\varphi\}$$

Performing a skip instruction does not change the value of any program variable. This is reflected in the axiom, which takes the same formula as both the precondition and postcondition.

Left strengthening rule

This rule is used for strengthening preconditions. That is, $\{\varphi'\}S\{\psi\}$ was proved, and one wants to strengthen the precondition φ' into φ (recall that this means that $\varphi \to \varphi'$).

$$\frac{\varphi \to \varphi', \{\varphi'\}S\{\psi\}}{\{\varphi\}S\{\psi\}}$$

To justify this rule, consider any state that satisfies φ. Then, according to the implication, it also satisfies φ'. But then, according to $\{\varphi'\}S\{\psi\}$, if S starts from that state and terminates, ψ holds at its completion. Hence $\{\varphi\}S\{\psi\}$.

This rule is often used together with the assignment axiom. If we want to prove $\{\varphi\}v := e\{\psi\}$, we usually first obtain a precondition $\psi[e/v]$ that is weaker than φ, and then use the left strengthening rule to strengthen the precondition by showing that $\varphi \to \psi[e/v]$. Recall that in the Floyd proof system both proof steps are performed at the same time.

Derived proof rules are often added to the Hoare proof system. These additional proof rules combine several other proof rules and axioms into one rule, allowing simpler (and shorter) proofs. For example, one can combine the assignment axiom with the left strengthening rule, obtaining the following derived rule:

$$\frac{\varphi \to \psi[e/v],\ \{\psi[e/v]\}v := e\{\psi\}}{\{\varphi\}v := e\{\psi\}}$$

Right weakening rule

This rule is used for weakening the postcondition. That is, $\{\varphi\}S\{\psi'\}$ was proved, and we want to weaken the postcondition ψ' into ψ (recall that this means that $\psi' \to \psi$). Since $\{\varphi\}S\{\psi'\}$, if S starts from a state satisfying φ, and terminates, ψ' holds at its completion. But according to the implication, any state satisfying ψ' also satisfies ψ. Hence $\{\varphi\}S\{\psi\}$.

$$\frac{\{\varphi\}S\{\psi'\},\ \psi' \to \psi}{\{\varphi\}S\{\psi\}}$$

Notice that in the Hoare proof system, one can strengthen preconditions, and weaken postconditions.

Sequential composition rule

This rule allows us to prove partial correctness for sequential composition, i.e., $\{\varphi\}S_1; S_2\{\psi\}$, after proving partial correctness for the components S_1 and S_2, separately. This is done by using an assertion η that is both a postcondition of S_1 and a precondition of S_2.

$$\frac{\{\varphi\}S_1\{\eta\},\ \{\eta\}S_2\{\psi\}}{\{\varphi\}S_1;\ S_2\{\psi\}}$$

Verifying code by first verifying separately its components is a useful strategy, called *compositionality*. This is the case for the sequential composition rule, since the proofs for S_1 and S_2 are performed separately, and then the proof for $S_1; S_2$ is combined from these proofs.

Suppose that the postcondition of S_1 and precondition of S_2 are not the same, e.g., $\{\varphi\}S_1\{\eta_1\}$ and $\{\eta_2\}S_2\{\varphi\}$ were proved. One can still prove that $\{\varphi\}S_1; S_2\{\psi\}$ when $\eta_1 \to \eta_2$. This can be done by either using the right weakening rule to weaken the postcondition of S_1 from η_1 to η_2, or the left strengthening rule to strengthen the precondition of S_2 from η_2 to η_1. We can also derive an additional proof rule, which will do exactly that:

$$\frac{\{\varphi\}S_1\{\eta_1\},\ \eta_1 \to \eta_2,\ \{\eta_2\}S_2\{\psi\}}{\{\varphi\}S_1;\ S_2\{\psi\}}$$

If-then-else rule

To prove that $\{\varphi\}$*if p then S_1 else S_2 fi*$\{\psi\}$, we consider two cases:

- p holds. Thus, $\varphi \wedge p$ holds before S_1 is executed, and can be used as a precondition.
- p does not hold. Thus, $\varphi \wedge \neg p$ holds before S_2 is executed, and can be used as a precondition.

The premises to the rule show that in both cases ψ holds when the if-then-else construct terminates.

$$\frac{\{\varphi \wedge p\}S_1\{\psi\},\ \{\varphi \wedge \neg p\}S_2\{\psi\}}{\{\varphi\}\textit{if p then } S_1 \textit{ else } S_2 \textit{ fi}\{\psi\}}$$

While rule

The while rule uses an invariant φ. This invariant needs to hold before the execution of the loop, and at the end of each iteration of it. Before executing any iteration of the body of the loop, we also know that the loop condition p holds, since otherwise we would have exited the loop instead of executing the loop body again. Thus, we can use $\varphi \wedge p$ as a precondition for the body of the loop S. We prove that φ is an invariant by showing that φ holds after each execution of the body of the loop (from any statement satisfying $\varphi \wedge p$). Thus, when the loop terminates, φ must also hold. Moreover, we also know that upon termination, the loop condition p failed, thus, the loop postcondition is $\varphi \wedge \neg p$.

$$\frac{\{\varphi \wedge p\}S\{\varphi\}}{\{\varphi\}\textit{while p do } S \textit{ end}\{\varphi \wedge \neg p\}}$$

Begin-end rule

This proof rule reflects the fact that the begin and end statements behave just as parentheses in arithmetic, binding together structures without side effects.

$$\frac{\{\varphi\}S\{\psi\}}{\{\varphi\}\textit{begin } S \textit{ end}\{\psi\}}$$

Exercise 7.4.1. Consider the following Hoare-style proof rules. Some of them are not sound, allowing one to prove incorrect properties about programs. Find which proof rules below are not sound and explain.

$$\frac{\{\varphi'\}S\{\psi\},\ \varphi' \rightarrow \varphi}{\{\varphi\}S\{\psi\}}$$

$$\frac{\{\varphi\}S_1\{false\}}{\{\varphi\}S_1; S_2\{\psi\}}$$

$$\frac{\{\varphi \wedge p\}S\{\psi_1\}, \ \{\varphi \wedge \neg p\}S\{\psi_2\}}{\{\varphi\}S\{\psi_1 \vee \psi_2\}}$$

$$\frac{\{\varphi\}S\{\varphi\}}{\{\varphi\}while \ p \ do \ S \ end\{\varphi \wedge \neg p\}}$$

$$\frac{\{\varphi\}S\{\varphi\}}{\{\varphi\}while \ p \ do \ S \ end\{\varphi\}}$$

$$\frac{\{\varphi \wedge p\}S\{\varphi\}, \ (\varphi \wedge \neg p) \rightarrow \psi}{\{\varphi\}while \ p \ do \ S \ end\{\psi\}}$$

Example: Integer Division

The following program calculates the *integer* division of $x1$ by $x2$. This is the text version of the program verified in Section 7.1.

```
y1:=0;
y2:=x1;
while y2>=x2 do
    y1:=y1+1;
    y2:=y2-x2
end
```

First, we annotate the program with assertions, such that each statement will have a precondition and a postcondition. These conditions describe the relation between program variables at each control location in the program. Not surprisingly, these assertions are the same ones we used to verify the partial correctness of the flowchart program in Figure 7.2.

```
{x1 ≥ 0 ∧ x2 > 0}
y1:=0;
{x1 ≥ 0 ∧ x2 > 0 ∧ y1 ≡ 0}
y2:=x1;
{x1 ≡ y1 × x2 + y2 ∧ y2 ≥ 0}
while y2≥x1 do
    {x1 ≡ y1 × x2 + y2 ∧ y2 ≥ x2}
    y1:=y1+1;
    {x1 ≡ y1 × x2 + y2 − x2 ∧ y2 − x2 ≥ 0}
    y2:=y2-x2
    {x1 ≡ y1 × x2 + y2 ∧ y2 ≥ 0}
end
{x1 ≡ y1 × x2 + y2 ∧ y2 ≥ 0 ∧ y2 < x2}
```

Let S_1 denote the first two assignment statements, i.e., $y1:=0; y2:=x1$. S_2 denote the while loop, i.e., *while $y2{\geq}x2$ do $y1:=y1+1$; $y2:=y2-x2$ end.* and S_3 denote the two assignment statements inside the loop S_2, i.e., $y1:=y1+1$; $y2:=y2-x2$.

The proof will be done using backward reasoning, according to the proof tree in Figure 7.3. Edges from a node to its immediate successors mean that the node uses as its premises the consequents that are proved in the successors. We will not show here how simple implications of first order logic over the *naturals* are proved. We assume that they are proved using some appropriate first order proof system. We list the different goals of the system, according to their occurrence in the proof. We start each goal with a number, followed by the name of the proof rule or axiom used.

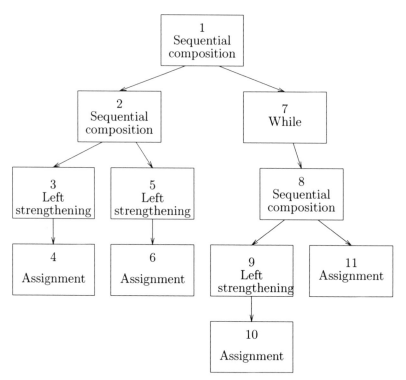

Fig. 7.3. A proof tree

Goal 1. Sequential composition

$$\frac{\begin{array}{c}\{x1 \geq 0 \land x2 > 0\}S_1\{x1 \equiv y1 \times x2 + y2 \land y2 \geq 0\} \\ \{x1 \equiv y1 \times x2 + y2 \land y2 \geq 0\}S_2 \\ \{x1 \equiv y1 \times x2 + y2 \land x2 > y2 \land y2 \geq 0 \land y2 < x2\}\end{array}}{\begin{array}{c}\{x1 \geq 0 \land x2 > 0\}S_1 \,;\, S_2 \\ \{x1 \equiv y1 \times x2 + y2 \land x2 > y2 \land y2 \geq 0 \land y2 < x2\}\end{array}}$$

Goal 2. Sequential composition

$$\frac{\begin{array}{c}\{x1 \geq 0 \land x2 > 0\}y1 := 0\{x1 \geq 0 \land x2 > 0 \land y1 \equiv 0\} \\ \{x1 \geq 0 \land x2 > 0 \land y1 \equiv 0\}y2 := x1\{x1 \equiv y1 \times x2 + y2 \land y2 \geq 0\}\end{array}}{\{x1 \geq 0 \land x2 > 0\}S_1\{x1 \equiv y1 \times x2 + y2 \land y2 \geq 0\}}$$

Goal 3. Left strengthening

$$\frac{\begin{array}{c}(x1 \geq 0 \land x2 > 0) \rightarrow (x1 \geq 0 \land x2 > 0 \land 0 \equiv 0) \\ \{x1 \geq 0 \land x2 > 0 \land 0 \equiv 0\}y1 := 0\{x1 \geq 0 \land x2 > 0 \land y1 \equiv 0\}\end{array}}{\{x1 \geq 0 \land x2 > 0\}y1 := 0\{x1 \geq 0 \land x2 > 0 \land y1 \equiv 0\}}$$

Goal 4. Assignment

$$\{x1 \geq 0 \land x2 > 0 \land 0 \equiv 0\}y1 := 0\{x1 \geq 0 \land x2 > 0 \land y1 \equiv 0\}$$

Goal 5. Left strengthening

$$\frac{\begin{array}{c}(x1 \geq 0 \land x2 > 0 \land y1 \equiv 0) \rightarrow (x1 \equiv y1 \times x2 + x1 \land x1 \geq 0) \\ \{x1 \equiv y1 \times x2 + x1 \land x1 \geq 0\}y2 := x1\{x1 \equiv y1 \times x2 + y2 \land y2 \geq 0\}\end{array}}{\{x1 \geq 0 \land x2 > 0 \land y1 \equiv 0\}y2 := x1\{x1 \equiv y1 \times x2 + y2 \land y2 \geq 0\}}$$

Goal 6. Assignment

$$\{x1 \equiv y1 \times x2 + x1 \land x1 \geq 0\}y2 := x1\{x1 \equiv y1 \times x2 + y2 \land y2 \geq 0\}$$

Goal 7. While

$$\frac{\{x1 \equiv y1 \times x2 + y2 \land y2 \geq 0 \land y2 \geq x2\}S_3\{x1 \equiv y1 \times x2 + y2 \land y2 \geq 0\}}{\{x1 \equiv y1 \times x2 + y2 \land y2 \geq 0\}S_2\{x1 \equiv y1 \times x2 + y2 \land y2 \geq 0 \land y2 < x2\}}$$

Note that we identify here $\neg y2 \geq x2$ with $y2 < x2$.

Goal 8. Sequential composition

$$\frac{\{x1 \equiv y1 \times x2 + y2 \wedge y2 \geq x2\}y1 := y1 + 1}{\{x1 \equiv y1 \times x2 + y2 - x2 \wedge y2 - x2 \geq 0\}}$$

$$\frac{\{x1 \equiv y1 \times x2 + y2 - x2 \wedge y2 - x2 \geq 0\}y2 := y2 - x2}{\{x1 \equiv y1 \times x2 + y2 \wedge y2 \geq 0\}}$$

$$\{x1 \equiv y1 \times x2 + y2 \wedge y2 \geq x2\}S_3\{x1 \equiv y1 \times x2 + y2 \wedge y2 \geq 0\}$$

Goal 9. Left strengthening

$$\frac{\begin{array}{c}(x1 \equiv y1 \times x2 + y2 \wedge y2 \geq x2) \rightarrow \\ (x1 \equiv (y1 + 1) \times x2 + y2 - x2 \wedge y2 - x2 \geq 0) \\ \{x1 \equiv (y1 + 1) \times x2 + y2 - x2 \wedge y2 - x2 \geq 0\}y1 := y1 + 1 \\ \{x1 \equiv y1 \times x2 + y2 - x2 \wedge y2 - x2 \geq 0\}\end{array}}{\begin{array}{c}\{x1 \equiv y1 \times x2 + y2 \wedge y2 \geq x2\}y1 := y1 + 1 \\ \{x1 \equiv y1 \times x2 + y2 - x2 \wedge y2 - x2 \geq 0\}\end{array}}$$

Goal 10. Assignment

$$\{x1 \equiv (y1 + 1) \times x2 + y2 - x2 \wedge y2 - x2 \geq 0\}y1 := y1 + 1$$
$$\{x1 \equiv y1 \times x2 + y2 - x2 \wedge y2 - x2 \geq 0\}$$

Goal 11. Assignment

$$\{x1 \equiv y1 \times x2 + y2 - x2 \wedge y2 - x2 \geq 0\}y2 := y2 - x2$$
$$\{x1 \equiv y1 \times x2 + y2 - x2 \wedge y2 \geq 0\}$$

There are several proof systems that extend the Hoare proof system for verifying concurrent programs [11, 48, 126]. Such proof systems provide axioms for dealing with shared variables, synchronous and asynchronous communication, and procedure calls. They are usually tailored for a particular programming language, such as concurrent Pascal or CSP. The interested reader is referred to the books listed at the end of this chapter.

7.5 Verification of Concurrent Programs

A generic proof system for handling concurrency was suggested by Manna and Pnueli [91]. This system is not directly connected to any particular syntax. Instead, it is assumed that the program under consideration is translated into a set of atomic transitions (see Section 4.4). This allows providing a uniform verification system, which can be used for different programming languages and concurrency paradigms. The proof rules also allow verifying various temporal properties, instead of only partial and total correctness.

An *entailment* is a formula of the form $\varphi \Rightarrow \psi$, which is shorthand for $\square(\varphi \rightarrow \psi)$. The notation $\{\varphi\}t\{\psi\}$ is an assertion that appears as a premise in some of the proof rules. It means that if t is executed from a state satisfying

φ, then a state satisfying ψ is reached. The notation reflects the fact that the premise behaves in a similar way to a Hoare triple. Consider a transition $t : en_t \longrightarrow (v_1, \ldots, v_n) := (e_1, \ldots, e_n)$. It behaves as passing a decision predicate, followed by a executing a multiple assignment. Consequently, a premise of the form $\{\varphi\}t\{\psi\}$ can be replaced by the following entailment:

$$(\varphi \wedge p) \rightarrow (\psi[e_1/v_1, \ldots, e_n/v_n])$$

We will present a set of proof rules in the style of Manna-Pnueli.

FOL: As in the Hoare proof system, the Manna and Pnueli proof system includes a sound and complete first order axiomatization for some underline first order over some structure S that is appropriate for the verified program. Each first order formula φ that holds for the structure S, i.e., $\models^S \varphi$, holds anywhere during the execution of any problem. Hence it is also an invariant (of any program).

$$\frac{\models^S \varphi}{\Box\varphi}$$

This rule can be used to lift formulas of the form $\varphi \rightarrow \psi$ that hold in S into entailments, i.e., $\Box(\varphi \rightarrow \psi)$.

INV: This rule is used to prove that an assertion η is an invariant. Recall that Θ denotes the initial condition of the program.

$$\begin{array}{ll} \text{I1} & \Theta \rightarrow \varphi \\ \text{I2} & \text{for each } t \in T,\ \{\varphi\}t\{\varphi\} \\ \text{I3} & \underline{\varphi \rightarrow \eta} \\ & \Box\eta \end{array}$$

The rule **INV** proves that η is an invariant by induction:

I1 This is the base of the induction. It asserts that φ holds initially.

I2 This is the inductive step. It asserts that if φ holds at some state during the execution, then it holds in the next state, for whichever transition was taken.

I3 This step shows that η holds whenever φ holds.

The proof rule **INV** may seem overly complicated at first; it looks like one can replace the formula φ, which appears in I1 and I2, by η itself. Then I3 seems to be redundant. The reason that this is not the case is that not every invariant can be proved in this alternative way, and we may need to strengthen η into φ. Consider the simplified proof rule **INV'**:

$$\begin{array}{ll} \text{I1'} & \Theta \rightarrow \eta \\ \text{I2'} & \underline{\text{for each } t \in T,\ \{\eta\}t\{\eta\}} \\ & \Box\eta \end{array}$$

To demonstrate that using **INV'**, together with the use of **FOL** for proving the necessary first order implication, may not be sufficient to prove invariants, consider a small (sequential) program over the *naturals*:

$$\text{Initially } x = 0, y = 0;$$
$$m1 : x := x + 1;$$
$$m2 : y := y + 1; \text{ goto } m1;$$

For this program, the initial condition is $\Theta : x \equiv 0 \wedge y \equiv 0 \wedge pc \equiv m1$. The two transitions are:

$$t1 : pc \equiv m1 \longrightarrow (x, pc) := (x + 1, \ m2)$$
$$t2 : pc \equiv m2 \longrightarrow (y, pc) := (y + 1, \ m1)$$

Consider the invariant $\eta = pc \equiv m1 \rightarrow x \equiv y$. This is indeed an invariant of this program. However, it describes only the states in which the program counter is at $m1$, and does not give information about the other states. This invariant will be too weak to be used directly in **INV'**, as we will now see. Consider $\{\eta\}t2\{\eta\}$. This becomes

$$((pc \equiv m1 \rightarrow x \equiv y) \wedge pc \equiv m2) \rightarrow (m1 \equiv m1 \rightarrow x \equiv y + 1),$$

which can be simplified into

$$((pc \equiv m1 \rightarrow x \equiv y) \wedge pc \equiv m2) \rightarrow (x \equiv y + 1).$$

As a first order logic assertion, this may not always hold, e.g., consider the assignment $\{pc \mapsto m2, \ x \mapsto 3, \ y \mapsto 3\}$. Thus, we cannot prove the premise **I2'** using **FOL**. The invariant η does not provide enough information to be used for the induction. We say that η is *not inductive*. To prove η, we need to strengthen it. For example, we can use in **INV**

$$\varphi = (pc \equiv m1 \rightarrow x \equiv y) \wedge (pc \equiv m2 \rightarrow x \equiv y + 1).$$

The proof rule **INV'**, together with **FOL** can be used to prove invariants of a program. These rules are sound. The problem is that they do not provide a complete set of rules for invariants.

Exercise 7.5.1. Prove $\Box\eta$ in the above example using **INV**.

NEXT: A proof rule for proving properties of the form $\varphi \Rightarrow \bigcirc\psi$.

$$\frac{\begin{array}{ll} \textbf{N1} & \varphi \Rightarrow \bigvee_{t \in T} en_t \\ \textbf{N2} & \text{for each } t \in T, \ \{\varphi\}t\{\psi\} \end{array}}{\varphi \Rightarrow \bigcirc\psi}$$

The premise **I1** asserts that there is at least one enabled transition in each state that satisfies φ. The premise **I2** establishes that each enabled transition from φ that is executed from a state satisfying φ ends in a state satisfying ψ. Thus $\varphi \Rightarrow \bigcirc\psi$.

FCS: The rule **FCS** is used to partition the set of states which satisfy the assertion φ into two sets, one set having states satisfying φ_1 and the other set having states satisfying φ_2. Then, proving $\varphi_i \Rightarrow \bigcirc\psi$ is done separately for the states satisfying φ_1 and the states satisfying φ_2. To obtain the effect of generalizing the rules for arbitrary number of formulas φ_i, the rules can be applied repeatedly.

$$\mathbf{FCS} \quad \begin{array}{c} \varphi \Rightarrow (\varphi_1 \vee \varphi_2) \\ \varphi_1 \Rightarrow \bigcirc \psi \\ \underline{\varphi_2 \Rightarrow \bigcirc \psi} \\ \varphi \Rightarrow \bigcirc \psi \end{array}$$

FIMM: This rule identifies $\varphi \Rightarrow \psi$ as a special case of $\varphi \Rightarrow \Diamond \psi$.

$$\frac{\varphi \Rightarrow \psi}{\varphi \Rightarrow \Diamond \psi}$$

FTRN: The rule **FTRN** allows proving $\varphi \Rightarrow \Diamond \psi$ by finding first an assertion ν satisfied by some intermediate states between φ and ψ, then proving $\varphi \Rightarrow \Diamond \nu$ and $\nu \Rightarrow \Diamond \psi$.

$$\begin{array}{c} \varphi \Rightarrow \Diamond \nu \\ \underline{\nu \Rightarrow \Diamond \psi} \\ \varphi \Rightarrow \Diamond \psi \end{array}$$

FPRV: This rule identifies $\varphi \Rightarrow \bigcirc \psi$ as a special case of $\varphi \Rightarrow \Diamond \psi$.

$$\mathbf{FPRV} \quad \frac{\varphi \Rightarrow \bigcirc \psi}{\varphi \Rightarrow \Diamond \psi}$$

FSPLIT: The rule **FSPLIT** allows splitting the proof of $\varphi \Rightarrow \Diamond \psi$ by decomposing the set of states that satisfy φ into states that satisfy φ_1, and states that satisfy φ_2. Then, one needs to prove separately $\varphi_i \Rightarrow \Diamond \psi$ for $i = 1, 2$.

$$\mathbf{FSPLIT} \quad \begin{array}{c} \varphi \Rightarrow (\varphi_1 \vee \varphi_2) \\ \varphi_1 \Rightarrow \Diamond \psi \\ \underline{\varphi_2 \Rightarrow \Diamond \psi} \\ \varphi \Rightarrow \Diamond \psi \end{array}$$

RESP: Let $(W, \succ)$ be a well founded domain and e an expression involving the program variables.

$$\begin{array}{ll} \mathbf{R1} & \varphi \Rightarrow (\psi \vee \eta) \\ \mathbf{R2} & \eta \Rightarrow e \in W \\ \mathbf{R3} & \underline{(\eta \wedge (e \equiv v)) \Rightarrow \Diamond(\psi \vee (\eta \wedge e \prec v\,))} \\ & \varphi \Rightarrow \Diamond \psi \end{array}$$

where v is a new variable that does not appear in the programs or in any of the formulas φ, ψ, and η or in the expression e.

Premise **R1** asserts that in every state in which φ holds either ψ or η hold. Premise **R2** asserts that when η holds, the value of the expression e is in the set W. Premise **R3** asserts that if η holds, and the expression e has some value v, then eventually, either ψ holds, or both η holds and there is an eventual decrease in the value of e, to some value less than v. Thus, according to R1, if φ holds but ψ does not hold yet, η must hold. According to R3, either eventually ψ holds, or there is another future state, where the expression e calculates to a smaller value. But, it is not possible that ψ will never happen, as otherwise there will be an infinite sequence of states satisfying η, with an infinitely decreasing sequence of values for e. This contradicts the fact that $(W, \succ)$ is a well founded domain. Thus, the well founded domain is used to show progress between a state in which φ held, and a state in which ψ will hold. The progress is measured by the decrease in the value of the expression η, and since this decrease cannot continue forever, ψ is eventually achieved. (Notice the similarity of this proof rule to the total correctness proof system for sequential programs, presented in Section 7.3.)

There are many other proof rules that can be used. Proof rules that prove eventualities under fairness are somewhat more complicated and can be found, e.g., in [92].

Finally, recall the safety properties, described in Section 6.12. There, a simpler model checking algorithm was provided for this special class of properties. Safety properties turn out to be simpler to deal with in the context of deductive verification as well.

One of the many ways to define the class of safety properties is as follows: add a new set of variables H called *history variables* to the program, and allow assigning to these variables arbitrary program expressions over the same or an extended signature of the program. (As a technical remark, for completeness we may need to be able to encode some sequences of values using these variables. It is possible to do this by adding variables that can hold sequences of values, or by having a domain that allows encoding sequences, such as the *natural* numbers.) These assignments allow keeping some indication of the history of the program, and thus behave in a way analogous to the states of the safety automaton described in Section 6.12. Then a safety property is any invariant φ that uses the program and the history variables, i.e., an LTL property of the form $\square\varphi$. In this case, the only temporal proof rules we need for proving safety properties are FOL and INV.

For more on this style of verification, including many examples, see, e.g., [91, 92, 93].

Exercise 7.5.2. A closer look at rule RESP shows that the consequent of this rule can be changed to an until ('U') property. However, rules such as FCS, FRTN and FPRV need to be adapted accordingly. Provide the appropriate proof rules.

Exercise 7.5.3. Prove the mutual exclusion property $\square\neg(pc_1 \equiv m5 \wedge pc_2 \equiv n5)$ for the mutual exclusion program from Section 4.6.

7.6 Advantages of Deductive Verification

Deductive verification is a comprehensive approach for establishing correctness. It is not limited to finite state systems (unlike most model checking techniques). It can handle programs of various domains (*integers, reals*) and data structures (stacks, queues, trees). It even allows the verification of parametrized programs, for example, programs with any number of identical processes. Automatic verification techniques are usually limited to checking particular instances of such programs, e.g., checking all the instances with one to seven processes. In addition for the undecidability results that show that in general one cannot automate the verification of parametrized programs [10], model checking is prone to state space explosion, which quickly limits the number of concurrent processes that can be checked.

The process of deductive verification often involves a great mental effort. It is frequently performed by people other than those that developed the code. This has the advantage of increasing the number of people who attempt to understand the intuition behind the programmed algorithm, and thus the chance of finding errors. On the other hand, deductive verification also involves introducing rigor and using mathematical theories, which sometimes leads to some rewarding consequences, such as:

- Finding errors in the code and correcting them.
- Generalizing the verified algorithm to capture new cases that were not anticipated.
- A better understanding of the verified algorithm.

In general, model checking provides useful evidence in the case where the program correctness fails to hold. Deductive verification provides intuition that explains why the program works. Hence, attempting both model checking and theorem proving in parallel, when possible, can provide important intuition in either case. (For an automatic generation of a proof that is constructed when model checking fails to find a counterexample, see [117].)

The theory of verification introduced various useful tools and concepts that can increase the reliability of developed code, even when the formal act of verification is not performed. One example is the notion of an invariant, i.e., an assertion that needs to hold throughout the execution of the code, usually relating the values of different variables to each other, and to particular locations in the code. One way to increase the reliability of the code is to require that the programmers provide invariants as part of the code development process. Invariants can be used for *runtime verification*, by inserting them as additional predicates in the code; if a certain invariant that is supposed to hold fails, the additional code will triggers an interrupt which does not allow the program to continue, and immediately reports the problem.

When it is difficult to verify the actual code, at least some increase in reliability can be gained by verifying an abstract, less detailed version. This is not very different from the prevailing practice in automated verification, where the actual code is often abstracted before the actual verification process. Although program verification can be difficult, verifying the *algorithm* behind it may be quite a reasonable task, and can provide much higher confidence in the code. Some critical and essential systems, where malfunction can cause great damage, may justify full verification, even when this involves nontrivial effort and resources.

Ideas from deductive formal verification can be used informally within software reliability methodologies such as the cleanroom method, presented in Section 10.3. Finally, deductive verification proof systems can also be viewed as mathematical definition for the formal semantics of programming language constructs. The Hoare proof system, presented in Section 7.4 is a classical example for this. It can stand as the formal semantic definition of pascal-like programming languages. This can help in developing cleaner and better understood languages. In principle, if a new programming construct is difficult to combine into a proof system, this may indicate that it is not completely understood or well-defined.

7.7 Weaknesses of Deductive verification

One problem in deductive verification is that it is highly time consuming. In a big project, deductive verification may become the bottleneck of the project. The rate of the verification is significantly slower than the typical speed of effective programming. Deductive verification is a much slower process than other formal methods techniques such as testing and model checking.

We often verify a simplified model of the code that may differ from the actual program. Even if we try to verify the actual code, the verification system may assume different semantics interpretation for the verified code. For example, the semantics given to the simple assignment $x := x + 1$ by the proof system may be of incrementing x. The actual code can be adding 1 to a 32-bit, two's complement register, and raising a flag (or causing an interrupt) when overflow occurs.

Errors may crop into the proof for other reasons. This can be the result, for example, of a faulty compiler (or in rare cases, even faulty hardware). It is almost impossible to verify all the layers on which the execution of the code depends. However, in some rare cases, such a verified hierarchy (hardware, compilers, code) has been obtained [19].

Development of computer programs scales up using constructs such as procedure calls and object-oriented code. Unfortunately, deductive verification has not proved itself able to scale up accordingly. Concurrent programs are much more error prone than sequential code, and thus have a greater need for verification. Such programs are in particular difficult to verify. In essence, the prover often has to use global knowledge about all the participating processes at the same time. Perhaps the way to attack the scalability problem is to try to develop not only better proof systems and mechanized theorem provers, but better programming languages and programming habits that take into account the need for verification. A step in that direction is the notion of invariant which has already diffused from program verification into the programming development community.

Deductive verification is mostly manual, and depends strongly on the ingenuity of the people performing the verification. The verifier, possibly assisted by the programmer or designer, needs to provide the appropriate invariants, i.e., claims that hold anywhere through the execution, and intermediate assertions, i.e., claims that hold at some points during the progress of the execution. Usually, it is not feasible to automatically obtain such assertions, although some heuristic techniques have been developed. Moreover, parts of the proofs, involving simple logical implications, cannot be automated, due to mathematically proven limitations of proof systems. Deductive verification requires a lot of expertise and extensive mathematical background. It may be difficult to find an appropriate knowledgeable person to perform the verification.

Proofs constructed manually may contain errors. Due to the difficulty of the entire verification process, and its detailed nature, the human verifier may be tempted to use 'shortcuts'; simple and unsuspicious looking implications (consider for example $x \geq y \rightarrow x > y$) or trivial pieces of code may be assumed to be correct and left unproved. Deductive verification that is supported by a tool may still raise the potential question of errors in the tool. The problem of taking account of quality of the job performed by the human verifier, or of the correctness of the verification tool is often referred to by the question "who will verify the verifier?"

Finally, a common error that occurs in deductive verification is asserting too many assumptions about the verified domain. The human prover tends to add more assumptions that seem to be obvious and can help shorten the proof, during the verification process. He can then mistakenly treat these assumptions as axioms. Such added assumptions may restrict the generality of the proof to some particular instances, where the added assumptions actually hold. Some mechanized theorem provers restrict the use of such added assumptions, by either forcing the user to prove each added assumption using the theorems that were already established with the tool, or by flagging as 'unsafe' proofs that use additional assumptions.

To conclude our discussion about the strengths and weaknesses of deductive verification, consider the following experience verifying an algorithm. The partial order reduction algorithm [67] that is used in SPIN was formally verified [26] using the theorem prover HOL. Since this algorithm is nontrivial, and is often used to verify or find errors in a model checking tool, it was considered to be important enough to invest the time and effort in formally verifying it. This took ten weeks of work for one person, and produced over 7,000 lines of HOL proof. Performing the proof was rewarding, as it resulted in the extension of the algorithm in a way that is useful for verifying embedded systems, which include both hardware and software. However, a year later, it was found that the specific implementation of this algorithm, in conjunction with the on-the-fly DFS used in SPIN caused an error [68]. This particular experience demonstrated the following points, which have been already discussed in this book:

- Deductive verification is time consuming and can be rather nontrivial.
- Abstraction of the algorithm may be required to facilitate the verification.
- The difference between the abstract version and the actual implementation may mean that although the proof is valid, the code, may still contain errors.
- Model checking tools, like any other software, may contain errors, and should themselves be subjected to verification and testing.

7.8 Soundness and Completeness of Proof Systems

Given a proof system, we want to make sure that only correct assertions can be proved. This is called the *soundness* of the proof system. When a proof system is given by a set of axioms and proof rules, soundness is proved by showing that

- all the axioms generate assertions that are correct, and
- for each proof rule, if the premises hold, then the consequent holds as well.

Observing, for example, the Hoare proof system, one may be able to convince oneself that the axioms and proof rules are correct in the above sense. However, how can this be formally proved? One possibility is that the Hoare axioms and proof rules are correct *by definition*. That is, they define how the programming constructs such as sequencing, *while* loops and *if-then-else* choices behave.

A different approach is to formally define the semantics of programming languages using some mathematical objects, e.g., map each program into a set of sequences of states, with each sequence representing an execution. Then, we need to show consistency between this definition and the proof system. Here, again, there is a gap between the program and its model, as the actual program may behave differently.

It is also important to have a realistic assessment of how likely it is that a proof system can prove a correct assertion. The ultimate goal of proof systems is to be *complete*, namely, be capable of proving every correct statement that can be expressed using the specification formalism. There are a few obstacles that prevent achieving this goal in program verification proof systems, in particular ones based on first order logic:

- The underlying logic, over some domain, may itself possibly fail to have a complete set of axioms and proof rules (see Section 3.6). We often want to use first order logic over the domains of the *naturals*. Gödel's famous incompleteness theorem shows that a complete proof system for the *naturals* cannot exist. Thus, in Hoare logic, we may get stuck in trying to prove first order implications that are required for the proof, e.g., in the left strengthening or right weakening rules.

- Invariants or intermediate assertions that are related to some locations in the program and are needed in the proof may not be expressible using the underlying (first order) logic. For example, suppose that the program uses some relation R and calculates its *transitive closure* R^*. That is, xR^*y exactly when there is a sequence of elements from x to y, with adjacent elements related by R. It can be shown that first order logic cannot express that x and y are related by the transitive closure of a given relation [38] (although it is simple to express in first order logic that a given relation R is already transitively closed).

The consequence of these obstacles is that, in most cases, complete proof systems for program correctness are not available. However, researchers identified a weaker notion called *relative completeness* of a proof system. This notion formalizes the property that any failure to achieve a proof is due only to the two reasons above, and not the part of the proof system that deals with programs. A proof system is relatively complete if, under the following two conditions, any correct assertion can be proved:

1. Every correct (first order) logic assertion that is needed in the proof is already included as an axiom in the proof system. Stated differently, there is an *oracle* (e.g., a human) that is responsible to decide whether an assertion is correct or not.
2. Every invariant or intermediate assertion that we need for the proof is expressive.

With these (sometimes unrealistic) assumptions one can prove, for example, the relative completeness of the Hoare, Floyd and Manna and Pnueli proof systems. This may seem at first sight to be a fruitless mathematical exercise, or an attempt of people developing proof systems to pass the responsibility of possible failure to other researchers. However, this is not the case; relative completeness is an important and profound notion for the following reasons:

- It identifies where exactly the problems in verification lie, and helps characterize what is possible and what is not.
- It may suggest ways to circumvent the problems. For example, when no multiplications are needed for the proof, one may use Presburger arithmetic, which is a decidable theory for natural numbers, with only addition, subtraction and constant multiplication. But notice that multiplication can be *programmed* using repeated addition.
- It gives hope that the correctness proof exists. Although one may not prove all the correct theorems of the underlying logic and domain, a written

program is most likely based on properties that were proven. Otherwise, there is no good reason to believe that it is indeed correct!

7.9 Compositionality

Being able to verify different components of a system separately, and then to combine the proof, is of course very desirable. This is called *compositional verification*. For sequential programs, one may regard the Hoare proof system as compositional: proving the sequential composition $\{\varphi\}S_1; S_2\{\psi\}$ can be done by finding an assertion η that is a postcondition of S_1 and a precondition of S_2, and then prove separately $\{\varphi\}S_1\{\eta\}$ and $\{\eta\}S_1\{\psi\}$. It is natural to seek an extension of Hoare's proof system that deals with concurrent programs in a compositional way. Idealy, we want to be able to combine separate proofs for different processes into a single proof of the complete system. We will now show that this goal incurs some difficulties.

Suppose that we want to prove for some concurrent system $P_1 \| P_2$ that the property $\varphi \wedge \psi$ holds, where φ refers only to variables of P_1 and ψ refers only to variables of P_2. A straightforward attempt is to prove that φ holds for P_1, and ψ holds for P_2, when they execute separately. This is hardly likely to succeed: in most programs, the interaction between P_1 and P_2 would have an important effect on their behavior. Each one of the processes may not even run to completion in isolation (e.g., it may wait forever for a message from the other process, or that the other process will change the value of some variable), and can behave differently when combined with the other process.

Another attempt for compositional verification is to replace P_2 with a smaller and less complicated process P_ψ that was proved to satisfy ψ, and prove that $P_1 \| P_\psi$ satisfies φ. Then do the symmetric proof replacing P_1 with P_φ, proving that ψ holds for the composition. However, the reasoning in this proof scheme is circular and may lead to wrong results.

Suppose for example that φ asserts that the value of the variable x is eventually changed from 0 to 1, and ψ asserts that the value of the variable y is eventually changed from 0 to 1. Now, suppose that the structure of P_1 is such that it first waits for a message from P_2 that implies that the value of y was change, before it changes the value of x. Similarly, P_2 waits for a message that implies that the value of x was changed, before P_2 changes y. Obviously, $P_1 \| P_2$ does not satisfy $\varphi \wedge \psi$. According to the suggested proof strategy, we may replace P_2 by a process P_ψ that changes y from 0 to 1 without waiting. Then $P_1 \| P_\psi$ satisfies φ. Similarly, we may replace P_1 by a process P_φ that changes x from 0 to 1 without waiting. Then $P_\varphi \| P_2$ satisfies ψ. This can lead to a wrong conclusion about $P_1 \| P_2$.

7.10 Deductive Verification Tools

Experiments with the Manna-Pnueli proof system can be performed through the STeP (Stanford Theorem Prover) tool, obtainable using the URL
http://rodin.stanford.edu
The TLV system can be used for deductive program verification (as well as model checking). It can be obtained using the URL
http://www.wisdom.weizmann.ac.il/~verify/tlv
Deductive theorem proves, such as the ones mentioned in Section 3.11 can also be used to verify properties of programs.

Notice: the use of formal methods systems often requires filling out and sending an appropriate release form, committing to some terms of use.

7.11 Further Reading

Two concise papers that survey the Hoare verification approach were written by K.R. Apt:

K.R. Apt, Ten years of Hoare's logic: A survey, part I, Transactions on Programming Languages and Systems, 3(4), 1981, 431–383.

K.R. Apt, Ten years of Hoare's logic: A survey, part II: Nondeterminism, Theoretical Computer Science 28, 1984, 83–109.

There are several books on Hoare style deductive theorem proving, including

N. Francez, *Program Verification*, Addison Wesley, 1992.

K. R. Apt, E.-R. Olderog, *Verification of Sequential and Concurrent Programs*, Springer-Verlag, 1991 (second edition, 1997).

F.B. Schneider, *On Concurrent Programming*, Springer-Verlag, 1997.

The latter covers also the Manna-Pnueli style verification method. A comprehensive book on the temporal verification of safety properties is

Z. Manna, A. Pnueli, *Temporal Verification of Reactive Systems: Safety*, Springer-Verlag, 1995.

The book by Kröger also describes the temporal verification approach.

F. Kröger, *Temporal Logic of Programs*, EATCS Monographs on Theoretical Computer Science, Springer-Verlag, 1992.

8. Process Algebra and Equivalences

"... Let me think: was I the same when I got up this morning? I almost think I can remember feeling a little different. But if I'm not the same, the next question is, Who in the world am I? ..."

Lewis Carroll, *Alice's Adventures in Wonderland*

Process algebras are formalisms for modeling the behavior of systems. Process algebraic techniques and algorithms can be used to show that two (models of) systems are related in some precisely defined way, e.g., that one of them can simulate the other. This can be useful in showing that one system is an *implementation* or a *refinement* of another. This ability to apply automatic or manual techniques for demonstrating the relation between pairs of systems can be used during a stepwise refinement software development process. According to this approach, the development starts with the specification, and gradually refines it into actual code, where in each stage the correctness is preserved by enforcing some equivalence relation. Refinement also allows describing a system in a hierarchical way, where each rank in the hierarchy is equivalent to the previous one in a formally defined way.

Since process algebra often deals with the issue of comparing different systems, choosing the right correspondence criteria between systems is of great importance. This choice directly affects the observations and the experiments one can make on systems, while comparing them, and the level of abstraction with which we describe systems.

To see why there may be more than one unique criterion for comparing systems, consider for example two simple transition systems, described in Figure 8.1. The system on the left starts by performing an action α. Then it makes a choice between executing action β or executing action γ. Then, in either case, an action τ, which returns the system to its initial state, is executed, and so forth. The system on the right makes a nondeterministic choice before the execution of α. After the execution of α, depending on the choice made, it allows only a β action or only a γ action. Then, in either case, it allows a τ action that returns the system to its initial state.

Suppose that these two transition systems describe (simplified) vending machines. (Vending machines are quite often used as examples in process algebra.) Assume that the action α means 'depositing a quarter', β means 'selecting a chocolate' and γ means 'selecting a candy'. In this case, it is likely that the user would prefer the machine on the left, since after depositing the quarter, she can choose between the chocolate and the candy. The machine on the right makes an internal nondeterministic choice, and subsequently, allows the user to obtain only one of them. Consider now stamp dispenser machines, behaving according to the transition systems in Figure 8.1, where β means dispensing a blue 33-cent stamp and γ means dispensing a red 33-cent stamp. (We ignored the possibility that the machines run out of candies, chocolates or stamps.) In this case, we may not care about this choice (except if we were stamp collectors), and may consider the machines to be equivalent to one another.

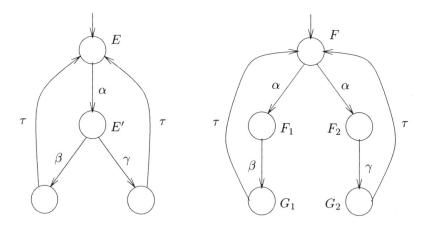

Fig. 8.1. Two simple systems

Process algebra was originally developed for the theoretical study of concurrent systems. For this reason, it employs only minimal notation. This fact makes it sometimes difficult to use for modeling real systems, and calls for extending it. One such extension is presented in Section 8.9. Process algebraic methods provide additional insight into the modeling of systems. For example, one can use process algebra to study the relationship between nondeterminism and concurrency.

The idea that the behavior of systems can be described and studied using algebraic methods was suggested by different researchers, most notably Hoare [64], Milner [100] and Park [112]. The theory of process algebras, and a variety of tools for using them for system comparison and verification were developed in parallel with model checking. In fact, it is interesting to observe that while model checking is more popular in North America, process algebra has extensive support in the European formal methods community.

8.1 Process Algebras

An *agent* in process algebra is an abstract description of a system. Process algebras suggest a *syntax* for describing agents. Agents are described as terms (just as in first order logic), using operators such as *sequential* and *parallel* composition, and *nondeterministic choice*. The semantics of process algebras describes how agents evolve (i.e., progress or change) during the computation. One goal in the study of process algebra is to investigate the properties of such operators and the interplay between them. For example, one may be interested in checking whether a nondeterministic choice construct is associative or commutative (see Section 4.9).

Another important ingredient of process algebra is a collection of *comparison criteria*, i.e., equivalence relations between agents. Each comparison criterion defines when two agents are considered to be so similar in their behavior that we would not like to distinguish between them. Comparison can be used as a correctness criterion when verifying that a system bears the required relationship to its design or specification. Tools, such as the Concurrency Workbench [31], were developed for checking that two given descriptions of agents are related by a given comparison criterion.

In process algebra, there is usually no explicit notion of a state as a mapping of variables to values. An agent is itself a representation of a state, in the sense that it dictates how the system will behave from the current point on; after executing an *action*, an agent *evolves* into another agent. The objects in focus in process algebra are therefore the actions rather than the states. For each action α from a given set of possible *visible* actions *Act*, there is a *co-action* $\overline{\alpha} \in Act$. We identify $\overline{\overline{\alpha}} = \alpha$. A complement pair α and $\overline{\alpha}$ can represent, for example, a synchronous communication, where α is the receive (input) action, and $\overline{\alpha}$ is the corresponding send (output) action.

In addition to the actions in *Act*, there is a special *invisible* (or *internal*, or *silent*) action τ, which is the complement of itself, i.e., $\overline{\overline{\tau}} = \tau$. This represents some internal action that is of no interest to the outside observer of the modeled system component. For example, the actions *Act* in both systems in Figure 8.1 are α, β and γ. Some process algebra equivalences distinguish between visible and invisible actions. Correspondingly, when using experiments to compare between different agents, one may have less control on invisible actions.

An *event*, denoted by $E_1 \xrightarrow{\alpha} E_2$, represents the fact that an agent E_1 evolves into another agent E_2 by executing some action $\alpha \in Act \cup \{\tau\}$. If $E_1 \xrightarrow{\alpha} E_2$ for some agent E_2, we say that α is *enabled* from E_1. If $E_1 \xrightarrow{\alpha_1} E_2 \xrightarrow{\alpha_2} \ldots \xrightarrow{\alpha_{n-1}} E_n$, we say that executing the sequence of actions $\sigma = \alpha_1\alpha_2\ldots\alpha_{n-1}$ from E_1 *leads to* E_n. We also denote this by $E_1 \xrightarrow{\sigma} E_n$.

The transition system on the left of Figure 8.1 represents an agent E that can perform the action α, and then evolve into another agent E'. The corresponding event is $E \xrightarrow{\alpha} E'$. The transition system on the right of Figure 8.1 can evolve from the agent F, by executing α, into either F_1 or F_2.

The corresponding events are $F \xrightarrow{\alpha} F_1$ and $F \xrightarrow{\alpha} F_2$. The left agent F_1 can perform only β, while the right agent F_2 can perform only γ.

Similar to the model of transition systems, we can define an *execution* of an agent E as a maximal sequence (i.e., infinite sequence, or finite sequence that cannot be extended) $E = E_1 \xrightarrow{\alpha_1} E_2 \xrightarrow{\alpha_2} \ldots \xrightarrow{\alpha_{n-1}} E_n \ldots$, such that for each $i \geq 1$, $E_i \xrightarrow{\alpha_i} E_{i+1}$ is an event. An execution is finite only if there are no enabled actions at the last agent in the sequence. In a similar way, we can define the *graph of E*. This is a graph whose nodes are the agents to which E can evolve, and whose edges represent the events and are thus labeled by actions. The agents in this graph are also called the *configurations* of E.

An *extended event* describes how an agent evolves via a (possibly empty) sequence of τ actions, followed by one or zero visible actions and by a (possibly empty) sequence of τ actions. We denote $G \xRightarrow{\varepsilon} G'$ when there is a (possibly trivial) sequence of invisible actions

$$G \xrightarrow{\tau} G_1 \xrightarrow{\tau} G_2 \xrightarrow{\tau} \ldots \xrightarrow{\tau} G_n \xrightarrow{\tau} G'$$

for some agents $G_1, \ldots, G_n$. Then, the extended event $E \xRightarrow{\alpha} E'$ denotes that there are some agents F and F' such that

$$E \xRightarrow{\varepsilon} F \xrightarrow{\alpha} F' \xRightarrow{\varepsilon} E'$$

for some agents F and F'. For example, in the right part of Figure 8.1, we have that $F_1 \xRightarrow{\beta} F$ and $G_2 \xRightarrow{\alpha} F_1$. We denote by $E \xrightarrow{\tau^\infty}$ the fact that one can perform infinitely many internal actions from agent E. In this case, we say that E *diverges*. One way to understand extended events is as a minimal visible part of an experiment. Consider an observer of the system that cannot perceive τ actions. Then, $F_1 \xRightarrow{\beta} F$, or $G_2 \xRightarrow{\alpha} F_1$ can represent some minimal observation that can be made about the system.

8.2 A Calculus of Communicating Systems

We use the syntax and semantics of CCS (calculus of communicating systems), as defined by Milner [100] (except that we denotes parallel composition with '$\|$' instead of '$|$'). Let α denote an arbitrary element of $Act \cup \{\tau\}$, R denote a subset of Act, f denote a mapping from actions to actions and C denote an *agent variable*. The agents can be defined in BNF as follows:

$$agent ::= \alpha.agent \ \Big| \ agent + agent \ \Big| \ agent \| agent \ \Big|$$
$$agent \setminus R \ \Big| \ agent[f] \ \Big| \ (agent) \ \Big| \ C \ \Big| \ 0$$

The restriction ('$\setminus$') operator has the highest priority among the different CCS operators. Next, in descending priority, come mapping ('[ ]'), sequential prefixing ('.') , parallel composition ('$\|$'), and nondeterministic choice ('+').

Notice that the prefixing operator '.' does not mean sequential concatenation (such as ';' in programming languages): in general, when E_1 and E_2 are process algebra expressions, we cannot write $E_1.E_2$. But we can write $\alpha.E_2$, for an action α. The agent '0' represents termination, i.e., there is no enabled action (including τ) from '0'. We will follow a common practice and omit the string '.0' or '.$(0||\ldots||0)$', from a description of an agent.

The semantic of an agent is described using *Structural Operational Semantics* (or *SOS*) rules, which resemble proof rules. This may seem surprising at first. Compare the situation to first order logic: axioms and proof rules are formed from *syntactic* objects. However, they manifest the semantics of the logic, by generating, in an effective way (i.e., through a proof) the valid formulas. Similarly, the Hoare proof system (see Section 7.4) can also be regarded as an axiomatic semantics of programs. In process algebra, proof rules prescribe how an agent can progress. One can obtain, through such a proof, a justification for an event, i.e., a proof that shows how an agent can evolve into another agent by executing an action.

Action Prefixing

The agent $\alpha.E$ where $a \in Act \cup \{\tau\}$ and E is an agent, performs first α and then behaves like E. This is captured by the axiom

$$\alpha.E \xrightarrow{\alpha} E \tag{8.1}$$

We can use this axiom to justify the event

$$\alpha.(\beta.(\delta||\bar{\delta}) + \gamma) \xrightarrow{\alpha} \beta.(\delta||\bar{\delta}) + \gamma$$

Choice

Executing $E + F$ is done by selecting nondeterministically between E and F and then behaving according to the selected agent. This is captured by the following two SOS rules, corresponding to either choosing to behave according to E or according to F.

$$\frac{E \xrightarrow{\alpha} E'}{E + F \xrightarrow{\alpha} E'} \qquad \frac{F \xrightarrow{\alpha} F'}{E + F \xrightarrow{\alpha} F'}$$

We can use the action prefixing axiom to justify

$$\beta.(\delta||\bar{\delta}) \xrightarrow{\beta} \delta||\bar{\delta} \tag{8.2}$$

Then, we can use the event (8.2) as the premise in the left choice SOS rule to justify the event

$$\beta.(\delta||\bar{\delta}) + \gamma \xrightarrow{\beta} \delta||\bar{\delta}$$

Notice that, in this case, executing β from $\beta.(\delta||\bar{\delta}) + \gamma$ means that the left side of the choice operator is taken, while executing γ means that the right side is taken. In case of an agent $\beta.\delta + \beta.\gamma$, executing β corresponds to either a left or a right choice.

Concurrent Composition

The agent $E||F$, representing the concurrent composition of the agents E and F. There are three choices for execution:

- The agent E takes some action $\alpha \in Act \cup \{\tau\}$. The agent F does not change. That is,

$$\frac{E \xrightarrow{\alpha} E'}{E||F \xrightarrow{\alpha} E'||F}$$

- The agent F takes some action $\alpha \in Act \cup \{\tau\}$ The agent E does not change. That is,

$$\frac{F \xrightarrow{\alpha} F'}{E||F \xrightarrow{\alpha} E||F'}$$

- The agent E takes an action $\alpha \in Act$, while the agent F takes its co-action $\bar{\alpha}$. As a result, E and F synchronize on this action, and the move is labeled with the invisible action τ.

$$\frac{E \xrightarrow{\alpha} E', F \xrightarrow{\bar{\alpha}} F'}{E||F \xrightarrow{\tau} E'||F'}$$

We can use the action prefixing axiom to justify the following events:

$$\delta \xrightarrow{\delta} 0 \tag{8.3}$$

and

$$\bar{\delta} \xrightarrow{\bar{\delta}} 0 \tag{8.4}$$

Then, using the events (8.3) and (8.4) as the premises in the latter concurrent composition rule, we can obtain the event

$$\delta||\bar{\delta} \xrightarrow{\tau} 0||0 \tag{8.5}$$

Restriction

Restricting an agent E by a set of actions $R \subseteq Act$ disallows executing any of the actions in R or their corresponding co-actions from any agent that is obtained from E by executing a sequence of actions.

$$\frac{E \xrightarrow{\alpha} E', \, \alpha, \, \overline{\alpha} \notin R}{E \setminus R \xrightarrow{\alpha} E' \setminus R}$$

We will denote the agent $\delta \| \overline{\delta}$ using the agent variable C. We can now use event (8.3) in the first concurrent composition rule to obtain the event

$$C \xrightarrow{\delta} 0 \| \overline{\delta}$$

This means that the concurrent agent C is ready to interact with an external co-action $\overline{\delta}$, as an alternative to the synchronized execution of the internal δ and $\overline{\delta}$. In a similar way, we can show that

$$C \xrightarrow{\overline{\delta}} \delta \| 0$$

Thus, the agent C is ready for interaction with an external action δ or $\overline{\delta}$.

We may want to prevent this from happening. That is, since both δ and $\overline{\delta}$ are co-actions enabled from C, we may want δ and $\overline{\delta}$ to interact *only* within the agent C, and not be available externally. We can achieve this by using the concurrent agent $C \setminus \{\delta\}$. This is an agent that hides the action δ (and its co-action $\overline{\delta}$) from the outside, hence cannot have an event labeled with δ or with $\overline{\delta}$.

We saw that using the third concurrent composition rule we obtain $C \xrightarrow{\tau} 0 \| 0$ (see (8.5)). The restriction of the singleton event set $\{\delta\}$ allows the internal interaction between δ and $\overline{\delta}$ inside the agent C, since it is applied to C, rather than to the concurrent components *within* C. When the interaction occurs, the combined effect of δ and $\overline{\delta}$ is labeled with τ, the invisible action, which is not, and cannot be, hidden. When we use the event (8.5) as the premise in the restriction rule, we obtain the consequent

$$C \setminus \{\delta\} \xrightarrow{\tau} 0 \| 0 \setminus \{\delta\} \tag{8.6}$$

Note that τ is the only action enabled from $C \setminus \{\delta\}$.

Relabeling

Let $m : Act \to Act$ be a mapping satisfying that $m(\overline{\alpha}) = \overline{m(\alpha)}$. That is, if m maps α to β, it also maps $\overline{\alpha}$ to $\overline{\beta}$ (therefore, if $m(\alpha) = \overline{\beta}$ then $m(\overline{\alpha}) = \beta$). Then $E[m]$ reflects the renaming actions.

$$\frac{E \xrightarrow{\alpha} E'}{E[m] \xrightarrow{m(\alpha)} E'[m]}$$

As a simple example, consider the mapping $m = \{\alpha \mapsto \beta, \beta \mapsto \alpha\}$. Then, using $\alpha \xrightarrow{\alpha} 0$ as the premise of the relabeling rule, we obtain as a consequent the event $\alpha[m] \xrightarrow{\beta} 0[m]$. For convenience, we will denote by $E[x_1/y_2, x_2/y_2, \ldots x_n/y_n]$ the relabeling which maps y_1 to x_1, y_2 to x_2, and so forth. Actions that do not appear within the square brackets are mapped to themselves.

Equational Definition

The part of CCS that was defined so far is not sufficient to describe agents with infinite behaviors. In order to create such agents, CCS also allows recursive definitions through a set of equations. An agent variable may thus be defined using a term that includes that name.

The notation is $A \triangleq E$, where A is an agent variable and E is an agent. The expression E may include the agent variable. Several agent variables can be defined with mutual references, for example, $A \triangleq \alpha.B$ and $B \triangleq \beta.A$. In this case, the agent A can perform α, and become B. The agent B can perform β and become A, and so forth.

Consider the two systems in Figure 8.1. The definition of the system on the left can be given as

$$\begin{aligned} E &\triangleq \alpha.E' \\ E' &\triangleq \beta.\tau.E + \gamma.\tau.E \end{aligned}$$

Equivalently, we can specify it in one line as

$$E \triangleq \alpha.(\beta.\tau.E + \gamma.\tau.E)$$

Note that the intermediate agent variable E' was eliminated in the latter representation. The definition of the system on the right can be given as

$$\begin{aligned} F &\triangleq \alpha.F_1 + \alpha F_2 \\ F_1 &\triangleq \beta.G_1 \\ F_2 &\triangleq \beta.G_2 \\ G_1 &\triangleq \tau.F \\ G_2 &\triangleq \tau.F \end{aligned}$$

Equivalently, we can specify it in one line as

$$F \triangleq \alpha.\beta.\tau.F + \alpha.\gamma.\tau.F$$

Care should be taken when using recursive definitions. Consider for example the agents $A \stackrel{\triangle}{=} B$ and $B \stackrel{\triangle}{=} A$. If we take this definition as an equation, we only know that A and B are the same, but have no restriction on how they behave. One possible restriction that is often imposed on equational definitions in order to prevent such a problem is that each right-hand side of the definition starts with a prefixing action or a nondeterministic choice, where each component is prefixed by an action.

The rule that defines the behavior of $A \stackrel{\triangle}{=} E$, where E is some agent, is

$$\frac{E \stackrel{\alpha}{\longrightarrow} E', A \stackrel{\triangle}{=} E}{A \stackrel{\alpha}{\longrightarrow} E'}$$

The combination of equations with concurrent composition allows one to denote agents with an unbounded number of concurrent components. For example, the equation $A \stackrel{\triangle}{=} \alpha || \beta.A$ denotes an agent that can evolve after executing the action β exactly n times into $n+1$ concurrent components: n of the components can only perform α and terminate, while the $n+1$st component can split again into a pair of components. A prefix of this execution appears in Figure 8.2

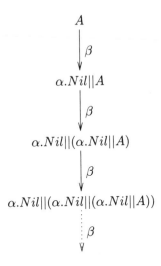

Fig. 8.2. Repeatedly executing β from $A \stackrel{\triangle}{=} \alpha || \beta.A$

To demonstrate how this sequence is formed, we will show how the event $\alpha || A \stackrel{\beta}{\longrightarrow} \alpha || (\alpha || A)$ is derived from the axiom and rules:

(1) $\beta.A \xrightarrow{\beta} A$ [Action prefixing]

(2) $\alpha||\beta.A \xrightarrow{\beta} \alpha||A$ [Concurrent composition and (1)]

(3) $A \xrightarrow{\beta} \alpha||A$ [Equational definition and (2)]

(4) $\alpha||A \xrightarrow{\beta} \alpha||(\alpha||A)$ [Concurrent Composition and (3)]

An agent represents a *finite state system* if it can evolve into finitely many different agents. Otherwise, it represents an infinite state system. Clearly, the agent $A \stackrel{\triangle}{=} \alpha||\beta.A$ describes an infinite state system.

The Agent 0

There is no axiom or rule for the agent 0. Hence, such an agent does not allow any action, and cannot be transformed into any other agent.

Figure 8.3 describes the graph of the agent $\alpha.(\beta.(\delta||\bar{\delta}) + \gamma)$. Some of the events were already justified using the above axiom and proof rules. Since no equational definitions were used, there are no infinite executions from this agent, and accordingly, no cycles in this graph.

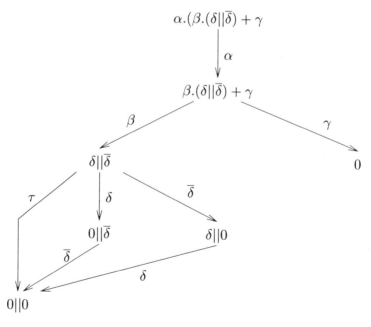

Fig. 8.3. The graph for $\alpha.(\beta.(\delta||\bar{\delta}) + \gamma)$

Value Passing Agents

In order to describe some more realistic systems, actions and agent variables are allowed to be parametrized. For example, the agent $a(x).P$ first performs an input where a value is being received into x, while the agent $\bar{a}(y).Q$ performs first an output where the value of y is being transmitted. An interaction between both actions binds the variable x to the value y inside P.

As an example, consider the agent

$$buy(x).(\overline{insure}(x).(\overline{drive}(x)))$$

There, some value is input into x, and is later output by the actions $\overline{insure}(x)$ and $\overline{drive}(x)$, in that order. For more information about value passing process algebra, see e.g., [21].

8.3 An Example: Dekker's Algorithm

We represent here the mutual exclusion algorithm of Dekker, presented in Section 4.6, as a CCS agent.

The first point is related to the representation of states in process algebra. Recall that a state in CCS is merely an agent, i.e., an expression that can evolve to other expressions. In order to represent variable values in this way, we first construct for each variable that has two possible values, e.g., $c1$, $c2$ and $turn$, an automaton with two states. These states correspond to the variable values. The automaton for $c1$ appears in Figure 8.4. This automaton uses the following co-actions:

$\overline{set\_0\_C1}$ Setting the value of $c1$ to zero. This will move the automaton to its state $C1\_0$ (meaning $c1$ is 0) if it is not already in that state.

$\overline{set\_1\_C1}$ Setting the value of $c1$ to one. This will move the automaton to its state $C1\_1$ (meaning $c1$ is 1) if it is not already in that state.

$\overline{is\_0\_C1}$ This edge is a self loop on the state $C1\_0$. It allows checking that the value of $c1$ is indeed 0.

$\overline{is\_1\_C1}$ This edge is a self loop on the state $C1\_1$. It allows checking that the value of $c1$ is indeed 1.

The automaton for $c1$ is implemented as an agent that starts as $C1\_1$. This agent can interact with other agents that are using the actions corresponding the above listed co-actions. The agent $C1\_1$ can become $C1\_0$ by performing a $\overline{set\_0\_C1}$. The agent $C1\_0$ can become $C1\_1$ by performing $\overline{set\_1\_C1}$. Another agent representing the process $P1$ or $P2$ can set the value of $c1$ to either 0 or 1, or wait until it has one of these values.

We define the three processes (agents) that represent the variables $c1$, $c2$ and $turn$.

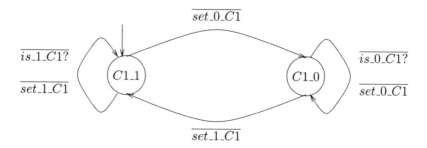

Fig. 8.4. An automaton representing a binary variable $c1$

c1

$$C1\_0 \overset{\triangle}{=} \overline{is\_0\_C1?}.C1\_0+ \qquad C1\_1 \overset{\triangle}{=} \overline{is\_1\_C1?}.C1\_1+$$
$$set\_1\_C1.C1\_1+ \qquad\qquad set\_0\_C1.C1\_0+$$
$$set\_0\_C1.C1\_0 \qquad\qquad set\_1\_C1.C1\_1$$

c2

$$C2\_0 \overset{\triangle}{=} \overline{is\_0\_C2?}.C2\_0+ \qquad C2\_1 \overset{\triangle}{=} \overline{is\_1\_C2?}.C2\_1+$$
$$set\_1\_C2.C2\_1+ \qquad\qquad set\_0\_C2.C2\_0+$$
$$set\_0\_C2.C2\_0 \qquad\qquad set\_1\_C2.C2\_1$$

turn

$$TURN\_1 \overset{\triangle}{=} \qquad\qquad TURN\_2 \overset{\triangle}{=}$$
$$\overline{is\_1\_Turn?}.TURN\_1+ \qquad \overline{is\_2\_Turn?}.TURN\_2+$$
$$set\_2\_Turn.TURN\_2+ \qquad set\_1\_Turn.TURN\_1+$$
$$set\_1\_Turn.TURN\_1 \qquad set\_2\_Turn.TURN\_2$$

We can now define the processes $P1$ and $P2$. Encoding these processes is a little tricky because CCS does not contain a sequential composition operator. Each selection made according to the value of a variable is represented here using a choice operator. Each choice is prefixed by an action. For example, if we want to check whether the value of the variable $c1$ is 0 or 1, we use a choice between the actions $is\_0\_C1?$ and $is\_1\_C1?$. The actions $critical1$ and $critical2$ describe the execution of the critical sections in the two processes, respectively. Similarly, $noncritical1$ and $noncritical2$ describe the execution of the noncritical parts in the two processes.

P1

$P1 \stackrel{\triangle}{=} noncritical1 \,.\, set\_0\_C1 \,.\, INSIDELOOP1$

$INSIDELOOP1 \stackrel{\triangle}{=} is\_1\_C2? \,.\, REST1 +$
$\qquad\qquad is\_0\_C2? \,.\, (\, is\_2\_Turn? \,.\, set\_1\_C1 \,.\, INNERMOST1 +$
$\qquad\qquad\qquad is\_1\_Turn? \,.\, INSIDELOOP1 \,)$

$INNERMOST1 \stackrel{\triangle}{=} is\_2\_Turn? \,.\, INNERMOST1 +$
$\qquad\qquad is\_1\_Turn? \,.\, set\_0\_C1 \,.\, INSIDELOOP1$

$REST1 \stackrel{\triangle}{=} critical1 \,.\, set\_1\_C1 \,.\, set\_2\_Turn \,.\, P1$

P2

$P2 \stackrel{\triangle}{=} noncritical2 \,.\, set\_0\_C2 \,.\, INSIDELOOP2$

$INSIDELOOP2 \stackrel{\triangle}{=} is\_1\_C1? \,.\, REST2 +$
$\qquad\qquad is\_0\_C1? \,.\, (\, is\_1\_Turn? \,.\, set\_1\_C2 \,.\, INNERMOST2 +$
$\qquad\qquad\qquad is\_2\_Turn? \,.\, INSIDELOOP2 \,)$

$INNERMOST2 \stackrel{\triangle}{=} is\_1\_Turn? \,.\, INNERMOST2 +$
$\qquad\qquad is\_2\_Turn? \,.\, set\_0\_C2 \,.\, INSIDELOOP2$

$REST2 \stackrel{\triangle}{=} critical2 \,.\, set\_1\_C2 \,.\, set\_1\_Turn \,.\, P2$

The graph for the concurrent agent $P1$ appears in Figure 8.5. The agent $P2$ can be obtained in a similar way (after replacing e.g., $C1$ with $C2$, etc). The nodes that are labeled in Figure 8.5 correspond to agent variables in the above definition.

Dekker's algorithm

In many CCS descriptions of systems, certain actions may not be of interest to external observers. Such actions will therefore be restricted. This is not only for the purpose of cleaning up the process algebra description. It also serves to remove the executions where actions that are supposed to be involved only with internal interaction are available for alternative interaction with the environment or other processes. Let R be the following set:
$\qquad \{ is\_0\_C1?, set\_0\_C1, is\_1\_C1?, set\_1\_C1, is\_0\_C2?, set\_0\_C2, is\_1\_C2?,$
$\qquad\quad set\_1\_C2, is\_1\_Turn?, is\_2\_Turn?, set\_1\_Turn, set\_2\_Turn \}$

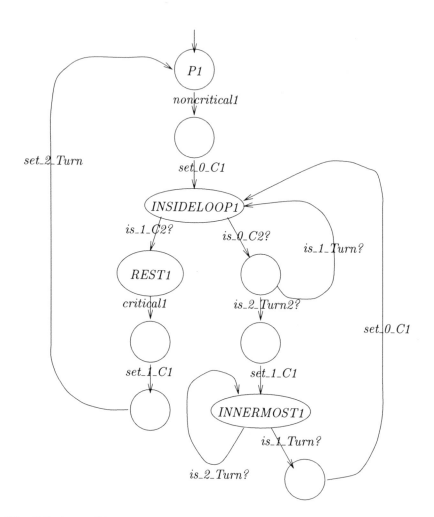

Fig. 8.5. Agent *P*1

Dekker's algorithm can be defined in process algebra as follows:

$$DEKKER \stackrel{\triangle}{=} (C1\_1 \| C2\_1 \| TURN\_1 \| P1 \| P2) \setminus R$$

Exercise 8.3.1. Describe Dekker's algorithm in a more compact way using value passing agents.

Exercise 8.3.2. Model the communication protocol from Section 4.15 in process algebra.

Exercise 8.3.3. Translate Dijkstra's provisional mutual exclusion algorithm from Section 4.6 into process algebra.

8.4 Modeling Issues

There are a several subtle points in modeling systems that can be demonstrated using the Dekker's algorithm example.

Consider the *wait* statement in the concurrent process appearing in Section 4.6, e.g., *wait until turn=1*. The way this is modeled corresponds to busy waiting: the process $P1$ checks in *INNERMOST1* repeatedly the value of *turn* using the actions *is_1_Turn?* and *is_2_Turn?*. If *turn* is 1, it continues to set $c1$ to 0, using *set_0_C1*. Otherwise, it returns to *INNERMOST1*. Alternatively, this statement can be implemented in such a way that process $P1$ freezes itself, making it the responsibility of the operating system to wake it up when *turn* is set to 1 by process $P2$. This can be modeled by removing the self loop labeled with the action *is_2_Turn?*. The resulting expression is then

$$INNERMOST1 \stackrel{\triangle}{=} is\_1\_Turn?.set\_0\_C1.INSIDELOOP1$$

In this case, there is no alternative to the action *is_1_Turn?*. Executing Dekker's algorithm with busy waiting allows the system to stay forever at the *INNERMOST1* loop. This cannot occur in the alternative definition of *INNERMOST1* above, where $P1$ freezes itself until *turn* is set to 1.

A similar observation affects the modeling of the noncritical sections. In our translation of the algorithm given in Section 4.6 to process algebra, the noncritical section was represented as a single action, *noncritical1* or *noncritical2*. However, the mutual exclusion algorithm should also work when a process decides to stay within its critical section forever. To allow this, we can change the expression $P1$ (and $P2$, correspondingly) into

$$P1 \stackrel{\triangle}{=} noncritical1.P1 + set\_0\_C1.INSIDELOOP1 \qquad (8.7)$$

Both of the above busy waiting loops should not delay the other process from entering its critical section if it wishes to do so. However, a naive verification of this property (e.g., using model checking tools, or tools for process algebra) may find that getting into the critical section is not guaranteed. The reason for this is that verification tools usually do not assume any fairness on the execution. Without assuming any fairness, a verification attempt can return a counterexample, showing, e.g., that $P2$ may not get into its critical section due to process $P1$ staying forever in its *Inntermost1* loop. In this case, the value of *turn* is 2. At some point, $P1$ performs indefinitely the action *is_1_Turn?*. Due to lack of fairness, process $P2$ does not have the chance to progress into and the out of its critical section, and set *turn* to 1, allowing $P1$ to get out of its *INNERMOST1* loop.

Weak fairness guarantees that while process $P1$ waits for *turn* to become 1 in the *INNERMOST1* loop, process $P2$ progresses and set it to 1, bailing process $P1$ out of the loop. Similarly, under weak fairness it is possible to verify that $P2$ is able to enter its critical section if it so wishes, even if $P1$ is staying in its *noncritical* loop (under the alternative definition in (8.7)) forever.

Unfortunately, some verification tools lack the ability to enforce fairness altogether, or include a prescribed fairness that does not match the one required by the user. This is due to the fact that fairness increases the complexity of verification [78]. In fact, the original semantics of CCS does not assume any fairness. We can still use a verification tool that does not assume fairness to verify some temporal property φ. Instead of using a built-in fairness assumption to verify φ under ψ, we can verify the property $\psi \to \varphi$ without assuming fairness.

Exercise 8.4.1. Even when the two busy waiting loops discussed in this section are eliminated, fairness is still required in order to show that a process will eventually get into its critical section when it wishes to do so. Show a scenario where this problem appears. One way to find such a scenario is by using model checking or process algebra tools (for a list of tools, see the end of Chapter 6, or the end of the current chapter). Hint: one such scenario includes the actions *is_0_C2?* and *is_1_Turn?*.

8.5 Equivalences between Agents

Comparison between agents is useful, for example, when one of them represents a system or an implementation and the other represent some abstract specification. It is also useful for showing that one system is a refinement of another. This is an important criterion when development is done by constructing increasingly more detailed systems. As we will see, there is more than one way to compare agents, and it is highly important to choose the right comparison criterion. The difference between the comparison criteria can be quite subtle, and will be demonstrated and motivated using examples. There is no widespread agreement on the right comparison criterion.

Each comparison criterion is given as an equivalence relation between agents, namely a reflexive, symmetric and transitive relation (see Section 2.1). Thus, showing the equivalence between pairs of increasingly detailed systems guarantees the equivalence between the first (least detailed, usually the specification) and last (most detailed, usually the implementation) one.

One can form a hierarchy (a partial order) between the different equivalence. An equivalence '$\equiv_1$' is *more refined* than another equivalence '$\equiv_2$' if any two agents that are equivalent according to '$\equiv_1$' are also equivalent according to '$\equiv_2$', but not necessarily vice versa. We follow van Glabbeek [53] and show part of his hierarchy of process algebra equivalences.

8.5.1 Trace equivalence

In process algebra, a *trace* is a finite sequence of actions that can be performed from a given agent.[1] Let $T(E)$ be the set of all the traces that can be performed from an agent E. Then, E is *trace equivalent* to F, denoted $E \equiv_{tr} F$ when $T(E) = T(F)$.

There are different variants of the definition of trace equivalence. One possibility is to consider both finite and infinite traces. It can be shown that if E and F are finite state systems, then $T(E) = T(F)$ implies also that the sets of infinite traces of E and F are the same. The proof of this fact, presented in the next paragraph, can be safely skipped.

Assume that $T(E) = T(F)$. Consider the branching structures obtained from E and F and their unfoldings into trees. In these unfoldings, E and F are the respective roots, and every node represents an agent obtained by executing the trace on the path leading to it from the corresponding root. Suppose that E has an infinite trace σ that F does not have. Since $T(E) = T(F)$, F has every finite prefix of σ that E has. We will construct a new tree rooted with F from prefixes of σ: this tree contains the agent F, the agents obtained from F after executing the first action α in σ (note that because of nondeterminism, there may be several ways to execute an α from F), the agents obtained from the latter agents after executing the second action, and so forth. This is an infinite tree, as there are infinitely many prefixes to the infinite σ. Each node has finitely many immediate successors, since this is a finite state system. According to König's Lemma (see Section 2.3), there must be some infinite sequence from the root F of the newly constructed tree. According to the construction, this sequence must be labeled with σ, a contradiction.

If process algebra agents are redefined to allow infinitely many immediate successors (e.g., by allowing an unbounded, parametrized nondeterministic

---

[1] This is a little misleading in that there is a different notion of a trace in concurrency theory, due to Mazurkiewicz [96]. A Mazurkiewicz trace is defined over an alphabet and a binary relation over the alphabet called *independence*. A Mazurkiewicz trace is a maximal set of sequences obtained by repeatedly commuting independent letters in a word.

choice operator), then trace equivalence does not imply having the same sets of infinite traces. König's Lemma does not hold in this case, due to the possibility of infinitely many successors. Moreover, even in the case of agents with finitely many successors, if there are added fairness constraints imposed on the executions, trace equivalence between two agents does not imply that they have the same set of infinite sequences. Such constraints can, for example, force each execution to pass infinitely often through a certain configuration, in a similar way to acceptance conditions in Büchi automata.

Another version of trace equivalence requires that in addition to having the same set of traces, the agents will have the same set of *terminating traces*, i.e., finite traces that cannot be extended with an enabled action. This leads to an equivalence that is finer than trace equivalence.

8.5.2 Failure equivalence

A *failure* of an agent E is a pair $\langle \sigma, X \rangle$, where σ is a trace of E such that executing σ from E leads to some agent F where none of the actions of X are enabled at F. Notice that the definition of failure allows actions that are not in X to be disabled in F as well. As a direct consequence of the definition, if $\langle \sigma, X \rangle$ is a failure of E, and $Y \subseteq X$, then $\langle \sigma, Y \rangle$ is also a failure of E. It is important to note that even if $\langle \sigma, X \rangle$ is a failure of F, then due to nondeterminism, one may be able to perform actions according to σ from E and reach another agent $F' \neq F$, where some actions from X can be performed. Let $Fail(E)$ be the set of failures of agent E. We define $E \equiv_{fl} F$, and say that E and F are *failure equivalent* when $Fail(E) = Fail(F)$.

It is easy to see that failure equivalence is a refinement of trace equivalence: $Fail(E)$ includes all the pairs $\langle \sigma, \emptyset \rangle$, where σ is a trace of E. Hence, $Fail(E) = Fail(F)$ implies $T(E) = T(F)$. The following example shows that failure equivalence may distinguish between agents that are equivalent under trace equivalence. Figure 8.6 shows two agents that have the same traces (and even the same terminating traces), but differ on their failures. The left-hand agent $\alpha.(\beta + \gamma)$ can always perform γ after executing α. The right-hand agent $\alpha.\beta + \alpha.(\beta + \gamma)$ has the failure $\langle \alpha, \{\gamma\} \rangle$, since it can choose its left α branch from which it cannot perform γ.

To gain an intuition as to why such a distinction may be important, assume that the two agents describe simple vending machines. Their actions are the following:

α insert a coin.
β select a chocolate.
γ select a candy.

The machine $\alpha.(\beta + \gamma)$ allows the user to make a selection between a chocolate and a candy, after inserting a coin. The machine $\alpha.\beta + \alpha.(\beta + \gamma)$ makes a nondeterministic choice after the coin is inserted. One of the nondeterministic choices of the latter machine allows the user to select only a

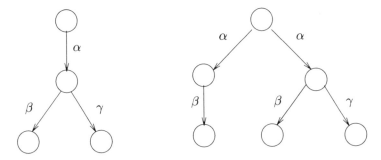

Fig. 8.6. Agents $\alpha.(\beta + \gamma)$ and $\alpha.\beta + \alpha.(\beta + \gamma)$

chocolate, while the other choice allows him to select either a chocolate or a candy. This nondeterministic choice may reflect some hidden internal details. For example, after the coin was entered, the latter machine may have checked and discovered that it has run out of candies.

A different way of defining the same equivalence appears in [105]. It defines pairs $\langle \sigma, X \rangle$, called *must-pairs*: in each agent obtained after executing the sequence of actions σ, from an agent E, at least one of the actions in X is enabled. Denote by $M(E)$ the set of must-pairs from E. Here, if $\langle \sigma, X \rangle$ is a must-pair for E and $Y \supseteq X$, then $\langle \sigma, Y \rangle$ is also a must-pair for E. Then, $E \equiv_m F$ exactly if $M(E) = M(F)$.

We will show that the definitions of failure equivalence $\equiv_{fl}$ and must equivalence $\equiv_{mu}$ are the same. That is, $E \equiv_{fl} F$ exactly if $E \equiv_{mu} F$. This is because for every sequence of actions σ that can be performed from E and and every subset X of the actions Act, $\langle \sigma, X \rangle$ is a must-pair from E exactly when it is *not* a failure from E.

8.5.3 Simulation Equivalence

In the following definitions of equivalence relations, we will implicitly assume a given set of agents S, and a set of actions Act. We say that an agent F simulates an agent E when there exists a binary relation $\mathcal{R} \subseteq S \times S$ over the set of agents, satisfying that

1. $E \mathcal{R} F$.
2. If $E' \mathcal{R} F'$ and $E' \xrightarrow{\alpha} E''$, then there exists some F'' such that $F' \xrightarrow{\alpha} F''$, and $E'' \mathcal{R} F''$.

According to this definition, $\mathcal{R}$ establishes how F simulates E. Suppose that E evolves into E' (by executing some sequence of actions), and F evolves into F', where E' and F' are related by $\mathcal{R}$. Then F' simulates E', i.e., $E'\mathcal{R}F'$. Executing any action α from E', obtaining some agent E'' can be simulated by an execution of α from F', obtaining some agent F''. Then F'' simulates

E'', i.e., $E''\mathcal{R}F''$, and the definition can be repeatedly applied to the latter agents.

There are some immediate consequences of the definition of simulation: if $E'\mathcal{R}F'$, then

- any sequence of actions taken from E' can also be taken from F'.
- all the actions enabled at E' are also enabled at F' (thus, all the actions disabled from F' are also disabled from E').

If both E simulates F and F simulates E, then we write $E \equiv_{sim} F$ and say that E and F are *simulation equivalent*. (Formally, we need to prove first that $\equiv_{sim}$ is an equivalence relation. This follows easily from the definition.) Note that in establishing that $E \equiv_{sim} F$ there is no requirement that the relation $\mathcal{R}$ that simulates E by F agrees with a relation $\mathcal{Q}$ that simulates F by E. That is, it does not have to be the case that $\mathcal{Q} = \mathcal{R}^{-1}$.

Simulation equivalence is finer than trace equivalence, since by repeatedly applying the above definition of the relation $\mathcal{R}$, if $E \equiv_{sim} F$, any trace of E can be simulated in F, and vice versa. Thus, E and F have the same traces. The example in Figure 8.7 shows two agents that are trace equivalent but not simulation equivalent. According to both agents, some choice will result in that eventually only γ or only δ is enabled. However, the nondeterministic choice is done at different points in the two agents. In the left-hand agent, this choice is made at the beginning, when executing α, while in the right-hand agent, this is done when the action β is executed.

The right agent, $\alpha.(\beta.\gamma.Nil+\beta.\delta.Nil)$, simulates the left agent, $\alpha.\beta.\gamma.Nil+\alpha.\beta.\delta.Nil$. This can be justified using the simulation relation

$$\mathcal{R} = \{(s_1,r_1),(s_2,r_2),(s_4,r_3),(s_6,r_5),(s_3,r_2),(s_5,r_4),(s_7,r_6)\}$$

On the other hand, we will show that the left agent cannot simulate the right agent. Suppose that there is a simulation relation $\mathcal{Q}$ from configurations evolved from the right agent to configurations evolved from the left agent such that $r_1\mathcal{Q}s_1$. Then, since α is enabled from both s_1 and r_1, we must have $r_2\mathcal{Q}s_2$ or $r_2\mathcal{Q}s_3$, or both. We will refute $r_2\mathcal{Q}s_2$. Refuting $r_2\mathcal{Q}s_3$ is done symmetrically. Suppose then that $r_2\mathcal{Q}s_2$. Since β is enabled from r_2, we must have both $r_3\mathcal{Q}s_4$ and $r_4\mathcal{Q}s_4$. However, $r_4\mathcal{Q}s_4$ cannot hold, since only δ is enabled from r_4, while only γ is enabled from s_4, a contradiction.

The two agents in Figure 8.7 can also be shown to be failure equivalent. We present now an example for two agents that are simulation equivalent but are not failure equivalent. Figure 8.8 shows the agents $\alpha.\beta + \alpha$ and $\alpha.\beta$. It is easy to see that there are simulation relations in both directions. From left to right we have the relation $\mathcal{R}$ such that $q_1\mathcal{R}l_1$, $q_2\mathcal{R}l_2$, $q_3\mathcal{R}l_2$ and $q_4\mathcal{R}l_3$. It is not a problem that q_3 is simulated by l_2, since the lack of an enabled action from q_3 does not mean that l_2 needs to have no enabled actions.

In the other direction, we have the simulation relation $\mathcal{Q}$ such that $l_1\mathcal{Q}q_1$, $l_2\mathcal{Q}q_2$ and $l_3\mathcal{Q}q_4$. Notice that q_3 cannot simulate l_2: the action β is enabled

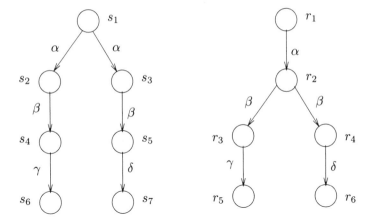

Fig. 8.7. Agents $\alpha.\beta.\gamma.Nil + \alpha.\beta.\delta.Nil$ and $\alpha.(\beta.\gamma.Nil + \beta.\delta)$

at l_2 but not from q_3. The simulation relations $\mathcal{R}$ and $\mathcal{Q}$ are unique, i.e., they cannot be replaced by other relations that will establish the simulation between these two systems. The two agents are not failure equivalent: $\alpha.\beta+\alpha$ has the failure $\langle \alpha, \{\beta\}\rangle$, while $\alpha.\beta$ does not.

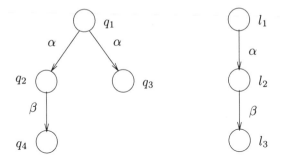

Fig. 8.8. Agents $\alpha.\beta + \alpha$ and $\alpha.\beta$

Exercise 8.5.1. Consider the two agents in Figure 8.9. Describe them using CCS expressions. Prove that the left agent cannot simulate the right agent. Can the right agent simulate the left one?

8.5.4 Bisimulation and Weak Bisimulation equivalence

Simulation equivalence was defined using two relations: $\mathcal{R}$ simulates the left agent by the right agent, and $\mathcal{Q}$ simulates the right agent by the left one.

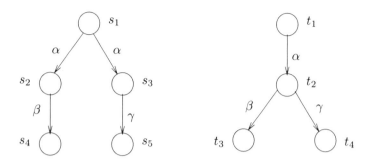

Fig. 8.9. Two agents for Exercise 8.5.1

Recall that these simulation relations do not have to agree, namely to satisfy that $Q = \mathcal{R}^{-1}$. For example, the agents in Figure 8.8 are simulation equivalent since there is a simulation relation in each direction. However, recall that in this example, the unique simulation relations from left to right and from right to left do not agree. In particular, $q_3 \mathcal{R} l_2$, but it is not the case that $l_2 Q q_3$. Thus, it is impossible to find a single relation that simulates in both directions.

Formally, $E \equiv_{bis} F$ iff there exists a binary relation $\mathcal{R} \subseteq S \times S$ over a set of agents S, satisfying that

1. $E \mathcal{R} F$.
2. For any pair of agents E' and F', and an action α, the following hold:
   a) If $E' \mathcal{R} F'$ and $E' \xrightarrow{\alpha} E''$, then there exists some F'' such that $F' \xrightarrow{\alpha} F''$ and $E'' \mathcal{R} F''$.
   b) If $E' \mathcal{R} F'$ and $F' \xrightarrow{\alpha} F''$, then there exists some E'' such that $E' \xrightarrow{\alpha} E''$, and $E'' \mathcal{R} F''$.

It follows directly from the definition that if two agents are bisimilar, then they are also similar; just use the relations $\mathcal{R}$ and $\mathcal{R}^{-1}$ in the two directions of the simulation. The discussion at the end of Section 8.5.3, related to the two non-agreeing simulation relations between the agents in Figure 8.8 shows that simulation and bisimulation equivalences are not the same. Thus, bisimulation equivalence is a *proper* refinement of simulation equivalence.

We prove that bisimulation is a refinement of failure equivalence. Let $\langle \sigma, X \rangle$ be a failure of E. We will show that if $E \equiv_{bis} F$, then $\langle \sigma, X \rangle$ is also a failure of F. Let $\mathcal{R}$ be a relation witnessing the bisimulation between E and F. Let E' be an agent obtained from E by executing σ such that all the actions in X are not enabled from E. By using the definition of bisimulation repeatedly, we can show that there is an agent F' that is obtained from F by executing σ, such that $E' \mathcal{R} F'$. Then none of the actions in X is enabled at F'. Otherwise, there must be an agent $F' \xrightarrow{\alpha} F''$, where $\alpha \in X$. But then there must be a state E'' such that $E' \xrightarrow{\alpha} E''$ and $E'' \mathcal{R} F''$, a contradiction to $\langle \sigma, X \rangle$ being a failure of E. Thus, every failure of E is also a failure of F, and by a symmetrical argument, every failure of F is also a failure of E. Consequently, E and F are failure equivalent.

The two agents in Figure 8.7 provide evidence that bisimulation equivalence is also *proper* refinement of failure equivalence. It was shown in Section 8.5.3 that these two agents are failure equivalent but not simulation equivalent. Since bisimulation equivalent agents are also simulation equivalent, these two agents cannot be bisimulation equivalent.

In the presence of invisible actions, requiring bisimilarity between agents may be too strong a criterion. It allows distinguishing between systems that differ from one another merely by the number of times that invisible actions are performed. *Weak bisimulation equivalence* is defined in a similar way to bisimulation equivalence, but with respect to the extended event relation. It allows reasoning about the modeled systems on a level of abstraction that does not count how many times invisible actions occur repeatedly. Formally, $E \equiv_{wbis} F$ when there exists a relation $\mathcal{R}$ between agents such that

1. $E \mathcal{R} F$.
2. For each pair of agents E' and F', and $\alpha \in Act \cup \{\varepsilon\}$, the following conditions hold:
   a) If $E' \mathcal{R} F'$ and $E' \overset{\alpha}{\Longrightarrow} E''$, then there exists some F'' such that $F' \overset{\alpha}{\Longrightarrow} F''$, and $E'' \mathcal{R} F''$.
   b) If $E' \mathcal{R} F'$ and $F' \overset{\alpha}{\Longrightarrow} F''$, then there exists some E'' such that $E' \overset{\alpha}{\Longrightarrow} E''$, and $E'' \mathcal{R} F''$.

Another interesting variant of the definition of bisimulation adds the condition that $E' \overset{\tau^\infty}{\longrightarrow}$ iff $E' \overset{\tau^\infty}{\longrightarrow}$. This means that for equivalent agents, either both can diverge by executing infinitely many τ actions, or neither one can diverge.

8.6 A Hierarchy of Equivalence Relations

Figure 8.10 depicts the hierarchy of the equivalences discussed here. For a more complete hierarchy, which contains more equivalences, see [53]. An edge from one equivalence relation to another means that the former is a *proper* refinement of the latter. That is, any two agents that are equivalent under the latter relation must be also equivalent under the former one; furthermore, there exists a pair of agents that are equivalent according to the latter relation but not according to the former one. In other words, the former equivalence relation is stronger than (implies) the latter one. In [54], equivalences that are based on the extended event relations (such as the weak bisimulation, mentioned above) are added to the hierarchy.

It is interesting that this hierarchy strongly depends on the fact that actions can be nondeterministic. That is, executing the same actions from

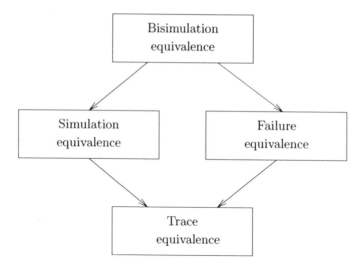

Fig. 8.10. A hierarchy of equivalences

some agents can lead to more than one successor agent, as in $\alpha.\beta + \alpha.\gamma$. If such nondeterministic actions are not allowed, all the equivalences described above are identified with each other. In fact, one can then use the simple criterion of language equivalence instead. Notice that disallowing nondeterministic actions does not mean abolishing nondeterminism altogether: the system can still decide nondeterministically between executing an action α and a different action β as in $\alpha + \beta$.

8.7 Studying Concurrency using Process Algebra

The framework of process algebra allows us to study the properties of different constructs such as the combination of nondeterministic choice and concurrency. For example, one can prove the following equivalences for bisimulation relation:

Commutativity $A + B \equiv_{bis} B + A$, $A||B \equiv_{bis} B||A$.
Associativity $A + (B + C) \equiv_{bis} (A + B) + C$, $A||(B||C) \equiv_{bis} (A||B)||C$.
Idempotence of nondeterministic choice $A + A \equiv_{bis} A$.

A weaker equivalence relation includes all the equivalences of the stronger relation, and possibly additional equivalences. For example, for weak bisimulation relation, in addition to the above equivalences, we have that

$$\tau.A \equiv_{wbis} A \tag{8.8}$$

One interesting phenomenon that is studied using process algebra is the notion of a *congruence*. A congruence is an equivalence relation that also preserves replacement under any context. Let A, B and C be three agents. Denote by $A\{C/B\}$ the agent obtained from A by substituting C for any occurrence of B. For example, let A be $\alpha + \beta$, B be β and C be $\tau.\beta$. Then, $A\{C/B\}$ is $\alpha + \tau.\beta$. A congruence relation between agents needs to satisfy that substituting an agent B with an agent C that is congruent to B results in an agent that is congruent to A. Formally: if '$\cong$' is a congruence relation between agents and $B \cong C$, then $A \cong A\{C/B\}$.

It is possible to show, using induction on the structure of agents, that the bisimulation equivalence is a congruence (see [100]). On the other hand, the weak bisimulation equivalence is not a congruence. Observe that, according to (8.8),

$$\beta \equiv_{wbis} \tau.\beta \tag{8.9}$$

However, it is easy to show that

$$\alpha + \beta \not\equiv_{wbis} \alpha + \tau.\beta \tag{8.10}$$

We can apply to the right agent in (8.10) the extended event ε, obtaining an agent where only β is enabled. Applying the extended event ε to the left agent in (8.10) results in no change, allowing α to be performed first. Thus, setting $A = \alpha + \beta$, $B = \beta$ and $C = \tau.\beta$ provides a counterexample showing that weak bisimulation equivalence is not a congruence [100].

Another interesting phenomenon that can be demonstrated using process algebra is the deficiency of the interleaving semantics in dealing with action refinement. Notice that the concurrent composition rules impose the *interleaving* semantics on concurrent composition. The expression

$$E = \alpha || \beta.\gamma \tag{8.11}$$

can evolve after executing α into $0||\beta.\gamma$, or after executing β into $\alpha||\gamma$. One can therefore show that E is equivalent (under bisimulation equivalence) to the expression

$$E' = \alpha.\beta.\gamma + \beta.\alpha.\gamma + \beta.\gamma.\alpha \tag{8.12}$$

The sequences allowed are hence $\alpha\beta\gamma$, $\beta\alpha\gamma$ and $\beta\gamma\alpha$, interleaving the action α of the left process with β and later γ of the right process.

Consider now the operation of *action refinement*, where an action can be replaced by a finite sequence of actions (separated from each other using the '.' operator) in an agent. Action refinement can be used for example to describe the stepwise refinement of a system. We can now use process algebra to demonstrate that interleaving semantics is *not closed* under action refinement. Consider the agent

$$F = \alpha || \delta \tag{8.13}$$

It allows the actions α and δ to be performed concurrently. Hence, according to the semantics of CCS, in any interleaving order. Again, we can convert the concurrent composition into an equivalent nondeterministic agent

$$F' = \alpha.\delta + \delta.\alpha \qquad (8.14)$$

Now, if we refine δ in agent F (Equation (8.13)) to be replaced by the sequence $\beta.\gamma$, we obtain the agent E from Equation (8.11) (which is equivalent to E', in Equation (8.12)). But if we apply the same refinement to the agent F' in Equation (8.14), which is equivalent to E, we obtain

$$C = \alpha.\beta.\gamma + \beta.\gamma.\alpha \qquad (8.15)$$

The latter agent C is not equivalent (under any of the equivalences presented in this chapter) to E, as it does not allow the sequence $\beta\alpha\gamma$, i.e., interleaving α in between β and γ. This is demonstrated in Figure 8.11.

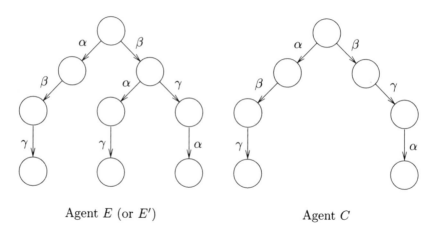

Agent E (or E')   Agent C

Fig. 8.11. Agents E and C

Example

In the following example [18], a two place queue is defined in two different ways, and the relationship between them are studied. The first definition is as follows:

$$
\begin{aligned}
Empty2 &\overset{\triangle}{=} put.Half2 \\
Half2 &\overset{\triangle}{=} put.Full2 + get.Empty2 \\
Full2 &\overset{\triangle}{=} get.Half2
\end{aligned}
$$

The state space of this queue is shown on the left side of Figure 8.12.

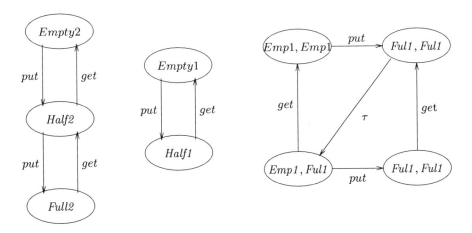

Fig. 8.12. Process algebra queues

The second definition is indirect. We first define a one buffer queue as follows:

$$Empty1 \quad \overset{\triangle}{=} \quad put.Full1$$
$$Full1 \quad \overset{\triangle}{=} \quad get.Empty1$$

The state space of this queue appears in the middle of Figure 8.12. We create two copies of the one place queue, and link them together. To do that, we rename (through relabeling) the *get* action of the first queue as *link*, and the *put* action of the second copy as $\overline{link}$. Then we combine the two copies using the concurrent operator '||'. Synchronized occurrences of *link* and $\overline{link}$, representing the synchronization of a *get* of the first copy and a *put* of the second, will be replaced by the invisible action τ. To prevent unsynchronized occurrences, we use the hiding operator.

$$B1 \quad \overset{\triangle}{=} \quad Empty1[link/get]$$
$$B2 \quad \overset{\triangle}{=} \quad Empty1[\overline{link}/put]$$
$$Queue2 \quad \overset{\triangle}{=} \quad (B1||B2) \setminus \{link\}$$

The state space of *Queue2* appears on the right side of Figure 8.12.

According to the definitions of the above equivalences, it is possible to show that the two implementations of the two place queue (*Empty2* and *Queue2*) are not bisimilar. In particular, *Queue2* includes the invisible action, which *Empty2* does not. However, the two agents are equivalent according to weak bisimilarity.

8.8 Calculating Bisimulation Equivalence

Consider the case of finite state agents. If bisimulation equivalence is used as the correctness criterion for comparing an implementation against a design, an effective way of checking it is needed.

We present a classical algorithm for checking bisimulation equivalence between agents E and F. We start by constructing the state space $\langle S, \Delta \rangle$, where S is the finite set of agents that can evolve from either E or F (thus, $E, F \in S$), and Δ is the transition relation between agents, i.e., $\Delta \subseteq S \times (Act \cup \{\tau\}) \times S$. The algorithm repeatedly partitions the states of S into disjoint subsets. It starts with one subset, consisting of all the nodes in S, and refines the partition, i.e., breaks subsets of nodes into smaller subsets until each subset $P \in \mathcal{P}$ includes agents that are bisimulation equivalent to each other. That is, for each $G_1, G_2 \in P$, $G_1 \mathcal{R} G_2$.

It is often possible to satisfy the definition of bisimulation relation on (S, Δ) in more than one way, i.e., there is more than one relation $\mathcal{R} \subseteq S \times S$ that satisfies the definitions of bisimulation equivalence. One trivial example is an equivalence relation that relates every agent only to itself. This is of course not an interesting equivalence relation. There is always a maximal (i.e., coarsest) such relation, i.e., one that includes the largest such bisimulation equivalence classes partitioning S. We are interested in finding the maximal relation $\mathcal{R}$ that is used in the definition of bisimulation. Then one checks whether E and F are within the same subset of the partition or not.

The partitioning algorithm is as follows:

1. Create the initial partition $\mathcal{P} = \{S\}$.
2. Repeat until there is no change:
   Find if there are two (not necessarily different) elements T_1, T_2 (i.e., two sets of agents) in the partition P and an action $\alpha \in Act$ such that the following holds: one can split the set of agents T_1 into two nonempty and disjoint subsets S_1, S_2 such that

   - For each agent $E \in S_1$ there exists an agent $E' \in T_2$ such that $E \overset{\alpha}{\longrightarrow} E'$.
   - There is no agent $E \in S_2$ such that for some agent $E' \in T_2$ it holds that $E \overset{\alpha}{\longrightarrow} E'$.

   If there are such sets, replace T_1 in $\mathcal{P}$ by the subsets S_1 and S_2.

According to the algorithm, one way of distinguishing between agents, hence putting them in different subsets, is when there is an event labeled with some action α from one agent while no event labeled with α exists from the other agent. A second way to partition the agents is to take an event labeled with α from both agents, but this will result in two agents that were already shown to be in different subsets of the partition.

One can show by a simple induction on the number of splits performed that at any stage in the execution of the algorithm, if a subset of agents is split into two subsets, then one can distinguish between these agents in a way that they cannot be bisimilar. Conversely, one can show by induction on the length of the splitting that at any stage of the algorithm, any bisimulation on (S, Δ) is a refinement of the current partition (including, in particular, the final partition). This means that the bisimulation obtained by the algorithm is the maximal one. The number of splits is bounded by the size of S, as each subset must contain at least one agent. If n is the number of agents in S and m is the number of actions in Δ, then the time complexity is $\mathcal{O}(m \times n)$.

Consider the two agents $A \stackrel{\triangle}{=} \alpha.((\beta) + (\gamma.\delta.A))$ and $B \stackrel{\triangle}{=} \alpha.\beta + \alpha.\gamma.\delta.B$. We denote their graphs in Figure 8.13. Each node corresponds to either one of the above agents or one that is evolved from it. The node s_0 corresponds to $A \stackrel{\triangle}{=} \alpha.((\beta) + (\gamma.\delta.A))$, while the node r_0 corresponds to $B \stackrel{\triangle}{=} \alpha.\beta + \alpha.\gamma.\delta.B$. The edges in the graph correspond to events and the nodes correspond to agents. For example, since s_1 is obtained from s_0 by executing an α action, s_1 corresponds to $(\beta) + (\gamma.\delta.A)$. The edge between r_0 and r_1 corresponds to taking the left α choice in B. Thus, r_1 corresponds to the agent β. The edge from r_0 to r_4 corresponds to selecting the right α choice in B and results in the agent $\gamma.\delta.A$.

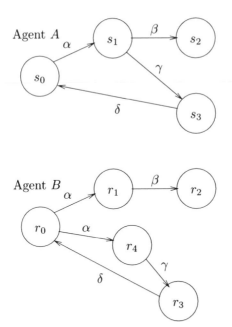

Fig. 8.13. The state spaces for agents A and B

We start the algorithm by putting all the nodes in one set:

$$S = \{s_0, s_1, s_2, s_3, r_0, r_1, r_2, r_3, r_4\}$$

Similarly, we set Δ to be the set of transitions of both state graphs:

$$\Delta = \{\ s_0 \xrightarrow{\alpha} s_1, s_1 \xrightarrow{\beta} s_2, s_1 \xrightarrow{\gamma} s_3, s_3 \xrightarrow{\delta} s_0,$$
$$r_0 \xrightarrow{\alpha} r_1, r_0 \xrightarrow{\alpha} r_4, r_1 \xrightarrow{\beta} r_2, r_4 \xrightarrow{\gamma} r_3, r_3 \xrightarrow{\delta} r_0\ \}$$

We choose to split first according to the action α. Only nodes s_0 and r_0 can perform α. Hence we obtain the following partition into two subsets:

$$\{s_0, r_0\}$$
$$\{s_1, s_2, s_3, r_1, r_2, r_3, r_4\}$$

We split the second subset according to the action β, which can be performed only from nodes s_1 and r_1, obtaining,

$$\{s_0, r_0\}$$
$$\{s_1, r_1\}$$
$$\{s_2, s_3, r_2, r_3, r_4\}$$

Next, we partition the second set according to the action γ. The node s_1 can perform a γ action, while r_1 cannot.

$$\{s_0, r_0\}$$
$$\{s_1\}$$
$$\{r_1\}$$
$$\{s_2, s_3, r_2, r_3, r_4\}$$

Now, we partition the fourth set according to γ. The only node in this set that can perform a γ action in that set is r_4. Hence it becomes a singleton set, separated from the others.

$$\{s_0, r_0\}$$
$$\{s_1\}$$
$$\{r_1\}$$
$$\{s_2, s_3, r_2, r_3\}$$
$$\{r_4\}$$

Next, we split the fourth set according to δ. The nodes s_2 and r_2 cannot perform the action δ, while s_3 and r_3 can.

$$\{s_0, r_0\}$$
$$\{s_1\}$$
$$\{r_1\}$$
$$\{s_2, r_2\}$$
$$\{s_3, r_3\}$$
$$\{r_4\}$$

We now split the first set according to α. Both s_0 and r_0 can perform the action α. However, executing α from s_0 results in the state s_1, while executing α from r_0 results in the state r_1. Since these two states belong to different subsets in the partition, we have to split s_0 from r_0.

$$\{s_0\}$$
$$\{r_0\}$$
$$\{s_1\}$$
$$\{r_1\}$$
$$\{s_2, r_2\}$$
$$\{s_3, r_3\}$$
$$\{r_4\}$$

By now we know that A and B are not bisimilar, as they are represented by states s_0 and r_0, respectively, which belong to different subsets in the partition. If we are still interested in continuing the partitioning process, we can split the 6th set according to δ, separating s_3 from r_3. The reason is that from s_3 we get to s_0 and from r_3 we get to r_0 which reside now in different subsets.

$$\{s_0\}$$
$$\{r_0\}$$
$$\{s_1\}$$
$$\{r_1\}$$
$$\{s_2, r_2\}$$
$$\{s_3\}$$
$$\{r_3\}$$
$$\{r_4\}$$

We cannot partition further: there is only one subset that has more than one node, which includes s_2 and r_2. These nodes are inseparable by any action since no action is enabled at each one of them.

Checking for weak bisimulation equivalence between finite state agents E and F can start by calculating the state space for E and F. Then the extended action relation is calculated. This is done using algorithms similar to ones for calculating the *transitive closure* of a relation. Such an algorithm, e.g., the Floyd and Warshall algorithm [145] can be done in time cubic in the size of the graphs (i.e., $\mathcal{O}(m^3)$).

These complexities are given as a function of the sizes of the state spaces that are compared. As argued in Section 6.9, this is a rather biased way to measure the size of the input, since the state space can be exponentially bigger than the process algebra description of the system. A more efficient algorithm, whose time complexity is $\mathcal{O}(m \times \log n)$ is given in [111].

8.9 LOTOS

LOTOS (Language Of Temporal Ordering Specification) is a process algebra standard, developed by the ISO (International Standard Organization) [72].

It contains ideas from the process algebra CCS, with data types based on algebraic specification [44]. In this section we will describe the main features of LOTOS and compare them to CCS. For a more comprehensive description of LOTOS see e.g., [17].

In LOTOS, agents are called *processes*. A process is defined as follows:

process *process_name* [*actions_list*]:=*behaior_expression* **end proc**

The action list is separated by commas. Unlike CCS, LOTOS does not have co-actions.

Some of the operators in a LOTOS *behavior_expression* have direct counterparts in CCS, although the notation is usually a little different. The action prefixing operator in LOTOS is ';', instead of '.'. The nondeterministic choice is '[]' instead of '+'. The invisible action is **i**, instead of τ. Restriction is denoted in LOTOS using '\', just like in CCS; however, a list of actions in LOTOS is surrounded by square brackets, '[' and ']', instead of braces. The termination notation is **exit** instead of 0. The execution of **exit** results in the special action δ.

LOTOS provides three ways to combine concurrent processes:

- *Full synchronization*, denoted using the operator '||', allows the involved processes to evolve only upon executing exactly the same actions. Thus, $a; B||a; C$ can evolve into $B||C$ upon executing a, while $a; B||d; C$ by both concurrent components cannot progress.

- *Pure interleaving*, denoted using the operator '|||', allows selecting an action from either one of the concurrent processes, while the other process remains unchanged. Thus, $a; B|||d; C$ can evolve to $B|||d; C$ upon executing a, or to $a; B|||C$ upon executing d. Under the pure interleaving composition, there is no synchronization between the different occurrences of the same action. Thus, the process $a; B|||a; C$ can evolve into either $B|||a; C$ or to $a; B|||C$ upon executing a, but unlike the concurrent composition of CCS, it cannot evolve to $B|||C$.

- *Selective synchronization* is denoted using the syntax

$$process\ |[actions\_list]|\ process$$

The left and right processes can synchronize on the actions in the list, or interleave on the other actions. Thus, $a; B|[a]|a; C$ can evolve into $B||C$ upon executing a. The process $a; B|[a]|d; a; C$ can evolve only to $a; B|[a]|a; C$ upon executing d. It cannot evolve by executing a, since the synchronization between the two concurrent processes is made on a, while a is enabled by only one of the processes. However, after d is performed, both processes can synchronize on executing a.

LOTOS has some constructs that are not available directly in CCS. The *enabling* operator '≫' allows sequential composition. Thus, $A \gg B$ behaves as A, and afterwards, if A terminates successfully, i.e., ends with **exit**, it behaves like B. Between the execution of A and B there is an occurrence of the invisible action i, instead of the special action δ that corresponds to the **exit** at the end of A. The *disruption* operator '[>' allows specifying interrupts. Thus, $A[> B$ starts behaving like A. At any point during the execution of A, it can be interrupted, and the execution of B begins. If A terminates successfully, i.e., with **exit**, then B cannot be performed any more. If A terminates unsuccessfully, then B has to be performed. The **hide** operator has the following syntax:

hide [*actions_list*] **in** *process*

It replaces the actions in *actions_list* by the invisible actions i. Both hiding and restriction are used for disallowing interactions with certain actions of the process. However, restriction disallows executions that contain the restricted actions, whereas hiding allows them to perform and subsequently replaces them by the invisible action.

8.10 Process Algebra Tools

The *concurrency workbench* is available from the University of Edinburgh using the URL
http://www.dcs.ed.ac.uk/home/cwb
The FC2Tools package is available from INRIA using the URL
http://www-sop.inria.fr/meije/verification
The PSF toolkit is available from the University of Amsterdam using the URL
http://adam.wins.uva.nl/~psf
Notice: the use of formal methods systems often requires filling out and sending an appropriate release form, committing to some terms of use.

8.11 Further Reading

Classical books on process algebra by Robin Milner include:

R. Milner, *Communication and Concurrency*, Prentice-Hall, 1995.
R. Milner, *Communicating and Mobile Systems: the π-calculus*, Cambridge University Press, 1999.

A recent extension of process algebra, which allows *mobility*, i.e., the dynamic change of communication topology, is the π-calculus. The second books in the above list includes the description of both CCS and the π-calculus.

A recent book on communication protocols, which contains a description of LOTOS, as well as other ISO standards, such as SDL and ESTELLE is:

R. Lai, A. Jirachiefpattana, *Communication Protocol Specification and Verification*, Kluwer Academic Publishers, 1998.

Other books on process algebra include

J. C. M. Baeten, W.P. Weijland, *Process Algebra*, Cambridge Tracts in Theoretical Computer Science, Cambridge University Press, 1990.

J. C. M. Baeten, ed., *Applications of Process Algebra* Cambridge Tracts in Theoretical Computer Science, Cambridge University Press, 1991.

G. Bruns, *Distributed System Analysis with CCS*, Prentice-Hall, 1996.

M. Hennessy, *Algebraic Theory of Processes*, MIT Press, 1988.

An extensive treatment of different process algebras, and comparisons between them can be found in the following two papers:

R. J. van Glabbeek, The Linear Time-Branching Time Spectrum (Extended Abstract), CONCUR 1990, Theories of Concurrency, Amsterdam, The Netherlands, Lecture Notes in Computer Science 458, Springer-Verlag, 1990, 278–297.

R. J. van Glabbeek, The Linear Time–Branching Time Spectrum II, E. Best (ed.), 4th international conference on Concurrency theory, CONCUR 1993, Lecture Notes in Computer Science 715, Springer-Verlag, Hildesheim, Germany, 66–81.

9. Software Testing

... and tied round the neck of the bottle was a paper label, with the words "DRINK ME" beautifully printed on it in large letters. It was all very well to say 'Drink me,' but the wise little Alice was not going to do that in a hurry. 'No, I'll look first,' she said, 'and see whether it's marked "poison" or not'.

Lewis Carroll, *Alice's Adventures in Wonderland*

Testing is the process of sampling the executions of a system according to some given criterion. Each execution is compared with the specification, and any mismatch is reported as an error. Since testing is usually based on sampling of the system executions, rather than on systematically checking all of them, it is not considered to be an exhaustive check guaranteed to cover all possible errors. It provides a lesser guarantee than the more comprehensive formal methods presented in previous chapters. Thus, some researchers do not even include testing within formal methods. However, testing does provide a practical solution in the case where a given system is so large that it defies manual or automatic verification. In fact, testing is by and large the most commonly used method for enhancing the quality of software.

Obviously, even the most rigorous testing technique may not *guarantee* that the checked system will behave correctly in all possible circumstances. For example, the testing process may be ignorant of some internal parameters such as temperature or humidity. Checking that a vending machine produces a chocolate bar ten times in a row, when the right amount of money is being inserted, the right button is pushed, and a chocolate bar is available, does not guarantee that the machine will do so the eleventh time. It merely enhances the expectation that it will do so. It is possible, although unlikely, that the machine would do so only until 5 P.M., when it starts dispensing popcorn instead. Nevertheless, verifying the design of the system using some of the methods described in previous chapters and testing the actual system for correct behavior can certainly decrease the possibility that the system will behave in some wrong and unexpected ways.

Testing is not intended to prove that there are no errors in the tested program, nor can it guarantee that the program performs its intended goal correctly. Testing does not guarantee to find all the errors (or even some); there are never sufficiently many tests that will guarantee that. Testing is merely the process of executing the checked program under certain specified conditions and parameters in an attempt to find errors.

In some sense, the goal of the tester is opposite to that of the programmer: a successful tester is one who shows that an error exists. Therefore, at least in theory, a programmer should not test his own code. In practice, programmers are often requested to test their own code.

Although testing is not guaranteed to necessarily detect all the errors in a given program, it is simple enough and increases the quality assurance at a reasonable cost. In particular, testing takes much less time to perform, and requires less human resources than deductive verification. It is applicable even in cases where verification is too hard to perform, and model checking is not feasible (for example, in the presence of an infinite or a huge state space, or complicated data structures).

There are several different levels and phases in software testing:

Unit (module) testing. The lowest level of testing, where one tests small pieces of code separately.

Integration testing. Testing that different pieces of the code, including code written by different groups, work well together.

System testing. Testing the system as a whole. System testing usually inspects the *functionality* of the software.

Acceptance testing. Usually performed by the customer, who needs to check that the developed system fits his needs.

Regression testing. Performed during maintenance, after changing, correcting or updating part of the system to check whether the system still functions correctly. Regression testing is typically used when adding a new feature to an already tested system. In this case, one usually repeats the tests performed previously to check that the existing features still operate correctly.

Stress Testing. Testing the system under extreme conditions, e.g., with an unusually high number of users, or with vast quantities of data.

White box testing is a technique for debugging systems based on inspecting their internal details, e.g., the code. Some practitioners do not like the term *white box* and use the more intuitive term *transparent box* to emphasize the visibility of the code in the testing process. An *execution path* consists of a sequence of control points and instructions appearing in the tested code. We can regard an execution path as a path in the flowchart of the tested code. A program may have an unbounded, or at least a very large, number of execution paths. Walking through all of the program paths is usually infeasible, due to their large number. In order to cope with this limitation, different coverage criteria suggest ways to check a relatively small number of paths, while trying to achieve a relatively high degree of probability of finding potential errors. *Code coverage analysis* can be used to obtain a quantitative and qualitative measurement of the quality of the coverage. Such an analysis predicts the chance that errors may still be present in the code after the testing process.

Unlike white box testing, *black box testing* is not based on the internal structure of the system, which may be unknown or inaccessible. Instead, black box testing can use experiments allowed by the known interface with the tested system. Sometimes, one performs black box testing even if part or all of the structure of the tested system is known, in order not to be influenced by and biased by the actual implementation.

Since white box testing deals directly with the code, it is better suited to handle lower level testing, such as unit testing and integration testing. Black box testing is more appropriate for checking the functionality of the system, hence better suited for system testing and acceptance testing. However, it can be applied to unit testing as well.

Finding errors during unit or integration testing helps to point out where the errors are, whereas higher-level testing only gives a rough idea where one should investigate further. It is cheaper to find an error earlier and fix it immediately. In addition, lower level testing, such as unit testing, allows developing and testing different parts of the software simultaneously.

Testing is based on automatically or manually performed *experiments* applied to the system under test. By applying some testing method (and, possibly by using some testing tools) to generate a set of test cases, the tester obtains a *test suite*. Test execution involves interaction with the system under test, performing the individual tests in the test suite. The *test environment* must allow the tester to perform the steps of the experiments, and make observations about them. Obtaining an appropriate test environment may involve adding code to the tested software. The actual testing process may involve providing user inputs to the program at certain predefined locations, and observing the printed result at the end of its execution. In other cases, testing may involve forcing the program to start from a particular state, or comparing some values of some internal variable when reaching a particular point in the execution. Then, special code that allows making such experiments and observations must be provided in order to perform the test.

We will start by presenting various white box testing techniques, and return to black box testing in Section 9.9.

9.1 Inspections and Walkthroughs

Inspections and *walkthroughs* are manual testing methods, carried out by a small team of people during a meeting, which typically lasts one to two hours. Experiments show that in such peer review meetings, 30% to 70% of the errors that exist in the code are found.

In *code inspection*, one of the team members is the *moderator*. He distributes the material, controls the session and records the errors. The testing process mostly involves a programmer explaining the inspected program line by line. The team members raise and discuss questions taken from a comprehensive list of potential errors. Some examples of such questions, relating to typical programming errors, are:

> Are there variables that are used before being initialized?
> Are there subscripts of array variables that are out of bounds?
> Are all the variables declared?
> Do procedure calls and procedure declaration match in number of parameters and types?
> Is there a division by zero?

There are several factors that contribute to the quality of code inspection:

- The preparation period for the review is critical. In the case that the code is completely new, the programmers may be asked to give a short lecture about the code. In this case, a code walkthrough, as described below, may be called for.
- The number of reviewers and the mix of programmers and external reviewers is important to achieve a high quality brainstorming meeting.
- The moderator has to make sure that the important issues are recorded and that the appropriate people know how they are responsible for taking care of the issues that were raised during the inspection.
- The number of errors found can be used as a measure of the success of the inspection. For various kinds of systems there are statistics that show the typical number of errors.

Code *walkthroughs* are also performed by small teams, similar in arrangement to the ones that are used for code inspection. Again, the moderator controls the session and records the errors. The testers simulate the behavior of the computer by following some previously constructed test cases. The test cases are described in standard documents.

The success of both of these testing methods depends on the preparation and collaboration of the team members. The moderator is supposed to set up the appointment and distribute the tested code to the team members in advance. The other team members need to get acquainted with it before the meeting. Several psychological factors are often very important in such human interaction. These are, for example, the lack of personal tension between the group members, the length of the meeting (which directly affects the ability to concentrate for such a brainstorming session), and the ability to manage the opposite goals of the group members (i.e., finding errors in the code on the one hand, and defending the code from possible criticism on the other).

9.2 Control Flow Coverage Criteria

In unit testing , a test case usually corresponds to the selection of an execution path. The path can be selected, e.g., by fixing the initial values and the inputs requested during the execution. (However, when nondeterminism is allowed, e.g., due to concurrency, the initial values and the inputs provided by the user during the execution may not be enough to fix the entire execution.) The tester can execute a path and compare the output to the expected behavior. It is assumed that the tester knows what the correct behavior of the tested system should be, and can detect possible deviations from the actual behavior tested.

During testing, one can seldom check all the executions of a system in a comprehensive way. Thus, testing is often done based on *coverage criteria*. Coverage criteria allow collecting sets of executions that are likely to present the same errors. (In practice, this is not always the case, and can be a source of failure to find errors during testing.) One then checks one sample execution out of each such set. For example, one can group together the executions that progress along the same path in the flowchart that correspond to the tested software.

In general, the larger the collected sets, the smaller the number of test cases that are included. It is usually (but not always) the case that a criterion that prescribes checking more executions will have a better chance of finding potential errors, at the expense of having to do more work. The criteria, some of which are presented below, can be viewed as heuristic methods for checking the code.

We will present the main coverage criteria and demonstrate the differences between them using a small example. Consider the flowchart in Figure 9.1, which is a part of a program. This is a simple case that does not involve requesting input from the user. We will give example test cases for the flowchart in this figure, based on the presented criteria.

To best emphasize the difference between the coverage criteria in this particular example, the test cases will be described using the state of the variables just prior to the decision predicate $x \equiv y \land z > w$, i.e., right after incrementing y. However, in general, it is much more reasonable to specify the test cases as assignments at the *beginning* of the paths, since this allows us to properly initialize the test. Propagating the test cases specification to the beginning of the path will be described in Section 9.4. In what follows, we use the terminology *condition* to refer to a simple first order formula (see Section 3.3), i.e., an application of a relation to first order terms.

Statement Coverage

Each executable statement of the program (e.g., assignment, input, test, output) appears in at least one test case.

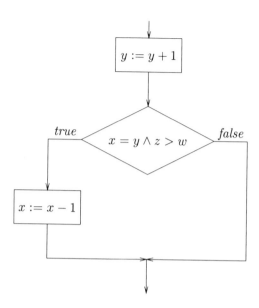

Fig. 9.1. A part of a flowchart

For statement coverage, we will make both conditions $x \equiv y$ and $z > w$ of the decision predicate evaluate to TRUE, by setting

$$\{x \mapsto 2,\ y \mapsto 2,\ z \mapsto 4,\ w \mapsto 3\}. \tag{9.1}$$

Notice that this does not cover the case where the decision predicate is interpreted as FALSE. Thus, it may miss some needed calculations that are required in the case that the *false* edge is taken, but were omitted from the code.

Edge Coverage

Each executable edge of the flowchart appears in some test case.

In particular, under this coverage criterion, one needs to include both of the edges marked by *true* or *false* of each decision predicate of the checked program (for example, in an if-then-else command, or a while loop). This coverage criterion is often called *branch coverage* or *decision coverage*.

For edge coverage, we have to add to the test case (9.1) another test case, which checks the case where the decision predicates is evaluated to FALSE, and therefore forces choosing the *false* edge out of the decision node. This can be done by setting

$$\{x \mapsto 3,\ y \mapsto 3,\ z \mapsto 5,\ w \mapsto 7\}. \tag{9.2}$$

The tests (9.1) and (9.2) cover the decision predicate $x \equiv y \wedge z > w$ as a single unit. But they do not exercise the two conditions $x \equiv y$ and $z > w$ separately. The selection of the *false* out-edge in the latter test case is because $z > w$ does not hold. It may be that the condition $x \equiv y$ was wrong, e.g., it should have been $x \geq y$ instead, and consequently, when $x > y$, the statement decrementing x should still be executed. Yet this case is not being tested.

An example of the problem with testing the decision predicate as one entity occurs in programming languages that allow 'short circuiting' of Boolean operators. That is, a decision of the form $A \wedge B$, where A is interpreted as FALSE would evaluate to FALSE without evaluating B. Similarly, a decision of the form $A \vee B$, where A is interpreted as TRUE would be interpreted as TRUE without evaluating B. Consider the decision predicate $A \vee (B \wedge C)$, where C is a Boolean function call with some side effects. Then, assigning TRUE to A, or FALSE to both A and B would guarantee that the decision predicate will be tested with both truth values. However, in both cases, the call to C was not exercised even once.

Another weakness of edge coverage is that it considers only the Boolean values of conditions: $x \equiv y$ can be falsified in different ways, and adding only the case where $x > y$ does not necessary reflect the case where $x < y$. The short circuiting problem is addressed by using a more exhaustive condition coverage such as edge/condition coverage, or combination coverage.

Condition Coverage

Each decision predicate can be a (possibly trivial) Boolean combination of simple first order formulas. This includes the comparison between two expressions, or the application of a relation to some program variables. Each executable condition appears in some test case where it is calculated to TRUE, and in another test case where it is interpreted as FALSE, provided that it can have these truth values.

For condition coverage we will use the test case (9.2) which guarantees that $x \equiv y$ is TRUE and $z > w$ is FALSE. We add to it the case where $x \equiv y$ is FALSE, while $z > w$ is TRUE. This can be done by the assignment

$$\{x \mapsto 3,\, y \mapsto 4,\, z \mapsto 7,\, w \mapsto 5\}. \tag{9.3}$$

Notice that in both of these cases (9.2) and (9.3), the overall decision predicate is interpreted as FALSE and we miss checking the decrement statement.

Edge/Condition Coverage

This coverage criterion requires the executable edges as well as the conditions to be covered.

According to the edge/condition coverage criterion, we can select the three test cases (9.1), (9.2) and (9.3). This will guarantee both that the decision will take both the positive and negative outcome, and that each separate condition $x \equiv y$ and $z > w$ will be calculated as both TRUE and FALSE.

Multiple Condition Coverage

This is similar to condition coverage, but instead of taking care of each single condition, we require that each Boolean combination that may appear in any decision predicate during some execution of the program must appear in some test case.

Thus, if a decision predicate is of the form $A \wedge (B \vee C)$, and each of the conditions A, B and C can be calculated independently to TRUE or FALSE, we need to check $2^3 = 8$ combinations. If such a decision node appears twice on the flow chart path, there can be $8 \times 8 = 64$ different combinations and so forth. It is not necessarily the case that each combination is possible. We may have some dependency between the conditions, e.g., A is TRUE whenever B is TRUE.

Multiple condition coverage is an even more exhaustive criterion than condition coverage. It adds to the cases (9.1), (9.2) and (9.3) the following case, which makes both $x \equiv y$ and $z > w$ evaluate to FALSE.

$$\{x \mapsto 3,\ y \mapsto 4,\ z \mapsto 5,\ w \mapsto 6\} \tag{9.4}$$

The main disadvantage of multiple condition coverage is that it involves an explosion of the number of test cases.

Path Coverage

This criterion requires that every executable path be covered by a test case.

Unfortunately, the number of paths for a given piece of code can be enormous. Since loops may result in infinite or an unfeasible number of paths, we cannot impose testing of all possible sequences including repetitions.

Some paths may never execute. Some decision predicates or simple first order formulas may never calculate to a given Boolean value, and some pieces of code may never be reached (i.e., *dead code*). For these cases there are obviously no corresponding *successful* test cases. We recognize this fact either when preparing the test cases, or during testing itself. In general, the problem of analyzing a system for finding dead code, or predicates that cannot take some truth value, is undecidable. Identifying, during testing or test preparation, that some part of the code is not executable, is itself valuable information about the tested code. During testing, it is possible to check how much coverage was actually obtained. This information can give some feedback about the quality of the testing process, and may be used to decide whether to perform further tests. Later we will discuss how to automatically calculate test cases, based on techniques similar to the ones used in deductive verification of programs.

Control flow coverage techniques have various limitations. First, the coverage is hardly comprehensive: it is usually impossible to cover all paths, and thus errors may be left unfound, as an existing error can occur on a path that was not covered. Another problem is that even if we do use a good test suite, we are merely executing the code according to the paths in the flowchart. It is not always easy to check during testing that the path covered does exactly what it should do.

Covering the program using its structural information can also be biased towards the way the code was already written (as opposed to the way the code should have been written). For example, consider the case where there are two executions that follow exactly the same sequence of instructions, and succeed and fail in exactly the same decision predicates, or even in the same conditions within the predicates. Hence, we may select a test case that corresponds to one of these executions, omitting the other. It still is possible that one of the executions is erroneous and the other is error free. This potentially indicates that the programmer should have distinguished between these cases and have forced different execution paths to be taken for the two cases. Unfortunately, the selected coverage criterion may result in the erroneous execution not being covered.

The effectiveness of different coverage criteria is difficult to assess, although some collected experimental statistics exist. One may argue that coverage techniques should be analyzed using probabilistic methods (see Section 9.10). However, techniques for increasing program reliability based on such analysis are usually of rather theoretical value. The main obstacle is that it is usually impossible to assign a reasonable probability distribution to programs. We do not usually have a good idea of what an 'average' program looks like, e.g., what is the likelihood of a condition to be evaluated as TRUE at a certain point in an execution.

Comparison Between Different Coverage Criteria

There are some obvious relations between the different coverage criteria. We say that one criterion *subsumes* another, if guaranteeing the former coverage also guarantees the latter. This means that the former is the more comprehensive criterion, and thus is more likely to find errors, at the cost of additional work. Notice that it can happen that due to a lucky selection of the test cases, a less comprehensive coverage will find errors that a more comprehensive approach will happen to miss.

It is easy to see that edge coverage subsumes statement coverage. We also have that edge/condition coverage subsumes edge coverage (and hence also statement coverage) and condition coverage.

Path coverage clearly subsumes edge coverage. Moreover, multiple condition coverage subsumes edge/condition coverage (and hence also any criterion that the latter subsumes). Path coverage does not subsume multiple condition coverage, since we can execute all the paths without exercising all the conditions in the decision predicates. Conversely, with multiple condition coverage we may not cover all the paths (e.g., due to loops).

The above examples can be used to show that condition coverage does not subsume edge coverage nor does edge coverage subsume condition coverage. Even more surprisingly, condition coverage does not even subsume statement coverage. This is due to possible dead code.

These relations appear in Figure 9.2, where a coverage criterion that subsumes another appears above it, with an arrow from the former to the latter.

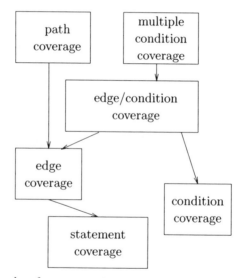

Fig. 9.2. A hierarchy of coverage criteria

Loop Coverage

The above coverage criteria (except the exhaustive, and usually impractical, path coverage) do not treat loops adequately: they do not include provisions for checking multiple traversals of a loop. There are several, mostly ad hoc strategies for testing loops:

- Check the case where the loop is skipped.
- Check the case where the loop is executed once.
- Check the case where the loop is executed some typical number of times (but notice that it is often difficult to assess what is typical).
- If a bound n of the number of iterations of the loop is known, try executing it $n - 1$, n and $n + 1$ times.

Testing loops become all the more difficult when nested loops are involved. The number of tests can grow up exponentially with the number of nestings. Therefore, testing nested loops is done in an even less comprehensive way than testing a single loop.

9.3 Dataflow Coverage Criteria

Dataflow analysis is often used within compilers to perform static analysis of the program. That is, analyzing the code based on its structure, without executing it first.

One common problem that is checked using dataflow analysis is the (improper) use of a variable in an expression before is is being initialized. This can be done using a backwards search on the flowchart of program. A variable is *live* in a statement when it is used to calculate some expression, e.g., in an assignment or a decision predicate. Progressing backwards in the flowchart graph, a variable remains live if it is not being assigned to within the current flowchart node. It remains live also if it is used, but also being assigned to, at the same node, as in $x := x + 1$. If it is only being assigned to, but not used, it becomes *dead*. For a decision node, which forks into two possibilities, a variable is live if it is used in the predicate of this node, or is live in at least one of the successor nodes (note that our analysis proceeds backwards from these successor nodes to the decision node). If we reach the starting point of the program with some live variables, then these variables are suspected as being used before being initialized. Of course, without executing the code, we may have some false alarms here; some of the paths in the search may not correspond to actual executions. Still, the compiler can issue a warning.

The aim of the coverage criteria is to minimize the number of test cases, while still maintaining a good probability of finding the errors in the tested code. A shortcoming of control-flow-based coverage criteria, discussed in the previous section, is that the generated test cases do not necessarily conform with how some of the program data is being processed later. In the control flow coverage criteria presented in Section 9.2, one may easily fail to include some execution sequence in which some variable is set to some value for a particular purpose, but later that value is misused. According to the control flow coverage criteria (except for path coverage), setting the variable to a particular value, and later using or checking the contents of that value, may not be represented at all in the selected test cases. Rapps and Weyuker [121] suggested several coverage techniques that are based on paths between definitions (assignments to) and uses of variables.

We provide some simple definitions that are required in order to present the dataflow coverage criteria. For each variable x, define the following sets of nodes in the flowchart (corresponding to statements and conditions of the program):

$def(x)$ the nodes where some value is assigned to x (e.g., in an assignment or an input statement).

$p\text{-}use(x)$ nodes where x is used in a predicate (e.g., in *if* or *while* statements).

$c\text{-}use(x)$ nodes where x is used in some expression other than a predicate (e.g., within an expression that is assigned to some variable).

The paths $def\text{-}clear(x)$ are defined to be those that include only nodes where x is not defined. For each node $s \in def(x)$, we define two sets of nodes corresponding to later uses of the variable x:

$dpu(s, x)$ includes nodes s' such that there is a $def\text{-}clear(x)$ path from s to s' (except for the first node, since $s \in def(x)$), and s' is in $p\text{-}use(x)$. That is, there is a path that starts with an assignment to x, progresses while not reassigning to x, and ends with a node where x is used within a predicate.

$dcu(s, x)$ includes nodes s' such that there is a $def\text{-}clear(x)$ path from s to s', and s' is in $c\text{-}use(x)$.

We can define now the various dataflow coverage criteria. Each criterion defines the paths that should be included in a test suite. Thus, for each program variable x, and for each statement s in $def(x)$, one needs to include at least the following paths, which are $def\text{-}clear(x)$, except for the first node s, as subpaths in the test suite:

all-defs Include one path to some node in $dpu(s, x)$ or in $dcu(s, x)$.

all-p-uses Include one path for each node in $dpu(s, x)$.

all-c-uses/some-p-uses Include one path for each node in $dcu(s, x)$, but if $dcu(x)$ is empty, include at least one path to some node in $dpu(x)$.

all-p-uses/some-c-uses Include one path to each node in $dpu(s, x)$, but if $dpu(x)$ is empty, include at least one path to some node in $dcu(x)$.

all uses Include one path to each node in $dpu(s, x)$ and to each node in $dcu(s, x)$.

all-du-paths Include all the paths to each node in $dpu(s, x)$ and to each node in $dcu(s, x)$.

These paths should not contain cycles except for the first and last nodes, which may be the same. This is important, since an assignment such as $x := x + 1$ both defines and uses x in some expression; the $c\text{-}use$ of this the expression $x + 1$ in assignment statement refers to a *previous* definition of the variable, not the current one. Thus, we allow the previous definition to be

another occurrence of the same assignment statement. The hierarchy of the
dataflow coverage criteria appears in Figure 9.3

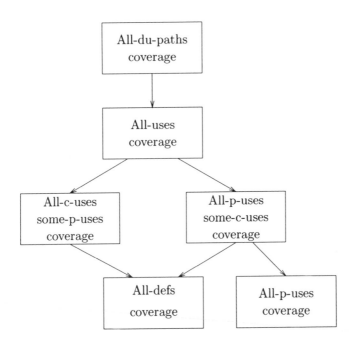

Fig. 9.3. A hierarchy of dataflow coverage

9.4 Propagating path conditions

The examples of test cases given in Section 9.2 for different ways to cover the
piece of code in Figure 9.1 were described using assignments to the program
variables just prior to the decision node included in each path. This was done
to better illustrate the differences between the coverage criteria. However,
giving the values of variables in the middle of the test case is obviously not
a reasonable way to specify it. Test cases can be specified, e.g., by listing the
paths together with the starting condition for the program variables. If the
path includes some user input, each test case should also specify the values
that need to be be entered by the user according to their requested input
order along the tested path. If the path starts from a different point than
the entry point to the tested program, the starting location must also be
supplied. These values need to guarantee the execution of the selected path
in the flowchart.

Consider first the statement coverage criterion. Assume that one picks up a set of paths that include every statement in the program under test. This can be done based on graph algorithms such as the Chinese Postman tour, which will be discussed further in Section 9.9. For each path, we need to find a test case in the form of an assignment to the variables at the beginning of the path, which will guarantee executing the path. In some cases, no such assignment exists. For example, consider a path of some flowchart that includes assigning the value 2 to the variable x and then testing whether $x > 7$, and proceeds according to the *true* edge of the test. Static analysis may help detect such paths. Otherwise, they can be detected during testing.

Consider the simple case where the flowchart does not include input statements. We would like to calculate a condition at the beginning of a given path, which will guarantee that we will execute that path. Then we can select values that satisfy this path precondition, and use them to test the path. The following algorithm can generate a path precondition η. It guarantees that when the control of the program is at the beginning of the path, the path is executed, and that at the end, some given condition φ will hold. The condition η calculated by the algorithm is in fact the *weakest* such precondition. That is, it is the one describing exactly *all* assignment to the program variables that will guarantee executing the path and obtaining φ upon its termination.

The algorithm traverses the given path backwards. It starts with some postcondition φ, and calculates at each point in the path the weakest (i.e., most general) condition to complete the path such that φ will hold at the end. We saw in Section 7.1 that the weakest precondition for executing an assignment $v := e$ and reaching a state satisfying φ is $\varphi[e/v]$, i.e., φ where each free occurrence of v is substituted by e. The weakest precondition for the traversal of the *true* edge of a decision predicate p is $p \wedge \varphi$. This is because calculating the truth value of the predicate does not change any variable (except for the program counter, which is not included here), thus φ must also hold before its execution. Furthermore, p must also hold in order for the execution of the test to succeed. In a similar way, the weakest precondition for traversing the *false* edge of a decision predicate p is $\neg p \wedge \varphi$.

Let $\xi = s_1 s_2 \ldots s_n$ be a sequence of nodes. For each node s_i on the path, we define the following notation:

$type(s_i)$ is the type of the transition in s_i. This can be one of the following: *begin, end, decision, assign.*

$proc(s_i)$ is the process to which s_i belongs.

$pred(s_i)$ is the predicate s_i, in the case where s_i is a decision node.

$branch(s_i)$ is the label on the outgoing edge of the node s_i (*true* or *false*), if s_i is a *decision* and it has a successor in the path that belongs to the same process. Otherwise, it is *undefined*. Note that if the path ends with a decision node, then the outgoing edge of that node is not included in the path. In this case, the decision predicate of that node does not affect the calculated path condition.

$expr(s_i)$ is the expression assigned to some variable, in the case where s_i is an *assign* statement.

$var(s_i)$ is the variable assigned, in case s_i is an *assign* statement.

$p[e/v]$ is the predicate p where all the (free) occurrences of the variable v are replaced by the expression e.

```
for i := n to 1 step -1 do
    begin
        case type(sᵢ) do
            decision⇒
                case branch(sᵢ) do
                    true⇒
                        current_pred := current_pred ∧ pred(sᵢ)
                    false⇒
                        current_pred := current_pred ∧ ¬ pred(sᵢ)
                    undefined⇒
                        current_pred := current_pred
                end case
            assign⇒
                current_pred := current_pred [ expr(sᵢ)/var(sᵢ) ]
            begin, end⇒ no_op
        end case;
        simplify (current_pred)
    end
```

The procedure **simplify** is used to simplify the formula obtained at each iteration of the main loop of the algorithm. There are various heuristics for this, e.g., combining together constants in $x + 3 - 2$, resulting in $x + 1$. Simplifying formulas is a difficult problem. It can be shown that in general it is undecidable whether a given first order formula over the *integers* (or other commonly used structures) is equivalent to the simple formula *true*, or to *false* (see [95]). The former means that the path will be executed independent of the values of the program variables. The latter means that the path cannot be executed at all. However, there are some structures where this problem is decidable. As an example, consider Presburger arithmetic, i.e., the *naturals* (or the *integers*) with addition, subtraction and comparison (see Section 3.6).

Given a path, we apply the above algorithm with *current_pred*= *true* as a postcondition to the path. The algorithm only finds a precondition, but does not find an assignment that satisfies it.

Consider the above example of an excerpt from a flowchart in Figure 9.1. To cover both the statement incrementing y, and the statement decrementing x, we need to follow a path with three nodes that selects the *true* edge of the decision. Applying the above algorithm, we start with a postcondition *current_pred=true*. The last node of the selected path is the decrement $x :=$

$x-1$, i.e., an *assign* node. Then *current_pred* gets the value $true[x-1/x]$, which is *true*. Continuing to traverse the path backwards, we reach the *test* node, which has the predicate $x \equiv y \wedge z > w$. Since we pass through the *true* edge, we conjoin this predicate to the value *true* in *current_pred*, obtaining $x \equiv y \wedge z > w$ as the new value for *current_pred*. Finally, we pass through the node that increments y. Thus, *current_pred* becomes $x \equiv y \wedge z > w[y + 1/y]$, which is $x \equiv y + 1 \wedge z > w$. The assignment

$$\{x \mapsto 2,\ y \mapsto 1,\ z \mapsto 4,\ w \mapsto 3\} \tag{9.5}$$

satisfies the later path precondition. Notice that this assignment corresponds to the case (9.1), which was given with respect to the values of the variables *before the test* rather than at the beginning of the path.

The test suite for edge coverage can be calculated in a similar way, selecting paths so that both *true* and *false* edges of each condition will be covered. For example, the path condition for the path with two nodes that includes the assignment statement $y := y + 1$, and the decision node, with its *false* outgoing edge in the above example is calculated as follows. We start with *current_pred*= *true*. Passing through the false outgoing edge of the decision node, which has the predicate $x \equiv y \wedge z > w$, we obtain *current_pred*= *true* $\wedge \neg(x \equiv y \wedge z > w)$, which can be simplified to $(x \neq y) \vee (z \leq w)$. Passing through the node that increments y, we obtain *current_pred*= $((x \neq y) \vee (z \leq w))[y + 1/y]$, i.e., $((x \neq y + 1) \vee (z \leq w))$. An assignment corresponding to the test case (9.2) above is

$$\{x \mapsto 3,\ y \mapsto 2,\ z \mapsto 5,\ w \mapsto 7\}. \tag{9.6}$$

Test cases do not necessarily have to start from the entry point of the tested program. They can start at some intermediate point, with some values specified to the program variables (including the program counter). Forcing the test cases to always start from the entry point will naturally tend to cover the statements near the beginning of the code much better than the other statements. This may involve more testing than necessary. On the other hand, the risk in not starting the test cases from the entry point of the program is that such test cases may start with states that can never be reached in an actual execution. In particular, one may force testing a program starting at a statement that belongs to some dead code. Of course, testing a program from any point other than its beginning may require adding special code that will allow that.

Exercise 9.4.1. Change the above algorithm to support condition coverage. (Hint: preprocess the selected path by changing the decision predicates.)

Example: GCD program

The following PASCAL program accepts two *natural* numbers $x1$ and $x2$. It calculates the *greatest common divisor* (GCD) of them, i.e., the largest *natural* number that divides both. The result appears, at the end of the calculation, in the variable $x1$ (and in $x2$, as at termination, $x1 = x2$).

while not $x1=x2$ do
  if $x1 > x2$ then $x1:=x1-x2$
    else $x2:=x2-x1$
end

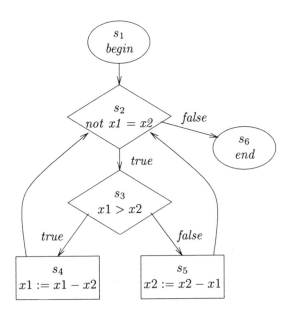

Fig. 9.4. A flowchart for the GCD program

This program can be translated into the flowchart in Figure 9.4. We will cover all edges of this program using the following paths: $\xi_1 : s_1, s_2, s_3, s_4$, $\xi_2 : s_1, s_2, s_3, s_5$ and $\xi_3 : s_1, s_2, s_6$.

We can calculate the path conditions for each one of these paths according to the above algorithm. We demonstrate this calculation in a table. The calculation goes backwards, starting with the postcondition *true* at the end of each sequence. Then at each step the postcondition is relativized with respect to one additional statement, and a precondition is calculated. Then the condition is simplified. The conditions calculated during the execution for the path ξ_1 is given in Table 9.1.

Exercise 9.4.2. Provide similar tables for the paths ξ_2 and ξ_3. Provide a table for the path $\xi_4 : s_1, s_2, s_3, s_4, s_2, s_3, s_5$.

Node	Statement	Post cond	Pre cond	Simplified
s_4	$x1 := x1 - x2$	$true$	$true$	$true$
s_3	$x1 > x2$	$true$	$x1 > x2$	$x1 > x2$
s_2	$x1 \neq x2$	$x1 > x2$	$x1 > x2 \wedge x1 \neq x2$	$x1 > x2$
s_1	$begin$	$x1 > x2$	$x1 > x2$	$x1 > x2$

Table 9.1. The conditions calculated for path ξ_1

Exercise 9.4.3. Find a set of paths and starting conditions for these paths, which will guarantee an edge coverage for the program in Figure 7.2.

Paths with Input Statements

The above test cases include assignments and decisions, but do not include requesting input from the user. To construct test cases with user input, requested via an *input x* command, where x is some program variable, we need to change the algorithm slightly [59]. Again, we will traverse the selected path backwards as before (according to the coverage criterion selected). When we reach an input command for a variable x, we observe the path precondition φ calculated so far. This is the condition to traverse the path from the current state to its end. We need to select a value for x so that it will conform with φ, i.e., we need to provide an input value of x that will satisfy φ. Let $y_1 \ldots y_n$ be all the other variables appearing (free) in φ.

Then, we need to select an input value x such that $\exists y_1 \ldots \exists y_n \varphi$ holds. Notice that here, again, finding such a value is in general undecidable. We select such a value n. This value is recorded to be the input value that must be provided by the tester when the test case will reach the current input point. The path is modified by replacing the occurrence of the input command by the assignment $x := n$ (since this, in effect, is what will happen in this test case). Thus, the precondition of the input statement is $\varphi[n/x]$. Now the algorithm continues as before. Notice that in this way, the input values are generated in reverse order, i.e., the last input is generated first.

Exercise 9.4.4. Change the above algorithm for calculating the path condition, presented in this chapter, to deal with the following cases [59]:

- Concurrency, i.e., allowing an interleaved path from multiple processes, with variables shared between the processes. Notice that in this case, due to possible nondeterminism, the precondition calculated does not *force* the execution of the interleaving path, when control is at its initial locations. Rather, it *allows* executing it, as other nondeterministic choices may be alternatively taken.
- Message passing.

9.5 Equivalence Partition

It is a common practice in specification and verification to partition the executions into sets of executions that should not be distinguished from each other. Then, instead of taking care of all the executions, we take care of at least one sequence from each such set. This usually allows simplifying the verification or testing process.

In verification, both deductive and automatic, we sometimes use an equivalence between interleaved sequences that result from the same partial order execution. The given specification often does not distinguish between them. In these cases, we can exploit this equivalence between sequences to provide a more convenient proof system, allowing reasoning only about some of the interleaved sequences [76, 55, 113, 142].

A similar principle of using equivalence between sequences is also used in testing. The motivation is the same as the one given for the coverage criteria; namely that checking all the executions of a program is impractical or impossible. We would like to group together into equivalence classes such that all the sequences in the same class are likely to either have no errors, or to have the same errors in them.

The process of equivalence partition testing is largely informal. We first take the specification of the input or initial condition of a system. We do not form explicitly the equivalence classes of the executions, but rather try to guess input values that will test each equivalence class, which when taken together, form the test suite. Suppose that the specification indicates that some conditions $\varphi_1, \ldots, \varphi_n$ must hold. Then, each condition φ_i partitions the set of executions to those that satisfy it and those that do not (we hope that the latter set is empty, of course). This is a partition of the executions to two sets exactly. Altogether, it can give us up to 2^n classes, where in each class some of the conditions hold and some do not.

Due to the large number of possible classes, we do not want to provide representatives to all of them. In addition, we would rather provide representatives to classes where one or a small number of the conditions do not hold; test cases that include a violation of many conditions are not as good as ones that include only a single one. This is because it would be difficult to pinpoint with the former the specific errors among all the ones that occurred in the same executions. We try to guess input values that would give test cases that would fail one (or a small number) of the conditions. In addition, we try to guess a test case that will satisfy all of the conditions.

9.6 Preparing the Code for Testing

The testers, or the programmers themselves, may need to make special preparation for testing, including the modification of the code. Such preparations can assist in automating the testing process, and in keeping track of the testing results and of statistics about the testing process. Preparing the software for testing may include creating an environment for it that allows the testing, often called a *test harness*. Additional code may, together with the original code, automatically apply the test cases and check the correctness of the testing results. This can involve forcing the program to start at particular locations (not necessarily the initial states) with some particular values for the program variables.

Such modification of the code can provide information about the quality of the coverage. Tables are allocated in secondary memory, to keep the information, while performing the different tests. Later, these tables are used to prepare the testing report. Such a table can include, for example, an entry for each statement in the program. Code is added in order to update each entry when the corresponding statement is executed. At the end of the testing, the table can be consulted to check whether complete coverage (in this case of the statements) was achieved. If not, new test cases are added, and the testing process repeats.

Adding such code can be done automatically at compile time, in the same way that debugging information is added by standard compilers (e.g., when compiling C programs with the UNIX command *cc -g*). As in the Heisenberg principle in quantum physics, performing the tests in this way modifies the behavior of the tested subject. The additional code will slow down the execution of the program, and change the memory allocation for the tested program. This is usually not a problem, except for special cases such as testing a time-critical embedded system.

Assertions can be inserted into the checked code. Additional code is responsible for checking these assertions, and informing the tester if they fail at run time. In this way, once such an assertion is violated, the tester is informed that the execution of the tested program from some given state violates an assumed relation between the program variables. One can generalize this technique to check whether safety properties of the program are violated. To do that, one can add several assertions to the code at different locations. The added code can be used to decide whether a safety property was violated, depending on the *combination* of the success and failure of the assertions during the test.

There are different kinds of dedicated software packages for assisting in the testing process:

Test case generation. These tools allow modeling the system. Then they use the model to automatically generate a set of tests according to some coverage criterion.

Coverage evaluation. Such tools check how much coverage is achieved by using a particular test suite, given some coverage criterion.

Test execution. These are tools that execute the test cases on the system under test, and report the test result. They may include interfacing with the system, e.g., through some communication queue, the internet or a file system. Another possibility is that test execution also involves a compilation of the system under test to include additional code required for performing the test, as described earlier in this section.

Test management. These tools maintain the different test suites, perform version control, and produce test reports. While executing one or even multiple tests can be performed using a test execution tool, this is often not enough. The results of testing should be carefully recorded and documented. Test cases need to be carefully maintained, so that regression tests can be repeated when the system is modified.

9.7 Checking the Test Suite

Testing seldom guarantees that all or even some of the design and programming errors will be found. One way of measuring the quality of a test suite is by performing *code coverage analysis*. This is done by comparing the test suite against the code according to the chosen coverage criterion. For example, it is possible to check what is the percentage of statements or edges that are covered. The result of the comparison is a quantitative measurement of the coverage, plus an indication of parts of the code (e.g., statements, conditions) that need to be exercised by adding further tests. In some cases, the coverage analysis can even identify redundant test cases that may not be required to achieve the desired coverage.

None of the coverage strategies described in this chapter guarantee a complete and thorough testing process. If a program P passed a set of tests, it is hard to provide an estimate about the quality of the testing process. The following simple idea can help in assessing the quality of a test suite:

A test suite is unlikely to be comprehensive enough if it gives the same results to two different programs.

This is based on the fact that different programs are most likely to perform different computations. This idea is used in *mutation analysis* [25]. Given a tested program P, one generates several mutations, i.e., variants of the program. The mutations can be driven by the possible questions raised in the inspection process, or by structural changes, such as changing labels, or replacing comparison symbols and logical operators.

The test cases for P are then applied to each such mutation P' in its turn. If some test case behaves differently on P and P', the mutation P' *dies*. At the end of the mutation analysis, if a considerable number of mutants remain live, one should regard the test suite as inappropriate: there is no reason to believe that any of the live mutations P' is less correct than the original program P, while there is a good reason to believe that either P or P' is incorrect. Of course, even if P passed all the tests, and all the mutations died, mutation analysis does not guarantee that the tested program P is error free.

9.8 Compositionality

Large software is usually developed by different teams, each responsible for a part of the code. This allows speeding up the development. The same principle can apply to software testing, as different pieces of code can be developed in isolation. The software testing process often begins even before all the development teams have completed their work.

Such a compositional approach has the additional advantage that keeping the size of the tested software down allows better management of its complexity. This allows the tester to concentrate on only part of the features required from the code. Another advantage is that finding an error in a small part of the code usually pinpoints the source of the error more accurately.

The main challenge here stems from the fact that different parts of a program often interact with each other. This makes it difficult to test one piece of code without already having the other parts ready for testing. Consider the case where there are different procedures, developed by different teams, with some hierarchy of calls between them. An example of such a hierarchy appears in Figure 9.5. There, the main procedure is A. It can call the procedures B, C and D. The procedure B can call E, while both C and D can call F.

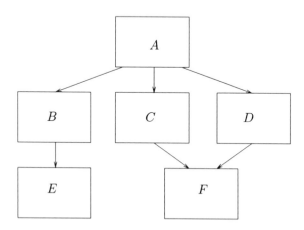

Fig. 9.5. A hierarchy of procedure calls

In order to test a procedure X that calls a procedure Y, we can use test suites for X, where calling Y is counted as one atomic operation. If Y is not available for such testing, we can write a short and simple version of Y called a *stub*, which is supposed to return values that will allow the testing of X. Similarly, if we want to test Y before X is available, we need to write some simple code that will simulate the calls that X makes to activate Y. Such code is called a *driver*. Thus, in the example in Figure 9.5, we may test A by writing stubs representing B, C and D. We may test E by writing a driver representing B. After the code is completed, the tests can be repeated with the actual code that was missing before.

Testing, like programming, is often done *bottom-up*, starting from the lowest levels in the hierarchy. In our example, the procedures E and F are tested first (they can be tested simultaneously by different groups). This requires coding drivers for the procedures B, C and D. Once the actual procedures are coded, they can be tested, using the already coded and tested procedures E and F, and a driver representing A. Finally, when the code for A is ready, one can test it, using calls for the rest of the procedures. To minimize the time needed for doing the testing in this example, we need three testing teams (the bottleneck is testing B, C and D simultaneously). There will be three consecutive testing phases. The number of drivers needed is 4, one for each node except the ones on the lowest level, which do not call any other procedure.

Testing can also be done *top-down*. In our example, this means starting with A, and writing stubs for B, C and D. Then, when these procedures are ready, we can test them, with appropriate new stubs for E and F. Finally, E and F can be tested, driven by real code for the procedures that can call them. Again, we need three testing teams to minimize testing time, and there are still three testing teams. The number of stubs needed is 5, one for each procedure except the top one, A.

Top-down and bottom-up are not the only two strategies that exist. One can test the code in an unstructured way. For example, test each one of the procedures A to F simultaneously, by adding the corresponding stubs and drivers for each. This strategy is called the *big bang*. For example, for testing C, we need both a driver representing A, and a stub representing F. The unstructured strategy allows reducing the testing time, since there are more procedures tested simultaneously. On the other hand, one needs to write a bigger number of drivers and stubs than in the structured strategies. In our example, this is 4 drivers and 5 stubs. Since drivers and stubs may deviate from the original code, having to use more drivers and stubs increases the chance of missing errors (or reporting incorrect errors, i.e., false negatives) during the testing processes.

It is natural to ask which testing strategy to use for a system composed of many procedures, tasks or modules. The answer is often that the testing strategy should fit the development strategy, as this is the order according to which the parts of the program are available to the testers.

9.9 Black Box Testing

Black box testing checks a system without considering its internal structure. Thus it is usually limited to checking the functionality or the features of a system. This is more appropriate for higher-level system testing, done at a later stage of the development. Another application is for menu driven systems. There, the tester may want to check that all the possible combinations of the options offered by the different menus behave according to the specification.

The intended behavior of the modeled system can be described in various distinct ways, such as text, message sequence charts (see Section 11.2), etc. State machines, or finite automata are quite useful for encapsulating the description of different executions of a system together. Many modern design systems and methodologies are based on the model of finite automata (state machine), or an extension of it. This model is appropriate for capturing the dynamic nature of a system. Finite automata are well studied and there is a growing number of tools that are based on it. In fact, automata are used within design tools (e.g., UML), testing tools (e.g., TESTMASTER) and model checking tools (COSPAN, SPIN, MURPHY). Using the same model for different purposes, e.g., design, simulation, testing and verification, is obviously desirable.

Black box testing is often based on modeling the tested system as a graph or an automaton, and using graph algorithms to construct the test suite. The first step is, as in model checking, modeling the system as an automaton. While in model checking we automatically check properties of the model, here we use the model to generate tests for the code. This distinction makes automata-based black box checking complementary to model checking. One can use a combined approach, where an abstract model for a system is formed. The model is used to perform tests on the program, comparing its behavior to the known variables of the system. Then, model checking techniques are applied to it, to automatically verify its properties [135]. This is demonstrated in Figure 9.6. In this view, the testing process is used to support the use of the model as a basis for automatic verification. Of course, one may not be completely satisfied with the fact that a system was *tested* to conform with a model. In this case, a more rigorous, though expensive approach for verifying the correspondence between a system and a model (e.g., deductive verification) may be preferred.

Since most software system are not limited to being finite state systems, the modeling process may require abstraction. One can also use *extended finite state machines*, which allow using conditions and assignments that involve variables. In this case, when considering also the values of the variables, there are possibly infinitely many states, but only finitely many *control states*.

After modeling the tested system as an automaton, one can use graph algorithms to generate the test suite. The setting is now different from model checking in the sense that the tester does not (and often cannot) perform backtracking when testing. Instead, when a different alternative of a previ-

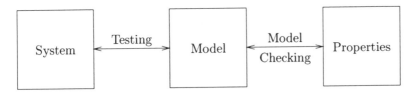

Fig. 9.6. A combined approach of testing and model checking

ously selected choice needs to be taken, the tester has to reset the system to its initial state, and reconstruct the experiment up to the point where the different choice needs to be taken.

Test generation algorithms use various coverage criteria to generate the test suite. Here too, it is usually impossible to cover all the paths, as there might be infinitely (or at least unreasonably) many of them. Thus, coverage criteria, similar to the ones discussed above, are used with respect to the finite state representation.

A typical automata-based test generation algorithm attempts to cover all the edges in the state space graph. For simplicity, one can assume that the state space consists of a single strongly-connected component. If this is not the case, one can add **reset** edges, which allow returning to the initial state. The **reset** edges force the graph to be a strongly-connected component, as the initial state is now reachable from every other reachable state (we assume that every state is reachable from the initial state). Alternatively, we may test each strongly-connected component separately, starting with a sequence from the initial state that brings us to that component.

Suppose we want to cover all the edges of the graph. A necessary and sufficient condition to visit each edge in a strongly connected graph exactly once, and return to the initial state is that for each node, the number of in-edges equals the number of out-edges. Not every graph satisfies this condition. If it does, the graph is said to have an *Euler cycle*. Checking this condition is simple, and if it holds, one can use an algorithm with linear complexity in the number of edges to construct such a path.

If the graph does not satisfy the above condition, one may want to find a path that includes every edge of the graph *at least* once. Since it is beneficial to minimize this effort, one would like to find a minimal number of paths that cover all the edges. This problem is called the *Chinese postman problem*. Solving this problem can be done based on the observation that instead of allowing an edge to repeat multiple times in the path, we can duplicate each edge according to the number of times it is supposed to occur in the path. After such a duplication, the Euler condition will hold. Then we can use an algorithm with linear time complexity [129] for finding an Euler cycle in the augmented graph. Finding the minimal number of times one needs to duplicate each node in order to satisfy the Euler condition can be solved in polynomial time using network-flow algorithm or linear programming [39].

Covering each edge at least once is not the only criterion used for constructing test suites. Some other possibilities include:

- Covering all the nodes.
- Covering all the paths (this is usually impractical).
- Covering each adjacent sequence of N nodes.
- Covering certain nodes at least/at most a given number of times in each sequence in the test suite.

Consider the graph in Figure 9.7. In order to cover all the states, it is sufficient to select two paths, e.g., $s_1, q_1, s_2, q_2, s_3, q_3, s_4$ and $s_1, r_1, s_2, r_2, s_3, r_3, s_4$. This does not cover all the edges. To do that, we can add the path s_1, s_2, s_3, s_4. To exhaustively cover all the paths, we need to test 27 paths. This is because there is an independent choice of three edges from each node s_1, s_2 and s_3.

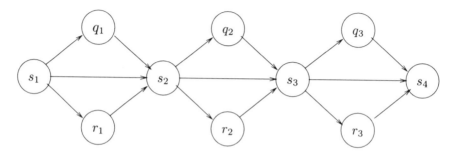

Fig. 9.7. A graph for testing

Notice that the coverage criterion used for testing may fail to guarantee finding all (or any of) the errors. Consider for example an error that is caused by the fact that a state r that satisfies some condition happens some time after another state s, satisfying another condition. Under a coverage criterion that guarantees to provide test cases that visit all the states of the system (or all the edges) we can still fail to find the erroneous executions. The two aforementioned states, s and r, may covered by some test cases. But each such test case contains only one of them (which by itself does not reveal the error).

A partial solution is to use the property checked when generating the test cases in order to target the testing towards finding errors according to the given property. For example, we can adopt the idea of automata-based model checking and use the finite automaton that represents the bad executions cases. Given a finite state model for the tested system, and the negated automaton, we can create the intersection, and use it to generate tests.

9.10 Probabilistic Testing

Software testing methods are based on a different philosophy than the one behind software verification: instead of trying to try to be exhaustive, we try to sample the executions of the software. The testing coverage criteria, presented earlier in this chapter, are an attempt to obtain a reasonable, yet practical coverability. To proceed further with this practical line of approach, we may abandon the goal of trying to be comprehensive and perform instead the tests based on the typical use of the software. The rationale behind this approach is that statistical studies showed that every software product is amenable to errors. Even after applying various formal methods techniques (typically, software testing), there are still some errors remain. With that in mind, we should aim at using the time allocated for checking the software in the most efficient way. Accepting the fact that after testing, there will still be some errors remaining in the software, we can try to maximize the 'minimal time to failure' (MTTF).

In order to base the testing on anticipated typical use, we can employ *probabilistic testing*. The model we use for probabilistic testing is an extension of the state space or finite automata model called a *Markov chain*. In addition to the states and the transitions, it also includes the *probability* of taking a particular transition from a given state. The probability is a *real* number between 0 and 1. In addition the sum of the probabilities of the transitions that exit from each state must be exactly 1.

In Figure 9.8, we have a model of a spring (see Figure 5.1, and the description in Section 5.2), in which probabilities were added. Since there is only one transition out of state s_1, and one transition out of s_3, the probabilities of these transitions must be 1, and thus, were not mentioned. From state s_2, there are two transitions: to s_1 and to s_3. The former has probability 0.8, and the latter has probability 0.2. We can express the probabilities in terms of percents by multiplying them by 100. So, each time we are in state s, there is an 80 percent chance of moving to state s_1, and a 20 percent chance of moving to state s_3.

In the Markov chain model, the probability of moving from one state to another depends only on the current state, and not on the history of the execution so far. The probability of executing a path is the multiplication of the probabilities along the path. Thus, the probability of executing the path $s_1 s_2 s_1 s_2 s_3$ in Figure 9.8 is $1 \times 0.8 \times 1 \times 0.8 \times 1 \times 0.2 = 0.128$, or 10.8 percent chance.

Notice that a Markov chain is merely a model. It does not necessarily reflect the actual system precisely. In fact, one may criticize the use of this model in the above case of a spring as follows:

- In a Markov chain, the probability of moving from one state to another depends only on the current state. This does not necessarily reflect the actual property of the system. In the spring example, the probability of

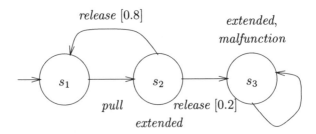

Fig. 9.8. A simple Markov Chain

the spring remaining extended may depend on its entire history, namely on the number of times it was pulled.

- Typically, there is a difficulty in providing the probabilities. This is true, in particular, when the system that is developed is new, and no prior statistics on its use are available. In the case of the spring, it is possible that the manufacturer may provide the probabilities, due to a study that was previously conducted. However, it is quite unlikely that such information exists. Instead, the probabilities usually reflect only a rough estimate.

The testing algorithm can use a Markov chain by simulating it according to the given probability. Programming languages often have a *random()* construct to generate a simulated random number, e.g., between 0 and 1. Assume a given list of transitions from a state s, numbered 1 to n, with probabilities $p_1, p_2, \ldots p_n$, respectively. We can partition the values between 0 and 1 into intervals of the form $(\Sigma_{i=1}^{i=j} p_i) \leq x < \Sigma_{i=1}^{i=j+1}$ (we can decide that the intervals are closed from below and open from above, except for the last interval, which is also closed from above), where $j \in \{0, \ldots, n-1\}$, and setting p_0 to 0. For example, in the spring example we have two intervals: $0 \leq x < 0.8$ and $0.8 \leq x \leq 1$. Then, if we are in state s, and the *random()* construct returns a value in the jth interval, we take the jth transition from s.

Assuming a non biased implementation of the random generator function, such a simulation would statistically conform with the probabilities of the checked model, and hence should give a preference for the more likely executions.

9.11 Advantages of Testing

Although testing is not as exhaustive as deductive verification or model checking, it is still the most popular method used for enhancing the quality of software. The main reason is that it is simple, feasible and gives a high cost/performance ratio.

Verifying software usually involves a lot of investment, more than it takes to consider it as a regular activity in developing software. Model checking has proved itself effective in verifying finite state systems such as hardware verification and communication protocols. However, it quickly reaches its limits when programs with *integer* or *real* variables and data structures such as stacks or trees are considered. In actual systems, a single state can consist of a large part of the computer's memory. Storing several states at the same time and comparing between them, as required by model checking algorithms, might not be practical. In contrast, testing usually requires a reasonable investment in time and human resources. It can be performed directly on the system under test.

9.12 Disadvantages of Testing

Testing is often done with less rigor than deductive verification and model checking. In essence, testing means sampling the execution of the checked programs. Since testing is applied directly to actual programs with a huge or infinite number of states, it is impossible or impractical to check all the executions of a program in a systematic way. Unfortunately, each one of the coverage methods can be shown to miss erroneous executions.

White box testing uses the code of the program to derive the test cases, according to the coverage criterion selected. This already introduces a bias towards the particular way that the system was implemented. Consider for example the criterion of edge coverage. The edges along some path of the flowchart are covered by an execution that passes through them. Such an execution is obtained based on inspecting the assignments and decision predicates that were used in the program. Thus, in essence, the code of the program, and the coverage criterion suggest a partitioning of the executions of the program, and testing follows this partitioning and checks a single execution from each equivalence class. Consider an execution that passes through the flowchart according to a particular path. Suppose that a the tested program has an error and that there are two possibilities covered by the same path, where one of them is correct and one of them is incorrect. The suggested partitioning may include, by chance, an execution that is correct, failing to include a test case for the incorrect execution.

A similar problem occurs in black box testing using a finite state machine model. The choice of model, which is based on the tester's conception of the correct and incorrect behaviors of the system, directly affects the choice of the test suite.

9.13 Testing Tools

Testing tools are less frequently available free of charge for academic purposes. Instruction for obtaining the GCT (Generic Coverage Tool) by Brian Merick is available from

ftp://cs.uiuc.edu/pub/testing/GCT.README

Notice: the use of formal methods systems often requires filling out and sending an appropriate release form, committing to some terms of use.

9.14 Further Reading

The classical book on software testing is still Myer's:

G. J. Myers, *The Art of Software Testing*, Wiley, 1979.

Several comprehensive books on testing were written by Beizer:

B. Beizer, *Black-Box Testing*, Wiley, 1995.

B. Beizer, *Software Testing Techniques*, 2nd edition, Van Nostrand Reinhold, 1990.

10. Combining Formal Methods

However, this bottle was NOT marked 'poison,' so Alice ventured to taste it, and finding it very nice, (it had, in fact, a sort of mixed flavor of cherry-tart, custard, pine-apple, roast turkey, toffee, and hot buttered toast,) she very soon finished it off.
Lewis Carroll, *Alice's Adventures in Wonderland*

Each one of the software reliability methods presented in this book has several typical advantages and disadvantages. Automatic verification methods are desirable since they are exhaustive and require minimal human intervention. However, the effectiveness of such methods decreases rapidly with the size of the checked system. Theorem proving can be applied to infinite state systems, but is slow and requires extensive human skills. Testing can be applied directly to a system, but is not comprehensive, hence may omit detecting some errors. Integrating different formal methods to work together may allow combining their strengths, while alleviating some of their weaknesses.

10.1 Abstraction

Verifying a system in its original form is frequently too complicated to perform. One often applies *abstraction*, i.e., obtain a simpler version of the checked system, by reducing the number of details that need to be taken care of. One successful approach for dealing with the complexity of systems is to simplify them into manageable versions, which preserve their essential properties. There are two verification tasks that are involved:

- Proving that the essential properties (including all the ones that we want to verify) are preserved between the original system and its simpler version.
- Proving the correctness of the simplified version. This task may be achievable after the simplification through model checking.

Abstraction can sometimes be used to relate an infinite state system with a finite state version in order to apply model checking. This is described in Figure 10.1. Even finite state systems may require abstraction for reducing the size of the state space of the original system into one that is manageable by existing model checking tools. Abstraction is usually based on using additional human knowledge via manual or semiautomatic tools. However, we cannot ignore the mathematical fact that in general verification of programs is undecidable, nor can it systematically reduce the complexity of model checking. Thus, we may fail to find an appropriate abstraction, or fail to formally prove the correspondence between the original system and its abstract version.

In this section, we will show some formal connection between a system and its abstract version, and the conclusions that can be drawn when first abstracting the system and then verifying the abstract version.

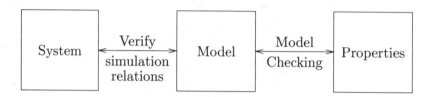

Fig. 10.1. A combined approach of verification and model checking

Consider a concrete transition system P (its structure will be given later) whose state space is $\mathcal{A}^P = \langle S^P, \Delta^P, I^P, L^P, \Sigma \rangle$, where S^P is its (finite or infinite) set of states, $\Delta^P \subseteq S^P \times S^P$ is the immediate successor relation, $I^P \subseteq S^P$ are the initial states, and L is some labeling function on the states over some alphabet (state labels) Σ. The abstract version O of P has a corresponding state space $\mathcal{A}^O = \langle S^O, \Delta^O, I^O, L^O, \Sigma \rangle$.

We saw in Chapter 8 how various notions of equivalences can be used to show the correspondence between process algebra agents. We can also use the notion of simulation between state spaces of systems. The abstraction will be presented using two simulation relations: a forward simulation $\mathcal{R} \subseteq S^P \times S^O$ and a backward simulation $\mathcal{Q} \subseteq S^O \times S^P$.

The forward simulation relation $\mathcal{R}$ must satisfy the following conditions:

- For each initial state $\iota^P \in I^P$, there exists at least one initial state $\iota^O \in I^O$, such that $\iota^P \mathcal{R} \iota^O$.
- If $r \mathcal{R} s$, then $L^P(s) = L^O(r)$.
- If $r \mathcal{R} s$, and $(s, s') \in \Delta^P$, then there exists at least one state $r' \in S^O$ such that $(r, r') \in \Delta^O$ and $r' \mathcal{R} s'$.

Notice the additional requirement that related states have the same labeling. Given the above conditions for $\mathcal{R}$, it is easy to see that for every execution σ of $\mathcal{A}^P$, there exists an execution $\hat{\sigma}$ of $\mathcal{A}^O$, that has a labeling matching the labeling of σ. That is, $L^P(\sigma_i)$, the labeling of the ith state of σ, is the same as $L^O(\hat{\sigma}_i)$. Thus, σ and $\hat{\sigma}$ satisfy the same linear temporal logic or Büchi automata properties.

Viewing the state spaces $\mathcal{A}^P$ and $\mathcal{A}^O$ as automata (not necessarily finite) over a mutual alphabet Σ, let $\mathcal{L}(\mathcal{A}^P)$ and $\mathcal{L}(\mathcal{A}^O)$ be the languages of $\mathcal{A}^P$ and $\mathcal{A}^O$, respectively. Then, the simulation relation implies that $\mathcal{L}(\mathcal{A}^P) \subseteq \mathcal{L}(\mathcal{A}^O)$. Let φ be a specification, and $\mathcal{L}(\varphi)$ the set of executions satisfying φ. If we verify that the abstract version $\mathcal{A}^O$ satisfies φ, namely that $\mathcal{L}(\mathcal{A}^O) \subseteq \mathcal{L}(\varphi)$, we can conclude using the transitivity of the inclusion relation '$\subseteq$' that $\mathcal{L}(\mathcal{A}^P) \subseteq \mathcal{L}(\varphi)$. That is, that the original system satisfies the verified property. However, there can be executions of $\mathcal{A}^O$ that do not have a matching execution in $\mathcal{A}^P$. Thus, if a counterexample that does not satisfy φ is found for the abstract version $\mathcal{A}^O$, we still need to check whether it also belongs to $\mathcal{A}^P$. (In fact, $\mathcal{A}^P$ is itself just a model of the system, thus one has to compare the correspondence of the counterexample to an actual execution of the modeled system.)

As an example, consider a representation of a buffer with 4 slots, in Figure 10.2. The states labeled by *empty* represent an empty buffer, while the states labeled by *full* represent a full buffer. The states labeled by *quasi* represent a buffer that is neither full, nor empty. On the left, we have a state space $\mathcal{A}^P$ for the buffer, while on the right we have an abstraction $\mathcal{A}^O$ of it. The arrows from the left to the right part of the figure correspond to the abstraction relation. Consider first the following property:

$$\varphi = \Box((quasi \to \bigcirc(quasi \vee empty \vee full)) \wedge$$
$$(empty \to \bigcirc quasi) \wedge (full \to \bigcirc quasi))$$

This property holds for $\mathcal{A}^P$, and is preserved by $\mathcal{A}^O$. Model checking $\mathcal{A}^O$ instead of $\mathcal{A}^P$ can establish, due to the existence of the simulation relation, the correctness of φ in $\mathcal{A}^P$. Note that the abstract version in the right part of Figure 10.1 abstracts away the number of slots. Thus, it can be considered to be an abstraction of a collection of models, each with a different number of slots. Consider now a second property:

$$\psi = \Box(empty \to \neg \bigcirc full \wedge \neg \bigcirc \bigcirc full \wedge \neg \bigcirc \bigcirc \bigcirc full)$$

This property asserts that an empty buffer cannot get full in three steps, i.e., it has at least four slots. It certainly holds for $\mathcal{A}^P$, but trying to prove it for the abstract version $\mathcal{A}^O$ fails. One counterexample is a sequence that has three consecutive states labeled with *empty*, *quasi* and *full*, respectively. However, this counterexample is not in the language $\mathcal{L}(\mathcal{A}^P)$. Thus, ψ is an example of a property that holds for $\mathcal{A}^P$ but is not preserved by the abstraction.

In fact, the model on the left in Figure 10.2 is itself an abstraction, as it ignores the data that is stored in the buffer. In the trivial case where the data is one bit, i.e., 0 or 1, the more detailed model describing the system is as in Figure 10.3. Notice that the first slot of the buffer to get filled is the leftmost empty one. Removing an element from the buffer consumes the

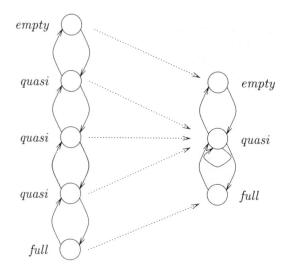

Fig. 10.2. An n slot buffer and its abstraction

element in the leftmost slots, and shifts the rest of the buffer one place to the left. In this figure, the buffer contents is denoted by a sequence of the symbols 0, 1 and E (for an 'empty' slot). According to the abstraction, the state $EEEE$ corresponds (via a simulation relation) to the *empty* state of the model on the left in Figure 10.2. The states with no empty slots, i.e., the states at the bottom of the figure, correspond to the state *full*, and the other states correspond to the states labeled with *quasi*.

Further, the latter model of Figure 10.3 is itself an abstraction of an infinite state system; in the original system, each buffer slot may store some unbounded value over some domain, say, the *integers*. Although in actual implementations, the values stored are bounded, their actual range may be prohibitively big for automatic verification. Moreover, an algorithm can be designed for the unbounded case, and may need to be verified without taking the actual word-size limit of a particular implementation.

The backward simulation relation $\mathcal{Q}$ must satisfy the following conditions:

- For each initial state $\iota^O \in I^O$, there exists at least one initial state $\iota^P \in I^P$, such that $\iota^O \mathcal{Q} \iota^P$.
- If $r\mathcal{Q}s$, then $L^O(r) = L^P(s)$.
- If $r\mathcal{Q}s$, and $(r, r') \in \Delta^O$, then there exists at least one state $s' \in S^P$ such that $(s, s') \in \Delta^P$ and $r'\mathcal{Q}s'$.

Given the above conditions for $\mathcal{Q}$, for every execution $\hat{\sigma}$ of $\mathcal{A}^O$, there exists an execution σ of $\mathcal{A}^P$, which has matching labeling, state by state. We have that $\mathcal{L}(\mathcal{A}^O) \subseteq \mathcal{L}(\mathcal{A}^P)$. This means that every counterexample showing that a verified property φ does not hold for the abstract version $\mathcal{A}^O$ (i.e., showing

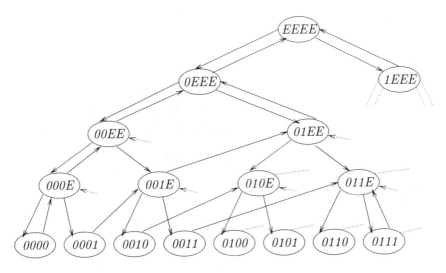

Fig. 10.3. A 4 slot buffer of bits

that $\mathcal{L}(\mathcal{A}^O) \not\subseteq \mathcal{L}(\varphi))$ is also a counterexample for the original version $\mathcal{A}^P$. On the other hand, even if all of the labeled executions of $\mathcal{A}^O$ satisfy the specification φ, i.e., $\mathcal{L}(\mathcal{A}^O) \subseteq \mathcal{L}(\varphi)$, one cannot conclude that this is also the case for $\mathcal{A}^P$, since there can be labeled executions of $\mathcal{A}^P$ that do not have a matching execution in $\mathcal{A}^O$.

Having to prove the simulation conditions for $\mathcal{R}$ on the state spaces (automata) $\mathcal{A}^P$ and $\mathcal{A}^O$ is often not practical. Thus, we attempt to prove it on the level of the transition systems. Assume two nondeterministic transition systems are given in the form presented in Section 4.7. We thus have two transition systems; the concrete one, $P = \langle \mathcal{S}^P, \varphi^P, \Theta^P \rangle$ and the abstract one, $O = \langle \mathcal{S}^O, \varphi^O, \Theta^O \rangle$, corresponding to the automata $\mathcal{A}^P$ and $\mathcal{A}^O$, respectively.

Denote an ordered list of the program variables of P, before executing a transition, by $\bar{x}$, and the corresponding list of variables, after executing a transition, by $\bar{x}'$. (Recall that nondeterministic transitions, defined in Section 4.7, use two copies of corresponding variables to relate the values before and after executing each transition.) Accordingly, we write the formula that represents the transitions as $\varphi^P(\bar{x}, \bar{x}')$. Similarly, we use $\bar{y}$ and $\bar{y}'$ to represent an ordered list of variables of O before and after executing a transition. Thus $\varphi^O(\bar{y}, \bar{y}')$ represents the transition relation of O. We assume $\bar{x}$ and $\bar{y}$ to be disjoint, which may be enforced by renaming variables. We abuse notation and denote $\exists \bar{x}$ or $\forall \bar{y}$, instead of listing each variable separately.

Let $R(\bar{x}, \bar{y})$ be a formula describing the abstraction $\mathcal{R}$, i.e., the relation between states in P and O. This formula is expressed over a signature that includes $\mathcal{G}^P$ and $\mathcal{G}^O$ and interpreted over a structure that includes $\mathcal{S}^P$ and $\mathcal{S}^O$. Then, the following two conditions are sufficient (but not necessary, i.e., may be too strong) for proving the simulation $\mathcal{R}$ between the two state spaces generated by P and O:

1. $\forall \overline{x}(\Theta^P(\overline{x}) \rightarrow \exists \overline{y}(\Theta^O(\overline{y}) \wedge R(\overline{x}, \overline{y})))$
2. $\forall \overline{x} \forall \overline{x}' \forall \overline{y}((R(\overline{x}, \overline{y}) \wedge \varphi^P(\overline{x}, \overline{x}')) \rightarrow \exists \overline{y}'(\varphi^O(\overline{y}, \overline{y}') \wedge R(\overline{x}', \overline{y}')))$

Notice that the above conditions are established for each possible value of $\overline{x}$. This may include some values that correspond to unreachable states. Thus, the conditions may fail to hold even if the abstraction is correct. Suppose we could use an invariant $In(\overline{x})$ of P, i.e., a formula that holds for all the reachable states of P. Notice that $In(\overline{x})$ may also allow (i.e., be satisfied by) states that are not reachable. Then, we can have the following, weaker conditions:

1. $\forall \overline{x}((In(\overline{x}) \wedge \Theta^P(\overline{x})) \rightarrow \exists \overline{y}(\Theta^O(\overline{y}) \wedge R(\overline{x}, \overline{y})))$
2. $\forall \overline{x} \forall \overline{x}' \forall \overline{y}((In(\overline{x}) \wedge R(\overline{x}, \overline{y}) \wedge \varphi^P(\overline{x}, \overline{x}')) \rightarrow \exists \overline{y}'(\varphi^O(\overline{y}, \overline{y}') \wedge R(\overline{x}', \overline{y}')))$

We strive to obtain the strongest possible invariant $In(\overline{x})$. An invariant that is satisfied by *exactly* the reachable states (and by no other state) will make the above reformulated pair of conditions necessary and sufficient for proving the simulation. Unfortunately, such an invariant is not always available to us. Another problem is that in order to use $In(\overline{x})$ in the reformulated conditions, we need to prove it as an invariant of P. This can be done, e.g., using the Manna-Pnueli proof system, and in particular, the proof rule INV, presented in Section 7.5. However, the proof must be performed for the concrete transition system P, which can defy the benefit of the abstraction.

Obviously, in order to be able to deduce correctness *and* rely on counterexamples, one needs to have both forward and backwards simulation relations. In practice, one may decide to apply abstraction when only one of these relations can be found. Then, care must be taken to make the right conclusions from the results of model checking: if only a forward simulation relation is established, one needs to check each counterexample found against the original system, in order to make sure it is not a false negative. If only a backward simulation relation is used, then the counterexamples can be trusted, but verifying a property of $\mathcal{A}^O$ does not entail its correctness for $\mathcal{A}^P$.

Abstraction is often done in an informal way, by the person who performs the verification, based on his own intuition and experience. In this case, it is not safe to draw conclusions from the automatic verification results of the abstract versions. Obtaining a formal connection between the system (which is often a detailed model, rather than the actual code) and its abstract version can be established by using deductive verification tools. We need to verify the abstraction conditions for $\mathcal{R}$, $\mathcal{Q}$ (or using only one of them in case the other is not available) in some proof system, using a theorem prover. There are many other ways to define abstraction.

There is usually no guidance for selecting the abstraction. Showing that the abstraction preserves the simulation relations (or the bisimulation relation) requires ingenuity. There are different 'generic' abstraction methods that work for a multiplicity of cases. There are also some useful theorems that attempt to characterize cases where the use of various data types can lead to automatic abstraction. Such *data independence* theorems [148] can be used to automatically translate a given model into a finite state system. Data independence can be used in a program that uses some unbounded data structure but never makes a decision depending upon it. An example of data independence is the modeling of a finite buffer over some unbounded domain (say, the *integers*). If the property that is to be checked does not depend on the value of the elements in the buffer, one may abstract these values out, using, e.g., a finite state space model, as in the left side of Figure 10.2 (or even a more abstract model, as in the right side of that figure). Some heuristics were suggested for automatically obtaining correct abstractions, see e.g., [15, 104, 56]. The following exercise gives some intuition about such transformations.

Exercise 10.1.1. Consider the following suggestions for a transformation of transition systems, and check whether they preserve forward, backward simulation or bisimulation. For both of the suggested transformations, consider a transition system T, consisting of deterministic transitions, as presented in Section 4.4. Let $\bar{z}$ be a subset of the variables participating in the transition system, satisfying the following:

If x is any program variable that may be assigned a value that depends on some other variable y in $\bar{z}$ (i.e., in the expressions defining some transition in T, there is one, assigned to x which includes y), then x is also in $\bar{z}$. For example, because of the transition

$$pc \equiv m1 \land x1 \geq 7 \longrightarrow (pc, x1) := (m2, y3 + 4). \qquad (10.1)$$

if $y3$ is in $\bar{z}$, then $x1$ must also be in that set.

First, we remove all the variables $\bar{z}$ from the transition system, including the expressions assigning values to them. The above transition (10.1) would then become

$$pc \equiv m1 \land x1 \geq 7 \longrightarrow pc := m2. \qquad (10.2)$$

We need also to change the conditions of the transitions. We suggest the following transformations for each condition c:

1. Substitute in c every occurrence of a first order formula that contains a variable from $\bar{z}$ with *true*. Thus, the transition (10.2) becomes

$$pc \equiv m1 \land true \longrightarrow pc := m2.$$

This can be simplified to

$$pc \equiv m1 \longrightarrow pc := m2.$$

2. Substitute in c every occurrence of a first order formula that contains a variable from $\bar{z}$ with *true*, obtaining $c1$. Substitute each such occurrence by *false*, obtaining $c2$. Then replace c by $c1 \vee c2$.

$$(pc \equiv m1 \wedge true) \vee (pc \equiv m1 \wedge false) \longrightarrow pc := m2$$

This also gets simplified into

$$pc \equiv m1 \longrightarrow pc := m2$$

(Show an example that 1 and 2 do not transform, after simplification, to the same transition.)
3. Work as in 1 above, but deal with one such occurrence at a time, until all such occurrences are replaced.
4. Work as in 2 above, but deal with one such occurrence at a time, until all such occurrences are replaced.

10.2 Combining Testing and Model Checking

Testing techniques are aimed at *sampling* the executions of the checked system and comparing them with the specified behaviors. Different coverage criteria were developed to cope with the tradeoff between the conflicting goals of minimizing the amount of time used for testing, and maximizing the probability of finding errors. However, testing does not provide an exhaustive coverage of the tested system. Model checking is exhaustive, but is applied to a *model* of the checked system, rather than to the system itself. Due to possible discrepancies between the model and the actual system, establishing that the model satisfies some property does not necessarily carry over to the actual system.

In this section we describe a technique [116] that combines the exhaustiveness of model checking, with the ability to check the actual system directly, as in testing. Combining the benefits of model checking and testing does not come for free; the resulting method is of a rather high complexity.

10.2.1 Direct Checking

Under certain (rather strong) assumptions, it is possible to *verify* that the tested system satisfies some specification, e.g., it conforms with another system, or satisfies some LTL properties. This technique can be viewed as a combination of black box testing and model checking techniques. There are two goals: achieving a comprehensive verification of the system, and performing the verification directly on the checked system (rather than on a model). These are obviously desirable goals. Unfortunately, the assumptions under which such methods work, and the high complexity of the relevant algorithms can be prohibitive, suggesting that model checking and testing may still be more feasible for detecting errors in software. Although such methods are often related to black box testing [84], we will use the term *direct checking*, to emphasize the difference from sampling based testing techniques.

Limitations of Direct Checking

Model checking and verification are usually performed on a model of the verified system, rather than being applied directly. One reason for this is that without introducing some abstraction, the amount of detail we need to consider quickly becomes extremely large.

However, even if a system is already of reasonable size, there are different requirements that usually prohibit it from being verified directly. Recall the different operations needed in model checking: in order to prevent infinite looping of the model checking algorithm, when a cycle occurs in the state space, we are required to identify that the current state is the same as a state that occurred previously. Obtaining information that can distinguish or identify two states encountered during a search of a system (as opposed to an idealized model) may be expensive, e.g., it may require comparing core dumps of the checked software. In some cases, the complete state information may even be unavailable. For example, in hardware or embedded systems, some state information may not be directly available at any one of the external ports.

Another difficulty for direct checking of systems is the possibility that applying the same action from a given state under different environmental parameters may lead to different states. Such action nondeterminism may be the result of some internal timing constraints or unforeseen external factor, such as the temperature or the humidity. The problem is that it is possible that all the experiments performed during testing will follow one of the possible nondeterministic choices, but when the system is deployed in the field, the different environment will cause another choice to be internally selected. In such cases, formal methods can provide little guarantee. One solution is to repeat the experiments while changing different parameters that may contribute to the nondeterministic choices. However, without the knowledge of the internal structure of the checked system, this cannot completely guarantee that all the choices are explored.

10.2.2 Black Box Systems

The literature on black box testing includes several variants of such systems. For example, a black box system may allow or disallow output, or an indication about the enabledness of actions from a given state. For simplicity, we will study one particular model, while the analysis for other variants is quite similar. In what follows, a black box system will be assumed to have the following characteristics:

- A finite state system with n states. One of the states ι is distinguished as the only initial state. Either the size n itself, or an upper bound of it is known. The system does not give any indication of the identity of the current state (except for the case of applying a **reset**, as described below).
- A finite alphabet Σ of *actions*, of size d. These are the possible inputs, which the user can apply to experiment with the system.
- A transition relation, where the transitions are labeled with actions from Σ.
- An indication of whether an action can execute from the current state or not (one can consider this indication as an output of 0 or 1) is available. If the action can execute, the system also moves to a successor state (which can be the same as the old one) according to the transition relation. If not, the system remains in the same state. In a more general setting, this can be replaced by a finite set of outputs.
- A reliable **reset** capability. Applying **reset** guarantees bringing the system to its unique initial state ι. That is, the reset is reliable. We will see in Section 10.2.6 why this assumption is important.

An *experiment* is a sequence of actions and **reset**s that are performed in order to verify some property of a black box system. The *complexity* of direct checking is defined to be the length of the experiment performed on the black box system. It is interesting to note that analyzing the complexity of direct checking is somewhat different from the usual analysis in complexity theory. This is because in usual algorithms, the input is known in advance, whereas in direct checking one performs experiments that change the internal data structure of the black box system without an full knowledge of it a priory. For this reason, modeling direct checking is often done using the theory of *games with incomplete information* [122]. We will provide here only an informal description of the complexity analysis.

10.2.3 Combination Lock Automata

Combination lock automata [102, 143] play a major role in proving lower complexity bounds on experiments with black box finite state systems. That is, they present a canonical example, which shows that direct checking can be highly time consuming. For each such automaton, there is some total order '$>$' on its states $s_1 > s_2 > \ldots > s_n$ with $s_1 = \iota$ the initial state, and the state s_n having no enabled transition. For each state s_i, $i < n$, there is a transition labeled with some $\beta_i \in \Sigma$ to s_{i+1}. For all other letters $\gamma \in \Sigma \setminus \{\beta_i\}$, there is a transition labeled with γ from s_i back to the initial state. Such an automaton is a *combination lock* for $\beta_1 \beta_2 \ldots \beta_{n-1}$. Figure 10.4 depicts a combination lock automaton for $n = 5$.

In a combination lock automaton, a sequence leading to the only state s_n without a successor, must have a suffix of length $n - 1$ that is $\beta_1 \beta_2 \ldots \beta_{n-1}$. This is a necessary, but not a sufficient condition. For example, the automaton

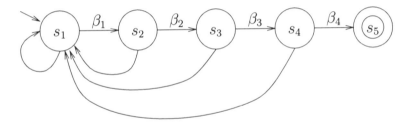

Fig. 10.4. A combination lock automaton

in Figure 10.4 does not reach a deadlock state as a result of the sequence $\beta_1\beta_2\beta_1\beta_2\beta_3\beta_4$ when $\beta_1 \neq \beta_3$ (or $\beta_2 \neq \beta_4$), since the second β_1 only causes it to return to its initial state.

10.2.4 Black Box Deadlock Detection

We study first a simple verification problem: given a deterministic black box finite state system B, with no more than n states, we want to check whether this machine deadlocks, namely reaches a state from which no input is possible. In this problem, part of the model is unknown and is learned via experiments.

The straightforward, inefficient solution is to checks systematically all the possible sequences of actions from Σ of length $n-1$, starting from the initial state. Notice that there are d^{n-1} different combinations of $n-1$ actions. It turns out that the problem is inherently difficult, and the lower bound, i.e., the worst case complexity does not allow for an algorithm that applies less than d^{n-1} actions altogether.

To see this, consider a black box automaton B that allows any input from any state (hence does not have a deadlock). Consider an experiment ρ, consisting of a sequence of actions from Σ and **reset**, applied during the check for deadlocks. Assume that ρ has fewer than d^{n-1} occurrences of actions. Then at least one sequence of actions $\beta_1\beta_2 \ldots \beta_{n-1}$ does not appear consecutively in the experiment associated with ρ. If instead of the above automaton B, we would have a combination lock automaton C for $\beta_1\beta_2 \ldots \beta_{n-1}$, the experiment ρ will give the same indications of success and failure of actions for both B and C. Since this does not distinguish between these two automata, we can mistakenly deduce that there is no deadlock in C. Since we have made an arbitrary selection of the experiment ρ, no such selection of length smaller than d^{n-1} is going to be sufficient. Checking more complicated properties is obviously not easier.

10.2.5 Conformance Testing

Conformance testing involves comparing a given model A of a system to a black box system B. If the comparison succeeds in showing that A and B allow exactly the same sequences, one can proceed to check the properties of B indirectly, using the model A. Recall that the black box automaton B has only deterministic transitions. It gives an indication of success or failure in applying an action α to the current state. Furthermore, it allows **reseting** it into its unique initial state. (Notice that since our model has only deterministic actions, the fact that the languages of A and B are equivalent implies that A and B are equivalent according to all of the equivalence relations given in Section 8.5.)

We will initially assume that B has no more states than A. The algorithm that will be presented is polynomial in the number of states of B. We will later show an algorithm that checks conformance between A and B when only an upper bound $m > n$, estimating the size of B, is known, where the number of states in the model A is still n. This algorithm will be exponential in the difference $m - n$. This is also the lower bound on conformance testing, which means that if the estimate m is considerably bigger than the actual number of states n, conformance testing is unreasonably hard to check.

If no estimate on the size of B is known, no finite experiment will guarantee that A and B are the same. To see this, consider Figure 10.5, where the left automaton represents a model A that includes a cycle of $\alpha\beta$ (denoted $(\alpha\beta)^*$ in the syntax of regular languages). If the length of the testing sequence is at most n, it is still possible that the actual system on the right has $\lceil n/2 \rceil - 1$ repetitions of $\alpha\beta$, and then closes the cycle with $\alpha\gamma$, instead of $\alpha\beta$.

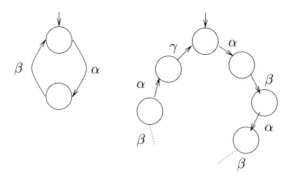

Fig. 10.5. Two nonconforming automata

Let S be the set of states of A with n elements, and Δ its (deterministic) transition relation. We can write *enabled*(s, α) if α can be executed from

s, and denote in this case the successor state by $\Delta(s, \alpha)$. Σ is the mutual alphabet of both A and B with size d.

We will assume that A is minimized, namely, there is no smaller automaton that recognizes the same sequences as A. If A is not minimized, it must have at least two states s and r that cannot be distinguished by any length of experiment (both s and r will allow exactly the same sequences). Minimizing deterministic automata can be done using the following algorithm, which is similar to the one used for checking bisimulation equivalence described in Section 8.8. (Indeed, the bisimulation equivalence algorithm is often used in model checking to minimize the state space, if properties that cannot distinguish between bisimulation equivalent structures are checked, e.g., branching temporal logic CTL, and the more expressive CTL* properties, see, e.g., [20, 30]). We use this algorithm here not only for minimizing the automaton A, but also because it generates, during its execution, a set of sequences distinguishing states of A from each other. These sequences will be used later within the conformance testing algorithm.

For each (unordered) pair of different states s and r, we keep a sequence $dist(s, r)$ that can distinguish s from r. That is, either s or r allows this sequence, and the other does not. Thus, $dist(s, r) = dist(r, s)$. If σ is a sequence of actions and α an action, then $\alpha.\sigma$ denotes affixing the letter α in front of σ.

Calculating distinguishing sequences

1. Initially, set $dist(s, r) := \varepsilon$ (the empty sequence), for each pair s and r.
2. For each pair of disjoint states $s, r \in S$ and action $\alpha \in \Sigma$ such that $enabled(s, \alpha)$ but not $enabled(r, \alpha)$, we set $dist(s, r) = \alpha$.
3. Repeat until there are no changes to the $dist$ entries.
   If there are of states $s, r \in S$ and an action $\alpha \in \Sigma$ such that
   a) $dist(s, r) = \varepsilon$,
   b) $enabled(s, \alpha)$ and $enabled(r, \alpha)$,
   c) $dist(\Delta(s, \alpha), \Delta(r, \alpha)) \neq \varepsilon$.
   Then set $dist(s, r) := \alpha.dist(\Delta(s, \alpha), \Delta(r, \alpha))$.

Thus, two states cannot be combined if they have some different actions that can be executed from them. Also, if one can separate s' from r' with some sequence σ and one can reach from s to s' and from r to r' with an action α, then one can separate s from r with $\alpha.\sigma$.

At the end of this algorithm, we can combine each maximal subset of states $C \subseteq S$ such that for each pair of states $s, r \in C$, $dist(s, r) = \varepsilon$ into a single state. Then it holds that if $s \in C$, $\Delta(s, \alpha) \in C'$, applying α to each one of the states in C will result in a state in C' (see e.g., [69]). These constructed *equivalence classes* of states are the states of the minimized automaton, and the transition relation between two subsets C and C' is according to any of the transitions between some state $s \in C$ and some state $r \in C'$. That is, if $s \xrightarrow{\alpha} r$ then $C \xrightarrow{\alpha} C'$. If the automaton A is already minimized, then the equivalence classes of states are singletons.

The *distinguishing set* for C is defined as

$$ds(C) = \{dist(s,r)|s \in C \wedge r \notin C\}$$

It is a property of the minimization algorithm that each state in C will allow or disallow exactly the same sequences from $ds(C)$. Furthermore, each other set of states C', will have at least one common sequence σ in both $ds(C)$ and $ds(C')$. All the states in C' will behave in an opposite way to the way the nodes in C will behave with respect to σ. That is, if σ can be executed from each of the states in C, then it cannot be executed from any of the states in C', and vice versa. It is important to note that each set $ds(C)$ can contain up to $n-1$ sequences (since there can be at most one distinguishing sequence for each state other than s itself). It can be shown that the above algorithm can be performed in at most $n-1$ phases in the following way: at each phase, the old entries $dist(s, r)$ of the previous phase are used to calculate the entries of the current phase. The new distinguishing sequences found in each phase are longer than the strings in the previous phase by at most one. Thus, each sequence in $ds(C)$ is of length smaller than n.

The distinguishing sets help to construct the conformance testing algorithm. We use the above algorithm to obtain these sets even if A is already minimized. In this case, each component C contains exactly one node. Since we will assume henceforth that A is minimized, we will denote the distinguishing set for a state s as $ds(s)$.

One task of conformance testing is to check that B has at least as many states as A. It is sufficient to check whether for each state r of A, there exists a state s of B, such that s and r are reachable from the initial states of their corresponding automata using the same sequence, and both states agree on allowing the execution of each sequence from $ds(r)$. To perform this check for a sequence $\sigma \in ds(r)$, we first **reset** B to its initial state, and perform on B the actions according to a path from the initial state of A to r. Then we can apply σ to B and see if B differs from A in accepting this sequence from the current state. We need to repeat this check for each sequence in $ds(r)$.

The construction of the distinguishing sets stipulates that for each pair of states s and r in A there exists at least one sequence in both $ds(s)$ and $ds(r)$ that is allowed from exactly one of these states but not the other. If B has passed the above tests and conformed with each one of the distinguishing sets of A, we have established that B has at least n different states. Since we know that n is also the upper bound on the size of B, B has exactly n states.

Another task is to check whether the transitions of B behave in the same way as those of A. Suppose there is a transition $\Delta(r, \alpha) = r'$ in A. We can repeat the following for each sequence $\sigma \in ds(r')$. First, we **reset** B. Then we pick a sequence of actions that moves A from its initial state to r and apply this sequence to B. Next, we apply α, and then apply σ to see if the obtained state behaves the same as r' with respect to the sequence σ.

To make all of the above checks systematically, we can construct a tree Tr for A that includes each node and each transition of A at least once. Such a tree is a part of a spanning tree for A from the initial state ι. Clearly the number of levels of Tr is bounded by n, since it is sufficient that on any path, at most one node (i.e., the last one) will repeat twice. We follow each (not necessarily maximal) path ρ in Tr and simulate it on the black box system B. Let r be the node that the model A reached after **reset**ings and executing ρ. We simulate on B each sequence σ in $ds(r)$ and compare it to A's behavior after **reset**ing and executing ρ followed by σ. Notice that we have to **reset** and simulate the path ρ to reach r again before checking each sequence in $ds(r)$.

The number of nodes in Tr is at most $2 \times n \times d$. For each node, we need to check at most $n - 1$ sequences. Each such sequence is of length at most $2n - 1$ (for the path on the tree, followed by a path from a distinguishing set). Thus, the length of the test sequence is $\mathcal{O}(d \times n^3)$.

Consider now the case where the number of states of B is known to be at most m for some $m > n$. It is possible that B is not minimized, but is still equivalent to A. A black box system that is difficult to check is described informally as follows: the black box B has n states that simulate the states of A. The extra $m - n$ states of B form a path $s_0, s_1, s_2, \ldots s_{m-n}$ that behaves in a way similar to a combination lock automaton. If we are not executing the combination, we move to one of the first n nodes, simulating the behavior of A. If we are executing the combination, we move from one node to the next, until we reach the last node s_{m-n}. That last node behaves in a different way than A. This is demonstrated in Figure 10.6. In order to detect such a sequence, one needs to reach the last state s_{m-n} by finding the combination.

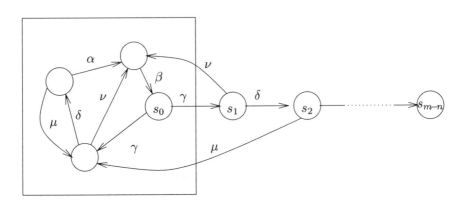

Fig. 10.6. A combination lock from a state of a black box automaton

The algorithm for this case constructs the tree Tr, but from each one of its nodes tries to perform any combination of $m - n$ or fewer actions. For each such combination, we check the last state reached. Let r be the state in A which we would have reached if we had executed a **reset**, followed by a path in Tr, followed by a sequence of $m - n$ letters from Σ. From this state, we compare the behavior of the sequences in $ds(r)$ in A and in B (notice that we need to repeatedly **reset** and reach this state for each sequence in $ds(r)$). This gives an experiment whose length is $\mathcal{O}(m^2 \times n \times d^{m-n+1})$.

10.2.6 Checking the Reliability of Resets

In the previous section we presented an algorithm for conformance testing, given a reliable **reset**. This means that we assume that applying **reset** guarantees to bring the black box system to the same initial state, each time it is applied.

We will now show, by means of an example, that for some systems, one cannot test for the reliability of a **reset**, even under the strong assumption that we know the internal structure of the system B. Of course, if we tested the **reset** several times, this would not guarantee that later it would behave the same. However, we will demonstrate that we cannot even present any evidence that during some experiment the **reset** behaved as it should.

Consider the system in Figure 10.7. Suppose the **reset** is not reliable, and can result in each one of the states of the system s_1, s_2 or s_3. If we apply **reset**, which brings us to either s_1 or s_3, and then apply the action α, we will be in state s_1 in both cases. So, any test that starts with α cannot help us separate these two cases from each other. If we apply **reset**, which brings us to either s_1 or s_2 and apply β, we will be in state s_2 in both cases. So, β cannot start such a separation experiment either.

Thus, applying either α or β does not guarantee to separate the cases of the possible states after a **reset** from each other. One has to choose the first action in the experiment, which has to be either α or β. That choice, if guessed incorrectly, may destroy the ability to make the distinction. This phenomenon was considered by Moore [102] to be a discrete counterpart of the Heisenberg uncertainty principle.

10.2.7 Black Box Checking

Model checking and testing, discussed in previous chapters, are two complementary approaches for enhancing the reliability of systems. Model checking usually deals with checking whether the *design* of a finite state system satisfies some *properties* (e.g., mutual exclusion or responsiveness). On the other hand, testing is usually applied to the *actual system*, often without having access to, or knowledge of its internal structure. It checks whether a *system* (or an *implementation*) *conforms* with some design (i.e., informally, has the same behaviors). Even if access to the internal structure of the tested system is possible, it is not always a good idea to use it when performing tests, as

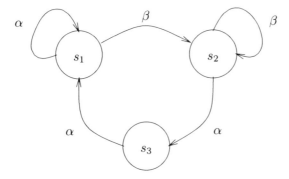

Fig. 10.7. A system where checking the reliability of **reset** is impossible

this may lead to a bias in the testing process. Furthermore, the whole system may be very large (e.g., millions of lines of code), while we are interested only in specific aspects of it. For example, in a typical telephony switch we may want to check that the implementation of a particular feature, such as 'call waiting', meets certain correctness properties. Extracting from the whole system the part of the code that is relevant, especially in the case of large legacy systems, is most probably infeasible (and is itself subject to errors).

Suppose one is interested in checking specific properties of some system such as a telephone switch. Model checking would be appropriate for checking properties of a model of the system, but not checking the system itself. On the other hand, testing methods can compare the system with some abstract design, but usually are not used for checking specific properties.

Black box checking [116], deals with the case where acceptance tests need to be performed by a user who has neither access to the design, nor to the internal structure of the checked system. It combines the two approaches, automatically checking *properties* of finite state systems whose *structure is unknown*. The assumptions about the structure are the same as in the previous black box conformance testing algorithm.

However, in addition, we have a specification automaton, representing the (negation of the) checked property. It is given directly, or translated from LTL into an automaton as shown in Chapter 6. This is an automaton that specifies the allowed sequences of transitions, as opposed to the state sequences that were used for modeling and specification so far. The problem of black box checking is a variant of the above model checking problem. We are given the automaton that represents the executions that are not allowed by the checked property. But the internal structure of the checked system is not revealed, and only some experiments, as described above, are allowed on it. Still, we want to check whether the system satisfies the given property.

The choice of an appropriate computational model is central to the issue of black box checking. Unlike standard algorithmic problems, the input is not given here at the beginning of the computation, but is learned through a sequence of experiments. Thus, the analysis is often done using the theory of *games of incomplete information* [122]. We will not discuss these issues here.

Given a specification Büchi automaton A with m states, and a black box implementation automaton B with no more than n states, over a mutual alphabet Σ with d letters, we want to check whether there is a sequence accepted by both A and B. The property automaton A accepts the *bad* executions, i.e., those that are *not allowed* (see Section 6.3). Thus, if the property is given originally e.g., using a linear temporal logic [119] property φ, then A is the automaton corresponding to $\neg\varphi$. Let k be the number of states of A. Notice that the automaton A need not be deterministic, and can have multiple initial states.

We will present here only a simple algorithm to perform black box checking [116]. It is not the most efficient one known, but is simple to understood, and demonstrates nicely the possible connections between techniques from testing and model checking.

The algorithm checks possible sequences of actions from Σ. For each sequence it changes the states of the known automaton A from some initial state, in parallel to making an experiment of the same sequence on the black box automaton B, after a **reset**. We want to check whether the intersection of A and B is not empty, and find a counterexample for that case. Notice that all the states in B are considered accepting, hence the acceptance of each state in the intersection is fixed by the acceptance of its A component. We repeat this experiment exhaustively, without repeating prefixes that were rejected by the black box automaton.

Each experiment consists of two paths of length bounded by $m \times k$ (since this is the number of states in the intersection). The first sequence σ_1 needs to terminate in a state whose A component r is accepting. The second sequence σ_2, starts executing in A from r and needs to terminate with r as well. For each such pair of sequences σ_1, σ_2, we apply σ_2 m more times. That is, we try to execute the sequence $\sigma_1(\sigma_2)^{m+1}$. If we succeed in reaching the state r in A at the end of each such iteration while the automaton B allows executing the sequence (after a **reset**), there must be a cycle in the intersection of the two automata through an accepting state. This is because the accepting state r can be paired up with any of the m (or fewer) states of B. In this case, $\sigma_1\sigma_2^{\omega}$ forms an infinite accepting path of the intersection, and thus can be given as a finitely generated counterexample.

The complexity is rather high, $\mathcal{O}(m^2 \times d^{2 \times m \times k} \times k)$. This is because there are $d^{2 \times m \times k}$ choices of such paths. Each is of length bounded by $m \times k$, and we repeat it $m + 1$ times. An algorithm that has better complexity appears in [116], and is based on learning the structure of the automaton [9], while performing experiments.

10.3 The Cleanroom Method

The *cleanroom method* [98] is a methodology for constructing reliable software, developed by a group of researchers at IBM's Federal Systems Division, led by Harlan Mills, starting in the late 1970's. The methodology includes elements from software verification and testing, and has been applied successfully to various projects. The main principles of the method are not very different from some of the methods that were described previously in this book. We will not provide exact details of the cleanroom method, but merely describe the main ideas. The interested reader can refer to the references or the book mentioned at the end of the chapter.

Verification

The cleanroom method proposes that the development of software will be done while verifying its correctness. However, the proof is done informally, without actually applying the axioms and proof rules. The actual proof system of the cleanroom method is somewhat different from Hoare's logic, described in Section 7.4 (see, e.g., [98]); instead of specifying the precondition and the postcondition of parts of the program, one specifies a single formula that expresses the relation between the variables at the beginning and the end of the execution of that program segment.

Proof Inspection

Instead of performing low level testing, and inspecting the *code*, the cleanroom method prescribes inspecting the *proof*. This is done by a team, similar to the one suggested for software inspections (see Section 9.1). The goal of the programmer is then to convince the team of the *correctness of his proof*, which would entail the correction of the code.

Testing

The cleanroom method prescribes performing high level testing, namely integration testing. It suggests that lower level testing is unreliable and biased, and is unnecessary in light of the more reliable verification and the proof inspection process. The actual testing is based on the principles of probabilistic testing, explained in Section 9.10.

Further Reading

A survey on algorithmic methods for black box testing appears in

D. Lee, M. Yannakakis, *Principles and methods of testing finite state machines - a survey*, Proceedings of the IEEE, 84(8), 1090–1126, 1996.

Black box checking algorithms are described in the following paper:

D. Peled, M.Y. Vardi, M. Yannakakis, Black box checking, Formal Methods for Protocol Engineering and Distributed Systems, Formal Methods for Protocol Engineering and Distributed Systems, 1999, Kluwer, China, 225–240.

The cleanroom method is described in the following book:

A.M. Stavely *Toward Zero-Defect Programming*, Addison-Wesley, 1999.

11. Visualization

'Well! I've often seen a cat without a grin,' thought Alice; 'but a grin without a cat! It's the most curious thing I ever saw in my life!'

Lewis Carroll, *Alice's Adventures in Wonderland*

Early formal methods were text-based. This included formal description of systems, the specification of system properties, the interaction with the tools and the testing and verification results. Researchers and practitioners have recently begun to realize that visual representation of software greatly enhances the effectiveness of software development. In many cases, one may obtain, by observing a visualization of the code, some new information, e.g., about the different program objects and their connection, the flow of control, and the pattern of communication. Such an intuitive understanding of the code may not be achieved by simply observing the linear text of the code.

The tendency to use visual formalisms is perhaps best reflected in the number of different diagrams that are included in software development methodologies, such as UML [46]. This includes diagrams for representing the system's architecture, the different processes or objects comprised in the system, the interaction between processes or objects, the transitions of the processes or objects, typical and exceptional executions, connections between system modules, and more. This chapter discusses ways in which formal methods can take advantage of visual representation.

The added benefit of visual systems is that they map a rigid syntax into some relation among graphical objects. Consider, for example, representing automata as a graph, versus representing it as a table of transitions and lists of initial states and final states. Visual representation has an advantage in demonstrating a dynamic process. For example, consider viewing a counterexample for model checking demonstrated by highlighting the execution path in its flowchart, as opposed to merely listing the text of the participating transitions.

11.1 Using Visualizations for Formal Methods

We already saw examples of notations that have both textual and a graphical representation. One of these notations was automata, which can be represented either textually, by listing its components, or as a graph. Another notation was flowcharts, representing programs using graphs.

Such notations exhibit a textual and a corresponding graphical representation. The translation between the two representations is formally defined. Formal methods tools often allow interaction with the graphical representation. Addition, removal, resizing or relocation of objects, changing of labelings, copying, are almost standard operations. Operations such as the selection of, or the updating of predefined entries that appear on the screen have a common look and feel, as a result of the vast use of the worldwideweb. This has the added benefit of reducing the time it takes a user to get acquainted with a new system.

Since computers still process textual data better than graphical representation, tools based on visual formalisms need a translation between the textual and the graphical representation. The textual representation is usually maintained within a text file. When the tool needs to use the representation, it compiles the text into the graphical representation and displays it. As a consequence of the user's interaction with the tool, the graphical representation is modified, which requires a corresponding change to the textual representation.

Any visual tool needs to interact with the user, and thus requires appropriate capabilities to respond to keyboard and mouse instructions, and to update the display. Powerful tools such as the X-windows system were developed for facilitating these capabilities. In recent years, there is a growing number of programming languages that simplify the programming of graphical interfaces, e.g., TCL/TCK [110].

11.2 Message Sequence Charts

The *Message Sequence Chart* (MSC) notation is becoming popular for describing executions of communication protocols. It is also closely related to use-cases, used e.g., in UML to describe the interaction between objects [46]. It enjoys an international standard called ITU-Z120 [73]. MSCs are among the standard description techniques used for designing communication systems [40], and a growing number of tools include an MSC interface [127].

Each MSC describes a scenario involving processes communication. It can be used to denote the communication structure of typical or exceptional executions of a system, or a counterexample found during testing or model checking. Such a scenario includes a description of the messages sent and received and the ordering between them. Figures 11.1 and 11.2 show corresponding graphical and textual representations of an MSC. In Figure 11.1, each process is represented by a vertical line with a top box that includes the process name. A message is represented by a horizontal or slanted arrow from the sending process to the receiving one. MSCs capture the events of sending and receiving a message. They often (but not necessarily) ignore other events such as decisions and assignments.

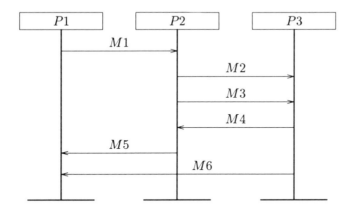

Fig. 11.1. A Message Sequence Chart

```
msc MSC;
inst P1: process Root,
     P2: process Root,
     P3: process Root;




     instance P1;
         out M1 to P2;
         in M5 from P2;
         in M6 from P3;
     endinstance;
```

```
instance P2;
    in M1 from P1;
    out M2 to P3;
    out M3 to P3;
    in M4 from P3;
    out M5 to P1;
endinstance;
instance P3;
    in M2 from P2;
    in M3 from P2;
    out M4 to P2;
    out M6 to P1;
endinstance;
endmsc;
```

Fig. 11.2. The ITU-120 textual representation of the MSC in Figure 11.1

Tools such as MSC [8], support representing message sequence charts. They allow both a graphical description of the MSC, and its standard textual representation [73]. Thus, an MSC can be obtained by either drawing it using the graphical interface, or by typing its textual description.

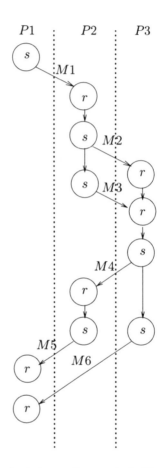

Fig. 11.3. The partial order between the events in Figure 11.1

We assign to each MSC its semantics denotation as a partially ordered set of events. The semantics of an MSC depends on some architectural parameters; it can differ between architectures with fifo (first-in, first-out) or non-fifo queues, or between architectures with one or multiple incoming message queues. This results in a slightly different behavior under each such choice [8].

Each MSC corresponds to a graph $(S, \prec)$. We will consider a semantic interpretation that assumes that for a pair of MSC events $p, q \in S$, $p \prec q$, i.e., p precedes q, in the following cases:

Causality. A send p and its corresponding receive q.

Controlability. The event p appears above q on the same process line, and q is a send event. This order reflects the fact that a send event can wait for other events to occur. On the other hand, we sometimes have less control on the order in which receive events occur.

Fifo order. The receive event p appears above the receive event q on the same process line, and the corresponding send events p', q' appear on a mutual process line, where p' is above q'.

Thus, a single MSC represents a partially ordered set of events, as discussed in Section 4.13. The partial order between the send and receive events of Figure 11.1 is shown in Figure 11.3. The MSC in Figure 11.1 describes an interaction between three processes, $P1$, $P2$ and $P3$. Process $P1$ sends the message $M1$ to $P2$. After receiving that message, process $P2$ sends two messages, $M2$ and $M3$ to $P3$. After receiving $M3$, process $P3$ sends the message $M4$ to $P2$ and later also sends the message $M6$ to $P1$. Process $P2$, after receiving $M4$, sends $M5$ to $P1$. The message $M5$ is received by process $P1$ before the message $M6$. The send events of the two messages, $M5$ and $M6$, are unordered.

One can apply some simple verification algorithms to MSCs. One such check is whether the MSCs contain *race conditions*. A race condition can result from the fact that we have only a limited control on the order between pairs of events that include at least one receive event (except for two receives corresponding to messages sent from the same process, according to the fifo semantics). For example, the MSC in Figure 11.1 contains two receive events of process $P1$ (of messages $M5$ and $M6$). Since each process line is one dimensional, the MSC notation forces choosing one of the receive events to appear above the other. However, these two messages were sent from different processes, $P2$ and $P3$, and it might happen that $M6$ arrives quicker than $M5$. Thus, there is no reason to believe that these messages must arrive in the particular order depicted using the MSC.

Formally, we can define a race as a pair of MSC events p, q, such that

- p and q appear on the same process line,
- p appears above q, and
- there is *no* path from p to q in the graph $(S, \prec)$.

Detecting races in an MSC is thus simple. All we need is to calculate the transitive closure $\prec^*$ of the relation $\prec$ among the MSC events. For two events $p, q \in S$, $p \prec^* q$ exactly when there is a path from p to q in the graph $(S, \prec)$. Then we can compare pairs of events that appear on the same process line with the transitive closure relation [8].

Exercise 11.2.1. Is there a race between the two receive events of process $P2$ in Figure 11.1? Explain.

The MSC standard allows combining simple MSCs using *high level message sequence charts* (HMSCs). These are graphs, where each node is a single MSC (or is itself a high level MSC), see Figure 11.4. Each path of this graph, starting from some designated initial state, corresponds to a simple visual concatenation of the MSCs that appear on it. That is, when concatenating an MSC S_1 with an MSC S_2, the messages of S_2 appear *below* the messages of S_1. With this capability, one can describe a large or even infinite set of scenarios, each one of which can be finite or infinite (due to loops in the graph). Using HMSCs allows the creation, debugging, organization, and maintenance of systems of message sequence charts.

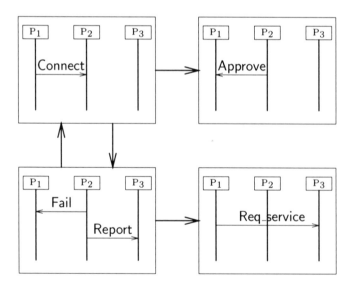

Fig. 11.4. An HMSC graph

One can add the ability to search an HMSC design for paths that match a given specification [87, 103]. The specification is also denoted using the same notation, as an MSC or an HMSC. However, the specification MSC (or HMSC) is a *template*, denoting a set of events (sending and receiving of messages) and their relative order; a specification *matches* any scenario that contains *at least* the events that appear in the template, while preserving the order between them. The matching path of the design can have *additional* events besides the ones appearing in the template. (The requirement that a specification HMSC is interpreted as a template is important, since the intersection of two HMSCs is shown to be undecidable [103].) At the conclusion of the search, the algorithm can either provide a matching scenario, or report the fact that no matching scenario exists in the checked graph.

The use of template matching allows one to mechanize such searches. The match can be used for determining whether MSCs with unwanted properties exist in the design. Another use is for determining whether a required feature is already included in the design or remains to be added.

An example of a template and a matching MSC scenario appears in Figure 11.5. In both charts, there are three processes, P_1, P_2 and P_3. The result of this match is that s_2 is paired with σ_1, r_2 with ρ_1, s_1 with σ_3, and r_1 with ρ_3.

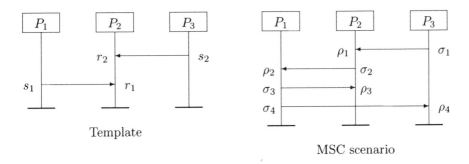

Fig. 11.5. A template and a matching scenario

11.3 Visualizing Flowcharts and State Machines

Displaying an automaton or a flowchart representing a program, and showing the progress from one state or node to another is an effective way to animate the executions of a system. One can simulate executions by highlighting the current node (changing the color or the tone of the node). When a transition is executed, the successor node of the one currently highlighted becomes accented instead.

Of course, displaying an entire state space is often impractical, since the number of states can be very large or infinite (though one may display only a part of the state space). A more practical approach is to display a graph consisting of the *control points* of the system. Each control point corresponds to a single value of the program counter (even if such values are implicit in the code of the program). For concurrent systems, one may display each process separately in a different window. In this case, the current location of the program is the combination of the program counter values in each process. Thus, when simulating an execution, at each point there is an highlighted node for every active process. Each transition is executed by one or more processes. In each of the processes involved in the execution of a transition, a successor of the current highlighted node is accented instead of the current one.

This visualization technique may not provide all the information about the current state. It may give only information about the current program counter(s). One may provide additional information, such as the values of the variables, or the message being sent or received. This can appear in a separate window. Such a visualization mechanism can be used for various purposes:

- Simulating different executions of the system. Special attention should be paid to nondeterministic choices made during the simulation. Such choices can be decided by the simulating tool by using a fixed criterion (e.g., enumerating the choices and always taking the first one), a pseudo random choice, or by delegating the decision to the user. Sometimes tools allow the user to program how nondeterministic choices are to be resolved, globally for the entire system or at each control point.

- Displaying a counterexample of model checking or testing. Counterexamples found during verification or testing can be represented textually, as a sequence of states and transitions. One can allow visualization of such executions.

- Selecting execution paths for testing purposes. Many testing coverage criteria are based on selecting paths through the code of the tested program. One can use visualization techniques that allow the user to select such paths in an interactive way.

Constructing a visual representation of a system can be done in different ways. One can use a compiler to translate the system's code into a graph [60]. Some tools allow the user to build and modify the graph while modeling the system or as part of the system design [127]. The graph may include additional information related to the nodes or the edges, including actual code for changing the value of variables, decision predicates and sent or received messages. We can use the visual interface in many stages of the system design, testing and verification. It can also serve as a very effective document of the development process.

The design of the system can start by using some visualization tools. Some of these tools automatically generate executable code. The user may not be able to use such code directly, but can modify it instead of starting to program the system from scratch.

Displaying graphs is a difficult problem, and an interesting research area by itself. One would like, for example, to minimize the number of edges crossing one another. There are programs that are specialized at allocating objects on a display for presenting graphs in a reasonable way, e.g., DOT [50], which is often provided as a part of the Unix system. Tools may also allow the user to move nodes from one place of the window to another, by dragging them with the mouse. In this case, the edges connected to the nodes must follow the new position of the nodes. In recent years we have seen advancement in programming languages and packages that support the easy implementation of such features, e.g., Java and TCL/TK [110]. The tools OBJECTIME [127] and OBJECTBENCH [128] are based on such a visualization mechanism. The UML approach [46], which is intended to standardize and unify a design methodology, advocates various kinds of graphs related to program execution, including state space graph, and message sequence charts.

The PET system was developed at Bell Labs [60]. It compiles processes, written in Concurrent Pascal, enhanced with interprocess communication, and produces a graph for each process. The edges and nodes of the graph are placed on the display using the DOT program. The system allows the user to select an interleaved path of the concurrent program. It calculates the path condition according to the algorithm presented in Section 9.4, and displays it.

Figure 11.6 represents the flowchart of the process $mutex0$ from the following attempt at solving the mutual exclusion:

$mutex0$::*while true do*
   begin
      while turn=1 do
         begin
            $x0:=x0$
         end;
      $y:=0;$
      $turn:=1$
   end

$mutex1$::*while true do*
   begin
      while turn=0 do
         begin
            $x1:=x1$
         end;
      $y:=1;$
      $turn:=0$
   end

The two processes are not supposed to reach the node labeled 3 at the same time, i.e., the assignment to the variable y. This is done using a *turn* variable, which contains the value 0 or 1, according to the process that has priority to enter the critical section. Each process performs busy waiting, represented by the loop that includes the nodes labeled with 1 and 2, when it is the other process' turn. It is interesting to notice for the following interleaved sequence

(mutex0 : 0), (mutex1 : 0), ⟨mutex0 : 5⟩, ⟨mutex1 : 5⟩, ⟨mutex1 : 2⟩, ⟨mutex0 : 2⟩, [mutex0 : 3], [mutex1 : 3].

For this path, the PET tool returns the condition $turn \neq 0 \wedge turn \neq 1$. This means that if $turn$ is, for example, 2, then both processes can enter their critical section at the same time. The mistake found in this case reflects the fact that each process should have performed busy waiting when it is not its own turn, not when it is not the other's turn. Of course, if we can be sure that the variable $turn$ is Boolean, and there are no other processes except for these two, this may not be a real error.

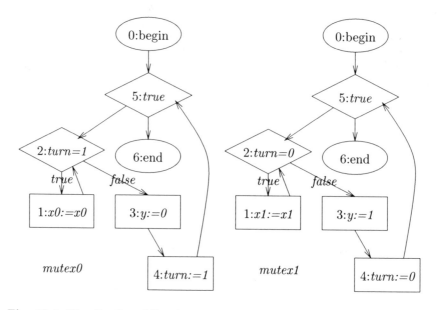

Fig. 11.6. Visualization of flowcharts

11.4 Hierarchical State Graphs

The large size of typical software, and its complex structure, limits the usefulness of simple state graphs in representing actual systems. Some of the frequently occurring deficiencies are:

- State graphs are *flat*. Hence they do not capture hierarchy in the structure of the system in a natural way.
- State graphs represent a *global view* of the modeled system. Thus, the concurrent composition of a system is represented by the product of the component state spaces (see Section 4.9). The concurrent structure is mostly lost.

- Due to the flat structure and global view, the state space is usually enormous. While the state space explosion problem is a big problem where verification is concerned, it is a huge problem for visualization: it is extremely hard to comprehend a graph that consists of more than a few dozens of nodes.
- The simplistic structure of graphs may introduce unnecessary redundancy. As an example, think about a system where an interrupt may occur from any state under a normal execution, leading to the execution of an interrupt procedure.

The use of *hierarchical state graphs* provides a good solution for the above mentioned problems. We will demonstrate a particular notation, called STAT-ECHARTS [61]. STATECHARTS allow grouping together several states (which will be called *substates*) into a *superstate*, as shown in Figure 11.7. It also allows the following features.

Hierarchical States

A state can cluster together a subgraph. The states in the subgraph of a state s are the *substates* of s. Then s is a *superstate* of the subgraph states. In Figure 11.7, the state C contains a subgraph which consists of the states A and B. One can enter a state s that contains a subgraph by either following an edge that enters one of the substates directly, as the edge from the state D to the state B in Figure 11.7. Alternatively, an edge can enter the superstate. In this case, there has to be a default initial state of the subgraph. This is denoted by a small full circle with an outedge that connects to that initial state. In Figure 11.7, the default initial state of the superstate C is A. Thus, the successor of the node E is the substate A. In the outmost level, the node E is the initial state.

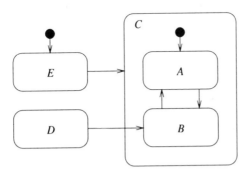

Fig. 11.7. A simple hierarchical graph

Uniform Exits and Entrances

A transition from a superstate replaces a transition from any of the substates that are included within it. Thus, in Figure 11.8, one can exit the superstate C, by moving from either the substate A or the substate B into the state D. This feature is in particular suited for specifying interrupts. The top black circle indicates that the superstate C is an initial superstate. The other black circle, with an edge to the substate A within C, is the default entrance node of C. Accordingly, when leaving D and entering C, we enter the substate A.

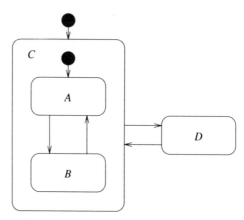

Fig. 11.8. Uniform exits

Concurrency

A superstate can include several concurrent components. When the system is in a superstate s with concurrent components, it must be in exactly one substate of each of the components. The different components are separated by dashed lines. In Figure 11.9, the superstate S includes two concurrent components, C and F. The component C includes a subgraph with two substates, A and B, while the component F includes a subgraph with two substates, D and E. Thus, while in S, we must be in exactly one of the following combinations: AD, AE, BD or BE. The concurrent components do not necessarily have to represent actual concurrency; they can be used to describe a subsystem that is decomposed into some orthogonal components, where each state is a combination of local states from the different components.

Inputs and Outputs

STATECHARTS are intended especially for specifying reactive systems. Thus, they need to include notation for inputs and outputs. Each transition, represented by an arrow, can include the name of an *input event*, received by the

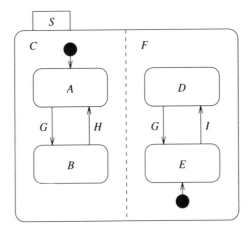

Fig. 11.9. Concurrency within a state

system, and an *output action*, performed by the system. These names appear separated by a '/' symbol. If no output action is specified, there is no need to include the '/'. There can be multiple output actions in an event, separated by semicolons (';'). In addition, a transition can include a condition. The condition appears on the left-hand side of the '/' symbol, inside square brackets ('[' and ']'). In order that a transition will execute, the (optional) input event associated with it has to occur and the (optional) condition has to happen. When executed, the (optional) actions associated with the transition occur.

A labeled transition is enabled when the (optional) action labeling it occurs, and the (optional) condition holds. If a single action labels several transitions in different concurrent components, the transitions can be executed together, in a synchronous way. If a single action appears only in a single concurrent component, the action labeled with it can occur independently (asynchronously) with the other components. Thus, in Figure 11.9, the moves from state A to B and from state D to E are performed simultaneously, since both actions are labeled with the input event G. Thus, if we are in the substates A and D, we move to the substates B and E. On the other hand, the transition from B to A is labeled with H, while the transition from E to D is labeled with I. Thus, if we are in the substates B and E at the same time, we can either move to A and stay at E, or stay at B and move to D. That is, one component will execute a transition, while the other component will not move.

A condition can refer to the latest transition in another concurrent component, i.e., $en(T)$ means that the last transition in another component was to *enter* the state T. Similarly, $ex(T)$ means that another component has most recently *exited* the state T. Finally, $in(T)$ means that the state in another component is T.

One can reuse the same names in different components. To disambiguate the names, it is possible to affix the name of a substate with the name of the superstate, separated by a dot. For example, in Figure 11.9, the state A in the C concurrent component of S can be also referred to by $C.A$ or by $S.C.A$.

11.5 Visualizing Program Text

Although the graphical representation of programs as flowcharts may be appealing, it has a severe limitation: nowadays programs are usually very large, with many lines of code and millions of states. One interesting approach is to use color to visualize program text [13]. Different shades can represent a scale of values, e.g., yellow shades represent lower values, red shades represent medium values, and brown shades represent the heighest values, etc. Darker shades can therefore represent pieces of code that

- were changed more recently than others, or
- were covered by more test cases than others, or
- were prone to more errors during development.

Such representation can give a good indication as to where one should focus in applying formal methods. For example, one may like to focus on those pieces of code that were more recently changed. One may also like to construct test cases that cover the pieces of code that were covered less. Interestingly enough, one might like to check the parts of the program where more errors were found: it has been found experimentally that with high probability, this is the place were additional errors will be found [101].

11.6 Petri Nets

An appealing visual representation for finite state programs is obtained via *Petri Nets* [118]. A Petri Net has a finite number of *places* P, denoted using circles, and *transitions* T, denoted using bars. Edges $E \subseteq (P \times T) \cup (T \times P)$ connect the places and the transitions, see Figure 11.10. A Petri Net contains a finite set of places and a finite set of transitions. A place p is called an *input place* of a transition τ if there exists an edge connecting p to τ. A place p is called an *output place* of a transition τ if there exists an edge connecting τ to p. The set of input places for a transition τ is denoted by $^\bullet\tau$, while the set of output places is denoted by $\tau^\bullet$. A place can be marked with a *token* or be unmarked. A transition is *enabled* if all its input places are marked and all its output places are unmarked. If a transition is enabled, it can be *fired* (executed). In this case, the token is removed from each of its input places and a token is put in each of its output places. We will only deal with *elementary net systems* [140] which can have no more than a single token in each place.

A (global) state G of a Petri Net is a subset of nodes from P. To represent that a Petri Net is in a global state G, the places in G are marked with tokens, denoted as small solid circles, while the places not in G are not marked. One state of is distinguished as the initial state. An execution of a Petri Net is a maximal sequence of states, starting with the initial state, such that each consecutive pair in the sequence is obtained through the firing of a single transition. Since there is a unique initial state, we can represent an execution as a sequence of transitions that were fired consecutively from the initial state.

Example. Consider the Petri Net , depicted in Figure 11.10. It has the states $p_0, \ldots, p_8$ and the transitions

$$T = \{\alpha_1, \, \alpha_2, \, \alpha_3, \, \beta_1, \, \beta_2, \, \beta_3\}.$$

We denote each state by a set of places that have a token in that state. The initial state, marked in the figure, includes exactly the places $G = \{p_0, \, p_1, \, p_2\}$.

Conforming with Section 4.4, we can represent places as two-valued variables. A place with a token represents the fact that the variable associated with the place has the value *true*. Otherwise, it has the value *false*. Define for each transition τ:

$$en_\tau = \bigwedge_{p \in \, {}^\bullet\tau} p \wedge \bigwedge_{q \in \tau^\bullet} \neg q$$

The transformation function f_τ assigns *false* to the variables ${}^\bullet\tau$ and *true* to the variables $\tau^\bullet$ while other variables remain unchanged.

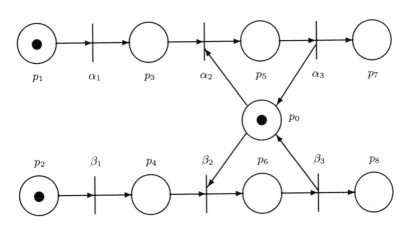

Fig. 11.10. A Petri Net

In order to represent the Petri Net as a transition system, we will use the variables $\{p_i \mid 0 \leq i \leq 8\}$. The initial state is $\{p_0, p_1, p_2\}$. The pairs of enabling conditions and transformation functions for each operation are listed below:

$$\alpha_1 : p_1 \wedge \neg p_3 \longrightarrow (p_1, p_3) := (false, true)$$
$$\alpha_2 : p_0 \wedge p_3 \wedge \neg p_5 \longrightarrow (p_0, p_3, p_5) := (false, false, true)$$
$$\alpha_3 : \neg p_0 \wedge p_5 \wedge \neg p_7 \longrightarrow (p_0, p_5, p_7) := (true, false, true)$$
$$\beta_1 : p_2 \wedge \neg p_4 \longrightarrow (p_2, p_4) := (false, true)$$
$$\beta_2 : p_0 \wedge p_4 \wedge \neg p_6 \longrightarrow (p_0, p_4, p_6) := (false, false, true)$$
$$\beta_3 : \neg p_0 \wedge p_6 \wedge \neg p_8 \longrightarrow (p_0, p_6, p_8) := (true, false, true)$$

One execution of this net is $\{p_0, p_1, p_2\} \xrightarrow{\beta_1} \{p_0, p_1, p_4\} \xrightarrow{\beta_2} \{p_1, p_6\} \xrightarrow{\beta_3} \{p_0, p_1, p_8\} \xrightarrow{\alpha_1} \{p_0, p_3, p_8\} \xrightarrow{\alpha_2} \{p_5, p_8\} \xrightarrow{\alpha_3} \{p_0, p_7, p_8\}$

In this example, the place p_0 represents a semaphore [37]. The operations α_2 and β_2 represent the acquisition of the semaphore, while α_3 and β_3 represent its release.

A Petri Net model for the provisional mutual exclusion protocol from Section 4.6 appears in Figure 11.11. The marking of the places represent the initial state of the system. Using the Petri Net representation is very convenient for visualizing the properties of the protocol. The safety property can be defined by requiring that a state where there is a token in both places *Critical section1* and *Critical section2* cannot be reached from the initial state.

One can demonstrate the possibility of deadlock in this algorithm by moving tokens according to the firing rules of the Petri Net. A deadlock occurs when there are no firable transitions. The transition marked with $c1 := 0$ is fired, removing the token from the places labeled as *Noncritical section1* and $c1 = 1$, and putting a token at the places labeled as *Try enter1* and $c1 = 0$. Symmetrically, The transition marked with $c2 := 0$ is fired, removing the token from the places labeled as *Noncritical section2* and $c2 = 1$, and putting a token at the places labeled as *Try enter2* and $c2 = 0$. Now, there are no firable transitions. In particular, the transition labeled $c2 = 1$? cannot be fired since there is no token in the place labeled $c2 = 1$. Similarly, the transition labeled $c1 = 1$? cannot be fired since there is no token in the place labeled $c1 = 1$.

Exercise 11.6.1. Model the Dekker mutual exclusion algorithm from Section 4.6 using Petri Nets.

11.7 Visualization Tools

The PEP tool [58] (Programming Environment based on Petri Nets) can be obtained from the University of Oldenburg, via the URL:
http://theoretica.informatik.uni-oldenburg.de/~pep
/HomePage.html

There are different versions of Petri Nets, geared towards modeling and verifying different systems. Some of the variations include:

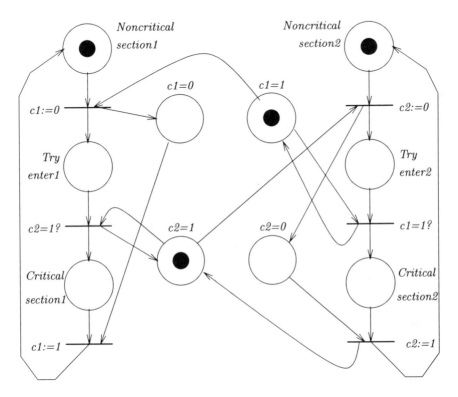

Fig. 11.11. A Petri Net for the provisional mutual exclusion algorithm

- Allowing a place to have more than a single token.
- Allowing a transition to transfer more than a single token.
- Adding *inhibitor* arcs, such that the input places connected to a transition with such arcs need to be empty for the transition to fire.
- Adding unquantified first order conditions to transitions.
- Distinguishing between tokens with different colors.

There are many verification algorithms for Petri Nets, varying according to the actual version of the model. The books suggested in the Further Reading section include surveys of such algorithms.

11.8 Further Reading

ITU standards such as SDL and MSC can be found in ISO documents, such as:

ITU-T Recommendation Z.120, Message Sequence Chart (MSC), March 1993.

The STATECHARTS approach is described in the book

D. Harel, M. Politi, *Modeling Reactive Systems with Statecharts*, McGraw-Hill, 1998.

There are many books on Petri Nets. For example:

K. Jensen, *Coloured Petri Nets : Basic Concepts, Analysis Methods and Practical Use*, Springer-Verlag, 1995.

W. Reisig, *Elements of Distributed Algorithms: Modeling and Analysis with Petri Nets*, Springer-Verlag, 1998.

W. Reisig, G. Rozenberg, eds. *Lectures on Petri Nets I: Basic Models*, Lecture Notes in Computer Science, Volume 1941, Springer-Verlag, 1998.

The *Unified Modeling Language* UML by Booch, Jacobson and Rumbaugh is one of the most popular visual modeling frameworks. There are several books dedicated to this method:

I. Jacobson, G. Booch, J. Rumbaugh, *Unified Software Development Process*, Addison-Wesley, 1999.

J. Rumbaugh, I. Jacobson, G. Booch, *The Unified Modeling Language, Reference Manual*, Addison-Wesley, 1998.

G. Booch, I. Jacobson, J. Rumbaugh, *The Unified Modeling Language User Guide*, Addison-Wesley, 1998.

12. Conclusions

Software systems have become so much an integral part in our lives that we now naturally interact with them on a daily basis. We buy merchandise using the worldwideweb, and obtain cash from automatic teller machines. We hardly use actual money any more; when we need to make a purchase, the sums of money are usually being transferred as data communication between distributed computer systems. Computers control traffic light systems, aircraft navigation and complicated medical equipment. We trust these systems to work properly. A computer printout is often brought as evidence to support some argument in a discussion or a dispute. We expect that for critical systems, the likelihood of making an error is smaller than the chance of a human operator making the same mistake.

Software development is nowadays a mature process. It is clear that although computer hardware is not likely to make an error (although sometimes it can), a programmer is highly likely to introduce mistakes into his code. Statistics can be given about the rate of errors per number of lines of code. Obviously, installing freshly written code directly in systems under production is not a good idea. This may lead to unpleasant and even catastrophic consequences. The number of incidents where severe damage is done by faulty software is constantly growing.

Formal methods are being used to enhance the quality of systems. They attempt to detect and eliminate errors. The software development process is usually accompanied by extensive testing. Testing is on the threshold of formal and informal methods. It can be performed by simply running arbitrary experiments on the software. However, testing can also involve tools and techniques based on mathematical analysis. This way, the chances of detecting problems with the code can increase significantly.

The deductive verification approach is a comprehensive method that uses mathematical logic for certifying the software. Model checking uses algorithmic methods to automatically verify finite state systems, while looking for counterexamples for its correctness.

Achieving absolute trust in a computer system is impossible. Formal methods help us to enhance our trust in software. Finding errors in code is a difficult problem. It was shown by mathematicians and computer scientists to be, in general, not completely solvable. It is thus not surprising that the different techniques suggest considerable tradeoffs.

Testing is based on sampling the executions of the code. Even when done formally, it allows some unchecked interactions to contain undetected errors. However, testing methods were shown to be efficient and effective in finding a *large portion* of the errors in programs. Model checking can be used for comprehensively checking whether the code satisfies a given property. It is mostly done automatically, and produces a counterexample when the correctness fails. However, it is usually limited to finite state systems, which rules out verifying algorithms with nontrivial data structures. Furthermore, the state space explosion problem limits the number of concurrent components that can undergo automatic verification. Deductive verification can handle infinite state systems, various data structures, and systems with any number of processes. However, the verification process is mostly manual, and is considerably slow.

Formal methods suffer from other limitations that need to be realized by their users. Even a careful verification can be subject to errors made by the human verifier. Using a model checking program or a mechanized theorem prover enhances the reliability of the verification. However, error are commonly found even in model checking and deductive verification tools. Moreover, it is often the case that the verification is not applied directly to the software, but rather to a manageable small model of it. The process of modeling is often done manually, and is subject to the introduction of discrepancies between the model and the actual system. Even if the modeling and verification are done correctly, an incomplete specification may result in some important aspects of the software being ignored.

Understanding the different techniques, their tradeoffs and their limitations, can help us in selecting the appropriate formal methods for a particular project. It may often be the case that the winning approach is a combination of methods. For example, in a banking system, one can perform tests on the complete system, model check some of the communication protocols used, and apply deductive verification to certify a critical kernel of the system involving large money transactions.

Current research is focused on tackling the limitations of available methods. Heuristics are suggested for automatic verification techniques, based on various observations about the nature of the verified systems. Various attempts are being made to combine deductive and automatic verification. For example, researchers study the use of deductive verification to justify abstractions, which produce small models of the software. Such a model can later be model checked, and the deductive verification is used to support the conclusion that the model checking results carry over from the abstract model to the actual software.

As formal methods techniques become mature, we are seeing a surge of software reliability tools. We now realize that the user interface is a key factor in such tools. The formal methods tools need to adopt the notation of the user, rather than trying to impose upon the user a new notation. Adding the use of new formal methods techniques to the process of software development may initially look like additional work to a developer. Therefore, software reliability tools need to attract the user by suggesting easy-to-use graphical interfaces, and performing some elaborate tasks automatically. Graphical interfaces and visual formal methods have proven to be big winners over text-based tools and methods.

Formal methods use a diversity of formalisms for describing systems and their properties. Selecting the appropriate formalism is based on several parameters such as conciseness, expressiveness and the availability of effective algorithms and tools. Tradeoffs need to be weighed when selecting a specification formalism. Achieving more conciseness or additional expressiveness may come at the expense of having a less efficient model checking algorithm, or even having to revert from automatic verification to manual deductive verification. Several attempts were made recently at standardization of formal description techniques, including notations such as SDL, LOTOS and UML. Building on past experience, such notations include both visual and textual representation.

Improving the efficiency of software reliability tools is a constant challenge for research in this area. The future may provide some new and exciting directions in formal methods techniques. One new and exciting direction in formal methods is verifying security protocols [123]. It is driven by the growing popularity of electronic commerce. Many companies and financial institutions are already offering a wide range of services over the web. One can make purchases, transfer money, gamble or play games remotely from his terminal at home. The availability of information such as bank accounts and credit card numbers, and the high connectivity of the worldwideweb makes it also a target for criminal activity. Such new applications and challenges call for the development of new software reliability techniques and tools.

References

1. M. Abadi, The power of temporal proofs, Theoretical Computer Science 65(1989), 35–83.
2. S. Abiteboul, R. Hull, V. Vianu, *Foundations of Databases*, Addison-Wesley, 1995.
3. S. Aggarwal, C. Courcoubetis, P. Wolper, Adding liveness properties to coupled finite-state machines, ACM Transactions on Programming Languages and Systems 12(1990), 303–339.
4. S. Aggarwal, R. P. Kurshan, K. Sabnani, A calculus for protocol specification and validation, H. Rudin and C. H. West, (eds.), Protocol Specification, Testing and Verification, North Holland, 1983, 19–34.
5. B. Alpern, F. B. Schneider, Recognizing safety and liveness, Distributed Computing 2(1987), 117–126.
6. R. Alur, D. L. Dill: A theory of timed automata, Theoretical Computer Science, 126(1994), 183–235.
7. R. Alur, T. A. Henzinger, O. Kupferman, Alternating-time Temporal Logic, 38th Annual Symposium on Foundations of Computer Science 1997, Miami Beach, FL, 100–109.
8. R. Alur, G. J. Holzmann, D. Peled, An Analyzer for Message Sequence Charts, Tiziana Margaria, Bernhard Steffen (Eds.), Tools and Algorithms for Construction and Analysis of Systems '96, Passau, Germany, Lecture Notes in Computer Science 1055, Springer-Verlag, 1996, 35–48.
9. D. Angluin, Learning regular sets from queries and counterexamples, Information and Computation, 75(1978), 87–106.
10. K. Apt, D. Kozen, Limits for automatic verification of finite-state systems. Information Processing Letters, 15, 307–309, 1986.
11. K. R. Apt, E. R. Olderog, *Verification of Sequential and Concurrent Programs*, Springer-Verlag, 1991 (second edition, 1997).
12. J. W. deBakker, *Mathematical Theory of Program Correctness*, Prentice-Hall, 1980.
13. T. Ball, S. G. Eick, Software visualization in the large, IEEE Computer 29(4), 1996, 33–43.
14. M. Ben-Ari, *Principles of Concurrent and Distributed Programming*, Prentice-Hall, 1990.
15. S. Bensalem, Y. Lakhnech, S. Owre, Computing abstractions of infinite state systems compositionally and automatically, International Conference on Computer Aided Verification 1998, Vancouver, BC, Lecture Notes in Computer Science 1427, Springer-Verlag, 319–331.
16. G. V. Bochmann, Finite state description of communications protocols, Publication No. 236, Departement d'informatique, Universite de Montreal, July 1976.
17. T. Bolognesi, H. Brinksma, Introduction to the ISO specification language LOTOS, Computer Networks and ISDN Systems, 14(1987), 25–59.

18. H. Brinksma, H. Hermanns, Stochastic process algebra: linking process description with performances, tutorial, Proceedings of Formal Methods of Protocol Engineering and Distributed Systems '99, Beijing, China, Kluwer, 1999.

19. B. Brock, M. Kaufmann, J. Moore, ACL2 theorems about commercial microprocessors, M. Srivas and A. Camilleri (eds.), Proceedings of Formal Methods in Computer-Aided Design (FMCAD'96), Lecture Notes in Computer Science 1166, Springer-Verlag, 1996, 275–293.

20. M. C. Browne, E. M. Clarke, O. Grumberg, Characterizing finite Kripke structures in propositional temporal logic, Theoretical Computer Science, 59(1988), 115–131.

21. *Distributed Systems Analysis with CCS*, Prentice Hall, 1997.

22. J. R. Büchi. On a decision method in restricted second order arithmetic, Proceedings of the International Congress on Logic, Method and Philosophy in Science 1960, Stanford, CA, 1962. Stanford University Press, 1–12.

23. S. Budkowski, P. Dembinski, An introduction to Estelle: a specification language for distributed systems, Computer Networks and ISDN Systems, 24(1987), 3–23.

24. J. R. Burch, E. M. Clarke, K. L. McMillan, D. L. Dill, L. J. Hwang. Symbolic model checking: 10^{20} states and beyond. Information and Computation, 98(1992), 142–170.

25. T. A. Budd, R. J. Lipton, R. A. DeMillo, F. G. Sayward, Theoretical and empirical studies on using program mutation to test the functional correctness of programs, Proceedings of the 7th conference on Principles of Programming Languages, January 1980, 220–233.

26. C. T. Chou, D. Peled, Verifying a model-checking algorithm, Tools and Algorithms for the Construction and Analysis of Systems '96, Passau, Germany, Lecture Notes in Computer Science 1055, 1996, 241–257.

27. A. Church, A formulation of the simple theory of types, Journal of Symbolic Logic 5 (1940), 56–68.

28. E. M. Clarke, E. A. Emerson, Design and synthesis of synchronization skeletons using branching time temporal logic. Workshop on Logic of Programs, Yorktown Heights, NY, Lecture Notes in Computer Science 131, Springer-Verlag, 1981, 52–71.

29. E. M. Clarke, O. Grumberg, D. E. Long, Model checking and abstraction., Transactions on Programming Languages and Systems, 16(1994), 1512–1542.

30. E. M. Clarke, O. Grumberg, D. A. Peled, *Model Checking*, MIT Press, 1999.

31. R. Cleaveland, J. Parrow, B. Steffen, The Concurrency Workbench: A semantics-based tool for the verification of concurrent systems. Transactions on Programming Languages and Systems 15(1993), 36–72.

32. W. F. Clocksin, C. S. Mellish, *Programming in Prolog*, Springer-Verlag, 4th edition 1994.

33. T. H. Cormen, C. E. Leiserson, R. L. Rivest, *Introduction to Algorithms*, MIT Press, 1990.

34. C. Courcoubetis, M. Y. Vardi, P. Wolper, M. Yannakakis, Memory efficient algorithms for the verification of temporal properties, Formal Methods in System Design, Kluwer, 1(1992), 275–288.

35. J. Davies, J. C. P. Woodcock, *Using Z; Specification, Refinement and Proof*, Prentice-Hall, 1996.

36. R. Diestel, *Graph Theory*, Springer-Verlag, 2nd edition, 2000.

37. E. W. Dijkstra, Cooperating Sequential Processes, Technical Report EWD123, Technological University, Eindhoven, The Netherlands, 1965, Reprinted in: F. Genuys (Editor), Programming languages, Academic Press, London, 1968, 43–112.

38. H. D. Ebbinghaus, J. Flum, W. Thomas, *Mathematical Logic*, Undergraduate Texts in Mathematics, Springer-Verlag, Second Edition 1994.
39. J. Edmonds, E. L. Johnson, Matching, Euler tours and the Chinese postman, Mathematical Programming, 5(1973), 88–124.
40. A. Ek, J. Grabowski, D. Hogrefer, R. Jerome, B. Kosh, M. Schmitt, SDL'97, Time for testing: SDL, MSC and Trends, Proceedings of the 8th DSL Forum, Elsevier, 1997, 23–26.
41. J. Elgaard, N. Klarlund, A. Moler, MONA 1.x: New techniques for WS1S and WS2S, 10th international symposium on Computer Aided Verification, Vancouver, BC, Lecture Notes in Computer Science 1427, Springer-Verlag, 1998, 516–520
42. E. A. Emerson, E. M. Clarke, Characterizing correctness properties of parallel programs using fixpoints, International Colloquium on Automata, Languages and Programming, Lecture Notes in Computer Science 85, Springer-Verlag, July 1980, 169–181.
43. E. A. Emerson, A. P. Sistla, Symmetry and model checking, Proceedings of the 5th Workshop on Computer Aided Verification, Elounda, Crete, Greece, Lecture Notes in Computer Science 697, Springer-Verlag, 1993, 463–478.
44. H. Ehrig, B. Mahr, *Fundamentals of Algebraic Specification*, Springer-Verlag, 1985.
45. R. Floyd, Assigning meaning to programs, Proceedings of symposium on applied mathematical aspects of computer science, J.T. Schwartz, ed. American Mathematical Society, 1967, 19–32.
46. M. Fowler, K. Scott, *UML Distilled : Applying the Standard Object Modeling Language*, Addison-Wesley, 1997.
47. N. Francez, *Fairness*, Springer-Verlag, 1986.
48. N. Francez, *Program Verification*, Addison Wesley, 1992.
49. D. Gabbay, A. Pnueli, S. Shelah, J. Stavi, On the Temporal Analysis of Fairness, ACM Symposium on Principles of Programming Languages, 1980, 163–173.
50. E. R. Gansner, E. Koustofios, S. C. North, K. P. Vo, A technique for drawing directed graphs, IEEE Transactions on Software Engineering 19(1993), 214–230.
51. M.R. Garey, D.S. Johnson, *Computers and Intractability: A Guide to the Theory of NP-Completeness*, W. H. Freeman, 1979.
52. R. Gerth, D. Peled, M. Y. Vardi,, P. Wolper, Simple on-the-fly automatic verification of linear temporal logic, Protocol Specification Testing and Verification '95, 3–18, Warsaw, Chapman & Hall, 1995.
53. R. J. van Glabbeek, The linear time-branching time spectrum (extended abstract), CONCUR 1990, Theories of Concurrency, Lecture Notes in Computer Science 458, Amsterdam, Springer-Verlag, 1990, 278–297.
54. R. J. van Glabbeek, The linear time - branching time spectrum II, E. Best (ed.), 4th international conference on Concurrency theory, CONCUR 1993, Theories of Concurrency, Hildesheim, Germany, Lecture Notes in Computer Science 715, Springer-Verlag, 1993, 66–81.
55. P. Godefroid, Using partial orders to improve automatic verification methods, Proc. 2nd Workshop on Computer Aided Verification, New Brunswick, NJ, Lecture Notes in Computer Science 531, Springer-Verlag, 1990, 176–185.
56. S. Graf, H. Saidi, Construction of abstract state graphs with PVS, 9th International Conference on Computer Aided Verification, Lecture Notes in Computer Science 1254, 1997, 72–83.
57. R. L. Graham, B. L. Rothschild, J. H. Spencer, *Ramsey Theory*, Wiley, 2nd edition 1990.

58. B. Grahlmann, E. Best, PEP - more than a Petri Net tool, TACAS 1996, Tools and Algorithms for the Construction and Analysis of Systems, Lecture Notes in Computer Science 1055, Springer-Verlag, 397–401

59. E. L. Gunter, R. P. Kurshan, D. Peled: PET: An Interactive Software Testing Tool, Internation conference on Computer Aided Verification 2000, Chicago, IL, Lecture Notes in Computer Science 1855, Springer-Verlag, 552-556.

60. E. L. Gunter, D. Peled, Path Exploration Tool, Tools and Algorithms for the Construction and Analysis of Systems (TACAS), Amsterdam, Lecture Notes in Computer Science 1579, Springer-Verlag, 1999, 405–419.

61. D. Harel, Statecharts: a visual formalism for complex systems, Science of Computer Programming 8(1987), 231–274.

62. O. Haugen, Special Issue of Computer Networks and ISDN Systems on SDL and MSC, 28(1996).

63. C. A. R. Hoare, An axiomatic basis for computer programming, Communication of the ACM 12(1969), 576–580.

64. C. A. R. Hoare, *Communicating Sequential Processes*, Prentice-Hall.

65. G. J. Holzmann, *Design and Validation of Computer Protocols*, Prentice-Hall Software Series, 1992.

66. G. J. Holzmann, Early Fault Detection Tools, Software Concepts and Tools, 17(1996), 63–69.

67. G. J. Holzmann, D. Peled, An improvement in formal verification, Formal Description Techniques '94, Bern, Switzerland, Chapman & Hall, 1994, 197–211.

68. G. J. Holzmann, D. Peled, M. Yannakakis, On nested depth first search, Second SPIN Workshop, American Mathematical Society, 1996, 23–32.

69. J. E. Hopcroft, J. D. Ullman, *Introduction to Automata Theory, Languages, and Computation*, Addison Wesley, 1979.

70. W. E. Howden, *Functional Program Testing and Analysis*, McGraw-Hill, 1987.

71. G. E. Hughes, M. J. Cresswell, *A New Introduction to Modal Logic*, Routledge, 1996.

72. ISO 8807, Information Processing Systems, Open Systems Interconnection, LOTOS - A formal description technique based on temporal ordering of observational behavior.

73. ITU-T Recommendation Z.120, Message Sequence Chart (MSC), March 1993.

74. L. Jategaonkar, A. R. Meyer, Deciding true concurrency equivalences on safe, finite nets, Theoretical Computer Science 154(1966), 107–143.

75. S. Katz, Z. Manna, Logical Analysis of Programs, Communication of the ACM, 19(1976), 188–206.

76. S. Katz, D. Peled, Defining conditional independence using collapses, *Theoretical Computer Science*, 101(1992), 337–359.

77. D. Kozen, Lower bounds for natural proof systems, 18th IEEE Symposium on Foundations of Computer Science, Providence, Rhode Island, 1977, 254–266.

78. O. Kupferman, M.Y. Vardi, Verification of fair transition systems, 8th International Conference on Computer Aided Verification, New Brunswick, NJ, Lecture Notes in Computer Science 1102, Springer-Verlag, 1996, 372–382

79. R. P. Kurshan. *Computer-Aided Verification of Coordinating Processes: The Automata-Theoretic Approach.* Princeton University Press, 1994.

80. R. P. Kurshan, V. Levin, M. Minea, D. Peled, H. Yenigun, Verifying hardware in its software context, ICCAD'97, San Jose, CA, November 1997, 742–749.

81. R. P. Kurshan, K. L. McMillan, A structural induction theorem for processes, Proceedings of the 8th Annual ACM Symposium on Principles of Distributed Computing, ACM Press, 1989, 239–247.

82. M. Z. Kwiatkowska, Fairness for Non–interleaving Concurrency, Phd. Thesis, Faculty of Science, University of Leicester, 1989.

83. L. Lamport, What good is temporal logic, R.E.A. Mason (ed.), Proceedings of IFIP Congress, North Holland, 1983, 657–668.

84. D. Lee, M. Yannakakis, Principles and methods of testing finite state machines - a survey, Proceedings of the IEEE, 84(1996), 1090–1126.

85. D. Gries, G. Levin: Assignment and Procedure Call Proof Rules. TOPLAS 2(1980), 564–579.

86. G. Levin, D. Gries, A proof technique for communicating sequential processes, Acta Informatica 15(1981), 281–302.

87. V. Levin, D. Peled. Verification of Message Sequence Charts via Template Matching, TAPSOFT (FASE)'97, Theory and Practice ofo Software Development, Lille, France, Lecture Notes in Computer Science 1214, Springer-Verlag, 1997, 652–666.

88. O. Lichtenstein, A. Pnueli, Checking that finite state concurrent programs satisfy their linear specification, 12th annual ACM symposium on Principles of Programming Languages 1985, New Orleans, Louisiana, 97–107.

89. N. A. Lynch, M. Merritt, W. Weihl, A. Fekete, *Atomic Transactions*, Morgan-Kaufmann, 1993.

90. Z. Manna, A. Pnueli, *The Temporal Logic of Reactive and Concurrent Systems: Specification*, Springer-Verlag, 1991.

91. Z. Manna, A. Pnueli, How to cook a temporal proof system for your pet language. 10th annual symposium on Principles of Programming Languages 1983, Austin, Texas, 141–154.

92. Z. Manna, A. Pnueli, Adequate proof principles for invariance and liveness properties of concurrent programs, Science of Computer Programming 4(1984), 257–289.

93. Z. Manna, A. Pnueli, Tools and Rules for the Practicing Verifier, In CMU Computer Science: A 25th Anniversary Commemorative, R.F. Rashid (ed.), ACM Press and Addison-Wesley, 1991, 125–159.

94. Z. Manna, R. J. Waldinger, Fundamentals of Deductive Program Synthesis. Transactions on Software Engineering 18(1992), 674–704.

95. Y. Matiyasevich, *Hilbert's 10th Problem*, MIT Press, 1993.

96. A. Mazurkiewicz, Trace theory, Advances in Petri Nets 1986, Bad Honnef, Germany, Lecture Notes in Computer Science 255, Springer-Verlag, 1987, 279–324.

97. T. F. Melham, *Introduction to Hol : A Theorem Proving Environment for Higher Order Logic*, Cambridge University Press, 1993.

98. H. D. Mills, The new math of computer programming, Communication of the ACM 18(1975), 43–48.

99. H. D. Mills, M. Dyer, R. C. Linger, Cleanroom software engineering, IEEE Software, September 1987, 19–24.

100. R. Milner, *Communication and Concurrency*, Prentice-Hall, 1995.

101. G. J. Myers, *The Art of Software Testing*, Wiley, 1979.

102. E. F. Moore, Gedanken-experiments on sequential machines, Automata Studies, Princeton University Press, 1956, 129–153.

103. A. Muscholl, D. Peled, Z. Su, Deciding properties for message sequence charts, FoSSaCS, Foundations of Software Science and Computation Structures, Lisbon, Portugal, Lecture Notes in Computer Science 1378, Springer-Verlag, 1998, 226–242.

104. K. S. Namjoshi, R. P. Kurshan, Syntactic program transformations for automatic abstractions, International Conference on Computer Aided Verification 2000, Chicago, IL, Lecture Notes in Computer Science 1855, Springer-Verlag, 2000, 435–449.

105. R. De Nicola, Extensional equivalences for transition systems, Acta Informatica 24(1987), 211–237.

106. T. Nipkow, Term rewriting and beyond – theorem proving in Isabelle, Formal Aspects of Computing, 1(1989) 320–338.

107. D. C. Oppen, A $2^{2^{2^{pn}}}$ upper bound on the complexity of Presburger arithmetic. JCSS 16(3): 323–332 (1978).

108. S. Owicki, D. Gries, An axiomatic proof technique for parallel programs, Acta Informatica 6(1976), 319–340.

109. S. Owre, S. Rajan, J. M. Rushby, N. Shankar, M. K. Srivas, PVS: Combining specification, proof checking, and model checking, International Conference on Computer Aided Verification 1996, New Brunswick, NJ, Lecture Notes in Computer Science 1102, Springer-Verlag, 1996, 411–414.

110. J. K. Ousterhout, *Tcl and the Tk Toolkit*, Addison-Wesley, 1994.

111. R. Paige, R. E. Tarjan: Three partition refinement algorithms. SIAM Journal of Computing 16(1987), 973–989.

112. D. Park, Concurrency and automata on infinite sequences, Theoretical Computer Science: 5th GI-Conference, Karlsruhe, Peter Deussen (ed.), Lecture Notes in Computer Science 104, Springer-Verlag, 1981, 167–183.

113. D. Peled, All from one, one for all: on model checking using representatives, Courcoubetis (ed.), 5th workshop on Computer Aided Verification, Elounda, Greece, Lecture Notes in Computer Science 697, Springer-Verlag, 1993, 409–423.

114. D. Peled, S. Katz, A. Pnueli, Specifying and proving serializability in temporal logic, International Symposium on Logic in Computer Science, Amsterdam, IEEE Computer Society Press, 1991, 232–244.

115. D. Peled, A. Pnueli, Proving partial order properties, Theoretical Computer Science, 126(1994), 143–182.

116. D. Peled, M.Y. Vardi, M. Yannakakis, Black box checking, Formal Methods for Protocol Engineering and Distributed Systems, Formal Methods for Protocol Engineering and Distributed Systems, 1999, Kluwer, China, 225–240.

117. D. Peled, L. Zuck, From model checking to a temporal proof, The 8th International SPIN Workshop on Model Checking of Software (SPIN'2001), Toronto, Canada, Lecture Notes in Computer Science 2057, Springer Verlag.

118. C. A. Petri, Kommunikation mit Automaten, Bonn, Institut für Instrumentelle Matematik, Schriften des IIM Nr. 2(1962).

119. A. Pnueli, The temporal logic of programs, 18th IEEE symposium on Foundation of Computer Science, 1977, 46–57.

120. J. P. Quielle, J. Sifakis, Specification and verification of concurrent systems in CESAR, Proceedings of the 5th International Symposium on Programming, 1981, 337–350.

121. S Rapps, E. J. Weyuker, Selecting software test data using data flow information, IEEE Transactions on software engineering, SE-11 4(1985), 367–375.

122. J. H. Reif, The complexity of two-player games of incomplete information, Journal of Computer and System Sciences, 29(1984), 274–301.

123. P. Ryan, S. Schneider, *Modelling and Analysis of Security Protocols*, Addison-Wesley, 2001.

124. S. Safra, On the complexity of omega-automata, Proceedings of the 29th IEEE Symposium on Foundations of Computer Science, White Plains, October 1988, 319–327.

125. W. J. Savitch, Relationships between nondeterministic and deterministic tape complexities. Journal of Computer and System Sciences 4(1970), 177–192.

126. F. B. Schneider, *On Concurrent Programming*, Springer-Verlag, 1997.

127. B. Selic, G. Gullekson, P. T. Ward, J. McGee, *Real-time object-oriented modeling*, Wiley, 1994.

128. SES Inc., *Objectbench Technical Reference*, Scientific and Engineering Software, 1997.

129. J. P. M. Silva, Search algorithms for satisfiability problems in combinatorial switching circuits, Phd. Dissertation, EECS Department, University of Michigan, 1995.

130. S. Singh, *Fermat's Enigma: The Quest to Solve the World's Greatest Mathematical Problem*, Walker and Co., 1997.

131. A. P. Sistla, Safety, liveness and fairness in temporal logic, Formal Aspects of Computing 6(1994), 495–511.

132. A. P. Sistla, E.M. Clarke, Complexity of propositional temporal logics. Journal of the ACM, 32(1986), 733–749.

133. A. P. Sistla, E. M. Clarke, N. Francez, Y. Gurevich, Can message buffers be characterized in linear temporal logic, ACM Symposium on Principles of Distributed Computing 1982, Ottawa, Canada, 148–156.

134. A. P. Sistla, M. Y. Vardi, P. Wolper, The complementation problem for Büchi automata with applications to temporal logic, Theoretical Computer Science, 49(1987), 217–237.

135. N. Sharygina, D. Peled, A combined testing and verification approach for software reliability, Formal Methods Europe 2001, Lecture Notes in Computer Science 2021, Springer-Verlag, 611-628.

136. G. Stalmark, M. Säfinnd, Modeling and verifying systems and software in propositional logic, Safety of computer control systems (SAFECOMP'90), Pergamon Press, 1990, 31–36.

137. A. Szalas, L. Holenderski, Incompleteness of first-order temporal logic with Until. Theoretical Computer Science, 57(1988), 317-325.

138. A. S. Tanenbaum, *Computer Networks*, Prentice-Hall, Third edition 1996.

139. R. E. Tarjan, Depth first search and linear graph algorithms, SIAM Journal of computing, 1(1972).,146–160.

140. P. S. Thiagarajan, Elementary net systems, W. Brauer, W. Reisig, G. Rozenberg (eds.), Proceedings of Advances in Petri Nets 1986, Lecture Notes in Computer Science 254, Springer-Verlag, 1987, 26–59.

141. W. Thomas, Automata on infinite objects, In Handbook of Theoretical Computer Science, vol. B, J. van Leeuwen, ed., Elsevier, Amsterdam (1990) 133–191.

142. A. Valmari, A stubborn attack on state explosion, 2nd Workshop on Computer Aided Verification, New Brunswick, NJ, Lecture Notes in Computer Science 531, Springer-Verlag, 1990, 156–165.

143. M. P. Vasilevskii, Failure diagnosis of automata, Kibertetika, 4(1973), 98–108.

144. M. Y. Vardi, P. Wolper, An automata-theoretic approach to automatic program verification, Proceedings of the 1st Annual Symposium on Logic in Computer Science IEEE, 1986, 332–344.

145. S. Warshall, A theorem on Boolean matrices, Journal of the ACM, 9(1962), 11–12.

146. C. H. West, P. Zafiropulo, Automated validation of a communications protocol: the CCITT X.21 recommendation, IBM Journal of Research and Development 22(1978), 60–71.

147. P. Wolper, Temporal logic can be more expressive. Proceedings of the 22nd IEEE Symposium on Foundations of Computer Science, Nashville, TN, October 1981, 340–348.

148. P. Wolper, Expressing interesting properties of programs in propositional temporal logic, Principles of Programming Languages 1986, Florida, ACM Press, 184–193.

149. P. Wolper, V. Lovinfosse, Verifying properties of large sets of processes with network invariants. Proceedings of the 1989 International Workshop on Automatic Verification Methods for Finite State Systems, Lecture Notes in Computer Science 407, Springer-Verlag, 1989, 68–80.
150. P. Zafiropulo, A new approach to protocol validation, Proceedings of the international communications conference, Vol II (ICC 77), Chicago, 1977.
151. H. Zhang, A decision procedure for propositional logic, Association for Automated Reasoning Newsletter, 22, 1993, 1–3.

Index

TEXTS IN COMPUTER SCIENCE

(continued from page ii)

Merritt and Stix, Migrating from Pascal to C++

Munakata, Fundamentals of the New Artificial Intelligence

Nerode and Shore, Logic for Applications, Second Edition

Pearce, Programming and Meta-Programming in Scheme

Peled, Software Reliability Methods

Schneider, On Concurrent Programming

Smith, A Recursive Introduction to the Theory of Computation

Socher-Ambrosius and Johann, Deduction Systems

Stirling, Modal and Temporal Properties of Processes

Zeigler, Objects and Systems